PERSONALITY, COGNITION, and SOCIAL INTERACTION

PERSONALITY,
COGNITION,
and
SOCIAL INTERACTION

Edited by
NANCY CANTOR
Princeton University

JOHN F. KIHLSTROM
University of Wisconsin

1981

LAWRENCE ERLBAUM ASSOCIATES, PUBLISHERS
Hillsdale, New Jersey

Copyright © 1981 by Lawrence Erlbaum Associates, Inc.
   All rights reserved. No part of this book may be reproduced in
   any form, by photostat, microform, retrieval system, or any other
   means, without the prior written permission of the publisher.

Lawrence Erlbaum Associates, Inc., Publishers
365 Broadway
Hillsdale, New Jersey 07642

Library of Congress Cataloging in Publication Data

Main entry under title:
Personality, cognition, and social interaction.

   Includes bibliographies and indexes.
   1. Social perception--Congresses.   2. Personality--
Congresses.   3. Cognition--Congresses.   4. Social
interaction--Congresses.   I. Cantor, Nancy.
II. Kihlstrom, John F.
HM132.P43   302   81-208
ISBN 0-89859-057-4   AACR2

Printed in the United States of America

Contents

Preface

PART VI DISCUSSION

Preface

Until very recently the scientific study of personality was primarily concerned with locating the individual with respect to a number of dimensions representing enduring characteristic dispositions, as formalized in the classic trait theories. In the 1950s and 1960s, however, a growing awareness that individual behavior was not highly consistent across different situations led many personologists to deemphasize generalized dispositions and focus instead on the impact of the social context in which social behavior takes place. This new personology favored constructs drawn from the behaviorist tradition in experimental psychology—particularly the notions of event–event and response–outcome contingency—as supplemented by new concepts such as vicarious learning, modeling, and self-reinforcement. The development of *social-learning* theory paved the way for an increasing interaction between personality and social psychology. If trait theorists tended to think of personality in terms of response tendencies that were stable across time and situations, social-learning theorists underscored the discriminativeness and flexibility of human behavior. Clearly, however, the operative factors in human behavior were not the objective stimulus conditions but the ways in which situations were perceived and the meanings attributed to them by the individual. Recognition of this fact led investigators to take seriously the cognitive processes by which the individual construes situations and plans behavior in a psychological environment. The resulting *cognitive* social-learning theory provides the basis for future links between personality and cognitive psychology.

This evolutionary trend—in which personality has "gone social" and "gone cognitive"—makes it quite difficult to draw sharp distinctions among the domains of personality, cognitive, and social psychology. Although some may see this ambiguity as posing difficulties, we do not think that such distinctions are necessary or even useful. Rather, in striving toward a definition of the field we think of personality (or any other subdiscipline of psychology) as a fuzzy set defined by a number of features none of which are necessary or sufficient. There was a time when the domain of personality was defined by, and restricted to, the study of individual differences. But the situation is now such that there are some individual differences—in the capacity of primary memory, for example—that do not clearly belong in the domain of personality and some general processes—such as those involved in the encoding and retrieval of social information—that clearly do belong there. Similarly, another traditional criterion for personality was a concern with cross-situational consistency. Now there is increasing recognition that consistency is an empirical question rather than a defining feature so that personologists are forced to consider the factors—dispositional or situational—that lead to consistency or specificity in behavior.

The present volume presents the domain of personality as a fuzzy set that includes features previously identified with cognitive and social psychology. Few of the individual contributions are centrally concerned with individual differences and cross-situational stability, but these traditional themes certainly appear in several of the chapters. The remaining chapters deal with the general processes mediating the interaction between the person and the social environment, filling out the fuzzy set of personality psychology.

Part I seeks to locate contemporary trends in the cognitive psychology of personality against a backdrop of historical events. Mischel briefly rehearses the conceptual and methodological problems associated with the differential and psychodynamic approaches to personality, at the same time as he discusses the relationship of cognitive approaches to Allport's idiographic psychology on the one hand and Lewin's field theory on the other. Most important, he makes clear that the conception of human behavior in the minds of cognitive-social learning theorists is not that of a passive victim of environmental forces but rather of an individual with a history and goals who creates the social world at the same time as he or she adjusts to it.

The chapters in Part II discuss some of the cognitive processes mediating social behavior. Cantor argues that social information is organized according to prototypes and discusses various ways in which these cognitive structures guide information processing and social behavior. Cohen shows how the schemata brought to bear on social information are themselves shaped by the individual's expectations and goals in particular social contexts. Similarly, Higgins and King discuss the way in which experience—over both short and long periods of time—influences the salience of the constructs by which we organize social perception and memory. Kihlstrom explores a wide range of topics in personality and memory, with a special emphasis on early recollections and other forms of autobiographical recall.

Part III contains contributions concerned with the rules by which people make judgments about objects in the social world. Borgida, Locksley, and Brekke present a theoretical framework for determining when widely shared sex-role stereotypes will be used to make predictions about individuals. Fiske and Kinder show that individual differences in political sophistication and involvement influence the way in which people make judgments about political topics.

The self, a dominant topic in personality theory and research, is treated extensively in Part IV. Rogers employs a variety of techniques familiar in experimental psychology to characterize the generalized self-concept as a cognitive structure. Kuiper and Derry extend this formulation to topics related to person perception and psychopathology. Markus and Smith consider self-knowledge within specific domains and also discuss the influence of self-schemata on the processing of information about others. Finally, Locksley and Lenauer propose a model, based on attribution theory, of the process by which we form impressions of ourselves.

Although many of the chapters are explicitly concerned with the relations between cognition and action—after all, most human interaction takes the form of judgments and communication—the contributions in Part V make the links to overt behavior. Athay and Darley outline within a social-exchange framework a number of interaction competencies important in resolving the tension between "routinizing" and "contextualizing" tendencies in behavior. Snyder presents a framework for understanding how individuals operate cognitively and behaviorally on situations in such a way as to support their characteristic dispositions and confirm their expectations and hypotheses about the social world.

Finally, Part VI offers two discussions of the previous contributions from the perspective of cognitive psychology. Glucksberg points out some hazards in forging too close a link, too soon, between personality and cognitive psychology: Although the cognitive psychology of personality may make profitable use of borrowed constructs pertaining to structure and process, borrowed paradigms may be much less helpful when—as so often happens—they are discredited. Posner draws attention to two other potential problems: the temptation to employ highly generalized cognitive constructs such as attention and schema without committing oneself to precise technical definitions; and a tendency to focus on mental constructs without linking them to overt social behavior.

It seems clear by now that the determinants of behavior and experience are so multifaceted and complex that the study of personality begs for an interdisciplinary approach. Personality psychology in its broadened form shares substantially with both cognitive and social psychology. The focus on cognitive mediation and on the role of goals, expectations, and inferences in shaping behavior joins personality and cognitive psychologists in common cause. Similarly, personality and social psychologists express a joint concern with the interactive nature of social behavior and the flexibility of the individual's response to even subtle situational variation. The new focus does not displace the old concerns with stability and psychodynamics. The intersection of personality, cognitive, and social psychology forces us to consider the reciprocal relations between relatively long-term social knowledge structures and behavioral dispositions and relatively short-term goals, expectations, and situational demands as they conspire together to shape social cognition and social behavior. The present volume is dedicated to dynamic interactionism as both a model of social behavior and a metaphor for the enterprise of personality research.

The chapters collected here are based on presentations at the Conference on Personality and Cognition held at Princeton University from March 30 to April 1, 1979. Support for the conference was generously provided by the Herbert Langfeld Fund administered under the auspices of the Department of Psychology, Princeton University. Walter Mischel and Mark Snyder expressed early enthusiasm for the idea of the conference; John Darley, Sam Glucksberg, Arlene Rakower, and Uta Runyan provided special organizational expertise and assistance necessary for its successful execution: we thank them all wholeheartedly. Finally, we are indebted to the Department of Psychology at Princeton for permitting 15 cognitive-social-personality psychologists to roam the environs of Green Hall for a long weekend. We stand firm in the belief that the nuclear accident at Three Mile Island was prevented from evolving into a full-scale tragedy as a result of our collective presence and united efforts.

Final preparation of this volume was supported in part by Grant #BNS-8022253 from the National Science Foundation; and by Grants #MH-29951 and MH-33737 from the National Institute of Mental Health.

Nancy Cantor
John F. Kihlstrom

PERSONALITY, COGNITION, and SOCIAL INTERACTION

HISTORICAL PERSPECTIVE

1 Personality and Cognition: Something Borrowed, Something New?

Walter Mischel
Stanford University

I hope that this volume is a step toward the increasing integration of orientations, insights, and methods from the subdisciplines of personality, cognitive, and social psychology. Like most (or all?) scientific developments, the progress reflected in the contributions that follow combines the new and old, a mix of innovation and recreation of elements whose historical roots may be discerned in earlier movements. In viewing these contributions, a proper evaluation of their originality lies somewhere between ''déjà vu'' and ''revolutionary.'' To help arrive at a reasonable perspective, I begin by commenting on what I see as some of the highlights of the field of personality, especially as they may relate to some of the major themes in the present volume.

SEARCHING FOR TRAITS

Historically, the field of personality has been influenced by a few main positions, of which one of the oldest and most enduringly influential is trait psychology. Beginning about the turn of the century, and inspired mostly by the success of the intelligence testing movement and especially by the work of Alfred Binet, psychologists became interested in seeing whether the success achieved with mental (i.e., ''cognitive'') measurement might be repeated if one tried to quantify social characteristics.

The trait theories of the 1920s and 1930s were primarily a psychology of common sense, in which the layperson's ''natural,'' everyday theory of what people are like became the scientific theory of what people are like. People were held to differ on dimensions such as friendliness, honesty, conscientiousness,

3

and aggressiveness. The scientific innovation—and it was a most important one—was the development of statistical methods to give dimension to these qualities systematically and to quantify them rigorously and carefully. The responses of the subject were primarily self-reports, sometimes ratings by others, represented by check marks on multiple choice or true–false inventories and questionnaires. Recall, for example, the Bell Adjustment Inventory, or the Woodworth Personal Data Sheet in World War I ("I am a good mixer"; "I am at ease with people"). These efforts began in a very reasonable way, intended as shortcuts for the actual sampling of behavior (for instance, the psychiatric interview).

I think a giant conceptual leap was taken at that time, perhaps without full realization of just how big a leap it was. This was the shift from sampling people's relevant specific *performance* by assessing what they could do (which was the heart of intelligence testing) to asking people to report about what they were like, in general, on such broad situation-free dimensions as friendliness, conscientiousness, or introversion. These responses were used not as *samples* of the respondents' relevant behavior but as *signs* or indicators of their generalized dispositions. This leap was not carefully thought through, and we have seen its implications over the last 10 or 20 years as we began to realize the conceptual and methodological problems that one gets into if one does not distinguish very carefully between people's subjective judgments about themselves and an objective sampling of what they actually do (their performance under specific circumstances). We see what people do, for example, when we ask them to count the beads or arrange the blocks or say the digits backward, or when we directly observe their behavior as it unfolds. Such specific behaviors are very different from how people characterize themselves globally as introverted, aggressive, or friendly, and the differences have serious measurement implications (Mischel, 1968).

Early trait psychology was a psychology guided mostly by words in the dictionary, as in Allport's (1937) search, yielding the hundreds of terms finally culled from an even larger number of adjectives. Other trait psychologists attempted to find ways to hone down this list more finely, using a variety of often ingenious techniques, most notably factor analysis. The struggle became an attempt to find a finite and, hopefully, relatively small taxonomy of the basic dimensions of personality and social behavior. This remains one of the main objectives of the field, with a distinctive methodology and, I think, with distinctive uses, contributions, and limitations.

The lone voice speaking out against this dimensionalization of personality with numbers was Gordon Allport, who, beginning in the 1930s, insisted on each person's uniqueness and individuality. Most who heard Gordon Allport were excited by the idiographic approach he espoused. But, curiously, his own work (Allport, Vernon, & Lindzey, 1960) inspired still more attempts to categorize people on slots or dimensions that were the preferred yardsticks of the psychologist rather than on the equivalence classes of the person being assessed. More forcefully than others before him, Allport (1937, p. 3) articulated the essence of the trait position, claiming that the individual is an "amazingly stable and self-contained system" that contains enduring generalized dispositions. Our task, in his view, was to search for those stable broad dispositions as manifested behaviorally, and that has been the major mission of trait psychology for many decades.

How fruitful has this search been? In trying to answer this question it is important to discriminate clearly between demonstrations of temporal stability on the one hand and cross-situational generality or consistency on the other. More than a decade ago the available research provided evidence for significant temporal stability but also—and far more surprising at the time—for discriminativeness or "specificity" in how behavior varies across situations. Summarizing those findings, I concluded: "Although behavior patterns often may be stable, they usually are not highly generalized across situations [Mischel, 1968, p. 282]."

In the long debate on this topic no one seriously questions that lives have continuity and that we perceive ourselves and others as individuals who maintain a stable identity over time, even when our specific actions change across situations (Mischel, 1968, 1973, 1977). Although temporal stability in the patterning of individual lives, in self-perceptions, and in how others view us seems evident, there is room for serious disagreement about the nature, degree, and meaning of the "erratic and uneven" relationships typically found when cross-situational consistency is studied with objective measures of behavior. To be sure, this result may reflect measurement problems, as Block (1977) and Epstein (1979) suggest. Better measures will surely provide better support for the existence of meaningfully organized behavior patterns. But, in my view, better measures and more fine-grained analyses should also make it even more apparent that individuals discriminate among situations according to subjective equivalences. Individual behavior is organized in terms of these personal meanings, not those of the trait psychologist. Although sometimes the subject's equivalences will coincide with the nomothetic trait categories of the assessor, often they will not (Mischel & Peake, work in progress). Whether or not the degree of correspondence is judged adequate and useful depends on a host of considerations, and especially on one's purpose (Mischel, 1979).

LIMITATIONS OF THE CLASSICAL APPROACH

The impact of trait psychology has been limited seriously because human consistencies and psychological equivalences are more complex and cognitively constructed than nomothetic trait theory suggests. Traditionally, the search for consistent personality traits and types has assumed well-defined, distinct, and nonoverlapping categories in which each member of a personality category has all the defining features of that category. But although such neatness and equality may be built into artificial, logical taxonomies, it does not seem to characterize the categories of objects, people, and situations encountered in the natural world. As Wittgenstein (1953) first noted, the members of common everyday categories do not share all of a set of singly necessary and jointly sufficient features critical for category membership. When one examines a set of natural objects all labeled by one general term, one will not find a single set of features shared by all members of the category; instead, one finds a *pattern* of overlapping similarities, a *family resemblance* structure.

Many linguists, philosophers, and psychologists following Wittgenstein (Labov, 1973; Lakoff, 1972; Lehrer, 1970; Rosch, Mervis, Gray, Johnson, & Boyes-Braem, 1976; Smith, 1976; Tversky, 1977) now suggest that natural semantic categories are "fuzzy sets" that violate the expectations of the classical all-or-none position: Natural categories are organized around *prototypical* examples of focal stimuli (the best examples of a concept), with less prototypical members forming a continuum away from the central prototypic exemplars (Rosch, 1975). Guided by this *prototypicality* view, and recognizing that person categories are "fuzzy sets," Nancy Cantor and I have been exploring the rules people use in making judgments about the clearest or most prototypical exemplars of such person categories as extraverts (Cantor, this volume; Cantor & Mischel, 1979). It is to be hoped that such studies of prototypicality rules and "family resemblance" principles will ultimately allow a better understanding of the nature of consistency and coherence extracted from variations in behavior. Someone who has seen a thousand Picassos, each of which is unique, can determine (usually quite easily) whether a previously unseen work is a true Picasso, an imitation, or the work of someone else. The same processes that allow this kind of pattern recognition—extraction of a central distinctive gist or unity from great diversity—must surely be basic for our recognition of identity and coherence in the face of behavioral variability.

Trait psychology has also been limited because its focus is not addressed at the flow of behavior nor in any way linked to the dynamic interactions that go on where people actually are living their lives. It has to do instead with the effort to taxonomize the world, to cut up human qualities and the stream of actions into neat dimensions, and to provide some kind of taxonomy which cuts people in their places—but on the psychologist's theoretically preferred favorite dimensions rather than on the person's. The result is a focus on between-person differences, between-person variance, rather than on *within-person* variance as it relates to environmental changes. These efforts have consumed much energy and yielded many interesting useful classification schemes (Guilford, 1975). Unfortunately these efforts do not address the processes underlying personality, tending rather to classify subgroups or people than to capture and explain the ongoing flow of their behavior.

Stimulated especially by the thoughtful writings of such personologists as Henry Murray (1938) and David McClelland (1951), some psychologists have long recognized these limitations and tried to move away from an exclusive person-focus to study the interactions of persons with their worlds in a more process-oriented fashion. Perhaps most influential in the discovery of the role of social contexts was Kurt Lewin's (1951) articulation of the field of forces operating in any given situation at the moment. Disappointment with the bundles of correlation coefficients yielded by traditional trait psychology added to the appeal of the experimental approach to the analysis of "basic processes" influencing attitudes and behavior espoused by the mainstream social psychology of Lewin's disciples (Festinger, 1957). Unfortunately, the personological concerns of this new breed of experimental social psychologists were generally limited to throwing in a few "personality measures" (often homemade and usually of unknown reliability) while searching for experimentally manipulated main effects in laboratory studies of interesting pieces of social behavior. For many social psychologists, individual differences at best became ancillary, minor data; at worst, they were error variance to be obviated by cleaner methodology and more potent independent variables. In the 1950s and 1960s, those who studied social processes experimentally thus tended to have little interest in personality, whereas those who were committed to studying persons found it most convenient to study them in relative isolation with the nonexperimental (i.e., correlational) methods. The rift between personality and social psychology widened, to the detriment of both endeavors.

THE PSYCHODYNAMIC SEARCH FOR UNDERLYING DISPOSITIONS

It is, I think, because of the static, descriptive, and nonanalytic quality of trait psychology that many of us were so excited when we first came across the psychodynamic approach. We found the writings of Freud and his followers to be an enormously stimulating, invigorating way of getting beyond labeling or groupings and into each person's unique psyche. For me, the appeal of the psychodynamic approach, when I first encountered it as a graduate student in the 1950s, was that at last there seemed to be a way of finding consistencies as they exist for the individual in a way that was not obvious at the level of surface behavior. These equivalencies were not documented by the kind of counting of specific behavioral similarities that characterized the work of Hartshorne and May (1928), who hoped to show that the child who is honest about not cheating when it comes to an arithmetic test is also honest about not cheating when it comes to a spelling test. Instead, psychodynamic theorists asserted that the relationship between indicators, intrapsychic dispositions, and overt behavior may not be cumulative and additive, as the trait approach had assumed. Rather, the relationship between sign and disposition may be subtle, indirect, and contradictory and may involve all kinds of transformations.

Indeed, much of the excitement of the psychoanalytic approach was that it provided the notion of transformation—the notion that the same motive could manifest itself in all sorts of ways, displaying a wide range of vicissitudes. Thus Joe, who repeatedly says he is very aggressive on questionnaires, may not be more aggressive than Charles, who claims to be unaggressive and endorses mostly timid adjectives; indeed, the more Joe insists on his aggressiveness, the *less* aggressive and the more passive–dependent he might really prove to be, whereas Charles, the ostensibly passive one, may indirectly reveal himself to be a cauldron of stifled aggressive impulses. The hope was that recognition of underlying "genotypic" equivalences would enable one to see the similarities uniting all kinds of phenotypic surface variations and seeming contradictions in behavior. The excitement here was that at last there was attention to causal dynamics, with a recognition that what people do is selective, motivated, and full of conflict, and has to be decoded in terms of what it really means rather than how it merely seems (Erdelyi & Goldberg, 1979).

Unfortunately, the initial exuberance and high promise of the psychodynamic approach was soon followed by a sobering and generally dismal empirical flood of studies that deeply questioned the nature, importance, and even the very existence of such basic psychodynamic processes as repression (Mischel, 1976). But because the studies themselves could readily be accused, often justifiably, of flaws and limitations in scope and in method, the psychodynamic approach itself tended to withstand the empirical assaults on its key constructs. The most serious disillusionment with psychodynamic approaches began to arise, in my view, not so much from the failure to validate crucial constructs experimentally as from the clinical experiences of the 1950s and early 1960s with clients seeking help. It was in that clinical context, not in the laboratory, that clinicians became increasingly dubious about the value of the psychodynamic portraits to which they were devoting so much of their time (Mischel, 1968; Peterson, 1968; Vernon, 1964).

Guided by the view that test responses are merely indirect manifestations of underlying psychodynamic processes, assessors had for years elicited signs such as picture drawings, associations to inkblots, or stories told to ambiguous pictures, whose demonstrable empirical relations to the individual's important life behaviors tended to be tenuous and remote. Skepticism about the utility of such assessments arose from a growing worry that the resulting psychodynamic personality diagnostics, too often formulated with little regard for the client's own construction of his life and his specific behaviors, might (like those of trait psychology) be exercises in stereotyping that miss the uniqueness of the individual and pin people instead on a continuum of theory-supplied labels while slighting their everyday problems of living. But a focus on the immediate behavioral troubles of the client was for many years widely regarded as naive and hazardous because these problems (phobias, sexual dysfunctions, fetishes) were construed merely as "symptoms" and even as manifestations of "resistances." Traditionally, the clinician's task had been to go beyond behavioral complaints to underlying psychodynamics, and the fear of symptom substitution led many to eschew direct behavior intervention. But these fears of "symptom substitution" turned out to be largely unjustified (Grossberg, 1964). Clients whose maladaptive behaviors were directly alleviated, rather than becoming victimized by substituted symptoms, appeared more likely to show generalized gains from overcoming their original handicaps (Bandura, 1969).

In the 1950s and 1960s many empirical studies carefully investigated clinicians' efforts to infer broad dispositions indirectly from specific symptomatic signs and to unravel disguises in order to uncover the hypothetical dispositions that might be their roots. The results generally indicated that the disillusionment beginning to be expressed by skeptics was empirically justified. The total findings questioned the utility of clinical judgments even when the judges were well-trained expert psychodynamicists working with clients in clinical contexts and using their own preferred techniques. On the whole, clinicians' assessments of underlying genotypic dispositions have not predicted behavior better than the person's own direct self-assessment, simple indices of directly relevant past behavior, or demographic variables (Mischel, 1968, 1972; Peterson, 1968). Moreover, to some degree, psychodynamic inferences, like dispositional attributions, appear to reflect illusory correlations perpetuated by shared semantic organizations and belief systems (Chapman & Chapman, 1969; D'Andrade, 1970; Shweder, 1975). Increasingly it appeared that the intriguing psychic structures and dynamics that clinicians elaborated at case conferences may have added more to the weight of the clients' diagnostic folders than to the design of treatments tailored to their specific needs and circumstances. As distressing as the failure to demonstrate the utility of the inferences and predictions of psychodynamically oriented clinicians was the evidence on the limitations of psychodynamic treatments. Although sometimes psychodynamic psychotherapy seemed better than no treatment at all, the approach lacked efficacy when compared to more parsimonious alternatives (Bandura, 1969; Kazdin & Wilson, 1978). Moreover, skeptics noted perceptively that dynamic therapy might lead to an ideological conversion to the belief system of the therapist rather than to a solution for the client's problems.

CONTEMPORARY COGNITIVE
SOCIAL-LEARNING APPROACHES

With the nomothetic trait orientation and the psychodynamic approach as the prevailing forces in personality and clinical psychology, the advent of social behavior theory in the 1960s seemed especially refreshing for many who were increasingly frustrated by both their correlation coefficients and their treatment experiences. For me, the original excitement of the social-learning behavior approach[1] (Bandura, 1969; Bandura & Walters, 1963; Mischel, 1968; Rotter, 1954; Skinner, 1953) lay in its promise to focus on the client-defined problematic behavior in its context rather than on the clinician's inferences about the symptomatic meaning of that behavior as a sign of generalized dispositions or psychodynamics. At last a person who complained, for example, of sexual performance problems or of fears of going outdoors might achieve help with the behaviors of concern rather than be given insights of uncertain validity into their hypothetical origins or symptomatic significance. In spite of all the ugly stereotypes so often associated with it, the behavioral approach at its best promised to pay more than lip service to each individual's uniqueness and to deal with behavior at the level at which the person categorized and lived it.

A behavior theory contribution of special interest for personality psychology is the view that behavioral discontinuities—real ones and not merely superficial or trivial surface changes—are part of the genuine phenomena of personality (Mischel, 1968, 1973). This perspective suggests that an adequate conceptualization of personality has to recognize that people change as the conditions of their lives change and that these changes are genuine, not merely phenotypic. In that view, an adequate account of human personality must have as much room for human discrimination as for generalization, as much place for personality change as for stability, and as much concern for one's self-regulation as for his or her victimization by either enduring intrapsychic forces or by momentary environmental constraints.

Early versions of the behavioral approach tended to focus on the role of external variables in the regulation of behavior (and hence emphasized contingencies in the environment). The rapid growth in recent years of the behavioral approach was soon accompanied by an increasing focus on the social and psychological environments in which people live, making distinctions between clinical–personality and social–experimental psychology increasingly ambiguous. As is true in most new fields, a first concern in the study of environments has been to try to classify them and provide taxonomies. Depending on one's purpose, however, many different classifications are possible and useful (Magnusson & Ekehammar, 1973; Moos, 1973, 1974). It may be as futile, then, to seek any single "basic" taxonomy of situations as it is to search for a final or ultimate taxonomy of traits: We can label situations in at least as many different ways as we can label people. We must not settle simply for a trait psychology of situations in which events and settings, rather than people, are subject to labeling. The naming of situations is no substitute for analyzing the process of *how*

---

[1]I refer here to the behavioral-learning approaches that began with an explicit break from the earlier Miller–Dollard translations of psychodynamic theory into the language of learning and that have become increasingly cognitive and social in orientation (Mischel, 1976).

conditions and environments interact with the people in them. That is, we must go beyond descriptions of the environment to the psychological processes through which environmental conditions and people influence each other reciprocally.

In the analysis of this interaction, contemporary behavior theorists moved rapidly beyond the objective environment and took increasing account of cognitive–symbolic processes, both as vital for social learning (Bandura, 1969) and as key components of individuality (Mischel, 1973). Moving beyond the habit-learning and drive formulations of earlier learning models, a focus on cognition generally and, specifically, on the role of subjective expectancies, values, and goals (Rotter, 1954) and of self-instructions, plans, and self-regulatory systems (Bandura, 1977; Meichenbaum, 1977, Mischel, 1973) has increasingly characterized applications of the behavioral approach to the study of persons.

Contemporary versions of behavior theory emphasize that what one does and experiences depends on self-evaluative processes, self-standards, and self-estimates and not merely on environmental and external circumstances (Bandura, 1977; Kanfer, 1975). They continue to cognitivize traditional behavior theory by emphasizing that how events are interpreted may be more crucial than the events themselves. Likewise, they view the individual's awareness of the contingencies in the situation (his or her understanding of what behavior leads to what outcome) as a crucial determinant of the resulting actions and choices. Finally, they stress that any given stimulus condition may have a variety of effects, depending on how the individual construes and transforms it (Mischel, 1974). The result is a much simpler and less mechanical view of the individual, with further evaporation of the boundaries between the personological, social, and cognitive domains. The result also is an emerging view of the person as a cognitive creature with both impressive cognitive competencies and substantial judgmental fallibilities.

For me, especially compelling evidence for the cognitive competencies of people (which we psychologists so easily underestimate) is found when we study young children's growing understanding of psychological principles underlying social behavior. Many of us have quipped at cocktail parties about how our grandmothers knew most of the things that psychologists labor so heavily to discover empirically. Lacking grandmothers, but having good access to young children, we decided to see which findings, if any, from the bedrock principles of our field would become known to youngsters early in the course of development (Mischel & Mischel, 1979). We constructed objective multiple choice tests that confronted children from preschool age through the sixth grade with highly specific questions requiring them to predict the probable outcome of classical experiments in psychology that we carefully described in detail, stripped of jargon, and phrased in age-appropriate ways. These experiments ranged from Asch's study on conformity through Bandura's work on modeling, Pavlov's classical conditioning, and Skinner's studies of reinforcement schedules. Perhaps we were naive, but we were surprised to find that by the time the children reached about age 10, they knew an impressive amount of psychology. They knew, for example, about the aggression-facilitating effects of watching aggressive models; they knew that live modeling with guided participation is a more effective treatment for phobias than either systematic desensitization or symbolic (film-based) modeling; they knew that Harlow's frightened monkeys would cling to the milkless terry cloth mother more than to the wire one with milk. And although fourth graders did not know that a bystander will be more likely to help when alone than when in a group, this ostensible nonobvious insight of social psychology was known to children by the time they reached the sixth grade.

Lest we decide to rely exclusively on our children's psychological knowledge, let me emphasize that their knowledge was not limitless: They were systematically wrong, for example, about conformity in the Asch situation and about the effects of cognitive dissonance, and they did not know Pavlov's discovery about classical conditioning. They did, however, know that intermittent reinforcement makes Skinner's pigeons peck longer after the food stops. The fact that by grade six we get correlations as high as .93 ($N = 10$) between knowledge and intelligence test scores makes us feel that spontaneous knowledge of psychological principles about social behavior may indeed be an important ingredient of personal and cognitive competence, and its developmental course may be worth pursuing systematically.

In my own version of the cognitive–social learning approach (Mischel, 1973, 1979), the person variables of special interest are the individual's competencies, encoding strategies, expectancies, values, plans–rules, and self-regulatory systems.[2] Even the mere listing of these variables should make it clear how far such a position is from the stereotyped view in which behavioral approaches leave the person a personality-less victim of every momentary situation and how heavy the reliance on cognitive constructs has become. It is equally far from the attempt to develop an exhaustive listing of individual-difference dimensions, motives, and defenses that characterized trait and psychodynamic approaches to personality. Nevertheless, it must be emphasized that the impact of these person variables on behavior hinges on specific interactions between the individual and the psychological conditions of his or her life. In my view, perhaps the greatest resistance to situational forces is shown by some of the individual's personal constructs. The "theories" we form about behavior (as in people's implicit personality theories about self and others) may be some of the most stable and situation-free constructions. That has double-edged consequences. On the one

---

[2]In my current research program I am especially concerned with how encoding strategies are influenced by affective states (Lewinsohn, Mischel, Chaplin, & Barton, 1980; Mischel, Ebbesen, & Zeiss, 1976) with the nature of everyday person-categories and their functions (Cantor & Mischel, 1979); and with the development of the individual's own knowledge and understanding of self-regulatory processes in particular and psychological principles more generally (Mischel, 1979).

hand, the tenacity of these constructions provides a needed degree of stability in an otherwise excessively complex, disorganized, and unstable world. On the other, they also may become hard to disconfirm and may lead us to badly misinfer, as we know from studies of the fallibility of the human judge and intuitive predictor (Nisbett & Ross, 1980).

COGNITIVE ECONOMICS

The same lines of research that help illuminate the nature and limitations of thought and judgment also are helping to clarify some of the puzzles that have made progress in personality and clinical psychology especially difficult. Studies of both clinical judgment and everyday social perception are teaching us much about how the constructs and expectations of the judge and structure interact with whatever data there might be "out there" in the world of the perceived. That is one of the fundamental, enduring messages that emerges from the fields of both personality and cognitive psychology. Indeed, beginning in the late 1940s with the "new look" (Bruner, 1957), we have come to recognize that there are cognitive heuristics (distortions, simplifications, and biases that channel what we expect and how we act) through which we go rapidly beyond the information given. Much in the present volume testifies to the continuation in new forms of this insight.

Especially in the last decade, research in cognitive and social psychology, most notably investigations of how people categorize, simplify, and process information when making social judgments, has begun to illuminate the cognitive bases for many of the enduring paradoxes and historical dilemmas of personality and clinical psychology (Nisbett & Ross, 1980; Tversky & Kahneman, 1971, 1974, 1979). For example, such studies have shown elegantly how certain everyday heuristics of inference may bias the judge (whether layperson or trained scientist) to ignore base rates (unless they are causally relevant) and the reliability of evidence. The "representativeness" heuristic, for instance, leads one to predict incorrectly extreme values and low probability events when they happen to resemble what one is trying to predict. The same heuristic also helps to account for other common judgmental embarrassments found in the literature on clinical inference (Mischel, 1968, Chapter 5). Thus the "illusion of validity" (Kahneman & Tversky, 1973, p. 249) arises and persists because the very factors that enhance the judge's subjective confidence—such as the consistency and extremity of the data—often are correlated negatively, in fact, with the accuracy of predictions, creating the paradox of confident predictors who persist in practices that are objectively unjustifiable. Moreover, the layperson, like the clinician, eagerly seeks *causal* explanations of events (Tversky & Kahneman, 1979) and in these explanations tends most readily and naturally to attribute causality to the enduring dispositions of actors rather than to the particular circumstances in which they act. The growing insights into our cognitive processes and our falli- bility as intuitive psychologists are an important part of the general recognition of what might be called "cognitive economics": the recognition that people (in- cluding scientists) are flooded by information that somehow must be reduced and simplified to allow efficient processing and to avoid an otherwise overwhelming overload.

These cognitive economics are a mixed blessing. On the one hand, categoriza- tions are the units essential for any kind of generalizing, providing the foundation of efficient information processing and thought. On the other hand, a reliance on preconceived typologies has its costs as well as its value, potentially encouraging attributions of the characteristics associated with a category to each member, even when those characteristics may not fit the individual. Such gratuitous at- tributions may constrain the subsequent behavior of the perceived as well as bias the perceptions and actions of the perceiver (Snyder, this volume; Snyder, Tanke, & Berscheid, 1977). A summary of the gist of diverse behaviors may undermine attention to their specific details and nuances. A tendency to exagger- ate and overgeneralize the structure that actually exists in the individual's be- havior may lead us to underestimate the incompleteness and flexibility in that structure. By searching for "good fits" to our general type categories, we may misjudge—and mistreat—people who poorly fit our preconceptions. The advan- tage of categorizing is that it allows thought and prevents us from being over- whelmed by a flood of stimuli. The disadvantage is that it allows stereotyping and may lead us to view and treat people on the basis of the types or categories into which we squeeze them rather than on the basis of each individual's unique- ness.

Much confusion in theorizing about personality may reflect a failure to recog- nize that categorizations are an inevitable, fundamental, and pervasive aspect of information processing, built into our cognitive economics. Such categorizations can be made at different levels, for different goals, and with distinctive gains and losses (Mischel, 1979). Categorizations about people at a fairly molar or global level, as in broad-trait ratings, can provide widely shared characterizations of what individuals "are like in general," and these characterizations of gist or central tendency may be stable and reliable over long periods of time. However, such broad categories will obscure the subtle interactions of the particular indi- vidual's behavior with particular contexts. Categorizations at a more molecular, context-bound, and behavioral level, on the other hand, tend to highlight the discriminativeness of behavior in relation to changes in the specific psychologi- cal situation, focusing on the within-person variance in behavior rather than on the mean (Mischel, 1968, 1973). A category that greatly helps us to see the fine-grain nuances of someone's behavior as it shifts with changes in life condi- tions may actually make it more difficult to see the overall gist of what they are doing "on the whole." In recent years, the importance of these categorization processes in everyday person perception has begun to be recognized, and provides one of the clearest interfaces of personality, social, and cognitive psychology (Cantor, this volume; Cohen, this volume; Higgins, this volume; Jeffery & Mischel, 1979).

For example, some research suggests that the strategy that perceivers use to process information about a person is affected importantly by their particular purposes. When their purpose is optimal recall, perceivers take account of both unifying traits and unifying contexts to the degree that they are "built-in" (intrinsic) to the actual structure of the information (Cohen, this volume; Jeffery & Mischel, 1979; Mischel, Jeffery, & Patterson, 1974). But when their purpose is either to form an impression or to make specific predictions, they tend to focus primarily on unifying traits, on the attributes of the person, glossing over common contexts. The cost of this strategy may be reduced recall of information about contexts or situations; the gain may be greater cognitive economy in the formation of a coherent person impression.

It also has become increasingly plain that the lay perceiver has a well-structured system of expectations in the form of "implicit personality theories" about what behavioral signs go with what dispositional qualities and about how these qualities, in turn, tend to cluster and co-occur in different kinds of people (Schneider, 1973; Shweder, 1975). There has been much debate about whether or not these configurations are merely illusions in the head of the perceiver. In my view, there certainly are significant, meaningful correlations among person attributes in the real world. For example, there probably is a tendency for sociable behavior to co-occur with talkative and active behavior in certain types of persons (e.g., extraverts), just as sweet songs, feathers, and wings tend to co-occur in certain kinds of animals (e.g., canaries). Structure, I believe, exists neither "all in the head" of the perceiver nor "all in the person" perceived; it is instead a function of an interaction between the beliefs of observers and the characteristics of the observed, in the person domain as well as in the common object domain. While I doubt the utility of broad-trait inferences for many purposes, and certainly do not regard traits as adequate units for the psychological explanation of behavior, I do not question their roots in the behavior of the persons perceived as well as in the cognitive structures of those who perceive them. Perceivers surely go beyond the information they are "given," but they just as surely do not invent regularly the information itself. Information in the head of the perceiver and in the world of the perceived interacts in the course of person perception. Thus, perceivers expect that certain behaviors go together: To some significant extent these co-occurrences do occur more often than by chance; in the search for the gist of another person's qualities, perceivers can discount molecular inconsistencies and exaggerate observed invariances to build meaningful coherences about the individual's distinguishing characteristics (Cantor, this volume). Instead of debating the existence or reality of such coherences, we need to continue to clarify with increasing depth their nature and organization and the rules through which they may be recognized.

THE RETURN OF THE SELF AND
PERSONAL CONSTRUCTS

Some anticipations of current developments at the personality–cognition interface may be found in the phenomenological and self theory of which perhaps the most influential modern spokesman was Carl Rogers. Beginning in the 1940s and 1950s, he adamantly asserted that our *perceptions* of events, more than their objective reality, guide how we act. Rogers was one of the first psychologists to recognize that the self provides a most important consistency-generating organizing unit. If I sense correctly what is happening in the field now (as reflected partly in this volume) one sees again a new concern not only with cognition generally but with the self particularly as an organizing structure that provides coherence and unity in the face of behavioral diversity (Kuiper & Derry, Locksley & Lennauer, Markus & Smith, and Rogers in this volume). It is to be hoped that the current approaches to the self will not endow it with the homunculus and will not create the tautologies that undermined the usefulness and credibility of the concept of self in earlier formulations.

George Kelly was another exciting historical force in the same vein, although his full influence is just beginning to be felt. Kelly (1955) noted in his personal construct theory that we perpetuate a curious dichotomy in how we practice psychology. When we scientists talk about other people, they are "subjects" whose behavior is governed by laws and depends on motives, contingencies, and reinforcement conditions. But when we talk about ourselves, we see ourselves as cognitive beings, who form and test hypotheses about the world. Kelly suggested, long before others, that the same orientation and principles ought to be used in talking about our "subjects" and about ourselves. He thus foreshadowed much in contemporary psychology, and his wisdom has not yet been fully recognized (Mischel, 1980). His notion that a person is capable always of constructive alternativism, of creating alternative worlds, is especially appealing to the present cognitive zeitgeist in psychology. He insisted that while cognition may not be able to change an event at all, one is always free to reconstrue what the event means and how it impacts. One can always recategorize the meaning of the event even if one cannot change its existence. I think that is an extremely important idea, introducing the possibility of freedom through reconstruing, through recategorizing, and through cognitive transformations that allow us to build alternative ways of seeing and being. It is this concern with personal meaning and understanding that serves as a main theme of the present volume.

PERSONALITY, COGNITION, AND
SOCIAL INTERACTION

In sum, the term "personality psychology" does not need to be limited to the study of differences between individuals in their consistent attributes, as it has been traditionally. Personality psychology ultimately must also encompass the study of how people's cognitive and behavioral activities, their understandings and actions, interact with—and shape reciprocally—the conditions of their lives.

A comprehensive approach to personality psychology, in my view, must emphasize the interdependence of behavior and conditions, mediated by the constructions and cognitive activities of the person who generates them (Mischel, 1973). It must recognize the human tendency to invent constructs and to adhere to them as well as to generate subtly discriminative behaviors across settings and over time. It must take account of the crucial role of situations (conditions) but recognize that they serve as informational inputs whose effect on behavior depends on how they are processed. Moreover, such an approach needs to recognize that the person's behaviors and expectations change situations as well as being changed by them in a reciprocal interaction (Athay & Darley, this volume; Snyder, this volume). The present volume should help to illuminate those reciprocal interactions while simultaneously bridging arbitrary divisions between personality, social, and cognitive psychology. The work reported in the following pages should nicely document the increasing fuzziness of those categories. I hope that this work also points toward a future in which both cognitive and social processes will become fully integrated into a coherent and comprehensive view of the person.

ACKNOWLEDGMENTS

I deeply appreciate the helpful comments of Nancy Cantor and John Kihlstrom on earlier versions of this chapter.

Preparation of this chapter was facilitated by Grant MH06830 from the National Institute of Mental Health and by Grant HD MH09814 from the National Institute of Child Health and Human Development.

Portions of this chapter are adapted from Mischel, 1979.

REFERENCES

Allport, G. W. *Personality: A psychological interpretation.* New York: Holt, Rinehart & Winston, 1937.
Allport, G. W., Vernon, P. E., & Lindzey, G. *A study of values* (3rd ed.). Boston: Houghton Mifflin, 1960.

Bandura, A. *Principles of behavior modification.* New York: Holt, Rinehart & Winston, 1969.

Bandura, A. *Social learning theory.* Englewood Cliffs, N.J.: Prentice-Hall, 1977.

Bandura, A., & Walters, R. *Social learning and personality development.* New York: Holt, Rinehart & Winston, 1963.

Block, J. Advancing the psychology of personality: Paradigmatic shift or improving the quality of research. In D. Magnusson & N. S. Endler (Eds.), *Personality at the crossroads: Current issues in interactional psychology.* Hillsdale, N.J.: Lawrence Erlbaum Associates, Erlbaum, 1977.

Bruner, J. S. On perceptual readiness. *Psychological Review,* 1957, *64,* 123-152.

Cantor, N., & Mischel, W. Prototypes in person perception. In L. Berkowitz (Ed.), *Advances in experimental social psychology* (Vol. 12). New York: Academic Press, 1979.

Chapman, L. J., & Chapman, J. P. Illusory correlations as an obstacle to the use of valid psychodiagnostic signs. *Journal of Abnormal Psychology,* 1969, *74,* 271-280.

D'Andrade, R. G. Cognitive structures and judgment. Paper prepared for T.O.B.R.E. Research Workshop on *Cognitive Organization and Psychological Processes,* Huntington Beach, Calif., August 16-21, 1970.

Epstein, S. The stability of behavior: I. On predicting most of the people much of the time. *Journal of Personality and Social Psychology,* 1979, *37,* 1097-1126.

Erdelyi, M. H., & Goldberg, B. Let's not sweep repression under the rug: Towards a cognitive psychology of repression. In J. F. Kihlstrom & F. J. Evans (Eds.), *Functional disorders of memory.* Hillsdale, N.J.: Lawrence Erlbaum Associates, 1979.

Festinger, L. *A theory of cognitive dissonance.* Stanford, Calif.: Stanford University Press, 1957.

Grossberg, J. M. Behavior therapy: A review. *Psychological Bulletin,* 1964, *62,* 73-88.

Guilford, J. P. Factors and factors of personality. *Psychological Bulletin,* 1975, *82,* 802-814.

Hartshorne, H., & May, M. A. *Studies in deceit.* New York: Macmillan, 1928.

Jeffery, K. M., & Mishel, W. Effects of purpose on the organization and recall of information in person perception. *Journal of Personality,* 1979, *47,* 397-419.

Kahneman, D., & Tversky, A. On the psychology of prediction. *Psychological Review,* 1973, *80,* 237-251.

Kanfer, F. H. Self-management methods. In F. H. Kanfer & A. P. Goldstein (Eds.), *Helping people change.* New York: Pergamon, 1975.

Kazdin, A. E., & Wilson, G. T. *Evaluation of behavior therapy: Issues, evidence and research strategies.* Cambridge, Mass.: Ballinger, 1978.

Kelly, G. A. *The psychology of personal constructs* (Vols. 1 & 2). New York: Norton, 1955.

Labov, W. The boundaries of words and their meanings. In C. J. Baily & R. Shuy (Eds.), *New ways of analyzing variations in English.* Washington, D.C.: Georgetown University Press, 1973.

Lakoff, G. Hedges: A study in meaning criteria and the logic of fuzzy concepts. *Papers from the 8th Regional Meeting, Chicago Linguistics Society.* Chicago: University of Chicago Linguistics Department, 1972.

Lehrer, A. Indeterminacy in semantic description. *Glassa,* 1970, *4,* 87-109.

Lewin, K. *Field theory in social science; selected theoretical papers.* D. Cartwright (Ed.), New York: Harper & Row, 1951.

Lewinsohn, P. M., Mischel, W., Chaplin, W., & Barton, R. Social competence and depression: The role of illusory self-perceptions? *Journal of Abnormal Psychology,* 1980, *89,* 203-212.

McClelland, D. C. *Personality.* New York: Holt, Rinehart & Winston, 1951.

Magnusson, D., & Ekehammar, B. An analysis of situational dimensions: A replication. *Multivariate Behavioral Research,* 1973, *8,* 331-339.

Meichenbaum, D. *Cognitive-behavior modification.* New York: Plenum Press, 1977.

Mischel, W. *Personality and assessment.* New York: Wiley, 1968.

Mischel, W. Direct versus indirect personality assessment: Evidence and implications. *Journal of Consulting and Clinical Psychology,* 1972, *38,* 319-324.

Mischel, W. Toward a cognitive social learning reconceptualization of personality. *Psychological Review*, 1973, *80*, 252–283.

Mischel, W. Processes in delay of gratification. In L. Berkowitz (Ed.), *Advances in experimental social psychology* (Vol. 7). New York: Academic Press, 1974.

Mischel, W. *Introduction to personality* (2nd ed.). New York: Holt, Rinehart & Winston, 1976.

Mischel, W. The interaction of person and situation. In D. Magnusson & N. S. Endler (Eds.), *Personality at the crossroads: Current issues in interactional psychology*. Hillsdale, N.J.: Lawrence Erlbaum Associates, 1977.

Mischel, W. On the interface of cognition and personality: Beyond the person–situation debate. *American Psychologist*, 1979, *34*, 740–754.

Mischel, W. George Kelly's anticipation of psychology: A personal tribute. In M. J. Mahoney (Ed.), *Psychotherapy process: Current issues and future directions*. New York: Plenum, 1980.

Mischel, W., Ebbesen, E., & Zeiss, A. R. Determinants of selective memory about the self. *Journal of Consulting and Clinical Psychology*, 1976, *44*, 92–103.

Mischel, W., Jeffery, K. M., & Patterson, C. J. The layman's use of trait and behavioral information to predict behavior. *Journal of Research in Personality*, 1974, *8*, 231–242.

Mischel, W., & Mischel, H. N. *Children's knowledge of psychological principles*. Manuscript in preparation, Stanford University, 1979.

Mischel, W., & Peake, P. *Correlates of children's delay behavior*. Work in progress, Stanford University, 1979.

Moos, R. H. Conceptualizations of human environments. *American Psychologist*, 1973, *28*, 652–665.

Moos, R. H. Systems for the assessment and classification of human environments. In R. H. Moos & P. M. Insel (Eds.), *Issues in social ecology*. Palo Alto, Calif.: National Press Books, 1974.

Murray, H. A. *Explorations in personality*. New York: Oxford, 1938.

Nisbett, R. E., & Ross, L. D. *Human inference: Strategies and shortcomings of social judgment*. Century Series in Psychology. Englewood Cliffs, N.J.: Prentice-Hall, 1980.

Peterson, D. R. *The clinical study of social behavior*. New York: Appleton, 1968.

Rosch, E. Cognitive reference points. *Cognitive Psychology*, 1975, *1*, 532–547.

Rosch, E., Mervis, C., Gray, W., Johnson, D., & Boyes-Braem, P. Basic objects in natural categories. *Cognitive Psychology*, 1976, *8*, 382–439.

Rotter, J. B. *Social learning and clinical psychology*. Englewood Cliffs, N.J.: Prentice-Hall, 1954.

Schneider, D. J. Implicit personality theory: A review. *Psychological Bulletin*, 1973, *73*, 294–309.

Shweder, R. A. How relevant is an individual difference theory of personality? *Journal of Personality*, 1975, *43*, 455–485.

Skinner, B. F. *Science and human behavior*. New York: Macmillan, 1953.

Smith, E. E. Theories of semantic memory. In W. K. Estes (Ed.), *Handbook of learning and cognitive processes* (Vol. 5). Potomac, Md.: Lawrence Erlbaum Associates, 1976.

Snyder, M., Tanke, E. D., & Berscheid, E. Social perception and interpersonal behavior: On the self-fulfilling nature of social stereotypes. *Journal of Personality and Social Psychology*, 1977, *35*, 656–666.

Tversky, A. Features of similarity. *Psychological Review*, 1977, *84*, 327–352.

Tversky, A., & Kahneman, D. Belief in the law of small numbers. *Psychological Bulletin*, 1971, *76*, 105–110.

Tversky, A., & Kahneman, D. Judgment under uncertainty: Heuristics and biases. *Science*, 1974, *185*, 1124–1131.

Tversky, A., & Kahneman, D. Causal schemata in judgments under uncertainty. In M. Fishbein (Ed.), *Progress in social psychology*. Hillsdale, N.J.: Lawrence Erlbaum Associates, 1979.

Vernon, P. E. *Personality assessment: A critical survey*. New York: Wiley, 1964.

Wittgenstein, L. *Philosophical investigations*. New York: Macmillan, 1953.

II

COGNITIVE PROCESSES IN PERSONALITY

2 A Cognitive–Social Approach to Personality

Nancy Cantor
Princeton University

An Interdisciplinary Approach to Personality

Personality psychology seems to be caught among conflicting goals, themes, and forces. On the one hand it is a psychology of "individual differences" with a commitment to an idiographic approach. On the other hand, the study of individual differences requires (at least initially) a focus on general processes, mechanisms, and dimensions of behavior (e.g., nomothetic traits, general principles of social learning). Similarly, personologists have been mainly attentive to the search for intraindividual stability, with the person as the main unit of analysis. Intraindividual behavioral stability, however, turns out to be heavily dependent on the social–situational context and subject to variation as a function of both cognitive and social–situational factors. Personality theorists increasingly embrace the view that individual social behavior is partially shaped by the expectations and observation of actors in social interaction settings (Magnusson & Endler, 1977; Mischel, 1973). Behavior may be determined as much by the inferences an actor draws about his/her own dispositions, the requirements of a situation, and the behavior of others as it is by fully formed predispositions or traits. A social psychological interpretation of personality focuses on the *dynamic* growth and development of consistent patterns of behavior over the course of a social interaction sequence (Darley & Fazio, 1978; Snyder & Swann, 1978a). A cognitive–social psychological interpretation supplements this position by focusing on the role of prior inferences and current perceptions about the self and others and the situation in shaping an individual's social responses.

The current broadening of personality psychology results in a discipline concerned as much with general processes as with specific dimensions of individual differences, a discipline as sensitive to the dynamic, interactional character of social behavior as it is devoted to finding underlying stability and generality (Magnusson & Endler, 1977). Personality psychology in its broadened form shares substantially with both social and cognitive psychology. The focus on cognitive mediation, the role of goals, expectations, and interpretations in shaping behavior joins personologists and cognitivists in common cause. Social and personality theorists similarly join forces in a concern with the subtle control of situational variables over behavior and the interactive, dynamic nature of social behavior. The intersection of the interests of all three areas involves the fundamental interaction between relatively long-term person variables like knowledge structures or dispositions and relatively short-term and immediate social-situational conditions as they conspire together to shape cognitive activity and social behavior (see, for example, the distinctions in the cognitive literature between top–down and bottom–up processing, the social psychological treatment of self-fulfilling prophecies, and the person–situation interactionism debate in personality psychology). Behavior occurs in a social context with other people, over time, and in actors who have well-structured beliefs and expectations about situations, people, and their typical behavior in similar social interactions. Dynamic interactionism involves sometimes complementary, sometimes conflicting interests—forces of the individual and the social situation, prior beliefs and the immediate reality, long-term stability and short-term specificity, as well as the constant interplay between affective reactions and cognitive mechanisms. The determinants of behavior are so multifaceted and complex that the study of social behavior and personality seems to beg for an interdisciplinary psychological approach.

FIGURE–GROUND MODEL OF
SOCIAL BEHAVIOR

Actors in a social interaction are constantly (and probably automatically) engaged in categorizing, testing, changing, and updating their theories about the ongoing "event" (its actors, setting, goals, outcome, etc.). A figure–ground model of personality sees social behavior as figure against a background of cognitive and affective activity within the individual. Such background cognitive activity may sometimes be in the direct service of planning behavior, but it may also simply be part of social reactions and occur almost automatically and quite nonstrategically. Social reactions are to some degree "theory driven"; we enter situations with expectations, form impressions of people quite quickly, and shape behavior with these in mind. However, there is also a fine and complex interplay between prior expectations and current perceptions. As the interaction unfolds, we are sensitive to the actual stimuli in the present context; expectations are changed and behavior is planned to fit both prior beliefs and current reality. The cornerstone of such a model is the dynamic interaction of prior beliefs/ expectations and current social conditions and perceptions. Consider the following personal example of behavior born of such an interaction.

A New York Subway Experience

Having read newspaper articles claiming an increase in subway crime in New York, I go in to the city and spend my entire time identifying potential muggers, rapists, and murderers. Riding downtown in the subway, I carefully consider each new person who enters the subway car, trying to abstract a total picture—physical appearance, facial expression, clothes, place that he/she got on, shopping bag that he/she is holding. I consider the various categories into which he/she might fit—for example, criminal type, ex-mental patient, or disgruntled graduate student down in the dumps over a rejection slip from *Journal of Personality and Social Psychology*. Having considered the possibilities, having matched the person's attributes to my prototype for each of these categories, and having seen that he/she better fits my criminal-type prototype than my angry-graduate-student one, I calmly inspect the distance between us, decide that he/she is ominously close, make a sudden decision to get off at Macy's instead of hitting the galleries in Soho, and leave the subway. As I exit, slipping calmly past the supposed criminal, I find that the suspicious looking shopping bag contains a plant, cat food, and the latest copy of *Science* magazine; that the ragged clothes are a N.Y.U. jogging outfit; and that the grubby haircut is the eastern version of the California laidback look. Thoroughly embarrassed, I stand like an idiot waiting for the next train and trying to think of a plausible excuse to give for my 20-minute delay enroute to Soho. Having totally failed in my "New York subway script," I vow to be more thorough in my assessments next time and consider revising my associations among the shopping bag, ragged sweat shirt, and the prototype for a criminal at large in New York—after all, New York criminal types are bound to be clever, having had so much experience, and I had better rethink their likely appearance in preparation for the ride home.

I am primarily concerned here with the cognitive components underlying social behavior. From this perspective the preceding example can be analyzed into at least three components: the structure of the cognitive system, the structure of the social context, and the cognitive processes operating on prior beliefs/ expectations and current social stimuli and perceptions that lead us from thought to action. The present chapter touches briefly on each of these three "cognitive" components; I use the "subway example" and references to empirical work on social categorization and theory-testing processes in order to illustrate the hypothesized role of each component in shaping an individual's social behavior. The empirical work places particular emphasis on three domains of social perception and interaction in which categorization and theory-testing processes seem salient: making psychiatric diagnoses, labeling other people as certain "types" and categorizing types of everyday situations. For example, I am concerned with the role of "cognitive structure," "input data," and "cognitive categorization processes'' as they determine the psychiatrist's choice of the label ''manic-depressive'' for a patient, the layperson's view of a friend as ''hyper,'' and my belief that New York subways are ''hectic–dangerous–stressful'' situations.

COGNITIVE STRUCTURE

The component labeled ''cognitive structure'' is clearly a broad and vaguely defined one; it should include the person's belief system and knowledge practically in its entirety. For the present purposes, it is used to refer to social *generalizations* that the actor–observer has drawn from direct personal experience or indirect exposure through the media and other institutions of culture. In particular, a categorical analysis of social knowledge focuses on the multiple categorization schemes that people frequently apply to people, to everyday social situations, and to their own feelings and behaviors. Associated with these social categories are beliefs about the attributes typically descriptive of category members. According to this view, cognitive–social structure consists of the (multitude of) ''*bins*'' into which the observer might sort his/her social experience and the *expectations* that are associated with each social category. For empirical research, cognitive–social structure can be sliced small or large. For example, one could study individual social categories such as beliefs about the class of extraverts (Ashmore & Del Boca, 1979; Cantor & Mischel, 1977; Cohen, 1977) or whole social taxonomies with multiple, interrelated categories of different amounts of inclusiveness (Cantor & Mischel, 1979; Taylor, 1979). Similarly, the expectations or generalizations about the typical category exemplar (member) are only relatively stable; they change and shift over the course of an individual's life, a culture's development, and even a single psychology experiment.

Returning briefly to my ''subway experience'': I had three categories of person types, I had primed my image of myself as a spineless weakling (and short to boot), and I had activated my category of stressful–dangerous situations—all this before I even entered the subway car. Further, I had activated abstract images (prototypes) of the physical and behavioral attributes common to these different types of people and situations. I had in my head a set of attributes that typically co-occurred with criminal types, depressed graduate students, and ex-mental patients, and I had a prototype for stressful situations like subways. In fact, my prototype of a ''criminal type'' is so strong that I would have been quite surprised to find one without a twitching face, shopping bag, and grubby appearance. I also have a clear affect—fear—associated with this collection of people. All this information was easily accessible and organized on the basis of previous experience, either direct or based on TV news and movies.

Turning from personal experience to empirical work, my research on cognitive structure has been primarily concerned with categories of psychiatric disorders, types of personalities, and everyday social situations (Cantor, 1979; Cantor

& Mischel, 1979; Cantor, Smith, French, & Mezzich, 1979). The strategy in this research has been to draw on work in the domain of object perception (Rosch, 1978; Smith & Medin, 1979; Tversky, 1977), particularly with regard to models for the representation and organization of knowledge about common objects like tables, cars, etc. The basic notion in this research has been that knowledge about categories may be internally represented and structured in terms of *prototypes* for the category. The category prototype, representing the meaning of the category, has been defined in many ways. The best choice of definition may ultimately come to depend on the domain under study. For example, prototypes have been variously defined as: (1) the central tendency of a set of geometric forms, defined as the mean value of the set of stimulus objects on each relevant feature dimension (Posner & Keele, 1968; Reed, 1972); (2) a representative set of exemplars of the category (Ebbesen & Allen, 1979; Medin & Schaffer, 1978; Smith & Medin, 1979; Walker, 1975), or (3) an abstract set of features commonly associated with members of a category, with each feature assigned a weight according to degree of association with the category (Cantor et al., 1979; Cantor & Mischel, 1979; Rosch & Mervis, 1975; Smith & Medin, 1979).

So, according to the *average value* view, my prototype of a "criminal type" would be a single composite representing the central tendency of the set of known "criminal types." Such a figure might have 8.7 years of education, have 2.3 children, be .25 white and .75 male with .35 of a twitch on its face, and so on. This central tendency prototype would not be descriptive of any actual individual. By contrast, the *exemplar* view would represent my knowledge of the category of "criminal types" by actual prototypical exemplars like "the son-of-Sam killer" or Charles Manson. The *abstract feature set* prototype is somewhat of a compromise between these two other views. It would contain a large set of features (like "shopping bag," "grubby appearance," and "twitch on the face") abstracted on the basis of direct or vicarious experience as both representative of "criminal types" and likely to distinguish criminals from other related person types (e.g., psychotics). (Each feature might also have a weight associated with it to indicate the frequency with which a particular feature is believed to occur in this category.) Although no individual criminal would be expected to possess all these features, any subset of features in the prototype might well describe a real "criminal," recognizable to all on the street. The abstract feature set prototype seems particularly suited to the domain of persons and social situations. It is descriptive of *real* people and situations (as contrasted with the average value one). Moreover, because it contains a large and varied set of features, it is less restrictive than one based on a few known exemplars; the abstract prototype can better represent the *variety* of possible subsets of features found in different persons or situations. For these reasons, I view the abstract feature set prototype as best suited to the social domain and my empirical work has emphasized this later conceptualization. (Of course, I would also expect a person to store in memory descriptions of highly familiar exemplars of particular person categories. I have a clear idea of the particular attributes of Charles Manson, in addition to thinking that a large set of attributes is descriptive of the general class of "criminal types.")

I have looked for evidence of rich and well-structured *consensual prototypes* (defined as sets of attributes that lay people tend to generate and agree upon in describing typical category members) in a variety of different social domains. For instance, Cantor and Mischel (1979) found that undergraduates can generate with relative ease lists of features common to exemplars of a variety of different personality categories like "jocks," "geniuses," "extraverts," and "phobics." The consensual features taken from these lists collectively characterize the category. We define the consensual feature list as the category prototype (Rosch, 1978). The individual features in the prototype list can also be assigned differential weight according to the number of subjects who had originally generated the feature or the percentage of category members with whom the feature is associated. Similar methods have been used to obtain prototypes in the psychiatric domain. Psychiatrists generate fairly rich consensual prototypes for standard diagnostic categories, prototypes that contain many clinical features not found in the professional diagnostic manuals (Cantor et al., 1980). Analyses of the content of the prototypes suggest that perceptual (visual appearance), functional (behavioral), and more abstract (dispositional) features are associated with categories in these domains. Prototypes can also be generated for categories of everyday social interaction situations—parties, classes, and political demonstrations. Content analysis suggests that our knowledge or beliefs about situation categories is tied in great measure to the (proto)typical behavior observed in these situations as opposed to other non-person–oriented features of a situation such as its physical structure (Cantor, 1979).

Pursuing this approach further, it is fruitful to analyze larger chunks of cognitive structure in each domain. One can compare the content, richness, and distinctiveness of prototypes for categories at different levels of inclusiveness in whole taxonomies. For example, Cantor and Mischel (1979) found that the lower levels of inclusiveness of social categorization (i.e., subordinate categories) emphasize the more perceptual and less abstract classes of features. Considering the three taxonomies illustrated in Table 2.1, more information about the typical visual appearance and function or behavior of category members is represented in the consensual prototypes for the less inclusive categories in these taxonomies (kitchen chair, door-to-door salesman, paranoid schizophrenic). The category prototypes for the most abstract categories in these taxonomies (furniture, extravert, functional psychotic) not only are less rich in concrete details but also are less rich in total number of features as well (Cantor et al., 1980; Cantor & Mischel, 1979; Rosch, Mervis, Gray, Johnson, & Boyes-Braem, 1976). The "middle"-level categories in these taxonomies (chair, p.r. type, schizophrenic) have both rich and distinctive prototypes. The prototypes for these categories were richer than those obtained for the most inclusive categories, and there was

TABLE 2.1
Sample Taxonomies

Common Object Taxonomy

furniture
- chair
  - kitchen chair
  - arm chair
- table
  - coffee table
  - dining table

Person-Type Taxonomy

extravert
- p.r. type
  - Madison Avenue advertising man
  - door-to-door salesman
- comic-joker type
  - TV comedian
  - Fraternity practical joker

Psychiatric Taxonomy

functional psychosis
- affective disorder
  - manic-depressive manic
  - manic-depressive depressed
- schizophrenia
  - chronic undifferentiated
  - paranoid schizophrenia

less overlap between the attribute lists for neighboring categories at this middle level than at the more detailed level of subordinate categorizations. Thus the middle level of categorization seems to be the one that provides rich, distinctive, and vivid social prototypes—a level that people presumably may find easiest and most convenient to use in everyday communication and thought. Research on this question may provide solutions to practical problems such as the most appropriate and useful levels of analysis for psychiatric diagnosis or personality assessment.

In addition to multiple levels of categorization, social experience can also be chunked and structured according to entirely different categorical schemes. The same experience can be organized, for example, around a "person focus"— serving to highlight different types of persons—or a "situation focus," which emphasizes the physical and psychological features of the interaction context. The potential for alternative constructions of the same social world raises again the issue of the relative utility of different categorical foci. In this case, utility is not measured by successful diagnosis or assessment procedures but rather by rich and easily accessible descriptions of social experience that might serve as guidelines for planning social behavior.

Reaction-time (RT) paradigms in which subjects are asked to form an image as quickly as possible describing a certain type of person or situation can provide a handle on questions of "construct accessibility" (see Higgins, Chapter 4, this volume) and the relative utility of constructive alternativism—"thinking in different ways" with different categorical organizations. These imagery–RT paradigms provide at least three sources of relevant data: (1) *Reaction-time* data can be used to assess ease of access of the relevant information via one or more types of categorical organization (e.g., person or situation images); (2) Data on the *length* of the images and the *number of information units* provide measures of the degree of articulation of these various categories of information; (3) *Content analyses* provide a measure of the kinds of attributes that one type of categorical focus (e.g., a focus on situations) would highlight as compared with an alternate categorical organization (e.g., a focus on people). Together, these data can provide some indication of the consequences of adopting a person or an environmental focus upon entering an everyday social interaction.

For example, Cantor, Mischel, and Schwartz (Cantor, 1979) recently asked people to use different categorical schemes to access social information. Specifically, they were asked to form visual images of persons (e.g., a jock), of situations (e.g., an athletic event), or of persons in situations (e.g., a jock at an athletic event). Substantial differences were observed in the time required to form the requested images and in the richness of the images. *Situation* images were actually easier to form and richer in content than *person-in-situation* ones, which in turn were more accessible and richer than simple *person* images alone. Content analyses of the *situation* images showed that participants in this condition had actually accessed a great deal of information descriptive of persons and behavior typically found in the situation. Hence, the content of the *situation* and *person* images overlapped considerably. However, it was easier (with regard to speed of accessibility) to organize and access this knowledge via situation labels (a social event) than via person labels (an extravert) or even *person-in-situation* labels (an extravert at a social event). These data suggest that situation categories and situation prototypes provide powerful cognitive guides for structuring and describing social experience. They may also serve as guidelines to socially appropriate behavior in many social interaction situations.

The aforementioned paradigm—combining a prototype and imagery–RT analysis—can also serve to underscore individual differences in social cognition. Knowledge about the social world can clearly be organized by different people around different focal concepts (e.g., typical people I interact with versus typical situations in which I find myself) and individual differences in preferred focus may be reflected in the accessibility and richness of images. For example, an individual differences analysis used by Snyder and Cantor (1979b) in an imagery paradigm revealed one class of people (low self-monitors) who find it easiest to image information about *themselves* compared to situations or abstract categories of people. Low self-monitoring individuals (as measured on the Snyder self-monitoring scale) formed richer images of "themselves" manifesting a variety of common traits in different situations than did high self-monitoring individuals. In contrast, high self-monitoring individuals formed richer images of the "prototypic person" in a variety of trait domains than did the low self-monitoring participants. These individual differences in preferences for different categorical organizations may also be associated with individual differences in social behavior in interactions (Snyder, 1979). For example, some people may most frequently choose to shape their behavior to be "true to their *self-image*" (e.g., focusing on self-categorizations); others may try to fit the personality and needs of the *other person(s)* in the interaction (e.g., focusing on other-person categorization); while still other individuals may try to be the "*prototypic person for the situation*" in which the interaction takes place (e.g., focusing on situation categorizations). To understand these cognitive–behavioral strategies, we need to know more about the richness and utility of information from these various sources, as well as the conditions under which people come to focus on particular kinds of categorization of experience.

How do social knowledge structures, as defined herein and investigated by cognitive and social psychologists, relate to the traditional concerns of personality psychologists? Following Bruner (1957), I see knowledge structures as providing an enormously rich and powerful constraint on individual behavior in social interactions. It is like a particularly dominant stage setting as the curtain rises on the opening scene (Goffman, 1974). Both the content of an individual's cognitive–social structure and his/her typical "encoding strategies" (Mischel, 1973) should be the focus of the personologist's attention if we are to be successful in predicting social behavior. Further, analyses of such powerful cognitive predispositions also provide a view in miniature of the tensions and issues in personality psychology. Cognitive structure is both a stable backdrop and a dynamic script full of emergent guidelines for action to come. It can be idiographically organized and yet faithfully mirror the nomothetic culture of the day. We call it *cognitive* structure and, even so, the beliefs I associate with subways and criminals are affectively "hot" (Abelson, 1976). By *structure* we imply stability and tradition; yet it is tradition waiting to be broken. The criminal type won't always have a scarred and twitching face and lunge at me in the expected manner, just as the person who scores high in extraversion may sometimes appear to be uncharacteristically introverted. A truly dynamic, idiographic yet nomothetic (idiothetic?) approach is clearly called for in a discipline that combines cognitive and social principles into a psychology of personality.

SOCIAL STIMULI IN THE INTERACTION SETTING

At the opposite pole from *cognitive structure* stands the *stimulus structure* and context sensitivity of social perception. Consequently, analysis of the contextual component involves moving from the observer's "head" to the observation situation. The structure of contexts make certain aspects of stimuli particularly salient and likely to receive attention (Tversky, 1977). The accessibility of particular categorization schemes is as much a function of contextual structure as of cognitive structure and expectations (Taylor & Fiske, 1978). Our interpretations of behavior are sensitive to the context in which the actions are observed (Cantor, 1978; Jones & Davis, 1965). So the crowded, dark, rushed subway atmosphere makes salient certain "menacing" features of other people and certain "fearful" aspects of my own affective and physical reactions. Similarly, a psychiatrist's interpretations of an intake interview is presumably as much a function of the filtering of data through the patient's report—an aspect of contextual structure—as it is shaped by the psychiatrist's theoretical preconceptions.

Social psychologists have acknowledged and investigated, for some time, the powerful influence over social behavior and perception of slight, often seemingly trivial, variations in the structure of a situation (Orne, 1962; Rosenthal, 1966). Though social-learning theorists have repeatedly stressed the need for functional and structural analyses of contexts (Mischel, 1976; Rotter, 1954), personologists have been slow to embrace the "situationist" perspective. However, recent attention to "situations" within the (PXS) interactionist camp suggests a shift in focus (Magnusson, 1980; Magnusson & Endler, 1977). As one example of the value of a serious analysis of situations, Price (1979) recently argued that preventative mental health programs could benefit as much by analyzing classes of "risky life situations" (e.g., divorce, pregnancy, change in jobs) as from a focus on high-risk groups of people. Similarly, Argyle (1979) tries to train his patients in "social skills" by focusing their attention on the social and physical structure (characteristics) of different everyday situations— the underlying normative rules of behavior for the situation. (Of course, the situational analyses may be more successful in England, where some structure remains constant and bound by tradition.) Clearly, personologists would be mistaken to "objectify" situational structure independent of the beliefs and perceptual proclivities of the observer and of his/her cultural heritage. It is absolutely essential that such analyses focus on the interactive construction of reality—both perceptions and behavior—as a function of both cognitive and contextual structure (Neisser, 1976). Hence, I turn now to the cognitive processes that unite those components.

COGNITIVE PROCESSES

At the outset of this chapter, I stress the growing concern expressed by personality psychologists for the dynamic, interactional aspects of "personality." Rather than being fixed by a set of clearly defined dispositions, personality—each individual's characteristic pattern of response to a situation—may evolve in a fluid manner as a function of a continual adjustment between the beliefs and expectations and desires of the individual and the social–situational forces in the social context. Social behavior may, at any given moment, reflect an adjustment between the cognitive and affective structure that the actor brings to an interaction and the social–situational structure that he/she finds in the interaction context. The "cognitive-process" component provides the dynamic, constructivist mechanism for such an adjustment process. According to the present position, actors in a social interaction are constantly engaged in a subtle adjustment process, "sizing up" the "interaction event," testing and updating their theories and expectations, and planning (more or *less* consciously or strategically) behavior to fit their current perceptions and goals. The importance, then, of cognitive processes in the shaping of dynamic, adaptive behavior patterns should not be underestimated.

Cognitive processes in social interaction can be thought of as a collection of subprocesses operating in tandem with mutual interrelations and influences. The present chapter considers briefly the role of three such subprocesses: cognitive focusing, social categorization, and theory revision.

Cognitive Focusing

The actor in a social interaction is faced with an overload of information and stimuli to receive attention. This overload occurs both with regard to the complex set of facts, beliefs, and feelings that the actor brings to the interaction and with respect to the complexities of the social–situational environment. Clearly, then, we must assume that as the interaction unfolds, certain "information domains" within the total setting and particular personal goals and feelings of the actor become the focus of special attention. For instance, Higgins (this volume) discusses the relative accessibility and salience of different constructs or expectations that the actor brings to an interaction; whereas Cohen (in this volume) emphasizes the shifting prominence of the various "observational goals" of the actor as the interaction unfolds. Returning to my "subway scene," I clearly brought to the interaction a focus on certain select–person categories— "abnormal" types like criminals, mental patients, and disgruntled graduate students. Further, as the subway ride wore on, I became increasingly focused on my goal of *remaining unharmed,* subjugating my other goal of *getting to my destination*—presumably something in the interaction between my prior "danger" focus on the contextual structure of the dark and crowded subway reinforced my self-protective goal at the expense of the more rational instrumental goal. *Focusing,* then, involves both the selective reinforcing of certain personal goals and expectations and the relative overemphasis on particular stimuli (or attributes of stimuli) in the environment.

Focusing processes are particularly important in that they have fairly direct and observable links to social behavior as it develops, changes, and unfolds. Consider, for example, the consequences for behavior of a choice between focusing on one's own inclinations or desires as opposed to focusing on the cues for socially appropriate behavior implicit in the interaction setting itself (see Snyder's self-monitoring work, reviewed in Snyder, 1979). My behavior in the "subway scene" would certainly have been different had I attended more closely to the *actual* situation and to the strong norm in New York subways to be nonchalant, read one's newspaper, and turn a cheek to all minor disturbances. I might even have noticed the two transit cops and recalled my knowledge of the low base rate of subway crime during afternoon hours had I adopted a more situation- rather than self-focused strategy. However, as we know from research on naive theory-testing strategies (Snyder & Cantor, 1979a; Snyder & Swann, 1978b; Wason & Johnson-Laird, 1972), people tend to focus on, search out, and retrieve from memory theory-confirming, not theory-disconfirming, instances. Therefore, given my general inclination to see the situation as a "dangerous" one and to focus on my own fears and the "creepy" people around me, it is not surprising that my behavioral choice was to "flee" rather than "tough it out."

Empirical research on "focusing strategies" reflects two themes that are central to personality psychology: (1) the constant interplay between general processes and individual differences; and (2) the complex adjustment between an individual's personal proclivities (predispositions) and forces in the social context. Focusing here on a single instance, both themes are addressed in research that Judith Schwartz and I have been conducting on people's naive theories about the relative utility of different pieces of information for predicting the outcome of a social interaction. The general paradigm used in this research involves the following setup: The subjects are asked to read about interactions between two persons and to play the role of one of the participants in the interaction. Each is to ignore his/her own personality and assume the stated character. For example, each one might be asked to play the role of a university student interviewing for a part-time job. Next, each is given three ''clues'' (bits of information about the interaction) and asked to rank order these clues in terms of their utility (informativeness) for predicting the outcome of the interaction. In the foregoing example this would mean that each person is to rank order the clues as to their relative utility for predicting whether the interviewer will agree to hire him/her. Subjects are told that another subject will actually be estimating the likelihood of the stated outcome on the basis of the one or two clues that they chose as most informative. The three clues are always of the following sort: (1) A SELF clue describes the character of the person the subject is role-playing. In the previous example, the student might be described as possessing excellent verbal skills, which help create an impression of real competence. (2) An OTHER person clue describes the personality of the other person in the interaction. In this case, the interviewer might be described as having a great liking for students from this university. (3) A SITUATION clue describes relevant features of the situation. For example, the particular office has no vacant positions at this time; a new position would have to be created. Subjects always receive one SELF clue, one OTHER person clue, and one SITUATION clue for each interaction item. However, these clues are varied according to the degree to which they are positive predictors of the occurrence of the relevant outcome. Each clue can be either a positive predictor of the outcome or a negative predictor of the outcome under consideration. For example, the SITUATION clue described in the foregoing is a negative predictor, or inhibitor, of the outcome in question (getting a job) and the SELF and OTHER clues are both positive predictors, or facilitators, of this outcome. Various combinations of inhibiting (negative) and facilitating (positive) SELF, OTHER, and SITUATION clues were used in the experiment.

Subjects' choices in this paradigm (we have used different variations on the general setup) reflect *generalized biases* against SITUATION clues as well as individual differences in the tendency to focus on SELF or OTHER person clues. We find a clear preference for SELF and OTHER clues over SITUATION clues under all circumstances. Subjects clearly are not willing to ascribe much predictive utility to situational factors in social interaction. However, there are individual variations in the preferences for SELF or OTHER person clues.

Similarly, the adjustment in general (or individual) focusing biases in the face of contextual information is also reflected here. For example, subjects often change from a SELF focus to an OTHER focus as a function of a change in the nature of the SITUATION clue. The SELF and OTHER clues are generally perceived as equally informative when all three clues are either positive or negative predictors of the outcome of the interaction. However, when the SITUATION clue is negatively related to the outcome and the other two clues both positively related to the outcome, the OTHER person clue is suddenly preferred over the SELF clue. This shift in preference occurs on the basis of a single change in the SITUATION clue, with the other two clues remaining the same. Focusing strategies, then, have both individualized and general features; they are stable to the extent that they reflect prior personal proclivities and yet fluid to the degree that they are sensitive to contextual variations.

Social Categorization

Social categorization processes are at the heart of a cognitive–social approach to the study of personality (Kihlstrom, in this volume; Mischel, 1979); the background cognitive behavior in a social interaction involves the actor as observer, "typing" and "sizing up" other people, the situation, and the self-in-that-situation. In so doing, the actor–observer makes contact between the stimuli in the external context (contextual structure) and his/her preconceptions or expectations (cognitive structure).

The particular model of categorization that has motivated my thinking and research in this area is derived from work on the categorization of common objects (Rosch, 1978; Smith & Medin, 1979; Tversky, 1977). This "prototype-matching" model assumes that in typing an object (person, situation, self) the perceiver estimates the degree of similarity between the object and a *prototype* for each category into which the object might plausibly fit. Categorization is a probabilistic process based on *degree* of overlap in features between the new object and the prototype for each different category. Thus, for example, in the subway I busily focus on each new target person, assessing the degree to which the person fits my "prototype" of a would-be mugger, a depressed graduate student, and an ex-mental patient. I look for evidence that the person shares a number of features "representative" of one of these categories and "diagnostic" with regard to distinguishing between categories—the disgruntled graduate student is far more likely (one assumes) to be carrying a large envelope from *JPSP* than is the would-be mugger or ex-mental patient. Of course this categorization decision is both difficult and risky. The prototypes for the three categories undoubtedly overlap considerably. The person's attributes are only partially known to me; I have to estimate the reliability of my first impression. Yet arguing against caution in categorization is my affective involvement in protecting myself; any one of these people could become the as–yet–unnoticed "son-of-the-son-of-Sam murderer." Whatever decision I make will be influenced by my personal concept of gains and losses—is it better to make a fool of myself calling a perfectly harmless New Yorker a crazy person than to take the chance of getting attacked? Further, my decision will be adjusted as a function of my own (minimal) degree of faith in my ability to appear calm and tough in the face of adversity. Clearly social categorization is a complex affair.

The prototype-matching model of categorization (Reed, 1972; Rosch, 1978; Smith & Medin, 1979) allows for considerable flexibility at two levels: (1) As described earlier, the particular structure of the category prototype may vary from domain to domain, category to category. (2) The particular processing rule used to assess degree of similarity to the category prototype(s) (i.e., degree of "prototypicality") can also vary across stimulus domains and theoretical models (Reed, 1972). One general class of rules considers similarity (prototypicality) to be an increasing function of the number of shared features and a decreasing function of the number of distinctive features in the target object and the category prototype(s) (Rosch & Mervis, 1975; Smith & Medin, 1979; Tversky, 1977). This general class of models has proved useful in the domain of personality and psychiatric categorizations (Cantor, 1978; Cantor & Mischel, 1979; Cantor et al., 1980). For instance, Cantor et al. (1980) found that trained psychiatrists were highly reliable, confident, and accurate in their diagnoses of patients who shared many features in common with the prototype for a diagnostic category. (These categorizations were made on the basis of actual case histories obtained from a hospital and presented in unaltered form to the psychiatrists.) The psychiatrists were considerably less reliable, confident, and accurate for judgments about less prototypical patients. Similar findings frequently have been reported for categorizations of common objects like tables and sports cars (McCloskey & Glucksberg, 1978).

Application of the prototype model to social categorization and psychiatric diagnosis has also brought to light factors that are not always considered in the study of other naturalistic categorization processes. For example, categorization judgments in the person (personality and psychiatric) domain are often made under less than optimal conditions: conditions in which a person is observed and/or discussed for a relatively brief amount of time in relatively restricted sets of situations. Judgments made under these degraded viewing conditions (e.g., first impressions or psychiatric case reports) differ considerably from those made on the basis of a full or extended view of the target stimulus (Cantor, 1978). The individual who has a brief glimpse of another person, or the diagnostician who briefly interviews a psychiatric patient, needs to decide whether the features that he/she is observing are even reliable characteristics of the target person (Jones & Davis, 1965; Kelley, 1967). *Inferences* about the target person's past and future behavior begin to enter into categorization decisions under these conditions (Cantor, 1978). The psychiatrist becomes engrossed in deciding whether the patient's symptoms (features) are chronic, cyclic, or in remission (Cantor et al., 1980). Similarly, the lay perceiver focuses more intently on the particular contexts in which a target person exhibits specific behaviors and on the cross-situational consistency of the behaviors (Cantor, 1978; Jones & Davis, 1965; Jones, Davis & Gergen, 1961). Of course, similar issues about the reliability of an impression and the context of an observation may intrude even in the study of common-object categorization (Barsalou, 1978; Labov, 1973; Tversky, 1977). However, such issues would seem to be more uniquely central to the study of person categorization.

Another potential area for divergence between the social and nonsocial domains is the degree of *dissimilarity* to a *category prototype* that will be tolerated in placing a particular item in a particular category. Because the variability in human behavior is quite large (Mischel, 1968), the categorizer of people may expect and tolerate more distortions from a category prototype than might the labeler of common objects. To study this, Cantor and Fitzgerald have been attempting to discover how much diversity, variability, and/or inconsistency people actually expect to find in other people's personalities. We present subjects with constellations of personality and behavioral descriptors and ask them to judge the "plausibility" of such a set of attributes as a description of a "real person." Similarly, we give subjects sets of attributes from standard personality inventories and ask them to create "plausible" and "implausible" persons. These studies of implicit theories of human variability complement studies of categorization in which we see how much variability people will accept and still ascribe a category label to the target person. For example, the prototypical extravert is frequently described as having a personality *dominated* by mostly extraverted attributes (Cantor, 1978). However, personality descriptions that include a much wider *variety* of trait dimensions are perceived as most plausible (i.e., likely to describe the personalities of real people).

These results, though admittedly preliminary, tell us something about the way in which people may use prototypes as standards of comparison in forming impressions and categorizing people they meet in the "real world." The lay perceiver may be willing to accept (and may expect to find) more variety of attributes and less strong domination by one class of attributes in real people as compared with the prototypical standard. The typical extravert may have many different qualities in addition to extraverted attributes, such that extraversion does not constantly dominate the personality. The modal extravert may be further from our image of a prototypical extravert than is the typical chair from the prototypical chair. Therefore, people may weaken their criterion for acceptable degrees of distance from a category prototype in categorizing people as opposed to objects. This divergence between the social and nonsocial domains may be intensified by the need to consider the role that cognitive schemata about the self (Markus, 1977; Rogers, Kuiper, & Kirker, 1977) may play as anchor points in the perception/categorization of people but not of common objects. Tolerance limits in the categorization of other people may be a reflection of the degree of perceived variability in one's own behaviors and attributes. For instance, psychiatrists' perceptions of the *degree* of abnormality of patients' behavior is influenced by their estimates of how unlikely it is that they themselves would engage in similar displays. Finally, as mentioned with regard to my subway experiences, tolerance limits on social categorization may be influenced by the urgency associated with such decisions. Social categorization judgments often have a certain urgency tied to them; somehow we may believe that it is more crucial to our security (as well as more central to planning behavior) to notice quickly that people around us have certain personalities or behavioral styles than to check out the tables and chairs and vegetables in the contextual background. The brief amount of time given people to figure out what is going on in social interactions suggests that in the real world social interaction is going to be guided more by first impressions than by carefully considered ones. In addition to making hasty social categorizations, these decisions may be more "affectively hot" than those typically associated with categorizations of common objects. Further research is needed to test the implications of "hot" as compared with "cold" categorization processes. Research on the meshing of affective–evaluative and cognitive processes may take us further from object categorization studies but closer to the dynamicism at the heart of social categorization.

Theory Revision

A large body of literature now exists that demonstrates the tenacity with which people hold on to pet theories and beliefs (Kuhn, 1962; Wason & Johnson-Laird, 1972) and the ease with which biased theory-testing strategies are applied to confirm these theories (Snyder & Cantor, 1979a; Snyder & Swann, 1978b). Yet people do change their beliefs; behavior is influenced and adjusted to fit the unique, unexpected aspects of each new context. Certainly the specificity and fluidity of individual *behavior* is a familiar, though irritating theme to personality psychologists (Mischel, 1968). Similar research is needed to uncover the conditions that encourage *cognitive fluidity* along with this behavioral flexibility.

The adjustment between prior beliefs/expectations and contextual stimuli (that results in a particular focusing–categorization–behavior strategy in an interaction) may also lead the observer/actor to *occasionally* revise his or her beliefs/ theories in anticipation of the next such encounter. So, standing hanging my head in shame on the subway platform, I might (and I emphasize *might*) just change my beliefs about the prototypical subway mugger. On my way back from Soho (having seen so many grubby shopping-bag people that I no longer believe them to be criminal, just boring) I may now scan the subway car for the hard-core criminal hiding in a three-piece suit, but wearing white socks—surely a clear giveaway! Clearly, we need to devote increased empirical attention to the way in which people reflect on their beliefs and revise theories on the basis of actual experience (Lingle & Altom, 1979).

Cognitive Processes and Behavior

Questions about "cognitive perseverance" and "behavioral variability" have frequently been addressed by social psychologists studying the complex relations between attitudes and behavior. It is clear that the links from thought to action are not entirely direct; stated beliefs and attitudes do not always predict behavior. Moreover, attitudes may persevere even when behavior changes and the available evidence is enough to induce correspondent change in beliefs (Ross, Lepper, & Hubbard, 1975). There are many (new) approaches to these (old) thorny questions: (1) It is clear that behavior is often "mindlessly" adapted to situational cues (Langer, 1978) and/or controlled by contingencies in the situation (Bandura, 1969). Given such behavioral conformity (to situational contingencies), it is not surprising that people do not always change their stated attitudes to be more in line with their past/present behavior—the attitudes reflect generalized expectations about their likely behavior in classes of situations or interactions (Ajzen & Fishbein, 1977), not particular instances in which their behavior was finely tuned to the contingencies perceived in a particular situation; (2) Considering the abundance of evidence recently in favor of the precedence of affectively "hot" reactions over more cool, strictly "cognitive" ones (Zajonc, 1978), we may need to consider that attitudes and beliefs ("cool cognitions") come after the fact, with behavior more directly controlled by mostly automatic affective or "hot cognitive" factors. Again, the after-the-fact generalizations that the actor draws and reports on the basis of social experience may be at a more abstract, "cooled-off" level of analysis than would be necessary to use in predictions of finely tuned behavior in vivo (Mischel, 1979); (3) The complexity of the links between cognitions and actual finely tuned behavior can also be addressed by an individual differences approach. For certain people, the preservation of stable self-images and clear correspondence between behavior and beliefs may be more characteristic; others may favor a more flexible, variable, situation-tuned strategy (Snyder, 1979). Of course, in both cases, cognitions and behavior are intertwined—however, in the former a self-focus replaces a situation-focus exhibited by the latter (Snyder & Cantor, 1979b).

The approach that I have begun to articulate in this chapter also speaks to issues surrounding the complex links between thought and action. The cognitive–social model of personality emphasizes the *dynamic* changing interaction between cognitive structure and contextual structure as mediated by cognitive processes such as focusing, categorization, and theory testing. As a social interaction unfolds, a fine adjustment process begins; behavior presumably grows out of this adjustment. Therefore, this approach places importance on the discovery of the social conditions that promote/inhibit various focusing strategies and consequently induce the actor to categorize the "event" in different ways over the course of the interaction.

The central assumption is that behavior can be better predicted on the basis of knowledge of the focus (and goals) of the actor; but to do this it is necessary to understand the conditions that elicit particular focusing strategies. Participants in social interactions do, on occasion, have the opportunity strategically to plan, control, and even shape or change the outcome of an interaction (for an experimental analog, see Snyder & Swann, 1978a). For example, one occasionally has the choice of behaving so as to "please another person" by acting according to that person's obvious personal style. Or, one could choose to follow one's own "real inclinations." Moreover, one can choose a course of behavior that fits the demands of the situation. In many cases the particular behavioral choice may depend jointly on the individual characteristics of the participant, the clarity of the other person's character, and the clarity of the situational demands. In other words, behavioral strategies may depend on factors influencing focusing and categorization activity.

This behavioral planning may seem instantaneous and automatic, but it is likely to require that the actor has achieved a sense of the characteristics of the people and the interaction situation. However, there is no reason to suppose that "background" cognitive activity cannot be very quick, continuous, and phenomenologically effortless (at least for some people, sometimes). (After all, a *long* reaction time in an imagery experiment is only a few seconds.) To be true to the dynamic quality of the cognitive adjustment process, we need to assume that behavior is *not* statically tuned to either prior beliefs or current contextual contingencies—our models need to be as spread out over time as is real behavior (Thomas & Malone, 1979; Thomas & Martin, 1976) in order to capture the intricate interconnections and contingencies between attitudes and actual behavior. If we assume that cognitive structure is static and try to predict molecular chunks of behavior on the bases of these molar cognitions, we should hardly be surprised to find inconsistencies between them.

Personality and Social Cognition

Throughout this chapter, I invoke my own subway behavior, dissecting the intricate processes underlying a simple overt chunk of cowardly behavior. What has this cognitive–social analysis told us about my "personality" that would (or should) be of interest to personologists? I believe that over the course of these pages we see the development of a "fearful" personality that is neither located solely in *me* or in the New York subways; this "fearful" personality is located exactly where it belongs: at the dynamic interface between my self-inferences and cognitive generalizations and the contextual structure of situations like New York subways (Magnusson & Endler, 1977; Mischel, 1979). To the extent that I respond in an equally cowardly, biased, and bizarre fashion each time I encounter similar situations and similar types of people, and to the extent that my self-inferences correspond to these attributions, I will tend to score high on a paper and pencil inventory measuring fearfulness; I will probably respond fearfully in situations that I perceive as similar to the New York subway; and I will be likely to evoke behavior from others that reinforces and bolsters my fear-responses (Snyder & Swann, 1978a). In other words, I will seem to be a "fearful" person. This is *not* to say that such a "trait" is insensitive to situational forces—the "right" conditions are required to elicit my fearful behavior—nor is it to say that such a "trait" exists independently of either my everchanging self-inferences or my focusing strategies. My personality is a dynamic (I hope) entity, cognitively, socially, and contextually created and molded—it changes; it won't be easy to pin down. At one molar level, I'm just like everyone else; lawful processes (of focusing, categorization, attribution, strategizing) and principles (like context-sensitivity and perseverance) characterize my behavior. But at another molecular level, my "fearful personality" is idiographically structured, and the particulars of how my beliefs interact with unique aspects of the contexts must be considered in order really to "know me" and predict my behavior. After all, who else thinks that men wearing three-piece business suits and white socks are highly likely to be New York subway muggers?

ACKNOWLEDGMENT

I would like to express my deep appreciation to John Kihlstrom for his insightful comments on earlier versions of this chapter.

REFERENCES

Abelson, R. P. Script processing in attitude formation and decision making. In J. S. Carroll & J. W. Payne (Eds.), *Cognition and social behavior.* Hillsdale, N.J.: Lawrence Erlbaum Associates, 1976.

Ajzen, I., & Fishbein, M. Attitude–behavior relations: A theoretical analysis and review of empirical research. *Psychological Bulletin, 1977, 84,* 888–918.

Argyle, M. *The experimental study of the basic features of situations.* Paper presented at The Stockholm Conference on the Situation in Psychological Theory and Research, Stockholm, Sweden, June 1979.

Ashmore, R., & Del Boca, F. Sex stereotypes and implicit personality theory: Toward a cognitive-social psychological conceptualization. *Sex Roles, 1979, 5(2),* 219–248.

Bandura, A. *Principles of behavior modification.* New York: Holt, Rinehart & Winston, 1969.

Barsalou, L. *Context dependent categorization.* Unpublished manuscript, Stanford University, 1978.

Bruner, J. S. On perceptual readiness. *Psychological Review, 1957, 64,* 123–152.

Cantor, N. *Prototypicality and personality judgments.* Unpublished doctoral dissertation, Stanford University, 1978.

Cantor, N. Perceptions of situations: Situation prototypes and person–situation prototypes. In D. Magnusson (Ed.), *The situation: An interactional perspective:* Hillsdale, N.J.: Lawrence Erlbaum Associates, in press.

Cantor, N., & Mischel, W. Traits as prototypes: Effects on recognition memory. *Journal of Personality and Social Psychology, 1977, 35,* 38–48.

Cantor, N., & Mischel, W. Prototypes in person perception. In L. Berkowitz (Ed.). *Advances in experimental social psychology* (Vol. 12). New York: Academic Press, 1979.

Cantor, N., Smith, E. E., French, R., & Mezzich, J. Psychiatric diagnosis as prototype categorization. *Journal of Abnormal Psychology, 1980, 89(2),* 181–193.

Cohen, C. *Cognitive basis of stereotyping.* Paper presented at the meetings of The American Psychological Association, San Francisco, August 1977.

Darley, J., & Fazio, R. *The origin of self-fulfilling prophecies in a social interaction sequence.* Unpublished manuscript, Princeton University, 1978.

Ebbesen, E. E., & Allen, R. B. Cognitive processes in implicit personality trait inferences. *Journal of Personality and Social Psychology,* 1979, *37,* 471–488.

Goffman, E. *Frame analysis: An essay on the organization of experience.* New York: Harper, 1974.

Jones, E. E., & Davis, K. E. From actors to dispositions: The attribution process in person perception. In L. Berkowitz (Ed.), *Advances in experimental social psychology.* New York: Academic Press, 1965.

Jones, E. E., Davis, K. E., & Gergen, K. J. Role playing variations and their informational values for person perception. *Journal of Abnormal and Social Psychology,* 1961, *63,* 302–310.

Kelley, H. H. Attribution theory and social psychology. In D. Levine (Ed.), *Nebraska Symposium on Motivation.* Lincoln: University of Nebraska Press, 1967.

Kuhn, T. *The structure of scientific revolutions.* Chicago: University of Chicago, 1962.

Labov, W. The boundaries of words and their meanings. In C. J. Baily & R. Shuy (Eds.), *New ways of analyzing variations in English.* Washington, D.C.: Georgetown University Press, 1973.

Langer, E. J. Rethinking the role of thought in social interaction. In J. H. Harvey, W. J. Ickes, & R. F. Kidd (Eds.), *New directions in attribution research.* Hillsdale, N.J.: Lawrence Erlbaum Associates, 1978.

Lingle, J., & Altom, M. *Processes of recategorization: When is a likeable person unlikeable?* Paper presented at the meeting of The American Psychological Association, New York, September 1979.

Magnusson, D. *The situation: An interactional approach.* Hillsdale, N.J.: Lawrence Erlbaum Associates, in press.

Magnusson, D., & Endler, N. (Eds.). *Personality at the crossroads: Current issues in interactional psychology.* Hillsdale, N.J.: Lawrence Erlbaum Associates, 1977.

Markus, H. Self-schemata and processing information about the self. *Journal of Personality and Social Psychology,* 1977, *35,* 63–78.

McCloskey, M., & Glucksberg, S. Natural categories: Well-defined or fuzzy sets? *Memory & Cognition,* 1978, *614,* 462–472.

Medin, D., & Schaffer, M. Context theory of classification learning. *Psychological Review,* 1978, *85,* 207–238.

Mischel, W. *Personality and assessment.* New York: Wiley, 1968.

Mischel, W. Toward a cognitive social learning reconceptualization of personality. *Psychological Review,* 1973, *80,* 252–283.

Mischel, W. *Introduction to personality* (2nd ed.). New York: Holt, Rinehart & Winston, 1976.

Mischel, W. On the interface of cognition and personality: Beyond the person–situation debate. *American Psychologist,* 1979, *34*(9), 740–754.

Neisser, U. Cognition and reality: Principles and implications of cognitive psychology. San Francisco: Freeman, 1976.

Orne, M. On the social psychology of the psychological experiment: With particular reference to demand characteristics and their implications. *American Psychologist,* 1962, *17*(11), 776–783.

Posner, M., & Keele, S. On the genesis of abstract ideas. *Journal of Experimental Psychology,* 1968, *77,* 353–363.

Price, R. *The strategic use of environmental information in the prevention of psychological distress.* Paper presented at The Stockholm Conference on the Situation in Psychological Theory and Research, Stockholm, Sweden, June 1979.

Reed, S. K. Pattern recognition and categorization. *Cognitive Psychology,* 1972, *3,* 382–407.

Rogers, T., Kuiper, N., & Kirker, W. S. Self-reference and the encoding of personal information. *Journal of Personality and Social Psychology,* 1977, *35,* 677–688.

Rosch, E. Principles of categorization. In E. Rosch & B. B. Lloyd (Eds.), *Cognition and categorization.* Hillsdale, N.J.: Lawrence Erlbaum Associates, 1978.

Rosch, E., & Mervis, C. Family resemblances: Studies in the internal structure of categories. *Cognitive Psychology,* 1975, *7,* 573–605.

Rosch, E., Mervis, C., Gray, W., Johnson, D., & Boyes-Braem, P. Basic objects in natural categories. *Cognitive Psychology*, 1976, *8*, 382–439.

Rosenthal, R. *Experimenter effects in behavioral research*. New York: Appleton-Century-Crofts, 1966.

Ross, L., Lepper, M., & Hubbard, M. Perseverence in self-perception and social perception: Biased attributional processes in the debriefing paradigm. *Journal of Personality and Social Psychology*, 1975, *32*, 880–892.

Rotter, J. B. *Social learning and clinical psychology*. Englewood Cliffs, N.J.: Prentice-Hall, 1954.

Smith, E. E., & Medin, D. *Representation and processing of lexical concepts*. Unpublished manuscript, Stanford University, 1979.

Snyder, M. Cognitive, behavioral, and interpersonal consequences of self-monitoring. In P. Pliner, K. R. Blankstein, I. M. Spiegel, T. Alloway, & L. Krames (Eds.), *Advances in the study of communication and affect* (Vol. 5). New York: Plenum Press, 1979.

Snyder, M., & Cantor, N. Testing hypotheses about other people: The use of historical knowledge. *Journal of Experimental Social Psychology*, 1979, *15*, 330–342. (a)

Snyder, M., & Cantor, N. *Thinking about ourselves and others: Self-monitoring and social knowledge*. Unpublished manuscript, University of Minnesota and Princeton University, 1979. (b)

Snyder, M., & Swann, W. Behavioral confirmation in social interaction: From social perception to social reality. *Journal of Experimental Social Psychology*, 1978, *14*, 148–162. (a)

Snyder, M., & Swann, W. Hypothesis-testing processes in social interaction. *Journal of Personality and Social Psychology*, 1978, *36*, 1202–1212. (b)

Taylor, S. E. A categorization approach to stereotyping. In D. L. Hamilton (Ed.), *Cognitive processes in stereotyping and intergroup behavior*. HIllsdale, N.J.: Lawrence Erlbaum Associates, 1979.

Taylor, S. E., & Fiske, S. T. Salience, attention, and attribution: Top of the head phenomena. In L. Berkowitz (Ed.), *Advances in experimental social psychology* (Vol. 11). New York: Academic Press, 1978.

Thomas, E. A. C., & Malone, T. On the dynamics of two-person interactions. *Psychological Review*, 1979, *86*(4), 331–360.

Thomas, E. A. C., & Martin, J. Analyses of parent–infant interaction. *Psychological Review*, 1976, *83*(2), 141–156.

Tversky, A. Features of similarity. *Psychological Review*, 1977, *84*, 327–352.

Walker, J. H. Real-world variability, resonableness judgments and memory representations for concepts. *Journal of Verbal Learning and Verbal Behavior*, 1975, *14*, 241–252.

Wason, P. C., & Johnson-Laird, P. N. *Psychology of reasoning: Structure and content*. London: Batsford, 1972.

Zajonc, R. B. *Exposure effect and its antecedents*. Paper presented at the meetings of the American Psychological Association, Toronto, August 1978.

3 Goals and Schemata in Person Perception: Making Sense From the Stream of Behavior

Claudia E. Cohen
Rutgers University

OBSERVATIONAL GOALS IN PERSON PERCEPTION

Making Sense from the Stream of Behavior

As perceivers of other people in our social world, we seem to operate much of the time without awareness of the processes that underlie our interpretation of their behavior. Perhaps only when the behavior of another person challenges or upsets our perceptions do we focus on the interpretation process. For instance, learning that a friend has betrayed a confidence may jolt us into examining our impression of him as trustworthy, and encourage us, in the future, to introspect more carefully when interpreting his actions. However, most of the time, as Tagiuri noted, our "evaluation of other persons, important as it is in our existence, is largely automatic, one of the things we do without knowing very much about the 'principles' in terms of which we operate (Tagiuri, 1958, [ix])."

Perhaps because perceivers are normally unaware of the *principles* or cognitive processes underlying person perception, we tend, both as professional and naive psychologists, to underestimate the complexity of the stimuli that we perceive as well as the difficulty of making sense from those stimuli.[1] For instance, much of the research in person perception has employed a paradigm in which subjects are *given* pieces of information about a target person (usually trait adjectives or brief behavioral descriptions) and are instructed to use the informa-

---

[1]It is unclear whether the lack of awareness of these processes is due to their genuine inaccessibility or to the perceivers' tendency to ignore the appropriate cues.

45

tion to form an impression or make other judgments about the person (Anderson, 1974; Wyer, 1974). Research in this paradigm has thus largely eliminated from study the processes that the perceiver uses to translate the stream of an actor's behavior into informational units. The need to consider the complexity of the behavioral stream has been similarly obscured (see Fiske & Cox, 1979, for a related discussion). Even in recent research, which focuses upon the role of preexisting knowledge structures in the processing of novel person information, the perceiver is usually presented with the stimulus information already extracted from the stream of an actor's behavior. As in earlier person perception research, the stimulus information is usually presented in the form of verbal descriptions and/or trait adjectives (Hamilton, Katz, & Leirer, 1980). It is suggested here that the tradition of bypassing the translation process, where the perceiver extracts and interprets information from the behavior stream, may have had several important consequences in person perception research.

First the range of categories of behavioral information that may be utilized in person perception has not been directly investigated.[2] Second, the units of information about a target person that are presented to subjects in person perception experiments may not be equivalent to the units of information that a perceiver extracts in various person perception situations. Finally, the relationship between cognitive (or other) properties of the perceiver and the extraction and interpretation of information from the actor's behavior has not been fully recognized as an important issue for study. Of particular importance to this chapter is the affect of the perceiver's *observational goal* upon his processing of the stream of an actor's behavior. This chapter explicitly considers the processes underlying the perceiver's extraction and interpretation of information from the actor's behavior.

Consider the process of observing a colleague who is giving a research colloquium. One is confronted with a stimulus that contains many different categories and levels of information. First, the speaker emits both verbal or linguistic and vocal or paralinguistic information. Verbal information may be interpreted by the perceiver at the level of phonemes, words, or clauses (Clark & Clark, 1977). Vocal information contains the pitch and the volume of the speaker's voice; the frequency with which he pauses; and so on (Apple, Streeter & Krauss, 1979; Kramer, 1963). Visually, the available categories of information seem even more diverse. Information about the speaker's physical appearance is continuously available to the perceiver (e.g., is his hair disheveled and are his clothes mismatched?); whereas details of his posture, gestures, and facial expression may change rapidly and thus add to the complexity of the stimulus. In addition, he may perform a series of actions that provide "higher-level" units of

---

[2]Although earlier work on perceivers' accuracy in the perception of emotions and traits (Hastorf, Schneider, & Polefka, 1970) as well as current research on nonverbal cue perception (Zuckerman, Lipets, Koivumaki, & Rosenthal, 1975) are relevant to this issue, the approaches taken differ substantially from the approach outlined in this chapter.

information (e.g., he may pick up a blackboard pointer, pace across the stage, or respond to a question from a member of the audience).

Observational Goals: A Tentative Taxonomy

How then *does* a perceiver make sense of the information contained in the stream of an actor's behavior without being overwhelmed by the diverse categories of inputs? It is suggested here that the *observational goal* of the perceiver serves the function of focusing him on those categories or features of behavior that are relevant to his or her purpose of the moment. *Observational goal* is defined as *the purpose for which an individual plans to use the information gathered from the observation of another's behavior*. Observational goals thus simplify the perceiver's task, possibly by determining the relative importance of various categories of behavioral information, as well as by providing a structure within which to interpret the information. If observational goals guide the processing of information from the behavior stream, and thus the observer's resultant perception of an actor, then it is obviously important to identify the observational goals that perceivers adopt.

A tentative taxonomy of observational goals is described here that derives from two different sources, one theoretical and one empirical. The theoretical source was a provocative paper by Jones & Thibaut (1958) that categorized perceptual goals in the context of social interaction. The empirical source was a review of some observational instructions given to subjects in previous person perception research. From a synthesis of these sources, three broad categories of observational goals are suggested: information-seeking or learning goals, personality analysis goals, and judgment goals. This system is in the initial stages of development and may well undergo future modification.

Information-Seeking or Learning Goals. For this category of observational goals, the actor's behavior serves mainly as a source of information for the perceiver about aspects of the social and nonsocial environment. Neither the personality of the actor nor the interpersonal implications of his behavior for the perceiver's behavior tend to be important. Three goals that may belong to this category, as suggested by instructions in previous research are recall of behavior, observational learning, and empathy (recall: see Anderson & Hubert, 1963; Dreben, Fiske & Hastie, 1979; Hamilton, Katz & Leirer, 1980; observational learning: see Bandura, 1965, Grusec & Mischel, 1966; empathy: see Fiske, Taylor, Etcoff, & Laufer, 1979; Galper, 1976; Regan & Totten, 1975).

Some real-life examples of goals in this category might include observing a friend serve the ball in tennis or empathizing with an acquaintance who has just lost his job.

Personality Analysis Goals.   Included in this category are goals that concern understanding what kind of a person the actor is. These goals may lead an observer to determine traits or underlying dynamics that motivate the actor, as well as to attempt to identify his emotions, attitudes, likes, abilities, and other qualities. Two goals from this category have been used in prior research: impression formation (Anderson, 1965; Asch, 1946; Hendrick & Constantini, 1970; Wyer, 1974) and behavior prediction (Jeffery & Mischel, 1979).

Intuitively, perceivers adopt personality analysis goals frequently. In order to "get to know" a neighbor or a colleague, perceivers presumably adopt goals from this category.

Judgment Goals.   Goals in this category are concerned with reaching a decision about the location of the actor's behavior along some dimension. Dimensions are probably often evaluative (i.e., good–bad), though not necessarily, and may vary in their level of abstractness—e.g., a likability judgment versus a dancing ability judgment (Anderson, 1965[3], 1974; Lingle & Ostrom, 1979). In naturalistic situations, judgments may range from whether to see an individual again socially to the guilt or innocence of a defendant in court.

Some examples of observational goals that perceivers may adopt have been provided and a system for classifying them suggested. Next, the role of observational goals in the person perception process is considered. Further issues concerning observational goal adoption are touched on in a later section.

A PERSON PERCEPTION FRAMEWORK

A person perception framework is described here, grounded in the current conceptual language of cognitive psychology. Despite evidence in the person perception literature that an observer's goal or purpose may influence processing of information about an actor (Jeffery & Mischel, 1979), no previous theoretical treatment has suggested specific mechanisms that might underlie this process.[4] The aim of this framework, then, is to incorporate observational goal as a hypothetical variable and to describe structural and processing mechanisms that may underlie its operation. As the theoretical work on cognitive social and personality processes proliferates, the importance of specifying assumptions about underlying structural and processing mechanisms seems more evident.

---

[3]Though the response dimension in this research was a likability judgment, the process by which subjects made the judgment was considered by the author to be in the domain of impression formation.

[4]In a very recent chapter, Wyer & Srull (1980) describe a processing system that acknowledges the importance of perceivers' objectives or goals.

Schemata: A Hypothetical Structure and Its Role in Processing

The term *schema* has been widely used by cognitive and social psychologists, though frequently without specifying its definition (Bartlett, 1932; Bobrow & Norman, 1975; see Taylor & Crocker, in press, for a review of social schemata). A schema is defined here as an hypothetical cognitive structure that represents associations among lower level units of information (i.e., the most concrete or closest to the peripheral perception), resulting in a functional higher-level cohesive and meaningful unit. Of interest here are schemata that represent portions of a perceiver's social world knowledge, that is, associations between behavioral and person-related elements that develop through experience and are stored in semantic memory. For example, an observer may have a schema for a "seductive facial expression," including pouting lips and widened eyes or, more mundanely, a schema for a telephone conversation that might include dialing a telephone number and speaking in turn. Obviously, to represent social knowledge adequately, an individual must have an enormous number of schemata, which reflect diverse contents. As noted elsewhere (Taylor & Crocker, in press), schemata may exist at varying levels of abstraction and complexity and may embody different kinds of associative relationships among their elements (e.g., in the "seductive expression" schema, the features occur contiguously; in the "telephone call" schema, the features occur in a specified temporal order).

A detailed discussion of the relationship between this schema definition and other references to schemata in the current literature is not attempted here (Hastie & Kumar, 1979; Taylor & Crocker, in press; Wyer & Srull, 1980), nor will distinctions among related constructs be offered (e.g., category).[5] The major value of the schema construct for the current discussion is that it provides a structural mechanism that represents prior experience and creates higher-level units that are operated upon by the processing system. However, one unique aspect of schema structure is made especially salient by the focus in this chapter upon "making sense from the stream of behavior." Schemata must be assumed to contain concrete, low-level behavioral "chunks" (e.g., pouting lips, widened eyes) and provide appropriate connections between them in addition to higher-level abstract "chunks" (e.g., "extravert" schema, Cantor & Mischel, 1977; implicit personality theory schema, Ashmore & Del Boca, 1979) that have received greater attention in other treatments.

Of critical importance is the assumption that schemata are *used* by the processing system to structure incoming information. The influence of schemata may occur at one or more of the three stages of processing frequently distin-

---

[5]It seems that an important issue for future research is the clarification of the respective meanings attached to the terms "schema," "category," "prototype," "script," and others by different investigators. Further thoughts on this issue are presented in Cohen, 1979, unpublished.

guished in models of cognition (Norman, 1976): encoding, storage, and retrieval. This influence can best be understood in terms of an activation model, in which "activation" refers to the stimulation of a concept or feature that is stored in long-term memory. (See Collins & Loftus, 1975; Wyer & Carlston, 1979, for descriptions of spreading activation models). Once an element has been activated due to veridical stimulus input (e.g., "pouting lips"), other elements that are represented within the same schema are also activated (e.g., "widened eyes") though probably not as strongly. Roughly, schemata operate in the course of processing as follows. First, a perceiver's operative schemata (i.e., the elements and relations among them) guide the way in which the stream of an actor's behavior is "chunked up" or encoded. Next, these schemata provide an interpretative framework for determining the "meaning" of the behavior and will influence what is stored from an actor's behavior. Finally, when a perceiver tries to retrieve information about the actor's behavior from memory, the relevant schemata will be reactivated and used to fill in forgotten or never seen behavioral features or relationships. The implications of these assumptions are very important: Schema-relevant information should be easier to process; the meaning extracted from a particular behavior should depend on the operative schemata; and memory should be best for, and err in the direction of, schema-relevant information. (See Taylor & Crocker's, in press, review of some empirical support for these assumptions.)

Observational Goals and Schema Activation

A central feature of this framework is that the *observational goal* of the perceiver is instrumental in *selecting* the person and behavior schemata that will be applied in a particular situation. It was stated earlier that observational goals focus the perceiver on those categories or features of behavior that are relevant to his or her purpose of the moment. Thus, the schema structure serves to implement the observer's goal through encoding, storing, and retrieving goal-relevant behavioral information.

As an example, consider the schema-selection operation of perceivers with two different observational goals: (1) an impression-forming perceiver watching a colloquium speaker giving a talk; and (2) a perceiver whose goal is to learn through observation how to give a good talk. First, each observer's goal-activated schemata should determine the behavioral features that are encoded, so the colloquium speaker's behavior may sometimes be "chunked up" differently by the two observers. The impression-forming observer might listen carefully to the speaker's voice tone and the talk-learning observer might attend more to the semantic relationships between the speaker's words. Next, the observers should interpret and store the information based on their goal-determined schema structures. If the colloquium speaker projects loudly, the first observer may interpret it as evidence of the trait of extraversion, and the second observer may categorize it as a technique for commanding attention. Finally, the two observers would tend to retrieve different information (e.g., the nervous gestures of the speaker versus the logical structure of the colloquium itself). This disparity could result from the initial difference in storage of information, compounded by the reconstruction or "filling in" of behaviors that were never actually seen (e.g., if the speaker's behavior was interpreted as nervous, the observer might inaccurately remember that the speaker's rate of speech was too rapid.)

OBSERVATIONAL GOALS AND ENCODING THE STREAM OF BEHAVIOR

First, the implications of this framework for encoding the stream of behavior is compared with a behavior perception theory described in some recent research conducted by Newtson and his colleagues (Newtson, 1973; Newtson, Engquist, & Bois, 1977). Then an experiment is described that investigated the influence of observational goals upon the encoding of behavior.

Behavior Perception and the Unitization of Action

In a series of provocative studies, Newtson and colleagues have (1) elaborated some theoretical assumptions about the principles of behavior perception; and (2) introduced a novel method for studying the "units" of behavior that perceivers extract. Central to their theory is the assumption that the behavior perception process consists of chunking the stream of behavior into *actions*. Their conceptual definition of an action has two important aspects. First, actions are always defined by *changes* in behavioral features, rather than static postures or "states" that may be meaningful to the perceiver. Second, actions are discrete and nonoverlapping, such that only one action occurs at a particular point in time. In addition, action units may be structured hierarchically with various levels of abstraction; and higher-level units often contain a series of embedded lower-level units. For example, a sequence of actions could be perceived as a high-level behavioral unit such as "closes the door," or alternatively it could be seen as a series of lower-level units, such as "gets up, walks toward door, and grasps doorknob" (see Newtson et al. 1977; Newtson, 1976, for a more complete description).[6]

---

[6]It should be noted that Newtson's assumption of hierarchically organized and embedded behavior units is based on evidence from studies where two groups of subjects were instructed to adopt two nearly identical goals (not Newtson's term). The instructions differed only in regard to the *size* of units they were told to identify (i.e., as "small" versus "large" as seems "natural and meaningful" [Newson, 1973]) supporting the inference that, although a hierarchical structure may exist between units defined by subjects with a common observational goal, it may not exist between units encoded under different goals.

For use in this research, a method for measuring subjects' "unitization" of the stream of behavior was developed (Newtson, 1973). Subjects observed a film or videotape of an actor engaged in a series of behaviors. They were instructed to press a button (attached to a continuous event recorder) when, in the subjects' judgments, "one meaningful action ends and a different one begins" (Newtson, 1976, p. 224). The intervals between button presses are considered to be equivalent to the perceptual "units" that a subject encoded from the stream of the actor's behavior.

Newtson's description of behavior perception (i.e., the chunking of behavior into discrete, nonoverlapping actions) is called into question when one considers the role of the perceiver's goal. First, when perceivers adopt certain goals, they may encode behavioral units that do not fit Newtson's description of an action. Rather, perceivers may encode features of an actor that are relatively static and thus violate the feature-change assumption (e.g., an observer whose goal is to form an impression of a derelict may encode static appearance features, such as shabby clothing or a dazed facial expression.) Second, and more important, by assuming discrete, nonoverlapping action units, Newtson's framework seems to ignore the possibility that observers with different goals may encode information from different categories of behavior. The "door closing" example was taken from Newtson's instructions to his subjects; he used it to demonstrate how meaningful actions may occur at varying levels of abstraction. Yet the information that is important for his "door closing" description comes from a limited range of behavioral categories (e.g., gross motor movements). For instance, behavioral information from categories such as facial expression or appearance is not relevant to the perception of this action. While a particular facial expression such as a smile may be part of a more abstract unit of information (cheerful demeanor), intuitively it shares few common features with actions such as closing a door. Thus, if two observers encode qualitatively different features (e.g., facial expression versus gross bodily movement), there seems no reason to expect a hierarchical relationship to exist between the units that they define. In sum then, when observational goals are taken into account, predictions about behavior perception and unitization emerge that contradict Newtson's assumptions. The accuracy of these predictions was explored in some recent research.

Observational Goals and the Unitization of Behavior

A study was conducted to test some hypotheses suggested by the person perception framework described here (Cohen & Ebbesen, 1979). The first hypothesis was that observers with different observational goals would encode the stream of an actor's behavior into different units. In addition, it was hypothesized that the units encoded by these two groups of observers would *not* necessarily be hierarchically related, contrary to the assumption of Newtson's theory.

The goals of *impression formation* and *observational learning* were chosen for several reasons. First, they were considered to be sufficiently dissimilar to allow for the encoding of different behavioral features. Also, as both of these goals have been used in previous research, the results could have implications for existing work in person perception. Finally, we could readily speculate about what sorts of information might be relevant for each goal, and how the information might be structured—e.g., trait information would be relevant for impression formation and would resemble a normative implicit personality theory structure (Rosenberg & Sedlak, 1972; Schneider, 1973).

Subjects were instructed either to "form an impression" of or to "learn the task" performed by an actor as they watched her engage in various activities. They viewed the actor in four brief behavioral videotaped sequences (each less than 2 minutes) that contained both personality and task-relevant information. For example, in one videotape the actor frowned, leafed impatiently through a magazine, sipped from a coffee cup, and then rose and paced the room, glancing anxiously at her watch. Subjects were told that they would later be tested to assess the accuracy of their impressions of her (or their knowledge about the tasks she performed).

All subjects were instructed to unitize the stream of the actor's behavior as they watched her. A unit was ambiguously defined so that subjects would impose their own interpretations when performing the task. Unlike previous unitizing research, no example was given to subjects, describing a potential "unit" (i.e., in Newtson's research subjects were given an example containing the behavior "to walk over and close the door" as a potential high-level unit and "to stand up" as a possible lower-level unit; see Newtson, 1973).

The unitization data strongly supported our hypothesis: Subjects whose goal was to form an impression unitized the stream of the actor's behavior differently from those subjects whose goal was to learn the tasks. Most simply, "task" subjects chunked the actor's behavior into a greater number of units than did "impression" subjects ($M = 11.1$ versus $M = 6.1$, $p < .001$). In addition, the relationship between the two sets of units was assessed. Although the *number* of units differed for subjects with different goals, if the unit boundaries lined up, then Newtson's assumption of hierarchical organization would be supported. However, less than 25% of the unit boundaries defined by task subjects "lined up with" (i.e., occurred within 1 second of) the unit boundaries defined by impression subjects. So, the two groups of subjects with different goals defined units that were apparently *not* hierarchically related. This result extends the findings from Newtson's research in which subjects' goals were not manipulated.

Unitization and Encoding of Behavioral Information

These data provide evidence that instructions to adopt a particular observational goal (e.g., impression; task) led subjects to unitize the stream of behavior around a series of behavioral features not shared by subjects with a different goal. However, one might question whether the unitizing data reflect the perceiver's actual *encoding* of behavioral information; that is, does the unitizing measure capture the form of the information that a subject records in memory? Although this question cannot be definitively answered here, the existing evidence suggests that the unitizing measure at least reflects the *location* of information in the behavior stream that is encoded by the perceiver. Cohen and Ebbesen (1979) demonstrated that subjects who differed in their unitization of a behavior sequence also differed in the behavioral information that they stored and retrieved. In addition, Newtson et al. (1977) found a relationship between unitization patterns and objective characteristics of a behavior sequence. Both of these studies support the existence of a link between unitization and actual information extraction.

However, the nature of the unitizing measure does seem to restrict the properties of the units that a perceiver may define. Thus, the unitization pattern may not always reflect the actual form of the encoded information. For example, it seems intuitively true that a perceiver may encode more than one "unit" of behavioral information at the same time (e.g., the actor simultaneously frowned and scratched her head in puzzlement). In addition, there may be instances where the perceiver encodes a very brief "unit" (e.g., a "fleeting facial expression") and then takes in no relevant additional information for a second or two. The current unitizing measure is designed to record continuous, nonoverlapping units of information; a button press signals the simultaneous end of one action and the beginning of another one. Therefore, a perceiver is unable to indicate instances where two units overlap or where there is a period of "noninformation." (See Ebbesen, 1980, for a more detailed discussion of the form of encoded information).

In sum, though the unitization measure may not always reflect the *form* of the information that a perceiver encodes, it seems that it does indicate the *location* of encoded information. Despite some possible interpretive limitations, the unitizing method seems useful for allowing subjects to indicate where goal-relevant information occurs in the stream of an actor's behavior.

OBSERVATIONAL GOALS, STORAGE AND RETRIEVAL OF BEHAVIORAL INFORMATION

A basic claim of this chapter is that observational goals help determine the schemata that guide a perceiver's encoding, interpretation and storage, and retrieval of information present in an actor's behavior. In the preceding section, evidence supporting the role of observational goals in *encoding* behavior was presented; in this section, the role of observational goals in the *interpretation* and *storage,* and *retrieval* of behavior is examined. First, some types of schemata that might be selected by two particular observational goals are considered and data supporting the processing role of these schemata are presented.

Then, some theoretical implications of goal-selected schematic processing are discussed.

Some Types of Schemata Selected by Observational Goals: Two Examples

What types of schemata are selected to facilitate a particular observational goal; that is, which categories of behavioral information are most relevant for which observational goals? Consideration of these questions serves two purposes. First, it provides a basis for an experiment, to be presented here, assessing the hypothesized processing role of goal-selected schemata in person perception. Second, there may be value in taking an almost anthropological interest in the content and structure of a perceiver's schemata. As schemata are assumed both to reflect a perceiver's acquired knowledge about persons and behavior and to shape future processing, some elaboration of schematic content may be important for fully understanding their operation. It should be clear, of course, that this discussion of goal-selected schemata is speculative and is not meant to be exhaustive or complete.

Impression Formation Schemata.   One suggested impression formation schema that researchers have long been concerned with is "implicit personality theory" (Rosenberg & Sedlak, 1972; Schneider, 1973), or perceivers' implicit notions about the normative co-occurrence of traits and related behaviors in people. Implicit personality theory (IPT) is viewed here as a high-level schema that represents the interrelationships between traits that are assumed by the perceiver (e.g., "clever" is closely related to "witty"). Each individual trait in IPT is viewed as a lower-level schema representing a variety of characteristics and behaviors that are indicative of the trait (e.g., a "clever" person may make comments that are nonobvious and make the perceiver laugh). Although trait-relevant information may be found in almost all behavior categories, certain categories like vocal information (e.g., voice tone; rate of speech) and nonverbal information (e.g., gestures; facial expressions) may be major sources. In addition to content, the particular structuring of the information in the perceivers' trait schemata makes it usable for forming an impression (e.g., a "deadpan" facial expression combined with comments of a particular evaluative tone indicates "wittiness"). The relationship between the behavior of an actor and the trait categories of the perceiver indicated by this behavior is obviously very complex (see Locksley & Lenauer, this volume).

Though most research into impression formation has investigated trait structure (Rosenberg & Sedlak, 1972) or the way in which perceivers combine trait information (Anderson, 1974), other person information schemata may be used in forming an impression. These include schemata related to knowledge about the actor's occupation (Cohen, in press; Rothbart, Fulero, Jensen, Howard, &

Birrell, 1978; Ostrom, Lingle, Pryor, & Geva, 1980); race or ethnic group (Brigham, 1971; McCauley & Stitt, 1978); sex or sexual preference (Ashmore & Del Boca, 1979; Snyder & Uranowitz, 1978); and other characteristics. Even though interest in the trait content of these alternative organizing structures has predominated, some studies have found schematic processing with nontrait personal characteristic information (e.g., physical appearance; preferences for books and music; social history (Cohen, in press; Snyder & Uranowitz, 1978). Hopefully, the current interest in cognitive processes underlying impression formation will lead to further investigation of these nontrait schemata.

Task Learning Schemas. The particular schemata that arise from a task-learning goal may depend on the type of task the perceiver wants to learn (e.g., subjects observing to learn a tennis serve will probably select different schemata from those observing to learn film developing). In general, task-learning schemata should contain information about *nonexpressive* features of verbal and nonverbal behavior (e.g., yells "15-love"; uses left hand). Task schemata may also include information about the relation between the actor and features of the nonsocial environment (e.g., picks up tennis racket; opens film cannister), as well as the temporal order in which actions normally occur—e.g., raises racket, tosses ball, brings arm over (Schank & Abelson, 1977; Schmidt, 1976).

Some tasks seem to require great attention to the specifics of behavioral detail and relatively little inference by the learner, either about the task's meaning or about the actor's phenomenology. Thus, goal-selected schemata should specify the required degree of memory for detail as well as the need for higher-level task inferences when required.

In sum, task-learning schemata may contain nonexpressive behavior features, relations between the actor and the environment, temporal order, and information about the degree of behavioral detail required in order to learn the task. This contrasts with the schemata presumably selected by an impression-forming goal: IPT; the individual trait schemata contained in IPT; and personal characteristic schemata, such as occupation or sex, which may contain both trait and nontrait (e.g., physical appearance) information.

Goal-Selected Schemata and the Processing of the Stream of Behavior. Having considered some types of schemata that might be associated with these two observational goals, we now can interpret some research in which these goals were manipulated. In the first study (Cohen & Ebbesen, 1979), subjects were instructed to adopt one of these two goals (i.e., form an impression of, learn a task). While viewing a videotape of an actor, they unitized her behavior. Afterward, they responded to questions about her: *Either* they rated her personality or they answered memory questions about her behavior. If the assumption of goal-selected schematic processing is valid, then the following hypotheses should be supported:

1. Impression subjects will form impressions that are more similar to IPT structure than will task subjects.
2. Task subjects will be more accurate at remembering task details performed by the actor than will impression subjects.

The experiment involved a 2 (observational instructions) × 2 (dependent measure) design. After viewing the videotapes of the actor (described in the previous section), subjects responded to one of the two dependent variables (i.e., trait ratings and memory for task-related behavior). Thus, half the subjects answered questions that were consistent with their observational instructions (impression instructions–impression questions, task instruction–task memory questions) while the other half answered questions that were inconsistent with their instructions (impression instructions–task memory questions, task instructions–impression questions).

A test of the hypotheses required that the performance of subjects with the two observational goals be compared on each of the dependent variables. To test if task subjects were more accurate at remembering task details, the task memory questions provided a straightforward comparison because objective accuracy could be easily determined. However, to test if impression subjects formed impressions that were more similar to IPT structure required a measure against which the structure reflected in subjects' trait ratings could be compared.

To determine how well they remembered the task information, subjects were asked to determine whether a particular action had been performed by the actor in one of the sequences. These memory questions were chosen to assess subjects' recognition accuracy for the kinds of behavioral features that were suggested by the goal instructions. For example, one question, referring to the pacing sequence described previously, was ''Did she look at the newspaper while sitting on the table?''. For the impression-dependent measure, eight personality trait ratings were chosen from Rosenberg and Sedlak's (1972) two-dimensional scaling configuration; the traits were selected both to have relevance to the actor's behavior and to represent a range of traits (i.e., both positive and negative social and intellectual characteristics). To measure the IPT structure presumably influencing subjects' trait ratings of the actor, judgments of expected trait co-occurrence were collected, as is done in IPT research (Rosenberg & Sedlak, 1972). Ten undergraduates from the same population as the previous subjects judged all possible pairs of the trait terms on how likely they were to co-occur in a typical person. For example, these subjects rated the likelihood that, in general, a person who is intelligent is also pessimistic. As these subjects did not view a videotape, their ratings presumably reflected the co-occurrence of traits represented in their IPT schemata, in the absence of behavioral information.

Did impression subjects form impressions of the actor that more greatly resembled their IPTs than did the respective impressions formed by task subjects? In order to test this hypothesis, co-occurrence matrices had to be constructed from the actual trait ratings of impression and task subjects, which could then be compared to the matrix representing IPT structure. To do this, all possible pairs of trait ratings were correlated across subjects, separately for each observational instruction condition. Then, these two matrices were compared with the IPT matrix and with each other by correlating the three matrices two at a time with one another. The impression subjects trait matrix was expected to be more highly correlated with the IPT-based structure than was the pattern generated by task subjects. The former correlation was in fact higher ($r = .48$, $n = 28$, $p < .01$) than the latter ($r = .30$, $n = 28$, $p < .10$), though this difference was not significant. In addition, the correlation between the patterns of ratings generated by subjects in the two observational instruction conditions was virtually zero ($r = .01$, $n = 28$, not significant), suggesting that there were major structural differences between the two sets of ratings. Moreover, this latter correlation was significantly less than the correlation between the impression matrix and the co-occurrence matrix ($p < .05$) but was not significantly less than the correlation between the task matrix and the co-occurrence matrix. Thus, these data support Hypothesis 1, though admittedly somewhat weakly.

Evidence about Hypothesis 2, that task subjects would be more accurate at remembering task-related behavior, was much easier to assess. As hypothesized, subjects who observed to learn the actor's tasks were better able to discriminate task-related behavior that had actually occurred in the videotape ($M = 70\%$ correct) than were subjects who observed to form an impression of the actor ($M = 58\%$ correct, $p < .05$). Obviously then, this supports the assumption that for a task-learning goal schemata were selected that facilitated observers' memories for an actor's task relevant behavior. Obviously, from these data alone we cannot determine how much the accuracy was due to the relative schematic influences on interpretation, storage, and retrieval of the behavioral information.

These memory data seem to contradict superficially some data reported recently by Hamilton et al. (1980). Subjects were presented with a series of "neutral" behavioral descriptions (e.g., "read the evening paper after dinner") and instructed either to form an impression of the person described in the sentences (impression) or to try to remember as many sentences as possible (memory). In a subsequent recall task, impression subjects recalled significantly more items than did memory subjects. Hamilton et al. (1980) attribute this result to "a higher degree of information organization inherent in the impression formation process [p. 9]" that presumably facilitates recall of the stimulus. An obvious difference between the two paradigms is that subjects in the Hamilton et al. study received a relatively simple stimulus (i.e., lists of sentences) in which the behavioral information had already been translated into words, whereas subjects in the Cohen and Ebbesen study (1979) received a more complex stimulus (i.e., a videotaped behavioral stream) which they translated for themselves into appropriate "chunks." Behavior sequences that are presented in sentence form may lack certain types of information (e.g., facial expression; posture) that enable subjects to organize the sequences into a more easily memorable structure. How-

ever, when behavior sequences are observed directly, as in the Cohen and Ebbesen study, the richness of the information may allow a wider, more successful
range of organizational strategies.[7]

In sum, the results from this study provided some reasonably good support for
the two hypotheses and, indirectly, for the framework and assumptions underlying it. The memory data were both easier to assess and slightly stronger than the
impression data. Yet, the impression result, that observers whose goal is to form
an impression are more strongly influenced by their IPTs than are other (task-
learning) observers is very intriguing and, if proved reliable, could have many
implications for understanding impression formation.

Therefore, a second study was conducted to attempt to replicate both the
impression and the memory results (Ebbesen, Cohen, & Allen, unpublished).
Some features of this study are irrelevant to this discussion and so only the
pertinent data are presented here. Eighty subjects watched a 7-minute videotape,
this time presenting two actors, a male and a female, interacting in a domestic
scene. As with the first videotape, the sequence contained what seemed to us to
be both personality-related and task-related behavior. Half of the subjects were
instructed to observe in order to form impressions of both actors and half were
instructed to remember the behavior of the actors. The latter instructions were a
slightly modified version that emphasized a goal to remember behavior rather
than a goal to perform the task. It was assumed these observational instructions
would conceptually replicate the instructions from the previous study. Subjects in
each instructional condition were given *both* dependent measures, in counterbalanced order.

The dependent measures were very similar to those in the previous study, but
with a few modifications. The memory measure was more extensive and presumably more powerful than in the previous study (i.e., 76 questions, half about each
actor); it was similarly presented in a recognition format. The impression measure was also more extensive (i.e., 39 items) and included items from the extremes of several personality dimensions used in IPT research (e.g., socially
good–bad, dominant–submissive). Again, independent trait co-occurrence
judgments were collected from subjects in the same population ($n = 20$), and
these were correlated with the matrices constructed by intercorrelating subjects'
trait ratings within the two instructional conditions.

Both major results from the Cohen and Ebbesen (1979) study were replicated.
First, observers whose goal was to remember what was done were more accurate
on the memory measure than were observers whose goal was to form an impression ($p < .01$). Further, these data provided even stronger evidence than in the
previous study that impression subjects' ratings more strongly reflected IPT
structure than did memory subjects' (impression subjects $r = .38$; memory sub-

---

[7]Later in their chapter, Hamilton, Katz, & Leirer (1980) concluded that memory subjects organized the information as highly as impression subjects, but the particular sort of organization was
less effective for enabling them to recall the information.

jects $r = .24$, $n = 1482$; $p < .01$). Therefore, the evidence supporting both hypotheses tested in the previous study is more convincing. Having demonstrated reliable support for the hypotheses in these two studies, and thus for the assumptions underlying the framework, we can now turn to some of its implications.

A PERSON PERCEPTION FRAMEWORK: SOME IMPLICATIONS AND SPECULATIONS

A Summary and Some Implications of Goal-Selected Schematic Processing

First, the person perception process as described here is summarized; then, some of the implications of this approach are considered. Perceivers' *schemata*, or their stored representations of person-related experiences, lend order and coherence to their processing of other people's behavior. In intuitive terms, schemata help to translate the ongoing stream of an actor's behavior into meaningful "chunks" of information, contribute meaning to the extracted information and facilitate memory for schema-congruent behavior. In addition, schemata at times fill in missing features of behavioral information, which the perceiver may not be able to distinguish from actually observed behavior. The *observational goal* of the perceiver, or the purpose for which he plans to use the behavioral information, serves the important function of schema selection, choosing those that will help the perceiver to achieve his goal. As a result, perceivers with different observational goals will, at times, chunk up the stream of behavior differently, interpret and store the information differently, and retrieve from memory different information about the actor. Goal-selected schemata will sometimes facilitate processing "accuracy," but, at other times, "accuracy" will be hindered. For example, data presented here indicated that perceivers whose goals encouraged attention to detail and minimal interpretation (i.e., task learning) more accurately remembered the actor's behavior. Perceivers whose goal encouraged interpretation (i.e., impression) were less accurate and more "stereotypic" in their descriptions of the actor.

One implication of this approach concerns the role of observational goals as a schema selection factor. Although the description presented here of schema structure and processing characteristics is generally consistent with the conceptualizations inherent in several recent treatments (Cantor & Mischel, 1979; Hamilton et al., 1980; Markus, 1977; Ostrom et al., 1980), no previous treatment has explicitly incorporated observational goals as a mechanism for schema selection. The need for such a mechanism is expressed by Taylor and Crocker (in press) who point out that little is currently known about the mechanisms that cause the application of particular schemata in particular situations. Of course, the role of observational goals in accounting for schema selection needs to be considered further in future research. Although an observer's goal may prove to be an important schema selection factor, it seems likely that other variables will influence this process as well. These additional variables may possibly be located in the perceiver (e.g., affect: Higgins, Kuiper, & Olson, in press) or located in the stream of behavior (e.g., similarity between a behavior and a schema: Cantor & Mischel, 1979). Even though the schema selection process may only be partially understood by considering the perceiver's observational goal, this approach should provide a first step toward predicting what information a perceiver will encode.

There are also some interesting theoretical implications about the role of IPT and other cognitive structures in person perception. First, impression information is placed within the context of other ways of observing and processing person information. This provides a basis for considering organizing structures perceivers may use in addition to trait terms and IPT. Evidence presented here (as well as other research) supports the assumption that perceivers do encode and process nontrait person information and may organize it with schemata other than IPT (Cohen, in press; Fiske & Cox, 1979; Hamilton et al., 1980; Jeffrey & Mischel, 1979). Therefore, research evidence that subjects relied upon IPT structure or organized behavior according to trait categories (Hastie & Kumar, 1979) should be conditionalized by noting the observational goal that those subjects had been instructed to adopt (i.e., to form an impression). An important direction for future research would be to investigate a wider variety of person information categories and organizational structures that perceivers use in processing information about other people. Including observational goal as a factor may facilitate this endeavor.

Second, most previous treatments do not specify where in the person perception process IPT has an effect; those that do have localized its effect in memory (D'Andrade, 1965; Shweder, 1972, 1977). In the current approach, perceivers' stored notions of behavior co-occurrence (i.e., their IPT schemata) are assumed to influence the processing of behavior as it unfolds. This assumption leads to the hypothesis, supported here, that impression-forming observers are more heavily influenced by their IPT than are observers with certain other goals (e.g., task learning). To the author's knowledge, previous research in IPT has not considered that perceivers' reliance on IPT may be determined by their goal. Because of the potential importance of this implication, further investigation is clearly needed. Future research should consider new, potentially more sensitive methods for assessing the influence of schemata (including IPT) on perceivers' processing of behavior.

Future Directions in Observational Goals Research

A tentative taxonomy of observational goals was described here. Three broad categories of goals were discussed (i.e., information seeking or learning, personality analysis, and judgment) and some more specific instances of goals within these categories were noted. Further investigation of these goals, at both levels of generality, may be valuable. To begin, analyses similar to those performed here for task-learning and impression-forming goals could be performed for the other goals identified here. Though these analyses do not claim to be definitive, the consideration of some goal-relevant schemata seems an important exercise. First, the description of goal-relevant categories of behavioral information provides a basis for studying the properties of schematic processing, as in the research described here. In addition, we may learn more about the relationship between goals assigned here to the same higher-level category (e.g., observational learning and memory are both information-seeking or learning goals). If these divisions are appropriate, observational goals within the same category should be more similar to one another than to those in different categories. In fact, there is already some evidence that impression-forming subjects and behavior-predicting subjects organize behavioral information more similarly than either group does with subjects with a memory goal (Jeffery & Mischel, 1979).

A remaining issue of importance concerns the perceiver's adoption of observational goals in real-life situations. If observational goals influence the perceiver's "construction" of an actor, then naturalistic goal adoption may be an important element in real-life person perception. Initially, two methods for determining the goals that subjects adopt in particular situations seem apparent. First, the method of self-report may be used; that is, subjects may simply be asked to describe which goal they have adopted. Of course, details of the way in which the question should be asked will require further consideration. Second, if enough of the content and structure of a particular goal were known, it might be possible to *infer* that that goal had been adopted by measuring the structure in the behavioral information that a subject had extracted. This strategy will, of course, require that precise methods for assessing schematic content and structure first be developed.

A final issue should be noted here. It is possible that perceivers may occasionally adopt multiple goals simultaneously: If so, what kind of relationship exists between these goals? For example, does a perceiver who is learning a task secondarily or intermittently process impression-relevant information perhaps because of its general usefulness? The possibility of multiple goals complicates the theoretical description offered here, but it may provide a more accurate picture of real-life processing. Further research is needed to clarify this issue.

OBSERVATIONAL GOALS, SOCIAL INTERACTION AND PERSONALITY

The focus of this chapter is to discuss the role of observational goals in person perception and to describe a framework, supported by some empirical evidence, to formalize this role. So far the discussion has focused on person perception situations in which one person (the perceiver) "processes" another person's (the actor's) behavior. It would be interesting to broaden the focus and consider the role of observational goals in situations where the perceiver also *interacts* with the actor. A second area for speculation concerns the relationship between observational goals and personality. Given the evidence that observational goals influence perceivers' processing of their social environment, consistent individual differences in observational goal adoption might be an important way in which individuals differ. The possible role of observational goals in both social interaction and personality is now briefly considered. Although a more programmatic consideration belongs in the domain of future work, it may be useful to extend our present discussion to include these potentially important issues.

Observational Goals and Social Interaction

The effects of observational goals upon social interaction may be realized in at least two different ways. First, the observational goal of the perceiver may directly influence interaction with the actor; that is, the observer may behave in order to promote the availability of information that is relevant to the goal. An obvious example of this is a personnel manager who is interviewing a prospective employee. Presumably the observational goal will be to form a judgment of the actor; and, a skilled manager will direct the course of interaction (e.g., through questioning and reacting) so that adequate information for making a judgment is obtained. A less formal example might be that of an observer whose goal is personality analysis and who directs interaction with an actor toward finding out why the actor dropped out of law school. This relatively direct link between social perception and social interaction has been noted as well by Jones and Thibaut (1958).

A less direct link between observational goals and social interaction is embodied in the assumption that an observer's perception of an actor will influence or possibly mediate the subsequent behavior of the observer. Of course, this assumption is widely shared by other theorists who are concerned with social perception and social behavior (Heider, 1958; Mischel, 1968; and most of the contributors to this volume). Empirical evidence in support of this assumption has been available for some time (Kelley, 1950; Taylor & Epstein, 1967) and has grown recently (Snyder & Swann, 1978; Snyder, Tanke, & Berscheid, 1977). The specific mechanisms may not be well understood, but it is hard to imagine a system where behavior, and hence the course of social interaction, is not influenced, at least to some degree, by an observer's perception of an actor. (See Taylor & Crocker, in press, for a discussion of the role of schemata in facilitating social action.) To the extent that observational goals mediate an observer's perceptions they should similarly play a role in the course of social interaction.

Observational Goals and Personality

The conceptual relationship between observational goals and personality, currently quite speculative, is interesting to consider. It is easy to imagine that perceivers will adopt a variety of different goals in response to situational demands (e.g., the personnel manager whose job is to make judgments). If, however, perceivers consistently adopt one or more types of observational goals, then their interpretations of other people and situations, and possibly their subsequent behavior, should be consistently influenced.

Several issues emerge here. One issue is whether observational goal adoption will prove to be a consistent individual difference. Evidence suggests that cross-situational behavioral consistency based on trait characteristics is not great. However, observational goal adoption falls into the category of cognitive style differences, the area for which the strongest consistency has been demonstrated (Mischel, 1968). This is not in itself evidence of stability, but it does suggest that observational goal adoption as an individual difference may be worth pursuing.

Second, this approach is consistent with previous work noting that different perceivers create alternative constructions of the social world (Kelly, 1958; Mischel, 1968). It would be premature to suggest how observational goal adoption may relate to other individual differences (e.g., cognitive complexity, Crockett, 1965) even though some conceptual relationships seem likely. Though following in the conceptual tradition of previous treatments, this current approach differs by incorporating current constructs and methods from cognitive psychology.

A final point concerns the relationship between observational goals and other recent approaches to individual differences that employ a schemalike construct. There has been considerable recent interest in self-schemata and how self-schema content relates to information processing (Markus, 1977; Rogers, Kuiper, & Kirker, 1977). In the current approach, the emphasis is less on differences in schematic content and more on alternative structures that perceivers use for interpreting person information, although content differences are implied here as well.

Some very tentative support for individual differences in goal adoption may be considered here. Intuitively, perceivers in similar situations do seem to adopt characteristically different observational goals. We all know of someone who seems to empathize with a wide range of people, no matter what the situation; we may know someone else who appears to use other people as sources for information gathering. Or, consider the very achievement-oriented salesman whose consistent goal is to judge others' salesmanship ability, and who constructs a social environment filled with information about others' strengths and weaknesses in that domain. Some initial empirical evidence exists for individual differences in goal adoption within the category of information seeking or learning (Mischel, 1976). For example, Gelfand (1962) found that individuals with a history of punishment for independence are relatively more likely to imitate the behavior of other people. If some degree of stable differences between people is found, then observational goal adoption may be a fruitful individual difference to pursue. It provides a mechanism through which a perceiver's cognitive structures will influence his processing of social information and assumes a link between this information processing and subsequent social behavior.

SUMMARY

In this chapter the construct of *observational goals* was introduced, and its possible role in person perception was explored. In the first section a tentative taxonomy of observational goals was described, and the role of a perceiver's goal in extracting information from the stream of an actor's behavior considered. In the next section, an information-processing framework for person perception was presented, incorporating observational goals as a variable and including the construct "schema" as a hypothetical structure used in processing. In the next two sections research designed to test some basic assumptions of the framework was described. Results from these studies support the role of observational goals in encoding, interpreting and storing, and retrieving from memory information about an actor's behavior. In the fifth section, several implications of this framework for person perception were discussed, and future directions for research in observational goals were considered. Finally, some speculations about observational goals in social interaction and personality were presented.

ACKNOWLEDGMENTS

The author wishes to thank Richard Bowers, Cindy Elgart, Don Kinder, and John Lingle for their helpful comments on an earlier version of this chapter. The research presented here was done in collaboration with Ebbe B. Ebbesen and Robert Allen and was conducted in part by Jeneva Lane. The research presented here was supported in part by Grant MH 26069 from the National Institute of Mental Health.

REFERENCES

Anderson, N. H. Primacy effects in personality impression formation using a generalized order effect paradigm. *Journal of Personality and Social Psychology*, 1965, *2*, 1-9.

Anderson, N. H. Information integration theory: A brief survey. In D. H. Krantz, R. C. Atkinson, R. D. Luce, & P. Suppes, (Eds.), *Contemporary developments in mathematical psychology*. San Francisco: Freeman, 1974.

Anderson, N. H., & Hubert, S. Effects of concomitant verbal recall on order effects in personality impression formation. *Journal of Verbal Learning and Verbal Behavior*, 1963, *2*, 379-391.

Apple, W., Streeter, L. A., & Krauss, R. M. Effects of pitch and speech rate on personal attributions. *Journal of Personality and Social Psychology*, 1979, *37*, 715-727.

Asch, S. E. Forming impressions of personality. *Journal of Abnormal and Social Psychology*, 1946, *41*, 258-290.

Ashmore, R. D., & Del Boca, F. K. Sex stereotypes and implicit personality theory: Toward a cognitive-social psychological conceptualization. *Sex Roles*, 1979, *5*, 219-248.

Bandura, A. Vicarious processes: A case of no-trial learning. In L. Berkowitz (Ed.), *Advances in experimental social psychology* (Vol. II). New York: Academic Press, 1965.

Bartlett, F. C. *Remembering*. Cambridge: Cambridge University Press, 1932.

Bobrow, D. G., & Norman, D. A. Some principles of memory schemata. In D. G. Bobrow, & A.

Collins (Eds.), *Representation and understanding: Studies in cognitive science.* New York: Academic Press, 1975.

Brigham, J. C. Ethnic stereotypes. *Psychological Bulletin,* 1971, *76,* 15–38.

Cantor, N., & Mischel, W. Traits as prototypes: Effects on recognition memory. *Journal of Personality and Social Psychology,* 1977, *35,* 38–48.

Cantor, N., & Mischel, W. Prototypes in person perception. In L. Berkowitz (Ed.), *Advances in experimental social psychology* (Vol. 12). New York: Academic Press, 1979.

Clark, H. H., & Clark, E. V. *Psychology and language.* New York: Harcourt Brace Jovanovich, Inc., 1977.

Cohen, C. E. Person categories and social perception: Testing some boundaries of the processing effects of prior knowledge. *Journal of Personality and Social Psychology,* in press.

Cohen, C. E. Prototypes: Some properties of person categories. In R. Hastie (Chair), *Categorical processing and representation of person information.* Symposium presented at American Psychological Association Convention, New York, 1979.

Cohen, C. E., & Ebbesen, E. B. Observational goals and schema activation: A theoretical framework for behavior perception. *Journal of Experimental Social Psychology,* 1979, *15,* 305–329.

Collins, A. M., & Loftus, E. F. A spreading-activation theory of semantic processing. *Psychological Review,* 1975, *82,* 407–428.

Crockett, W. H. Cognitive complexity and impression formation. In B. A. Maher (Ed.), *Progress in experimental personality research* (Vol. 2). New York: Academic Press, 1965.

D'Andrade, R. G. Trait psychology and componential analysis. *American Anthropologist,* 1965, *67,* 215–228.

Dreben, E. K., Fiske, S. T., & Hastie, R. Impression and recall order effects in behavior based impression formation. *Journal of Personality and Social Psychology,* 1979, *37,* 1758–1768.

Ebbesen, E. B. Cognitive processes in understanding ongoing behavior. In R. Hastie, T. M. Ostrom, E. B. Ebbesen, R. S. Wyer, Jr., D. L. Hamilton, & D. E. Carlston (Eds.), *Person memory: The cognitive basis of social perception.* Hillsdale, N.J.: Lawrence Erlbaum Associates, 1980.

Ebbesen, E. B., Cohen, C. E., & Allen, R. B. Cognitive processes in person perception: Behavior scanning and semantic memory. Unpublished manuscript, University of California at San Diego, 1979.

Fiske, S. T., & Cox, M. G. Person concepts: The effect of target familiarity and descriptive purpose on the process of describing others. *Journal of Personality,* 1979, *47,* 136–161.

Fiske, S. T., Taylor, S. E., Etcoff, N. L., & Laufer, J. K. Imaging, empathy and causal attribution. *Journal of Experimental Social Psychology,* 1979, *15,* 356–377.

Galper, R. E. Turning observers into actors: Differential causal attributions as a function of "empathy." *Journal of Research in Personality,* 1976, *10,* 328–335.

Gelfand, D. M. The influence of self-esteem on rate of verbal conditioning and social matching behavior. *Journal of Abnormal and Social Psychology,* 1962, *65,* 259–265.

Grusec, J., & Mischel, W. Model's characteristics as determinants of social learning. *Journal of Personality and Social Psychology,* 1966, *4,* 211–215.

Hamilton, D. L., Katz, L. B., & Leirer, V. O. Organizational processes in impression formation. In R. Hastie, T. M. Ostrom, E. B. Ebbesen, R. S. Wyer, Jr., D. L. Hamilton, & D. E. Carlston (Eds.), *Person memory: The cognitive basis of social perception.* Hillsdale, N.J.: Lawrence Erlbaum Associates, 1980.

Hastie, R., & Kumar, P. A. Person memory: Personality traits as organizing principles in memory for behaviors. *Journal of Personality and Social Psychology,* 1979, *37,* 25–38.

Hastorf, A. H., Schneider, D. J., & Polefka, J. *Person perception.* Reading, Mass.: Addison-Wesley, 1970.

Heider, F. *The psychology of interpersonal relations.* New York: Wiley, 1958.

Hendrick, C., & Costantini, A. F. Effects of varying trait inconsistency and response requirements on the primacy effect in impression formation. *Journal of Personality and Social Psychology,* 1970, *15,* 158–164.

Higgins, E. T., Kuiper, N. A., & Olson, J. M. Social cognition: A need to get personal. In E. T. Higgins, C. P. Herman, & M. P. Zanna (Eds.), *Social Cognition: The Ontario Symposium.* Hillsdale, N.J.: Lawrence Erlbaum Associates, in press.

Jeffery, K. M., & Mischel, W. Effects of purpose on the organization and recall of information in person perception. *Journal of Personality,* 1979, *47,* 397–419.

Jones, E. E., & Thibaut, J. W. Interaction goals as bases of inference in interpersonal perception. In R. Tagiuri & L. Petrullo (Eds.), *Person perception and interpersonal behavior.* Stanford, Calif.: Stanford University Press, 1958.

Kelley, H. H. The warm-cold variable in first impressions of persons. *Journal of Personality,* 1950, *8,* 431–439.

Kelly, G. A. Man's construction of his alternatives. In G. Lindzey (Ed.), *Assessment of human motives.* New York: Rinehart, 1958.

Kramer, E. Judgment of personal characteristics and emotions from nonverbal properties of speech. *Psychological Bulletin,* 1963, *60,* 408–420.

Lingle, J. H., & Ostrom, T. M. Retrieval selectivity in memory-based impression judgments. *Journal of Personality and Social Psychology,* 1979, *37,* 180–194.

Markus, H. Self-schemata and processing information about the self. *Journal of Personality and Social Psychology,* 1977, *35,* 63–78.

McCauley, C., & Stitt, C. L. An individual and quantitative measure of stereotypes. *Journal of Personality and Social Psychology,* 1978, *36,* 929–940.

Mischel, W. *Personality and assessment.* New York: Wiley, 1968.

Mischel, W. *Introduction to personality* (2nd ed.). New York: Holt, Rinehart & Winston, 1976.

Newtson, D. A. Attribution and the unit of perception of ongoing behavior. *Journal of Personality and Social Psychology,* 1973, *28,* 28–38.

Newtson, D. A. Foundation of attribution: The perception of on-going behavior. In J. H. Harvey, W. J. Ickes, & R. F. Kidd (Eds.), *New directions in attribution research* (Vol. 1). Hillsdale, N.J.: Lawrence Erlbaum Associates, 1976.

Newtson, D., Engquist, G., & Bois, J. The objective basis of behavior units. *Journal of Personality and Social Psychology,* 1977, *35,* 847–862.

Norman, D. A. *Memory & attention* (2nd ed.). New York: Wiley, 1976.

Ostrom, T. M., Lingle, J. H., Pryor, J. B., & Geva, N. Cognitive organization of person impressions. In R. Hastie, T. M. Ostrom, E. B. Ebbesen, R. S. Wyer, Jr., D. L. Hamilton, & D. E. Carlston (Eds.), *Person memory: The cognitive basis of social perception.* Hillsdale, N.J.: Lawrence Erlbaum Associates, 1980.

Regan, D., & Totten, J. Empathy and attribution: Turning observers into actors. *Journal of Personality and Social Psychology,* 1975, *32,* 850–856.

Rogers, T. B., Kuiper, N. A., & Kirker, W. S. Self-reference and the encoding of personal information. *Journal of Personality and Social Psychology,* 1977, *35,* 677–688.

Rosenberg, S., & Sedlak, A. Structural representation of implicit personality theory. In L. Berkowitz (Ed.), *Advances in experimental social psychology* (Vol. 6). New York: Academic Press, 1972.

Rothbart, M., Fulero, S., Jensen, C., Howard, J., & Birrell, P. From individual to group impressions: Availability heuristics in stereotype formation. *Journal of Experimental Social Psychology,* 1978, *14,* 237–255.

Schank, R., & Abelson, R. P. *Scripts, plans, goals, and understanding: An inquiry into human knowledge structures.* Hillsdale, N.J.: Lawrence Erlbaum Associates, 1977.

Schmidt, C. S. Understanding human action: Recognizing the plans and motives of other persons. In J. Carroll & J. Payne (Eds.), *Cognition and social behavior.* Hillsdale, N.J.: Lawrence Erlbaum Associates, 1976.

Schneider, D. J. Implicit personality theory: A review. *Psychological Bulletin*, 1973, *79*, 294–309.

Shweder, R. A. Semantic structures and personality assessment (Doctoral dissertation, Harvard University, 1972). *Dissertation Abstracts International*, 1972, *3*, 2452B. (University Microfilms No. 72-29, 584).

Shweder, R. A. Illusory correlation and the MMPI controversy. *Journal of Consulting and Clinical Psychology*, 1977, *45*, 917–924.

Snyder, M., & Swann, W. B., Jr. Hypothesis-testing processes in social interaction. *Journal of Personality and Social Psychology*, 1978, *36*, 1202–1212.

Snyder, M., Tanke, E. D., & Berscheid, E. Social perception and interpersonal behavior: On the self-fulfilling nature of social stereotypes. *Journal of Personality and Social Psychology*, 1977, *35*, 656–666.

Snyder, M., & Uranowitz, S. Reconstructing the past: Some cognitive consequences of person perception. *Journal of Personality and Social Psychology*, 1978, *36*, 941–950.

Tagiuri, R. Introduction. In R. Tagiuri, & L. Petrullo (Eds.), *Person perception and interpersonal behavior*. Stanford, Calif.: Stanford University Press, 1958.

Taylor, S. E., & Crocker, J. Schematic bases of social information processing. In E. T. Higgins, C. P. Herman, & M. P. Zanna (Eds.), *Social Cognition: The Ontario Symposium*. Hillsdale, N.J.: Lawrence Erlbaum Associates, in press.

Taylor, S. P., & Epstein, S. Aggression as a function of the interaction of the sex of the aggressor and the sex of the victim. *Journal of Personality*, 1967, *35*, 474–486.

Wyer, R. S. Changes in meaning and halo effects in personality impression formation. *Journal of Personality and Social Psychology*, 1974, *29*, 829–835.

Wyer, R. S., & Carlston, D. E. *Social inference and attribution*. Hillsdale, N.J.: Lawrence Erlbaum Associates, 1979.

Wyer, R. S., & Srull, T. K. The processing of social stimulus information: A conceptual integration. In R. Hastie, T. M. Ostrom, E. B. Ebbesen, R. S. Wyer, Jr., D. L. Hamilton, & D. E. Carlston (Eds.), *Person memory: The cognitive basis of social perception*. Hillsdale, N.J.: Lawrence Erlbaum Associates, 1980.

Zuckerman, M., Lipets, M. S., Koivumaki, J. H., & Rosenthal, R. Encoding and decoding nonverbal cues of emotion. *Journal of Personality and Social Psychology*, 1975, *32*, 1068–1076.

4

Accessibility of Social Constructs: Information–Processing Consequences of Individual and Contextual Variability

E. Tory Higgins
Gillian King
University of Western Ontario

> *Given a sensory input with equally good fit to two nonoverlapping categories, the more accessible of the two categories would "capture" the input.*
>
> —Bruner (1957, p. 132)

> *Once upon a time, Michael and Minnie, a happily married couple, went on vacation to a large island resort. There they met another couple, Donald and Daisy, and the two couples spent most of their vacation together. Michael and Minnie noticed that Donald spent a great amount of his time in search of what he liked to call excitement. During the vacation he climbed a steep mountain, drove in a demolition derby, and piloted a jet-powered boat—without knowing very much about boats. They watched him risk injury and even death a number of times. Michael and Minnie also noticed that once Daisy made up her mind to do something it was as good as done no matter how long it might take or how difficult the going might be. Only rarely did she change her mind, even when it might well have been better if she had. After Michael and Minnie arrived home from their vacation they got into a terrible fight. Minnie said she didn't like Donald because "he acts without thinking of the consequences," but Michael argued that "he has a great sense of fun." On the other hand, Michael didn't like Daisy because "she is never willing to admit when she is wrong," but Minnie liked Daisy because "she is there when you need her." Michael and Minnie now take separate vacations.*
>
> —Anonymous

INTRODUCTION

It is widely believed that our judgments and memory of others are based on whatever information about them has been available to us. Thus, reasonable people who are exposed to the same information about someone else should form the same judgments and remember the same facts. As exemplified in the preceding story about Michael and Minnie, however, people often form different judgments and recollect different facts, even when exposed to the same information. Why is this? What factors determine how people categorize and remember each other? What are the personal and interpersonal consequences of this, and what cognitive processes are involved?

These issues have a long history (Bartlett, 1932; Brown, 1958, Bruner, 1957; Kelley, 1950) and, under the influence of recent information processing approaches, are once again receiving increasing attention. A number of major directions have emerged concerning these general issues. One approach has been to consider the effects on memory of encoding stimulus information for different purposes or goals (Cohen & Ebbesen, 1979; Hamilton, Katz, & Leirer, 1980; Higgins, 1980; Jeffery & Mischel, in press). Another approach has been to consider the information-processing effects of drawing attention to different attributes of the stimulus information (McArthur, 1980; Taylor & Fiske, 1978). A third approach has been to consider the effects of the match between the attributes of the stimulus information and the content of particular constructs or schemata (Cantor & Mischel, 1977; Hastie, 1980; Snyder & Uranowitz, 1978; Tsujimoto, 1978). A fourth approach, and the major concern of this chapter, is to consider the effects of the relative accessibility of different categories that could be used to characterize the stimulus information (Higgins, Rholes, & Jones, 1977; Wyer & Srull, 1980). The effect of category accessibility, and individual differences in category accessibility, on judgments and memory of others is exemplified in the story of Michael and Minnie: Michael's accessible categories were "adventurous" and "stubborn" whereas Minnie's accessible categories were "reckless" and "persistent."

In this chapter, we propose a preliminary model of the role of construct accessibility in information processing. We first describe some basic concepts in the model and distinguish among different kinds of encoding processes. We then describe various factors that influence the accessibility of social constructs. Next, we discuss some consequences of construct accessibility for the general information-processing stages of input, consolidation, and output. Evidence supporting this model is presented throughout, including some recent studies by the authors and collaborators that have examined the information-processing effects of contextual *and* individual variability in construct accessibility. Finally, we consider the implications of such variability for a number of topics, such as cognitive therapy, interpersonal conflict and attraction, impression management, first impressions, and similarity in judgments of self and others. We also consider the possibility that individual variation in construct accessibility underlies some of the phenomena associated with various personality dimensions.

A PRELIMINARY MODEL OF
CONSTRUCT ACCESSIBILITY

In this section, we describe the basic concepts, determining factors, and processing consequences of construct accessibility. To begin, let us define *construct accessibility* as *the readiness with which a stored construct is utilized in information processing;* that is, *construct accessibility* is concerned with stored constructs, their utilization in information processing, and the likelihood of such utilization.

Recently, there has been an increasing tendency to use the terms *accessibility* and *availability* interchangeably. These terms, have traditionally been distinguished in the literature, however. Accessibility has referred to the readiness with which a stored construct is retrieved from memory and/or is utilized in stimulus encoding, whereas availability has referred to whether or not a construct is stored in memory (Bruner, 1957; Tulving & Pearlstone, 1966). Some overlap in the application of these terms was introduced in Tversky and Kahneman's (1973) description of the availability heuristic, where availability referred to the ease of retrieving construct instances. In the availability heuristic, however, availability also referred to the ease of constructing instances of novel classes and events, which is distinct from the traditional meaning of accessibility. Most recently, Nisbett and Ross (1980) have used availability as if it were a synonym for accessibility. The traditional distinction between availability and accessibility is useful, however, for considering various memory phenomena (for example, differences between free recall and cued recall). For our concerns in this chapter, then, accessibility is the appropriate term.

Basic Concepts

Psychological Constructs. The most general concept in the model is *construct,* which refers to coherent information about some entity typically derived from specific instances or occurrences. The two major types of constructs discussed in this chapter are *categories* and *proper constructs*. A *category* consists of information about a class of objects, events, or properties. A *proper construct* consists of information about a specific, individual object or event.[1] Social and personal categories include information about social groups (e.g., Protestants,

---

[1]The term *proper construct* was selected because of the conventional use of *proper name* to refer to labels designating some definite, individual entity without a limiting modifier.

Italians, and Blacks), social roles and occupations (e.g., mother, policeman, and friend), physical characteristics (e.g., attractive, skinny), traits and behaviors (e.g., intelligent, artistic, aggressive, and helpful), social types (e.g., introvert, social activist, neurotic, and redneck), and social events (e.g., making breakfast, going to a party, taking an examination, and meeting new people). Proper social constructs include information about individual people (e.g., Pierre Trudeau, your mother, Johnny Carson, and your kindergarten teacher), and individual places and events (e.g., the assassination of President Kennedy, your wedding day, Paris, and your hometown). In some cases, a proper construct may become a category, especially when communication and the media create a socially shared or conventional concept from a particular person or event. For example, actual persons (e.g., Florence Nightingale, Hitler) or fictional characters (e.g., Archie Bunker, Lolita) may become personality types (e.g., an Archie Bunker type). Actual places and events (e.g., Devil's Island) and fictional places and events (e.g., Utopia) may also become types that are used to categorize other places and events.

There is substantial agreement at present that the content of categories includes information about the essential and characteristic attributes of category members, the range of category attributes, and typical or prototypic exemplars of the category (Posner, 1978; Reed, 1972; Rosch, 1978; Rosch & Mervis, 1975; Smith, Shoben, & Rips, 1974). There is also general agreement that category attributes vary in their predictive validity (the probability that a target is a member of a category given that it possesses the attribute) and that category members may vary in their family resemblance (the number of attributes in common with other category members relative to the number of attributes in common with noncategory members) (Reed, 1972, Rosch & Mervis, 1975; Smith et al., 1974). There is less current agreement concerning the long-term representation of categorical information. Because the issues of concern in this chapter do not require subscribing to any particular model of representation, however, this is not a problem.

Both categories and proper constructs may be *structured* or *unstructured*. Structured constructs involve co-occurrence or redundancy of attributes (Neisser, 1967; Rosch, 1978). For example, the category *surgeon* or the proper construct *Johnny Carson* involves clusters of co-occurring behaviors, skills, appearance, and background. Trait categories, such as "happy," also involve the co-occurrence of particular behaviors, appearance, and state. However, some categories (e.g., skin textures) and proper constructs (e.g., an individual's voice quality) are unstructured because they involve, at least phenomenologically, a single attribute. The social constructs of concern in the present chapter are generally structured.

Identification as and Identification with.   The process of identifying a stimulus is central to this chapter. In general, identification involves an assessment of the similarity between the properties of a stimulus and the content of alternative constructs (Rosch, 1978; Tversky & Gati, 1978). The identification process that has received most attention in the psychological literature consists of recognizing a stimulus to be an instance of a proper construct and especially, classifying a stimulus as being a member of some category. The process in both these cases has usually been called *categorization*, even though only the latter process strictly involves categories. We continue this use of categorization in this chapter. Categorization consists of identifying a stimulus *as* an instance of some construct. Relatively little attention has been paid to an alternative process of identification—identifying a stimulus *with* some construct.

A stimulus may be *identified with* some construct when its properties are sufficiently similar to the construct to evoke the construct but not similar enough to be accepted as an instance of the construct. *Identification with* rather than *identification as* is especially likely when a stimulus has attributes that are characteristic of the construct but lacks at least some of the essential attributes of the construct. For example, one may meet a person who possesses many of the characteristic attributes of one's father but who lacks the essential attributes to be one's father. This person, therefore, would not be identified as one's father but may be identified with one's father. Similarly, a target person may be a psychology professor who displays some attributes thought to be characteristic of businessmen and thus may be identified with businessmen even though identified as a psychology professor. Abelson's (1976) description of the use of episodic scripts versus categorical scripts in decision-making also reflects this distinction between identification with versus identification as. When a stimulus is identified as belonging to a construct, the stimulus will be called an *instance* of the construct.[2] When a stimulus does not belong to a construct but is identified with the construct, the stimulus will be called an *analogue* of the construct. As discussed later, identifying a stimulus with a construct, as well as identifying a stimulus as a construct instance, has important implications for a person's memory and judgments of the stimulus. In fact, interesting judgmental errors can occur when people treat analogues of constructs as if they were instances of the constructs.

Active and Passive Processing.   In Kelley's (1950) classic study of labeling effects on impression formation, students' ratings of a new instructor were more favorable when the instructor was described as a "warm" person by the experimenter prior to the instructor's arrival to class than when the instructor was described as a "cold" person. There are a number of possible interpretations of these results. One possibility is that exposure to a particular label (e.g., "warm") activated the construct designated by the label (i.e., 'warm' disposition) as well as other constructs such as "friendly" and "helpful" that are closely associated with this construct. This prior activation in turn could have

---

[2]The term *instance* is preferred to *member* because it makes little sense to speak of an instance of an individual as being a member of the personal construct for the individual.

increased the likelihood that the instructor's behavior would be categorized in terms of these constructs (a *passive* priming effect). Another possibility is that the experimenter's prior description may have given the students a set to expect instances of the construct designated by the label as well as instances of other constructs assumed to be highly related to that construct (an *active* set effect). Given the design of the study, Kelley's set interpretation is the simplest explanation, although the findings are likely to have been multiply determined.[3]

In general, the social psychological literature has not distinguished between active and passive processing. In the cognitive literature, a detailed analysis of the active–passive distinction has been provided by Posner and Warren (Posner, 1978; Posner & Warren, 1972; Warren, 1972). They distinguish between active, conscious processes involving deliberate strategies and control versus passive, unconscious processes that occur automatically and are uncontrolled. (See also Shiffrin & Schneider, 1977.) According to Posner (1978), a critical feature of conscious attention is its limited capacity, such that its utilization for processing one type of stimulus reduces the efficiency with which a different type of stimulus can be processed. For this reason, when conscious attention is directed to a construct, subjects' processing of stimulus information matching the construct is facilitated but their processing of stimulus information not matching the construct is inhibited or impaired (i.e., benefits with costs). In contrast, when a construct is primed or activated without conscious attention being directed to the activated construct, subjects' processing of stimulus information matching the construct will be facilitated without inhibiting the processing of stimulus information that does not match the construct (i.e., benefits without costs). Posner (1978, p. 91) proposes three criteria for whether a process is automatic: The process may occur without intention, without giving rise to conscious awareness, and without producing interference with other ongoing mental activity. In fact, an automatic process may take place despite an intention to prevent it. *Set* is an active process in which conscious attention is deliberately directed toward the expected event (Posner, 1978), whereas *priming* through verbal exposure can involve passive, automatic activation of constructs (Higgins, Rholes & Jones, 1977; Warren, 1972).

Strong support for both Posner's (1978) analysis of active and passive processing and distinction between active set and passive priming is provided in a study by Neely (1977). In a word–nonword classification task, each visually presented target letter string was preceded by a signal word. In one condition, the signal word *body* was usually followed by the name of a building part as target (*door*). Thus, the signal word body should arouse the *set* to expect a member of the building category. On the other hand, the word body should also *prime* or activate members of the body category. In the condition where the target word

---

[3]It is also possible that the students were conforming to the experimenter's personal judgment of the target (Higgins, et al., 1977; Higgins, in press).

was unexpectedly a member of the body category (leg), the signal body had an inhibiting effect on responding when there was a long delay between signal word and target word (2000 msec) but a facilitating effect when there was a short delay (250 msec). These results implicate a set mechanism where it takes time for conscious attention to be directed toward the expected event and, once active, interferes with processing unexpected stimuli, as well as a rapid priming process that occurs automatically and facilitates processing stimuli associated with the prime.

In Kelley's (1950) study, the experimenter's label would facilitate the processing of those aspects of the instructor's behavior that matched the designated construct regardless of whether an active set or passive automatic process was involved. If an active set was involved, however, then the instructor's label should also have inhibited the processing of those aspects of the instructor's behavior that did not match the designated construct. No such inhibition should have occurred if a passive automatic process was involved. Unfortunately, critical data bearing on these alternatives are not available.[4] It would be very useful if future research were designed and analyzed to distinguish between active and passive processing.

Determinants of Construct Accessibility

In Bruner's (1957) seminal paper on construct accessibility, two general factors are proposed as influencing construct accessibility: (1) the subjective probability estimates of the likelihood of a given event; and (2) search requirements imposed by one's needs, task goals, etc. In the present model, the first factor is called *expectations* and the second is called *motivation*. In addition to these factors, *recency of activation, frequency of activation, salience,* and *relation to accessible constructs* will be considered. In some cases the influence on accessibility is *momentary,* whereas in other cases it is *prolonged*. In some cases the influence is active and controlled, whereas in other cases it is passive and uncontrolled. The factors are interrelated in that a change in one factor (e.g., motivation) may often cause a change in one or more other factors (e.g., expectations), but the factors are operationally independent with respect to the methods by which they can be manipulated.

Expectations.   The accessibility of a construct will increase when the estimate of the likelihood of occurrence of a construct instance increases. Bruner (1957) points out that expectations, and changes in expectations, may be produced either by gradual learning from sequential observations or by instruction. In fact, there are a variety of ways to acquire expectations, and the impact

---

[4]It is also not possible to test these alternatives in the Higgins et al. (1977) study because all the stimulus information presented was related to the primed constructs.

of an expectation on a construct's accessibility may vary depending on how it was acquired. For example, a self-generated expectation induced through successive, dispersed instances is likely to have a greater influence on a construct's accessibility than is an expectation acquired through propositional transmission from another person (Higgins, Kuiper, & Olson, 1980).

Some expectations have only momentary effects on a construct's accessibility, such as an expectation about which category will occur in the next presentation of a predictable sequence of categories. Momentary effects can also arise from instruction, as exemplified in many placebo studies, where experimentally induced sensations are interpreted by subjects in terms of internal state constructs that were made temporarily more accessible by experimenter-provided expectations (Ross & Olson, in press). Other expectations have a relatively prolonged effect on a construct's accessibility. For example, labeling the instructor as "cold" in Kelley's (1950) study would create an expectation for instances of the construct not only with respect to the immediately subsequent behavior of the instructor but also for his long-term behavior. Another example of prolonged effects are the expectations that experienced marihuana users provide new users concerning the ambiguous sensations produced by the drug (Becker, 1966), which increases the accessibility of certain internal state constructs (e.g., warm, exciting) relative to alternative constructs (e.g., hot, agitating). Expectations about occupational or social roles are also likely to have prolonged effects on construct accessibility, because the expected appearance or behavior is a requirement of appropriate role fulfillment. For example, Cohen's (1977) research on occupational roles suggests that behavior related to constructs made more accessible by role expectations may be better remembered than behavior unrelated to such constructs. In addition, expectations about individuals or group members rarely have momentary effects because of the tendency to attribute behaviors to stable, habitual dispositions (Jones & Davis, 1965).[5]

The influence of expectations on construct accessibility can lead to either active or passive information processing. As Bruner (1957) points out, categorizing is often a silent or unconscious process. The influence of momentary expectations on construct accessibility is more likely to yield active processing than the influence of prolonged expectations, because momentary expectations and their source are more likely to be conscious. Expectations arising from a momentary set to expect a construct instance or analogue given by an experimenter are especially likely to yield active processes. For example, active processing was

---

[5]This tendency has been referred to as "the fundamental attribution error" (Ross, 1977), and the error has often been described as attributing the cause of an act to the actor rather than the situation when the situation is as likely or more likely to have been the cause. It should be noted, however, that the immediate or proximal cause of an act is necessarily the actor's intent or plan to perform the act. The error arises from the assumption that this momentary or acute intent on the part of the actor reflects a chronic or prolonged disposition rather than a temporary response to momentary circumstances. Thus, it is the dispositional inference and not the person attribution that is in error.

likely to have arisen from the manipulation of expectations in Carmichael, Hogan, and Walter's (1932) classic study where the experimenter provided different subjects with alternative labels for an ambiguous drawing (e.g., eyeglasses versus dumbbell) prior to its presentation. In contrast, the processing effects of prolonged social expectations on the reconstruction of past events are likely to be relatively passive.

Motivation.   Another factor that can increase a construct's accessibility is motivation (goals, needs, values, affective state), which can affect people's preparedness for construct instances without necessarily affecting their estimate of the likelihood of construct instances. As Jones and Gerard (1967) point out, if instances of certain objects or events are comforting or satisfying, then it is to our advantage to be prepared to see them so they are not missed. If instances of other objects or events are disturbing or harmful and recognition is instrumental for effective action, then it is also to our advantage to be prepared to see them. Bruner (1957) suggests that a construct's accessibility may be increased when a person's needs or ongoing activities require construct-related information. In pursuit of specific goals (e.g., to satisfy one's hunger), instances of particular constructs (e.g., restaurants, grocery stores) are actively sought out, thus increasing the accessibility of those constructs. The goals may be short term or long term, causing momentary or prolonged increases, respectively, in construct accessibility. Such increased accessibility imposed by goals would lead to relatively active processing. For example, active information processing is likely to be involved when subjects are instructed that their task goal in watching or reading about a target's behavior is to form an impression of the target or to remember the details of the information provided (Cohen & Ebbesen, 1979; Hamilton, 1980; Jeffery & Mischel, 1979).

The influence of motivation on construct accessibility can also result in relatively passive information processing. In fact, such passive or "unconscious" processing was a major focus of the "new look" in perception (Allport, 1955). There is some evidence, for example, that moderate increases in hunger will increase the accessibility of food-related constructs such that food responses to food analogues (ambiguous drawings of food) or food labels are enhanced (Levine, Chein, & Murphy, 1942; Wispe & Drambarean, 1953). There is also evidence that inducing a positive or negative mood in subjects by manipulating their success or failure on a task will affect their recall of items presented in a previous task, with subjects' recalling more pleasant stimulus words when in a positive mood and more unpleasant stimulus words when in a negative mood (Isen, Shalker, Clark, & Karp, 1978). Similarly, Postman and Brown (1952) found that prior success (performing above one's level of aspiration) increased the ease of identifying success-related words (e.g., winner) and prior failure increased the ease of identifying failure-related words (e.g., unable). The increased accessibility of the stimulus words in those studies, however, could also be due in part to the activation of evaluative judgments during the success or failure experience causing closely related constructs to be activated—the "relation to accessible constructs" determinant described later. Prolonged passive effects of motivation can also occur. For example, in a study concerning long-held values, Postman, Bruner, and McGinnies (1948) found that the higher the value to a subject of the value construct to which a word was related, the more readily the word was identified. It is possible, however, that constructs of higher value to a person are also activated more frequently, which, as noted later, would also increase their accessibility.

Recency of Activation.   Recent activation of a construct can also temporarily increase its accessibility (Forbach, Stanners, & Hochhaus, 1974; Higgins et al., 1977; Huttenlocher & Higgins, 1971; Warren, 1972; Wyer & Srull, 1980). In the Higgins et al. (1977) study, for example, subjects were first unobtrusively exposed to either positive or negative personality trait terms (e.g., adventurous versus reckless) as part of a perception study (the priming task) and then participated in a supposedly unrelated reading comprehension study where they read evaluatively ambiguous descriptions of a stimulus person (the "impression formation" task). Exposure to the personality trait terms in the priming task increased the accessibility of the constructs designated by these terms, as indicated by subjects' tendency to use the primed constructs later to characterize the stimulus person in the impression formation task. Other methods of priming or activating constructs will also increase their subsequent accessibility, such as exposure to behavioral instances of a trait construct (Wyer & Srull, 1980).

Increased construct accessibility from recent activation can have both active and passive information-processing effects. With respect to active processes, for example, Salancik and Conway (1975) have shown that students' evaluations of a college course will vary depending on whether instances of procourse behaviors versus anticourse behaviors have been recently activated. According to Salancik and Conway's (1975) and Bem's (1972) account of such processes, subjects answer the attitude question by actively searching for relevant behavioral information and then responding so as to be consistent with the implications of the information retrieved. Recent activation can also yield passive processing effects. In the Higgins et al. (1977) study, for example, subjects were not attending to the previously primed constructs when they encoded the stimulus information in the second "unrelated" task. The passive nature of the processing was indicated both by subject's inability to guess the true purpose of the study and by the fact that the percentage recall of the experimental trait labels presented in the priming task was, if anything, slightly less than the percentage recall of some irrelevant filler labels. Additional evidence against an active, experimental demand interpretation of recent activation effects is provided in a recent study by Wyer and Srull (1980). They found that exposure to construct instances had no effect on judgments of the target when it occurred after the presentation of the stimulus information. Priming after stimulus presentation necessarily eliminates any construct accessibility effects on stimulus encoding, but should, if anything, increase demand effects. Finally, evidence that priming effects increase over time (Higgins et al., 1977; Wyer & Srull, 1980) is consistent with a passive-processing interpretation but not a demand-effects interpretation.

The increase in construct accessibility from recent activation generally has momentary effects that dissipate within 15 minutes or so (Forbach et al., 1974; Warren, 1972), although contextual support and frequent activation (to be discussed later) can cause the effects to persist for as much as a day (Wyer & Srull, 1980). A metaphor for the influence of recent (and frequent) activation on construct accessibility is an energy cell whose energy or action potential is increased whenever the cell is activated or excited and whose energy slowly dissipates with time. The more energy a cell contains, the greater is the likelihood of its utilization.[6] This contrasts with Wyer and Srull's (1980) metaphor of a layered storage bin in which the construct on top is utilized in processing. In Wyer and Srull's model, recent activation affects subsequent processing because a recently activated construct is placed on top of the bin. Recent activation effects decrease over time because, with the passage of time, other constructs are likely to be used and then deposited on top of the bin; therefore, in the absence of any intervening utilization of alternative constructs, the effects of recent activation should persist over time. In Wyer and Srull's model, recent activation effects need not be momentary, whereas we would predict that frequent activation is necessary for prolonged effects.

Frequency of Activation.   The more frequently a construct is activated, the more accessible it will become. If the repeated activation is massed over a short period, then the accessibility effects will be relatively momentary. If the repeated activation is dispersed over a long period, then the accessibility effects will be relatively prolonged (Higgins et al., 1980).

One conspicuous example of the relation between activation frequency and construct accessibility is the correspondence between a concrete word's frequency of occurrence in a language and the readiness with which the word is recalled (Paivio, 1971) or an instance of the word is labeled or identified (Howes, 1954). The labeling effect, however, could also be due to expectations, because words that have occurred frequently in the past also have a high likelihood of occurrence in the present. Fortunately, Wyer and Srull's (1980) study provides

---

[6]It should also be noted that the metaphor of an energy cell fits nicely with the *spreading activation* model of semantic processing discussed later (Collins & Quillian, 1969; Collins & Loftus, 1975), where activation of one construct excites other closely related constructs through a passive spreading process (Warren, 1972). We do not wish to suggest, however, that the metaphor of an energy cell is wholly adequate to capture all the features of construct accessibility. For example, this metaphor is not suitable with regard to the influence of salience on construct accessibility (discussed later).

evidence of the relation between activation frequency and construct accessibility that is not confounded with expectations. Using the *unrelated-studies* paradigm, they presented subjects in the initial priming study with 6, 12, 24, or 48 behavioral instances of a trait construct and found a positive, generally monotonic relation between the number of instances presented (the frequency of construct activation) and the extent to which a target person in the subsequent impression-formation study was characterized in terms of this construct.

According to Wyer and Srull's (1980) storage bin notion, frequency of activation increases the likelihood that, at any point in time, the construct will have been recently used and thus stored on top of the bin. According to our energy cell notion, the action potential of a construct increases as a function of frequency of activation. These notions make different predictions when frequency and recency of activation involve different constructs. Consider, for example, a study using the Higgins et al. (1977) paradigm where four of the priming labels presented in the first study designate one construct and its close synonyms (e.g., "reckless," "foolhardy," "rash") but the final priming label designates an evaluatively opposite construct (e.g., adventurous), and subjects in the subsequent impression formation study must characterize an ambiguous reckless/adventurous stimulus person. Presumably, the storage bin model would predict that the stimulus person would be characterized as "adventurous," whereas the energy cell notion would predict that the stimulus person would be characterized as "reckless."

Salience.   The accessibility of a construct is also affected by its salience in memory, where the salience of a construct depends upon both its *prominence* and *distinctiveness*. The prominence of a construct is determined by the quality of its attributes. Just as the attributes of an external stimulus can be more striking or attention grabbing than the attributes of other external stimuli because of their greater intensity, complexity, or vividness (McArthur, 1980; Nisbett & Ross, 1980), the attributes of a stored construct (and its instances) could be more striking than the attributes of other stored constructs because of their greater intensity, complexity, or vividness. Among Muppet proper constructs, for example, the relative accessibility of the Big Bird and Cookie Monster constructs are enhanced by the prominence of Big Bird's physical attributes (e.g., huge size, bright yellow and orange color) and Cookie Monster's behavioral attributes (e.g., intense eating behavior). Such inherent, prominent attributes or instances of a construct should yield relatively prolonged and passive accessibility effects. There has been very little experimental research concerned with the accessibility of stored constructs deriving from the prominence of their inherent attributes or instances. Instead, most research on salience has been concerned with the momentary salience of external, novel stimuli deriving from manipulations of subjects' viewpoint or attention, such as manipulations of visual access to target persons (McArthur, 1980; Taylor & Fiske, 1978).

The distinctiveness of a construct depends on both the uniqueness of its attributes and the degree to which it monopolizes its taxonomic level of inclusiveness.[7] As the overlap between a construct's attributes and the attributes of other constructs decreases, ease of identifying construct instances should increase and confusability with other constructs should decrease. Similarly, as the number of coordinate or alternative class members of a construct decrease, recall interference and confusability should decrease. The inherent distinctiveness of a construct should also yield relatively prolonged- and passive-accessibility effects.[8] The instances of a construct with relatively distinct episodes should be easier to retrieve, and this in turn should increase the frequency estimate of construct instances (Tversky & Kahneman, 1973). For example, Hamilton and Gifford (1976) presented subjects with a set of statements describing the desirable or undesirable behaviors of different group members, where either the desirable or undesirable behaviors occurred more often. As predicted, subjects' subsequent estimates of the frequency of the desirable and undesirable behaviors were significantly inflated for the relatively distinct types of behavior (the type of behavior with less instances).

Some recent research by Taylor, Fiske, Close, Anderson, & Ruderman (1977) suggests that momentary distinctiveness can also affect judgments of a target person. Subjects were shown videotaped discussions of groups that consisted of either a solitary black target in an otherwise white group or the same black target in a racially balanced group of blacks and whites. When the black target was the sole black, he was perceived as having been more influential in the group discussion than his coparticipants. The same target was not perceived as more influential when he was not distinctive. It is also possible that the accessibility of the general construct for blacks was temporarily increased in the imbalanced group by the visual prominence of the black-attribute instances embodied in the target, which could have affected the processing of information about this particular black. The influence of momentary distinctiveness (e.g., the sex composition of a group) on judgments and attitudinal responses has also been shown in other studies (Shomer & Centers, 1970).

There is also evidence that distinctiveness can cause increases in the accessibility of different aspects of a person's self-construct (McGuire, McGuire, Child, & Fujioka, 1978; McGuire & Padawer-Singer, 1976). For example, McGuire and Padawer-Singer found that the attributes elementary-school children included in their spontaneous self-descriptions depended on their distinctiveness within the classroom, with distinctive attributes being more likely to be mentioned (e.g., green eyes, foreign birthplace). For some attributes, such as green eyes, distinctiveness should have relatively prolonged effects on accessibility because the attribute is likely to be distinctive across many contexts. For other attributes, such as a person's sex, distinctiveness should have relatively

---

[7]For a discussion of levels of abstractions, see Rosch (1978) and Cantor and Mischel (in press).

[8]With increasing knowledge, the distinctiveness of most constructs is likely to decrease because both a construct's uniqueness and a construct's monopolization of its taxonomic level is likely to decrease.

momentary effects on accessibility because the distinctiveness of the attribute is likely to vary continually across different contexts. A recent study by McGuire, McGuire, and Winton (1979), however, suggests that multiple exposure to situations in which particular self-attributes are salient can yield persistent and relatively context-free increases in the accessibility of these attributes, presumably because the multiple exposure has caused frequent activation of these self-attributes. McGuire et al. (1979) found that school children were more likely to mention their gender in their spontaneous self-descriptions if they came from households where their gender was in the minority. Thus, household composition can yield prolonged individual differences in the accessibility of certain constructs.

Relation to Accessible Constructs.   The accessibility of a construct will also increase if the accessibility of a closely related construct is increased. The increase in accessibility can be momentary or prolonged, depending on whether the increased accessibility of the related construct is momentary or prolonged. With respect to momentary effects, the spreading-activation theory assumes that when a stored item is processed or activated, other items will be automatically (i.e., passively) activated to the extent that they are closely related to that item (Collins & Loftus, 1975). Evidence of this passive spreading-activation effect for conceptually related or semantically similar items is provided by a number of studies in the cognitive literature. For example, Loftus (1973) has shown that the latency to name an instance of a category (e.g., a fruit) decreases if another instance of the category has been named on a previous trial.[9] In a study by Warren (1972), subjects found it more difficult to ignore the meaning of a target word (e.g., tree) while quickly trying to name its ink color (the Stroop interference task), if they had been previously exposed to words closely related in meaning to the target (e.g., elm, oak) than words unrelated to the target, indicating that the accessibility of the target word's meaning was increased when closely related constructs were activated. It has also been shown that the time it takes to classify letter strings as words or nonwords is faster when the letter string (e.g., butter) is preceded by an associated word (bread) than an unassociated word (e.g., nurse) (Meyer, Schvaneveldt, & Ruddy, 1975).

One would expect the same spreading-activation effects for closely related social constructs (Higgins et al., 1977; Wyer & Carlston, 1979). In fact, there is evidence from the Higgins et al. (1977) study that exposure to a particular trait construct (e.g., reckless) increases the likelihood that an ambiguous behavioral description (a reckless/adventurous description) will be characterized in terms of closely related trait constructs (rash, crazy). Kelley's (1955) classic study on the

---

[9]This is true even when there has been an intervening trial where an instance from a different category is named, a result consistent with our energy cell notion.

effects of membership salience on resistance to attitude change also suggests that activating one social construct (reading about the life of Pope Pius XII) will increase the accessibility of closely related social constructs (the principles of the Catholic Church). More recently, Geller and Shaver (1976) found that increasing the salience of a person's physical self and current behaviors (by having subjects look at themselves in a mirror and telling them that they were being observed) increased the accessibility of self-relevant and self-evaluative words, as measured by the Stroop interference task.

Because there is evidence that constructs with similar evaluative tone are closely related (Wickens, 1972), an activated social construct (e.g., ugly) should also increase the accessibility of evaluatively similar social constructs (e.g., evil, gangster, mugging). Other constructs become closely related as part of people's implicit personality theories (Rosenberg & Sedlak, 1972; Schneider, 1973). For example, the constructs fat and jolly (or glamorous and dumb) are closely related in the minds of many people, even though they are neither semantically nor evaluatively similar. The learning of social scripts is yet another way that social constructs may become related (Abelson, 1975; Berne, 1964). Such interrelatedness among constructs suggests that by activating one construct (e.g., fat) included within a person's implicit personality theory or "personae" (Nisbett & Ross, 1980), other constructs related to this construct (e.g., jolly) will increase in accessibility, as evident, for example, in their increased use to encode subsequent stimulus information. Moreover, these effects are likely to be unconscious and uncontrolled (i.e., passive).

Relatedness to accessible constructs could result in long-term increases in construct accessibility as well as the short-term increases described previously. If there is a prolonged increase in a construct's accessibility (e.g., from frequent activation), prolonged increases in the accessibility of closely related constructs could occur. A more intriguing possibility is that a construct's accessibility could be increased for a prolonged period by increasing its association, or creating an association, to a highly accessible construct. For example, being told that someone you know only slightly at work is a lot like Archie Bunker at home could cause a prolonged increase in the accessibility of your construct for that person.

CONSEQUENCES OF CONTEXTUAL VARIABILITY IN CONSTRUCT ACCESSIBILITY

Contextual variability refers to differences in physical and social circumstances that tend to cause differences in the accessibility of particular constructs for any person in the situation (i.e., acute, context-dependent variability). Different situations, events, and circumstances vary with respect to the accessibility determinants described earlier. Some situations involve characteristic goals, expectations, or salient actions and objects (e.g., small talk, drinking, and meeting new people at cocktail parties). For these situations, there would be relatively prolonged accessibility of the associated constructs (Rosch, 1978). In other contexts, there may be momentary increases in a construct's accessibility due to the temporary salience of associated actions and objects or to the direct activation of the construct or associated constructs. Of course, even a momentary increase in a construct's accessibility can have long-term consequences for subsequent information processing. For example, a momentary increase in construct accessibility from recent activation (i.e., priming) has been shown to affect subjects' judgments of a stimulus person over a week later; in fact, the consequences increased over time (Higgins et al., 1977; Wyer & Srull, 1980).

This section considers the information-processing consequences of contextual variability in construct accessibility. The short-term and long-term consequences have been examined in a number of studies by the senior author and collaborators and are presented here. The implications of these and related studies are discussed in terms of the consequences of increased accessibility for the input, consolidation, and output stages of information processing.

Input

For most stimulus information, there are more aspects of the input to be noticed than one can possibly attend to and encode. Selectivity is forced upon us by our information-processing limitations (Bruner, 1958). One determinant of selectivity is whether or not a schema (or construct) is available to encode the information. Neisser (1976), for example, states that perceivers will "pick up only what they have schemas for and willy-nilly ignore the rest [p. 80]." Another determinant of selectivity is construct accessibility; that is, among stored constructs, some constructs are more accessible than others, and perceivers are more likely to pick up what they have accessible constructs for.

Selectivity effects of increased construct accessibility appear to be involved in a number of studies where role expectations have been manipulated. Zadny and Gerard (1974) found that subjects' recall of items in a live skit varied depending on the role that was attributed to the target actor. Items were better recalled when they were related to the target's role (e.g., chemistry items when the target was a chemistry major) than when they were unrelated to the target's role (e.g., chemistry items when the target was a music major). These results could also be due to retrieval effects of role expectations, but it is likely that subjects selectively noticed and encoded items related to the target's role. Selectivity effects of manipulating the role of the target actor have also been found by Cohen (1977) and may be involved in Langer and Abelson's (1974) finding that therapists evaluate a target as more disturbed if previously told that the target is a "patient" versus a "job applicant."

Using a different paradigm, Anderson and Pichert (1978) manipulated subjects' own role expectations by having them read a story containing information about a particular house from the perspective of either a burglar or a prospective home buyer. For the home buyer role, at least, the manipulation of role expectations appeared to have selectivity effects (as well as retrieval effects to be discussed later). Controlling for perspective at recall, a much higher proportion of home buyer-related items were recalled when subjects had been initially assigned the home buyer role than when subjects had been initially assigned the burglar role.

Selectivity effects could also arise from the influence of group composition on construct accessibility. With respect to the sex composition of a group, for example, gender should be more salient for a group member whose gender is in the minority than for a group member whose gender is in the majority. Increasing the salience of gender should, in turn, increase the accessibility of attributes associated with male and female gender.[10] Such increased accessibility should influence the processing of stimulus information exemplifying sex-linked attributes. For people with traditional views concerning the attributes of males and females, salient group sex composition should cause selective attention to aspects of a stimulus person (whether self or other) that are consistent with the conventional, stereotypic, sex-linked attributes (e.g., ambitious, scientific, and independent for males; sensitive, artistic, and nurturant, for females). For people with nontraditional or modern views concerning the attributes of males and females, salient group sex composition should cause selective attention to aspects of a stimulus person that in many cases are opposite to the stereotypic, sex-linked attributes (e.g., sensitive, artistic, and nurturant for males; ambitious, scientific, and independent for females).[11]

Most recent undergraduates at major universities are likely to have both the traditional and modern views available to them, having acquired the traditional view while growing up and the modern view while attending the university. In addition, most recent undergraduates subscribe to the modern view, especially in regard to people possessing the positive stereotypic traits of the opposite sex (Kravetz, 1976; Pleck, 1976). Therefore, when the accessibility of gender-related constructs is increased, undergraduates should selectively attend to in-

---

[10]In this study, as well as in the studies described later, the comparison is between those students in a group whose gender is in the minority versus those students whose gender is in the majority. The proposal is that gender is relatively more salient (and gender-related constructs are relatively more accessible) for those students in the group whose gender is in the minority. This does not necessarily mean that being in a group where one's gender is in the majority has no effect on the salience of one's gender. In fact, a person's gender under such conditions may be more salient than when the person is alone or in a group with an equal number of males and females.

[11]For a discussion of traditional and modern views of sex-linked attributes, see Kravetz (1976) and Pleck (1976).

formation about a stimulus person that is consistent with the modern view of sex-linked attributes because their sex-linked processing is under active control. Otherwise, undergraduates should selectively attend to information about a stimulus person that is consistent with the traditional view of sex-linked attributes because this view is likely to be more accessible during passive, uncontrolled processing due to its much longer history of activation. This hypothesis was examined in the following study by Higgins and Petty.[12]

Study 1:   Group Sex Composition Effects on Encoding the Sex-Linked Characteristics of a Target Person

Method.   One hundred and forty-six Princeton University undergraduates agreed to help serve as an adult comparison group for a future developmental study on the relation between object and person perception. The study involved two major experimental manipulations—sex composition of the groups and sex of target person. Three or four subjects were run at a time and were seated around a large table such that no subject could see another's responses. No talking was permitted. A female undergraduate experimenter conducted 20 groups of subjects each composed of two or three other females and one solitary male; a male undergraduate experimenter conducted 20 groups of subjects each composed of two or three other males and one solitary female. For each of these two types of groups, subjects in half of the groups read a paragraph supposedly describing a female undergraduate at Princeton (Barbara) and subjects in the other half of the groups read the same paragraph supposedly describing a male undergraduate (Bob). Following the procedure for constructing unambiguous descriptions outlined in Higgins and Rholes (1978), the paragraph contained descriptions exemplifying the following eight traits, selected to be neither redundant nor contradictory: two evaluatively positive, stereotypically male traits, (active, ambitious) and two evaluatively negative, stereotypically male traits, (aggressive, selfish); two evaluatively positive, stereotypically female traits, (polite, sensitive) and two evaluatively negative, stereotypically female traits, (emotional, dependent). The male and female traits were selected on the basis of previous reports concerning common sex-role stereotypes (Rosenkrantz, Vogel, Bee, Broverman & Broverman, 1968). In order to check whether the behavioral descriptions did exemplify these traits, 16 pilot subjects read each description separately and characterized the type of person described. On the average, the descriptions elicited the intended traits, or denotative and evaluative synonyms (e.g., moody instead of emotional), 76% of the time.

---

[12]This study was conducted as a Princeton University Senior Thesis by Cornelia J. Petty (1977) under the direction of the senior author.

The subjects were told that the information about Bob (Barbara) contained in the paragraph had been obtained from a variety of sources, including Bob's (Barbara's) application and interview for a summer job, and evaluations from some of Bob's (Barbara's) instructors or acquaintances. After reading the paragraph, the subjects were given a 20-minute "Hidden Pictures" filler task, ostensibly to compare object perception with person perception. They were then asked to reproduce the paragraph about Bob (Barbara) as best they could, word for word.

Results.   The reproductions were scored by a coder blind to experimental condition for the number of positive male stereotypes, the number of negative male stereotypes, the number of positive female stereotypes, and the number of negative female stereotypes included in each reproduction. A sex of subject $\times$ sex of target $\times$ distinctiveness of gender $\times$ sex of stereotype $\times$ desirability of stereotype analysis of variance yielded, as predicted, a significant sex of target $\times$ distinctiveness of gender $\times$ sex of stereotype interaction, $F(1, 135) = 9.62$, $p < .01$. As shown in Table 4.1, when the target was ostensibly a male, the subjects recalled less stereotypically male and more stereotypically female stimulus information when their gender was in the minority (i.e., high gender distinctiveness) than when their gender was in the majority (i.e., low gender distinctiveness); whereas when the target was ostensibly a female, the subjects recalled less stereotypically female stimulus information when their gender was in the minority than when it was in the majority. There was also greater recall of female stereotypes than male stereotypes, $F(1, 135) = 26.06$, $p < .001$. There was no sex of subject effect on memory for the stereotypically male and female descriptions.

The analysis of variance also yielded a significant sex of subject $\times$ sex of target $\times$ desirability of stereotype interaction, $F(1, 135) = 4.29$, $p < .05$,

TABLE 4.1
Mean Number of Male Stereotypes and Female Stereotypes
Reproduced as a Function of Sex of Target and Distinctiveness
of Gender

	Distinctiveness of Gender	
Sex of Target	*High (minority)*	*Low (majority)*
Male target		
Male stereotypes	.9	1.6
Female stereotypes	2.5	2.1
Female target		
Male stereotypes	1.9	1.9
Female stereotypes	2.0	2.4

reflecting the fact that female subjects recalled more positive stereotypes and slightly less negative stereotypes for the supposed female target than the supposed male target, whereas male subjects' did not evaluatively differentiate between the male and female targets.

The results of this study are consistent with our hypothesis that, for undergraduates, increasing the distinctiveness of gender increases the accessibility of the modern view of sex-linked attributes, leading to relatively greater attention to information about a stimulus person that is less traditionally sex linked.

Consolidation

At the input stage, the selectivity resulting from construct assessibility causes people to notice some aspects of the stimulus information while not noticing other aspects. At the consolidation stage, only those aspects of the stimulus information that have been noticed are encoded and stored. When the attributes of the stimulus are similar to the content of more than one construct and the match to these alternative constructs is approximately the same, the stimulus is likely to be identified with whichever construct is most accessible (Bruner, 1957). Consider, for example, the story at the beginning of the chapter. The ambiguous stimulus information about Donald and Daisy was identified differently by Michael and Minnie. Donald was identified as "adventurous" by Michael but as "reckless" by Minnie, and Daisy was identified as "stubborn" by Michael but as "persistent" by Minnie.

Similar behavioral information was used in the Higgins et al. (1977) study, and subjects' spontaneous characterizations of the stimulus person in the impression formation task varied as a function of whichever trait constructs had been made more accessible through recent activation in the previous priming task. These effects of recent activation on identification can, in turn, have rather dramatic consequences for subsequent information processing. In the Higgins et al. (1977) study, for example, subjects' attitudes toward the stimulus person were significantly affected by the trait priming, as discussed in the Output section later. Can even creative problem solving be influenced by such priming effects on identification? This question was addressed in the following study by Higgins and Chaires (1980).[13]

Study 2:   Priming, Identification, and Creative Problem Solving

One of the classic insight problems is Duncker's (1945) "candle problem." Subjects are seated at a table on which there is a cardboard wall, and, under a cover, a candle, a full book of matches, and a box filled with thumbtacks. They

---

[13]This study was conducted as a Princeton University Senior Thesis by William M. Chaires (1976) under the direction of the senior author.

are told that when the cover is removed their task is to affix the candle to the cardboard wall, as quickly as possible, so that the candle burns properly and does not drip wax on the table or floor. In order to solve the problem, subjects must tack the box on to the cardboard wall, place the candle on top of the box, and then light the candle. The difficult part of the problem is to think of using the box as a platform for the candle, rather than just as a container for the tacks. Most adults have great difficulty with this problem as many do not solve it at all within the 10- or 15-minute allotted time.

The results of an initial study indicated that labeling the box facilitated problem solving only when it clearly differentiated the box from the tacks (i.e., for the label "box and tacks" but not for the label "box of tacks"). The facilitating effects of labeling have previously been explained as being due either to the label calling attention to the key object (Glucksberg & Weisberg, 1966) or to the label directing subjects to the solution desired by the experimenter (Weisberg & Suls, 1973). These factors require that the box be labeled by the experimenter when the candle problem is presented. We reasoned, however, that if the facilitating effects were due to the label activating a differentiated categorization of the box, then it should be possible to obtain the same results by activating a general mode of categorization through verbal exposure in an extraneous task.

Method. Three groups of 10 undergraduates each (the "of" description, "and" description, and "no" description groups) were shown the same series of slides depicting 15 objects as part of a study on "long-term memory." Subjects were told they would be shown slides of common household objects to be recalled later after completing a problem-solving task designed to prevent rehearsal of the objects. Of the 15 items, 5 were objects that would normally be designated by a single word (comb, eyeglasses, scissors, football, and banana), and 10 were objects that would normally be designated by a phrase (e.g., tray containing tomatoes, bowl containing cereal, jar containing cherries, carton containing eggs, and bag containing vegetables). All subjects received the same random order of the slides. None of the objects used in the candle task was present in the slides. In the *of* condition, the phrase slides were all described by the experimenter with an *of* linguistic construction (e.g., a carton of eggs, a tray of tomatoes, a bag of vegetables) when they appeared on the screen. In the *and* condition, the slides were described with an *and* construction (e.g., a carton and eggs). In both conditions the "single-name" objects were described by their appropriate names. In the *no description* condition none of the slides was described by the experimenter.

In order to check whether exposure to differentiated labels would be effective in increasing the frequency with which subjects labeled the box of tacks in a manner differentiating the box from the tacks, 16 pilot subjects were asked to describe all the objects on the table before beginning the candle problem after exposure to either the *and* or the *of* descriptions. As predicted, a greater number of subjects in the *and* condition (5 out of 8) than in the *of* condition (0 out of 8) labeled the box of tacks in a manner differentiating the box (e.g., tacks, box; thumbtacks and box; small box, tacks in box), Fisher Exact Test, $p < .025$, one tailed. These results indicated that exposure to differentiated labels did increase the frequency of the subjects' labeling the box of tacks in a manner differentiating the box.

In the actual experiment, the subjects were not asked to describe the objects in the candle problem before beginning the problem, and thus the box of tacks was never overtly labeled by either the experimenter or the subjects. After subjects were shown the slides, they were given the candle problem ostensibly to prevent them from rehearsing the slide objects. They were told they would be timed and should try to solve the problem as quickly as possible. While a subject worked on the problem, the experimenter sat out of sight behind the subject and recorded the subjects' solution times (from the moment the cover was removed to the moment the box was tacked to the cardboard wall). There was a time limit of 10 minutes.

Results.   As shown in Table 4.2, the primed mode of categorization in the *and* condition greatly facilitated problem solution. With respect to solution time, subjects in the *and* condition solved the candle problem faster than subjects in both the *of* condition, Mann-Whitney $U = 13$, $p < .01$ one-tailed, and the *no description* condition, $u = 11$, $p < .01$ one-tailed. Moreover, a greater number of subjects in the *and* condition solved the problem within the allotted time period than subjects in both the *of* condition, Fisher Exact Test, $p < .025$ one-tailed, and the *no description* condition, Fisher Exact Test, $p < .025$ one-tailed. There were no significant differences between the *of* and *no description* conditions, suggesting that subjects in the *no description* condition spontaneously categorized the box in an undifferentiated manner.

In order to check whether subjects were aware that the experimenter's description of the slides was related to the candle task, subjects were asked at the end of

TABLE 4.2
Median Solution-Time Scores (in minutes)
and Percentage of Solvers
in Each Verbal Exposure Condition

Verbal Exposure Condition	N	Median Solution Time	Percentage of Solvers
And	10	4.1	80
Of	10	10.0	20
None	10	10.0	20

Note: The allotted time period for solving the problem was 10 minutes. Subjects who did not solve the problem were given a solution-time score of 10 minutes.

the study whether anything about the memory task interfered with or affected their behavior in the problem-solving task, because it was still easy for the procedure to be changed to avoid such problems. None of the subjects reported any relation between the tasks other than the candle task interfering with their memory for the slide objects. Thus, subjects expressed no awareness of having learned a mode of categorization that affected their performance.

These findings indicate that priming effects on mode of categorization can have substantial consequences even for creative problem solving. Moreover, these consequences arise from passive, unconscious processing effects of priming. The implications of these results for interrelational constructs (e.g., liking, dominance) and social problem-solving need to be explored (cf. Higgins & Chaires, 1980).

Levels of Going Beyond the Information Given

Construct accessibility not only increases the likelihood that the accessible construct will be used to encode a stimulus rather than an equally applicable alternative construct. As Bruner (1957) suggests, construct accessibility also reduces the amount of similarity between input and construct necessary for the input to be accepted as fitting the construct. Wyer and Srull (1980), for example, presented subjects with behavioral descriptions that were ambiguous instances of trait constructs and found that subjects were more likely to judge a description as being a clear instance of a trait if the trait's accessibility had previously been increased through recent activation.

Construct accessibility has still further consequences for the encoding and storage of stimulus information that derive from its influence on the identification process; specifically, the tendency for people to "go beyond the information given" once a stimulus is confidently identified (Bruner, 1958). There are basically three levels of going beyond the information given: inferring identifying attributes of the stimulus beyond those actually present in the stimulus; inferring nonidentifying attributes of the stimulus that constitute part of the activated construct but are not observable in the stimulus; and inferring additional attributes that are thought to co-occur with the attributes of the activated construct but are not part of the activated construct.

Identifying a stimulus as an instance of a construct does not require that all the construct's identifying attributes be present in the stimulus; a subset of identifying attributes is often sufficient to make an equivalence judgment or match. Once the stimulus is accepted as an instance, however, the remaining identifying attributes of the construct are usually assumed to be present in the stimulus. For example, if a person sees a woman dressed in a nurse's uniform and on this basis identifies her as a nurse, then the person is likely to infer that she also possesses the skills and training of a nurse; that is, functional attributes are inferred following identification from perceptual attributes. Similarly, if a person has been told that a woman is a nurse and sees, from a distance, the woman wearing white clothes, then the person may encode and store the fact that the woman was wearing a nurse's uniform even though she was actually wearing a spring outfit for a garden party. The process of identification not only leads to filling in missing identifying attributes but also to ignoring, omitting, or distorting attributes that do not match the construct's identifying attributes in order to create a better fit between the stimulus and the construct. In the opening story, once Minnie has categorized Daisy as "persistent," she is likely to delete or distort any evidence that is incongruent with this construct, such as those aspects of Daisy's behavior that suggest stubbornness more than persistence.

Once a stimulus has been identified as an instance of a construct, other nonidentifying properties of the construct are likely to be attributed to the stimulus. Miller (1978) distinguishes between lexical knowledge, required for linguistic communication, and practical knowledge. The identifying attributes of a construct are part of the lexical knowledge, because linguistic production and comprehension require the ability to identify instances of a construct. Constructs, however, also contain practical knowledge that is not necessary for identification; for example, the fact that a shoe can be used to hammer in tacks may be part of one's practical knowledge about shoes but would not typically be considered an identifying attribute of shoes. The processing of stimulus information may be affected by the application of such practical knowledge. For example, one's practical knowledge about headwaiters may include the fact that they treat a guest better if given a generous tip, and, thus, after giving a generous tip to a man identified as a headwaiter, one may encode and store his behavior as being more courteous and helpful than it actually is.

The third level of going beyond the information given is to assign those attributes to a stimulus that are thought to co-occur with the attributes comprising the identified construct. Social scripts (Abelson, 1975) are one source of naive knowledge about the co-occurrence of social attributes. The source that has received most attention in the literature is people's implicit personality theories; that is, people's assumptions about the associations among traits (Bruner & Tagiuri, 1954; Schneider, 1973). In the opening story, for example, Minnie's opinion that Daisy "is there when you need her" derives from Minnie's belief that reliability co-occurs with persistence. In Wyer and Srull's (1980) study, subjects' ratings of the target person along some additional trait dimensions evaluatively related to the primed trait were consistent with their ratings of the target person along the primed trait dimension, perhaps reflecting inferences from subjects' implicit personality theories.

Thus far, the discussion of the effects of identification has focused on the consequences of identifying a stimulus *as* an instance of a construct. People also go beyond the information given, however, when identifying a stimulus *with* a construct. For example, a person may identify a stranger with his father because of the stranger's striking resemblance to his father's physical appearance, and then, because of this identification, the person may assign dispositional traits to the stranger that are characteristic of his father. This process of judging and interpreting an individual in terms of the salient attributes of a significant other evoked by the individual is a major type of inferential process (Nisbett & Ross, 1980; Sarbin, Taft, & Bailey, 1960) but one that has rarely been investigated. Identification with significant others affects self-judgments as well as judgments of others. It is also one of the major processes involved in interpersonal influence (Kelman, 1958).[14]

An important difference between identifying a stimulus with a construct versus identifying a stimulus as a construct instance is that people are less likely to assign the missing essential or defining attributes of the construct to the stimulus when identifying a stimulus with a construct, because the stimulus is, in fact, not an actual instance of the construct. There may be less difference, however, in people's tendency to infer missing characteristic attributes and practical knowledge attributes of the construct.

The consequences of an active versus passive process of identification for subsequent inferences about a stimulus may also vary for these two kinds of identification. When a stimulus is identified as an instance of a construct, inferences will be made concerning missing construct attributes regardless of whether the identification process was conscious (e.g., a set) or unconscious (e.g., priming). When a stimulus is identified with a construct, however, it is possible that missing construct attributes will be inferred *only* if the identification process is unconscious. People, after all, are unlikely to assign the missing attributes of a construct to a stimulus when they are conscious of the fact that the stimulus is *not* an instance of the construct.

Output

Construct accessibility can have various consequences at the output stage of information processing. The identification of a stimulus during the consolidation stage can increase the accessibility at the output stage of those constructs arising from the identification (i.e., both perceived and inferred attributes). This has consequences for remembering the stimulus information, as well as for subsequent judgments about the stimulus, and these consequences tend to increase over time. The accessibility of a construct during retrieval also has consequences for memory and judgments that can be independent of any previous identification

---

[14]In fact, one could conceptualize a change from identification to internalization with respect to adopting others' values as involving a change from *identifying with* another's values to *identifying* one's own values *as* equivalent to these values.

of the stimulus material. Both of these kinds of output consequences of construct accessibility are considered in this section.

Consequences Arising from Prior Identification

During the consolidation stage of information processing, both details of the stimulus information as well as judgments of the stimulus will be stored. Memory and judgments of the stimulus information at the output stage are influenced by both the stored representation of the stimulus details and the prior judgments. There is a tendency for the original stimulus to be subsequently remembered and judged in a manner consistent with the denotative and evaluative implications of the prior judgments, especially if the representation of the input is incomplete or decayed (Bartlett, 1932; Higgins et al., 1977; Neisser, 1967; Spiro, 1977).[15] In addition, because the representation of the stimulus tends to decay rapidly over time, the delayed influence of accessible constructs on memory and judgments is often greater than the immediate influence (Bartlett, 1932; Higgins et al., 1977; Higgins & Rholes, 1978). These conclusions are supported by a number of studies.

Evidence is presented in the Higgins et al. (1977) study that subjects' later evaluation of the stimulus person was influenced by their prior judgments of the stimulus person and that this influence increased over a two-week period. First, evaluations of the stimulus person in the first session did not differ significantly as a function of their priming condition, but in the second session two weeks later, subjects who had been in the positive-priming condition rated the stimulus person as significantly more desirable than those who had been in the negative-priming condition. Second, in the first session, there was little relation between subjects' prior judgments of the stimulus person and their evaluations of the stimulus person ($r = .13$), but by the second session two weeks later, there was a significant positive relation between the positivity of subjects' prior judgments and the positivity of their evaluations ($r = .46$).

Wyer and Srull (1980) and Carlston (in press) have also found that the influence of subjects' previous ratings of a target person on their subsequent ratings of the target increases over time. Other studies provide evidence that prior judgments affect later evaluations, predictions, inferences, and behavior (e.g., Higgins & Rholes, 1978; Lingle & Ostrom, 1979; Ross, Lepper, Strack, & Steinmetz, 1977; Sherman, Ahlm, Berman, & Lynn, 1978). For example, Lingle and Ostrom (1979) found that judgments of the suitability of a target person for a particular occupation (e.g., judge) was based more on their prior judgment of the target's suitability for a similar or dissimilar occupation (e.g., lawyer versus

---

[15]It must be emphasized that the stored representation of the stimulus details is not necessarily an accurate reflection of the stimulus information because it can be, and often is, substantially altered by the processing involved in the input and consolidation stages.

store clerk) than on the input description of the target that was the basis for their prior judgment.

There is also evidence that prior judgments of stimulus information have an increasing impact over time on memory for the stimulus information. In a study by Higgins and Rholes (1978), subjects were asked to summarize ambiguous and unambiguous information about a stimulus person for a recipient who purportedly either liked or disliked the stimulus person. Subjects' labeling or categorization of the stimulus person was more positive when they thought the message recipient liked the stimulus person. As shown in Table 4.3, the subsequent reproductions of the stimulus information by subjects who wrote a message (the *message condition*) were more positive when subjects had written a message for a recipient who purportedly liked the stimulus person. In contrast, there was little effect for subjects who did not actually write a message (the *no-message condition*), either because they did not modify their categorizations of the stimulus person to suit the recipient or because their categorizations were less accessible by not having been overtly expressed.

The Higgins and Rholes (1978) study also provides evidence that the effect of prior judgments on memory for stimulus information can increase over time (especially for reproductions of unambiguous stimulus information). First, the amount of distortion in the reproductions of the unambiguous stimulus information toward the recipient's attitude was significantly greater for reproductions obtained 2 weeks after input than for reproductions obtained shortly after input. There was also a tendency for the overall evaluative tone of the reproductions to become increasingly consistent over time with the overall tone of the messages. Second, the correlation between the evaluative tone of the distortions in subjects' messages and the evaluative tone of the distortions in subjects' reproductions increased significantly from $r = .18$ (ns) for reproductions obtained shortly after message encoding to $r = .74$, $p < .001$, for reproductions obtained 2 weeks after message encoding.

The effects of stimulus identification on subsequent memory and judgments have been examined mostly with regard to trait and role constructs. However,

TABLE 4.3

Mean Number of Positive and Negative Distortions in Reproduction as a Function of Message Recipient Opinion and Communication Condition

	Message		No Message	
Message Recipient's Opinion of Stimulus Person	*Positive Distortions*	*Negative Distortions*	*Positive Distortions*	*Negative Distortions*
Like	2.4	0	0.8	0.6
Dislike	0.3	1.9	0.8	0.5

when a group construct is activated, beliefs associated with the group are activated, and this can also influence subsequent processing of construct instances.
Although the consequences on memory and judgments are probably due in part to
selectivity factors, consolidation and output factors are clearly implicated when
the effects increase over time. Unfortunately, very few studies have examined
the effects over time of activating beliefs associated with groups. In one relevant
study by Taft (1954), black and white teenagers heard a passage that contained
favorable and unfavorable items about a black baseball player and then were
asked to repeat as much about the passage as they could both immediately after
hearing it and again 3 days later. On the immediate recall, there was little
difference between the black and white subjects in the proportion of favorable
and unfavorable items they recalled. On the delayed recall, however, the proportion of favorable to unfavorable items recalled was significantly higher for the
black subjects than the white subjects, with the black subjects recalling an increasing proportion of favorable items over time and the white subjects recalling
an increasing proportion of unfavorable items over time. Similar results were
found in the following study by Higgins and Ross where white high school
students read about a target person who ostensibly was either black or white.[16]

Study 3:   Race of Target Effects on Memory
as a Function of Temporal Delay

Method.   Eighty white twelfth-grade students from Princeton Day School
agreed to act as an adult comparison group for a developmental study on perception. Subjects were seated so that they could not see each other's responses and
no talking was permitted. On entering the testing room, the subjects were randomly assigned to different seating areas for each of the eight between-subject
experimental conditions. The experimental task involved subjects reading a paragraph purportedly describing a student from another high school. The information was supposedly based on teacher observations of the student and interviews
with the student. After performing a "hidden figures" filler task, the subjects
were asked to reproduce the paragraph verbatim.

The paragraph about the target person, Michael, consisted of eight behavioral
descriptions moderately exemplifying the following traits, using the procedure
described in Higgins and Rholes (1978) for unambiguous traits: two positive,
stereotypically white traits (ambitious, practical) and two negative, stereotypically white traits (stubborn, conventional); plus two positive, stereotypically
black traits (sociable, athletic) and two negative, stereotypically black traits

---

[16]This study was part of Jenise A. Ross' Masters Thesis (1977) for the Department of Psychology, Princeton University, and was conducted under the supervision of the senior author.

(superstitious, ostentatious). These black and white stereotypic traits were selected on the basis of their having been found in several past studies to be commonly associated with blacks and whites, respectively (Bayton & McAllister, 1964; Brigham, 1973; Sigal & Page, 1971), as well as their being neither redundant nor contradictory. A pretest of the traits with another sample of subjects indicated that the assumed likability of the traits did, indeed, match the high school students' basic judgments of the positivity or negativity of the traits. The format of the character sketch was similar to an institutional record, as follows:

NAME: Michael Smith
DATE OF BIRTH: May 9, 1959   AGE: 17
SEX: Male X   Female____
CITIZENSHIP: U.S.A. X   Foreign____
ETHNIC BACKGROUND: White____   Black____   Asian____
Other____
MARITAL STATUS: Single X   Married____
EDUCATIONAL LEVEL: High School X   College____

The between-subject experimental manipulation of Race of Target consisted of placing either an X in the white blank or an X in the black blank. This demographic information was followed by the randomly ordered behavioral descriptions. The other two between-subject experimental manipulations were Overt Characterization and Temporal Delay. After reading the paragraph, half of the subjects in both the black target and white target conditions were asked to give their personal impression of the target person; the remaining subjects were not asked to characterize the target person. Because this manipulation of overt characterization had no effect on subjects' memory of the stimulus person, it will not be considered further. For the manipulation of temporal delay, half the subjects in each Race of Target condition received the reproduction measure a few minutes after reading the paragraph, and the other half received the reproduction measure a week later when they returned, supposedly for some additional visual perception tasks. Either before or after the reproduction measure, subjects were also asked to state how much they liked the target person on an 11-point scale ranging from +5 (extremely like) to −5 (extremely dislike). (There were no significant order effects of the dependent measures.)

Results.   The reproductions were scored by two independent judges, blind to experimental condition, for deletions and for evaluatively positive or negative distortions (Higgins & Rholes, 1978). The interjudge agreement was 100% for deletions and over 80% for the distortions. In cases of disagreement, a third judge chose between the alternatives. If a stimulus description was neither deleted nor evaluatively distorted in reproduction, it was coded as correctly recalled. Separate race of target × race of stereotype × desirability of stereotype × communication × temporal delay analyses of variance were performed for the deletion, distortion, and correct recall measures of reproduction.

On the deletion measure, there was a significant target race × race of stereotype × temporal delay interaction, $F(1, 70) = 4.61$, $p < .05$, indicating that for brief-delay reproductions but not for long-delay reproductions, subjects tended to delete more stereotypic white traits for the black target ($M = .5$) than the white target ($M = .2$), but more stereotypic black traits for the white target ($M = 1.8$) than the black target ($M = 1.0$). Thus, as least immediately, the stimulus information was reproduced in a manner that confirmed black and white stereotypes. On the correct recall measure, there was a significant target race × desirability of stereotype interaction, $F(1, 70) = 4.98$, $p < .05$, reflecting the fact that more positive stereotypes were correctly recalled for the white target ($M = 1.1$) than the black target ($M = .7$), and slightly more negative stereotypes were correctly recalled for the black target ($M = .7$) than the white target ($M = .6$). On the distortion measure, there was a significant target race × temporal delay × valence of distortion (positive versus negative) interaction, $F(1, 70) = 5.87$, $p < .02$. As shown in Table 4.4, for the black target, subjects' reproductions over time contained fewer positive distortions and many more negative distortions, whereas there was relatively little change over time for the white target.

A target race × communication × temporal delay analysis of variance on the liking measure revealed a main effect for race of target, $F(1, 70) = 4.34$, $p < .05$, reflecting the fact that subjects expressed greater liking for the white target ($M = 1.1$) than the black target ($M = 0.1$).

The results of this study indicate that prior activation of a group construct (i.e., black versus white) can affect people's memory and judgments of stimulus information about a target person, presumably by increasing the accessibility of

TABLE 4.4
Mean Number of Positive and Negative Distortions
in Reproduction as a Function of
Race of Target and Temporal Delay

Race of Target	Temporal Delay	
	Brief Delay (5 minutes)	Long Delay (1 week)
Black target		
Positive distortions	1.3	.4
Negative distortions	1.2	3.0
White target		
Positive distortions	1.6	1.2
Negative distortions	2.3	2.2

the beliefs associated with each group. Moreover, the study provides evidence that the consequences of such construct activation can increase over time; when subjects thought the target person was black, there was an increasing amount of negative distortion of the stimulus information over a 1-week period, as well as a decreasing amount of positive distortion.

Consequences of Accessibility at Time of Output

In addition to the influence of construct accessibility on subsequent processing that derives from prior judgments during consolidation, the accessibility of constructs at the time of output can directly affect memory and judgment. The more accessible a construct, the more likely it is that information relating to the construct will be retrieved. According to Tversky and Kahneman (1973), people judge the frequency or probability of classes, events, and co-occurrences by the ease with which related instances or associations come to mind. The importance of this judgmental strategy, the *availability heuristic,* for social judgment and decision making has been demonstrated in a number of recent studies (Chapman & Chapman, 1969; Hamilton & Gifford, 1976; Nisbett & Ross, 1980; Ross & Sicoly, 1979; Rothbart, Fulero, Jensen, Howard, & Birrell, 1978). Tversky and Kahneman (1973), for example, suggest that when clinicians attempt to predict the likelihood that a particular patient will commit suicide, they retrieve the most accessible analogue patient with whom the present patient can be identified and use the analogue's behavior as the basis for prediction. Sarbin et al. (1960) describe various ways in which people use analogues to predict the attributes of others. It is also possible that highly accessible instances of a construct are used when making predictions about the construct as a whole (Higgins, 1980b; Higgins, Feldman, and Ruble, 1980). For example, when predicting the attitudes of preschoolers, people may base their predictions on the attitudes of whichever preschooler most readily comes to mind (e.g., their own son or daughter, a young movie or television star, themselves at that age). Similarly, people may predict the behavior of blacks in general on the basis of information about a particular black who readily comes to mind.

Just as activation of constructs during input can influence the construction of stimulus information, activation of constructs during output can independently influence the reconstruction of stored stimulus information, especially if no prior stimulus judgments have been made. A number of studies have found that providing subjects with a construct after the presentation of stimulus material will affect how the material is remembered (Hanawalt & Demarest, 1939; Loftus, Miller, & Burns, 1978; Spiro, 1977). In Anderson and Pichert's (1978) study on role perspective and recall discussed earlier, half of the subjects took a different perspective on the second recall of the stimulus information (e.g., a burglar) than they had taken on the first recall (e.g., a home buyer). On the second recall, these subjects recalled significantly more information relevant to their new role than they had recalled in their previous role (for which the information had been irrelevant) and recalled significantly less information irrelevant to their new role than they had recalled in their previous role (for which the information had been relevant). Finally, Snyder and Uranowitz (1978) found that subjects' recognition memory for factual events in the life of a woman were affected by being told after reading about her life that she was currently living either a heterosexual or lesbian life-style, with subjects' recognition responses tending to support their beliefs about these different life-styles.

In many of these studies (Hanawalt & Demarest, 1939; Loftus et al., 1978), the method of activating the constructs could inject additional persuasive or interpersonal influence factors into the situation because the construct is provided by the experimenter as a fact about the stimulus that directly or indirectly relates to the factual material used in the memory task (Higgins, 1980a). For example, subjects in the Loftus et al. (1978) studies were shown slides of an accident and were then asked a question in which the presence of either a stop sign or a yield sign in the slides was presupposed (e.g., "Did another car pass the red Datsun while it was stopped at the stop sign?"). This "fact" about the accident was true for half the subjects and false for the remaining subjects. On a yes–no recognition test administered later, the misled subjects tended to recognize falsely the slide with the presupposed sign. If a subject could not confidently remember which sign had appeared, however, it would make sense to conform to the facts stated in the questionnaire because it was presumably written by an expert on the slide series.

An alternative method of activating constructs after the storage of stimulus information is to provide subjects with judgment scales that allow subjects *to decide themselves* whether or not a particular construct applies to the stimulus person. With this method, any effects of construct accessibility on reconstructive memory are unlikely to be due to interpersonal influence factors. In addition, if interpersonal influence were a determining factor, then the immediate effects of construct activation on memory should be at least as strong as the delayed effects. In contrast, if the determining factor is construct accessibility, the effects on memory should increase over time because the impact of an accessible construct increases as the representation of the stimulus details decays. The following study by Higgins and Rholes was designed to examine the effects of construct accessibility over time on reconstructive memory.

Study 4: Reconstructing Trait Information: Retroactive Effects of Current Construct Accessibility

Method.   Sixty-one Princeton University undergraduates were asked to read a paragraph ostensibly describing another student, Donald K., as part of a study on impression formation. They were told that the paragraph was based on information collected from interviews with Donald and from his responses to some personality tests. The subjects read the paragraph and then filled out a questionnaire in which they rated Donald on a variety of personality trait scales. Subjects were allowed to look back at the paragraph when answering the questionnaire.

All subjects were given the same paragraph, which contained eight behavioral descriptions of Donald taken from our previous studies (Higgins et al., 1977; Higgins & Rholes, 1978). There were four evaluatively ambiguous descriptions exemplifying "adventurous/reckless," "persistent/stubborn," "self-confident/conceited," and "independent/aloof," as well as two evaluatively positive unambiguous descriptions exemplifying "honest" and "athletic," and two evaluatively negative unambiguous descriptions exemplifying "irritable" and "messy."

The independent variables of the study were the type of questionnaire received (ambiguous/positive labels or ambiguous/negative labels) and the amount of delay between filling out the questionnaire and reproducing the paragraph (no delay, 20 minute, or 1 week). Ten or 11 subjects were assigned to each of the six conditions in this 2×3 between-subject design. The questionnaires contained eight 4-point scales from "not at all x" to "extremely x," where x was a personality trait label. (Less than 5% of subjects' responses were "not at all x.") The labels for the third, fourth, sixth, and eighth scales in both questionnaires were honest, athletic, irritable, and messy, respectively. Thus, both questionnaires had the same scales for the positive and negative unambiguous descriptions. The questionnaires only differed with respect to the labels for the ambiguous scales. In the ambiguous/positive questionnaire, the labels were independent, persistent, adventurous, and self-confident. In the ambiguous/negative questionnaire, the labels were aloof, stubborn, reckless, and conceited. In both questionnaire conditions, subjects were asked to reproduce the paragraph about Donald as accurately as possible, word for word, immediately after they finished filling out the questionnaire, 20 minutes later, or 1 week later when they returned supposedly for a different study.

Results. Subjects' reproductions were scored by a judge blind to experimental condition using the procedure reported in Higgins and Rholes (1978). In this study, however, only the reproductions of the ambiguous descriptions were of direct concern because only the labels applied to them were manipulated in the questionnaires. As shown in Table 4.5, exposure to different labels for the ambiguous stimulus information had substantial effects on subjects' recall of this information, with there being relatively more positive than negative distortions of the material when subjects responded on positive scales and relatively more negative than positive distortions of the material when subjects responded on negative scales, especially after a week delay. In order to measure the amount of distortion in each reproduction unconfounded with the amount of deletion and obtain a measure of the overall evaluative tone of the reproduction, the difference

TABLE 4.5
Mean Number of Positive and Negative Distortions of
Ambiguous Descriptions in Reproduction as a Function of
Labeling Condition and Temporal Delay

Temporal Delay	Positive Labeling		Negative Labeling	
	Positive Distortions	Negative Distortions	Positive Distortions	Negative Distortions
No delay	1.3	.4	.6	.6
Twenty minute	.9	.3	.7	.6
One week	.8	.4	0	1.3

Note: Scores could range from 0 to 4.

between the total number of positively distorted descriptions and the total number of negatively distorted descriptions was divided by the total number of descriptions included in the reproduction (both distorted and undistorted). The arcsine transformations of these proportions were then analyzed as a function of type of questionnaire labels and delay of reproduction. This analysis yielded a main effect of delay of reproduction, $F(2, 55) = 5.10$, $p < .01$, reflecting the fact that the reproduction distortions became significantly more negative over time. In addition, as predicted, there was a significant main effect of type of questionnaire labels, $F(1, 55) = 5.93$, $p < .02$, indicating that the reproduction distortions were significantly more positive when subjects responded on scales with positive labels than when they responded on scales with negative labels. There was also a nonsignificant tendency for this effect of scale labels to increase over time, with the difference in distortions being twice as great after a 1-week delay as after no delay or a 20-minute delay. There were no significant effects for the unambiguous descriptions.

The results of this study clearly indicate that manipulating people's characterizations of a stimulus person *after* exposure to information about the person can affect their memory of the person even when interpersonal influence factors are unlikely to be involved. Moreover, the effect of the labeling on memory is greater a week later than it is a few minutes later, which is consistent with a construct-accessibility interpretation but not with a demand–effect interpretation. The absence of any significant reproduction effects for the unambiguous descriptions is also more consistent with a construct-accessibility interpretation than a demand–effect or "halo effect" interpretation.

The accessibility of constructs at output could also be influenced by unobtrusive, nonverbal means. The results of Study 1, previously discussed, demonstrated that group sex composition can affect the accessibility of attributes associated with male and female gender. Increasing the accessibility of gender-related constructs through group sex composition should affect subjects' judgments of any target, whether self or other, and should affect information processing at any stage, whether input or output. Thus, consistent with our previous analysis of group sex composition effects on undergraduates' processing of information, when the accessibility of undergraduates' gender-related constructs is increased (i.e., in the high gender salience condition), their spontaneous self-descriptions should generally reflect selective retrieval of aspects of their self that are consistent with the modern view of sex-linked attributes because their sex-linked processing is under active control. Otherwise, their spontaneous self-descriptions should generally reflect the traditional view of sex-linked attributes because this view would be more accessible during passive processing due to its longer history of activation. This hypothesized output effect of group sex composition on self-judgments was examined in the following study by Higgins and Smith.[17]

Study 5:   Group Sex Composition Effects on Retrieving Sex-Linked Characteristics of Self

Method.   Fifty-eight Princeton University undergraduates were told that we needed more adult norms for a developmental study on the perception of self and others. The experimental manipulation involved the prearranged sex composition of the groups. Using the same procedure as in Study 1, a female undergraduate experimenter conducted eight groups of subjects each composed of two or three other females and one solitary male, and a male undergraduate experimenter conducted eight groups of subjects each composed of two or three other males and one solitary female. Thus, the independent variables of the study were *sex of subject* (male or female) and *distinctiveness of gender* (minority or majority). Because subjects' gender is more distinctive in groups where they are the only representative of their gender than in groups where their gender predominates, the minority and majority conditions were again used to manipulate high and low salience of sexual identity, respectively. After all subjects had arrived, they were given McGuire and Padawer-Singer's (1976) "Tell us about yourself" measure of spontaneous self-concept. Subjects were separated at the table so that they could not see each other's responses to this question.

Results.   Subjects' spontaneous self-descriptions were scored by judges blind to experimental condition in terms of the total number of male stereotypes and the total number of female stereotypes included in a subject's self-description (either as a label or as a descriptive statement). The male and female stereotypes

---

[17]This study was conducted as a Princeton University Junior Thesis by Julia C. Smith (1974) under the direction of the senior author. A discussion of the social implications of this and related research may be found in Ruble and Higgins (1976).

considered were those consistently reported in the literature (McKee & Sherriffs, 1959; Rosenkrantz, Vogel, Bee, Broverman, & Broverman, 1968). The intercoder correlations were .95 for female stereotypes and .84 for male stereotypes.

As evident in Table 4.6, the distinctiveness of subjects' gender had significant effects on whether male or female stereotypes were included in subjects' spontaneous self-descriptions. A subject sex × distinctiveness of gender × sex of stereotype analysis of variance yielded a significant three-way interaction, $F(1, 54) = 8.34$, $p < .01$; that is, males in the minority described themselves as more stereotypically female and less stereotypically male than males in the majority, whereas females in the minority described themselves as more stereotypically male and less stereotypically female than females in the majority. Thus, when subjects' gender was relatively distinctive, they were more likely to describe themselves in terms of traits stereotypically associated with the opposite sex than when their gender was not distinctive. The analysis also yielded a significant main effect for sex of stereotype, $F(1, 54) = 6.07$, $p < .02$, indicating that the subjects were more likely to describe themselves in terms of female stereotypes than in terms of male stereotypes. It was also clear from the self-descriptions that when subjects described themselves in terms of traits stereotypically associated with the opposite sex, the traits included were almost always positive (e.g., males describing themselves as sensitive and females describing themselves as independent). In general, there was an overwhelming tendency for subjects to describe themselves in terms of desirable traits, $F(1, 54) = 21.33$, $p < .001$.

The results of this study are strikingly similar to the results of Study 1. Once again, high gender distinctiveness led to relatively greater recall of information about a target person that was less traditionally sex linked. Otherwise, undergraduates' spontaneous self-descriptions reflect the traditional view of sex-linked attributes. In this study, however, subjects recalled information about themselves rather than another person.

TABLE 4.6
Mean Number of Male Stereotypes and Female Stereotypes
in the Spontaneous Self-Descriptions as a Function of
Sex of Subject and Distinctiveness of Gender

	Distinctiveness of Gender	
Subject Sex (self as target)	High (minority)	Low (majority)
Male Subjects		
Male stereotypes	1.1	1.7
Female stereotypes	2.4	1.5
Female Subjects		
Male stereotypes	2.4	1.2
Female stereotypes	2.3	2.5

The effect of manipulating gender distinctiveness has been interpreted as resulting from an increase in the accessibility of the modern view of sex-linked attributes, the view to which recent undergraduates at major universities subscribe (Kravetz, 1976; Pleck, 1976). The results of this study permit an alternative interpretation. It is possible that gender distinctiveness increased the accessibility of traits stereotypically associated with the dominant, majority gender in the group (or the experimenter's gender that was the same as the majority), with these traits being opposite to the traits stereotypically associated with the minority subjects' own gender. In Study 1, however, this interpretation would predict that minority members of groups with a male majority and a male experimenter (i.e., minority females) would recall stereotypically male behaviors, whereas minority members of groups with a female majority and a female experimenter (i.e., minority males) would recall stereotypically female behaviors. This would be reflected in a sex of subject × distinctiveness of gender × sex of stereotype interaction. Instead, it was the sex of target × distinctiveness of gender × sex of stereotype interaction that was significant, as predicted, where sex of target was manipulated independently of majority gender and sex of experimenter.

CONSEQUENCES OF INDIVIDUAL VARIABILITY IN CONSTRUCT ACCESSIBILITY

Individual variability refers to individual differences in the accessibility of particular constructs that are independent of any differences in the individuals' immediate circumstances and that persist across different circumstances (i.e., chronic, context-independent variability). The scarcity of research on the consequences of individual variability on construct accessibility precludes an analysis in terms of different stages of information processing. Instead, the literature concerned with individual differences in construct accessibility is briefly reviewed to provide some background for our own research on the consequences of such differences.

Because people differ in their experiences, expectations, goals, and so on, one would expect there to be individual differences in the accessibility of social constructs. Kelly (1955) suggests that individual differences in personal constructs might arise from differences in personal experiences of events and outcomes. Variation among people in verbal exposure should also lead to individual differences in construct accessibility. For example, the construct *attractive* is likely to become highly accessible for a child whose parents frequently comment on others' attractiveness. Moreover, individual differences in construct accessibility should be relatively prolonged and have passive effects on information processing.

There is, in fact, evidence from a number of studies that the accessibility of social constructs varies among people (Beach & Wertheimer, 1961; Dornbusch,

Hastorf, Richardson, Muzzy & Vreeland, 1965; Markus, 1977; Yarrow & Campbell, 1963). There is also evidence of considerable consistency over time in individuals' accessible constructs (Dornbusch et al., 1965; Fjeld & Landfield, 1961; Mitsos, 1961; Yarrow & Campbell, 1963). There is little evidence, however, that individual differences in construct accessibility affect the processing of social information. Dornbusch et al. (1965) and Yarrow and Campbell (1963) had children describe other children they knew and found more construct overlap in descriptions having a common perceiver but different targets than in descriptions having a common target but different perceivers. These results have often been taken as evidence of the judgmental consequences of individual differences in construct accessibility. Because the measure of individual differences in target judgments was based on the same data as the measure of individual differences in construct accessibility, however, it is inappropriate to draw any conclusion about the relation between these variables. In addition, because there was no control of the input information, it is possible that the individual differences in target judgments reflected differences in the actual behavior of the target persons revealed to different perceivers rather than individual differences in processing the same stimulus information; that is, the targets may have behaved differently in the presence of different perceivers because they were observed in different situations or different behaviors were elicited by the different attributes or interaction styles of the perceivers themselves. Moreover, a particular perceiver may observe the same behaviors from different targets because the targets were observed in the same situations or the perceiver's attributes or interaction style elicited the same behaviors from different targets.

In order to examine whether individual differences have information-processing consequences, it is necessary to have independent measures of construct-accessibility differences and target judgments. In a recent study by O'Keefe, Delia, and O'Keefe (1977), such independent measures were obtained. All subjects were given six traits, supposedly characterizing a college student. In one condition, the three positive and three negative traits were normatively determined; in another condition, the three positive traits were self-generated (i.e., relatively accessible) and the three negative traits were normatively determined (positive-own); and in the third condition, the three negative traits were self-generated and the three positive traits were normatively determined (negative-own). Subjects' evaluations of the target person were most positive in the positive-own condition and most negative in the negative-own condition, with this significant difference persisting for 8 weeks (although diminished in magnitude). Although suggestive, this study did not control the target information available to judges. It is possible that the traits used as subjects' own positive or own negative constructs were simply more evaluatively extreme than the normative traits. In studies of personal constructs, the following traits frequently occur: warm, intelligent, friendly, humorous, selfish, boring, conceited. These traits are much more evaluatively extreme than the relatively moderate normative traits used by O'Keefe et al. (1977): confident, idealistic, polite/ conforming, sarcastic, nosy. There is also no direct evidence in the O'Keefe et al. (1977) study that construct accessibility affected the actual processing of the stimulus information. The target traits could be encoded in a similar manner by all judges, with only the importance or weight assigned to different traits varying among judges. A study by Higgins, Mavin, and King attempted to overcome some of these methodological problems as well as to examine more directly the information-processing consequences of individual differences in construct accessibility.[18]

Study 6: Individual Construct Accessibility Effects on Person Memory and Impressions Over Time

Method.   Sixteen University of Western Ontario undergraduates participated in two supposedly unrelated studies. In the first *personality* study, they were given a modified form of Zajonc's (1960) card-sorting technique in which they were asked to write down the characteristics of two male friends, two female friends, and themselves. A trait was considered accessible for a subject if it appeared in the subject's description of both himself/herself and at least one of his/her friends or if it appeared in the subject's descriptions of 3 or more friends. Approximately 2 weeks later, the subjects were tested individually in a study on "person perception" ostensibly being conducted for a different researcher. All subjects were given the same paragraph supposedly describing another University of Western Ontario undergraduate, which contained behavioral descriptions moderately exemplifying five positive and five negative traits. The traits selected were those found to be accessible for several, but not all, of the subjects in the first session (e.g., intelligent, happy, thoughtless, and lazy), with different traits being accessible for different subjects. After a 10-minute delay in which subjects performed a nonverbal task, subjects were asked to reproduce the paragraph exactly, word for word. They were also asked to write down, as fully as they could, the sort of person they thought the target person was. Two weeks later, subjects returned supposedly for another part of the study and again were asked to reproduce the paragraph and give their impression of the target person.

Results.   Each subject's reproductions and impressions of the target information were scored for the number of deletions of those behavioral descriptions exemplifying the subject's accessible traits and the number of deletions of those behavioral descriptions exemplifying the subject's inaccessible traits. Interrater reliability for scoring 10 randomly selected reproductions was above 90%. Each

---

[18]This study was conducted as a University of Western Ontario Honors Thesis by Gregory H. Mavin (1978) under the direction of the senior author.

of a subject's reproductions and impressions was scored for the percentage of the subject's accessible essay descriptions that were deleted in output and the percentage of the subject's inaccessible essay descriptions that were deleted in output. In subjects' immediate reproductions, there was, as predicted, a higher percentage of deletions of inaccessible trait descriptions ($M = 35.3\%$) than accessible trait descriptions ($M = 17.7\%$), Wilcoxon test, $p < .05$ two-tailed, and within-subjects analysis of variance (with an arcsine transformation of the percentages), $F(1, 15) = 2.74$, $p < .12$. In subjects' immediate impressions, there was also significantly greater deletion of inaccessible trait descriptions ($M = 69.4\%$) than accessible trait descriptions ($M = 45.1\%$), Wilcoxon test, $p < .02$ two-tailed, and $F(1, 15) = 6.74$, $p < .02$. These differences in the percentage recall of accessible and inaccessible trait descriptions persisted over the 2-week delay period. In subjects' delayed reproductions, there was greater deletion of inaccessible trait descriptions ($M = 52.7\%$) than accessible trait descriptions ($M = 26.7\%$), Wilcoxon test, $p < .01$ two-tailed, and $F(1, 15) = 8.70$, $p < .01$. Finally, in subjects' delayed impressions, there was also greater deletion of inaccessible trait descriptions ($M = 75.2\%$) than accessible trait descriptions ($M = 53.9\%$), Wilcoxon test, $p < .05$ two-tailed, and $F(1, 15) = 3.51$, $p < .08$.

The results of this study suggest that individual variability in construct accessibility can cause differences in people's memory and impressions of a target person. Moreover, the results indicate that these consequences of individual construct accessibility persist for at least a 2-week period.

The procedure used in Study 6 to examine the consequences of individual variability in construct accessibility has some limitations. First, it does not ensure that the essay contains the same proportion of accessible and inaccessible traits for all subjects nor that it contains an equal number of accessible and inaccessible traits. Second, any particular trait description in the essay can, at least to some extent, be overrepresented as either an accessible trait or an inaccessible trait across subjects, which potentially confounds accessibility with content memorability. Third, the accessibility measure itself is based upon the frequency of a trait's occurrence across a subject's descriptions of friends and self rather than being based on a trait's order of appearance (i.e., the first trait that comes to mind), with primacy of output being, perhaps, a better operational definition of accessibility. The next study by Higgins and King was designed to overcome these limitations.

Study 7:   Individual Construct Accessibility Effects on Social Information Processing

Method.   Thirty-two undergraduates at the University of Western Ontario participated in two supposedly unrelated studies conducted by two different experimenters. The first study was ostensibly concerned with the relation among different measures of personality and cognitive style, and the second study, held a week later, was ostensibly concerned with psycholinguistics. In the first session, each individual's accessible trait categories were elicited. Subjects were asked to list the traits of: (1) a type of person that they liked; (2) a type of person that they disliked; (3) a type of person that they sought out; (4) a type of person that they avoided; and (5) a type of person that they frequently encountered. A modified form of Zajonc's (1960) card sorting technique was used that required subjects to write the traits that came to mind for a particular type of person on slips of paper lettered from A to J. These slips of paper were then placed in an envelope, one for each of the five persons. The order of the four affect questions (i.e., like, seek, dislike, and avoid) was counterbalanced across subjects, and half of the subjects received the frequency question (i.e., frequently encounter) before and half after the four affect questions. After writing each list of traits, subjects performed a 4-minute nonverbal task to reduce the possibility of prior responses affecting later responses.

A second experimenter conducted the second session, where each subject read a one-page essay describing various behaviors of a stimulus person. Following the procedure outlined in Higgins and Rholes (1978), each essay was constructed to contain 12 behavioral descriptions moderately exemplifying 6 traits that were relatively accessible for a subject and 6 traits that were relatively inaccessible. A subject's accessible traits were selected on the basis of the traits he/she listed in response to the questions in the first session, with an accessible trait defined as the *first* characteristic listed by a subject. One trait came from each of the four affect questions and two traits came from the frequency question. Because of occasional synonyms and antonyms, a method was used to ensure the distinctiveness of a person's six accessible traits. A subject's inaccessible traits were traits that did not appear in his/her responses to the questions in the first session. The inaccessible traits of one subject were selected from among the accessible traits of the other subjects. Again, one trait came from responses to each of the four affect questions and two came from responses to the frequency question. The 6 inaccessible traits were selected so that none of the 12 traits in a subject's essay would be either synonyms or antonyms. In addition, the inaccessible traits were selected to ensure that across all subjects one subject's accessible traits were another subject's inaccessible traits and vice versa. Thus, both the inherent accessibility, importance, or extremity of particular traits and the inherent memorability of the essay descriptions exemplifying particular traits were controlled with respect to the accessible versus inaccessible comparison. The order of the different types of trait descriptions (i.e., accessible-positive affect; accessible-negative affect; accessible frequently encounter; inaccessible-positive affect; inaccessible-negative affect; inaccessible frequently encounter) were also counterblanced across subjects.

After subjects finished reading the essay about the target person, they were given a 10-minute nonverbal interference task and were then asked to reproduce exactly, word for word, the essay describing the stimulus person. They were also asked to write down, as fully as they could, the sort of person they thought the target person was.

Results.   Each subject's reproduction and impression of the target information were scored for the number of deletions of those behavioral descriptions exemplifying the subject's accessible traits and the number of deletions of those behavioral descriptions exemplifying the subject's inaccessible traits. A second rater scored 10 randomly selected reproductions to check for scoring reliability. The interrater correlation was .93. In subjects' reproductions, there was, as predicted, significantly more deletions of inaccessible trait descriptions ($M = 2.9$) than accessible trait descriptions ($M = 2.4$), as analyzed both by a Wilcoxon test ($p < .05$ two-tailed) and an analysis of variance, $F(1, 31) = 4.62, p < .05$. In subjects' impressions, there was also significantly more deletions of inaccessible trait descriptions ($M = 4.7$) than accessible trait descriptions ($M = 3.9$), as analyzed both by a Wilcoxon test ($p < .03$ two-tailed) and an analysis of variance, $F(1, 30) = 6.38, p < .02$. In this study, therefore, there was approximately 20% greater omission of stimulus information related to a subject's inaccessible constructs than omission of stimulus information related to a subject's accessible constructs for both subjects' reproductions and impressions. Thus, two subjects with different accessible constructs could have quite disparate recollections and impressions of the target person.

The anonymous story at the beginning of the chapter exemplifies how individual differences in construct accessibility can lead to individual differences in memory and judgments of a target person. One would expect the effects of individual differences in construct accessibility to be especially evident for ambiguous stimulus information, such as that in the story, because ambiguous information is especially susceptible to change (Higgins & Rholes, 1978). The results of Studies 6 and 7, however, demonstrate that individual differences in construct accessibility can affect memory for even unambiguous information. In both studies, stimulus information about a target person was better remembered if it was related to a person's accessible constructs than if it was related to a person's relatively inaccessible constructs. The results of both studies also indicate that individual variability in construct accessibility has consequences for people's impressions of a target person. Finally, the results show that differences among people in construct accessibility can be chronic and context independent, and that the consequences of these differences can persist over a long period (Study 6).

GENERAL DISCUSSION

People's judgments about others' behaviors are affected by various factors. The attribution literature describes a number of factors that influence whether a dispositional or situational attribution will be made for another's behavior (Bem, 1972;

Jones & Davis, 1965; Kelley, 1967). The choice between a dispositional or situational attribution, however, is not the only choice a judge must make. Even if a judge decides to make a dispositional attribution, for example, there are often alternative ones that could be made (e.g., adventurous versus reckless). This chapter has been concerned with one factor that influences people's choices among alternative dispositional (or situational) attributions—the relative accessibility of the alternative constructs that could be used to characterize the behavior.

We have attempted to elaborate and extend Bruner's (1957) original account of construct accessibility in a manner that captures the full range of recent evidence concerning construct–accessibility effects on social information processing. Thus, "recency of activation," "frequency of activation," "salience," and "relation to accessible constructs" have been included as determinants of construct accessibility, in addition to the "expectations" and "motivation" determinants described by Bruner (1957). As well, the effects of construct accessibility on the output stage of information processing has been considered, in addition to Bruner's (1957) concern with the effects on input and consolidation (i.e., selective attention and categorization). Finally, a number of distinctions have been introduced into the model to highlight different issues and potential areas of research—distinctions between identifying a stimulus *as* an instance of a construct and identifying a stimulus *with* a construct, between active- and passive-processing effects of construct accessibility, and between context-dependent, momentary variation and context-independent, chronic variation in construct accessibility. Although the chapter has focused mainly on the implications of construct accessibility for processing social information, the determinants, consequences, and intervening processes have clear implications for processing nonsocial information as well (cf. Higgins & Chaires, 1980).

There are various features of our account of construct accessibility that have implications for other issues in personality and social psychology. Limited space precludes a detailed or exhaustive discussion of these implications, but some examples may suggest the potential importance of this variable. One feature is that there are a number of different determinants of a construct's accessibility. Awareness of this multiple determinism could be useful when trying to modify a person's accessible constructs in order to reduce their negative impact. Consider, for example, a person whose most accessible constructs are negative traits, thus increasing the likelihood that the person will negatively judge and remember both his/her own behavior and the behavior of others. These negative traits may have become more accessible for a number of reasons relating to the person's personal history and family background. The relative accessibility of the person's positive and negative traits, however, could be modified without having to probe into the person's background or intervene with respect to the original source of the problem; that is, an accessibility-modification technique, such as frequent activation of positive-trait constructs through unobtrusive verbal exposure, could be used to change the relative accessibility of positive and negative traits regardless of whether the technique matches the original source of the accessibility.

Whichever accessibility-modification technique is most economical and efficient could be used. Similarly, negative judgments of other people or groups that are mediated by construct accessibility (e.g., social stereotypes) could be changed by applying accessibility-modification techniques without any need to know the source of the accessibility. In some cases, of course, knowing the source of the accessibility could facilitate the modification process, because mode of acquisition can have additional implications for information processing (Higgins et al., 1980).

Another feature of our account of construct accessibility is the distinction between context-dependent, momentary variation in construct accessibility and context-independent, chronic variation in construct accessibility. Surprisingly, the implications and consequences of the latter type of variability have received little attention in the literature. Construct-independent, chronic variation is reflected in individual differences in construct accessibility. We have shown that individual differences in construct accessibility are related to individual differences in processing information about a target person. They are also likely to be related to individual differences in processing information about the self. Moreover, individual variation in construct accessibility could underlie some of the phenomena associated with various personality dimensions, such as repression-sensitization, depression, self-esteem, authoritarianism, locus of control. The difference between repressors' and sensitizers' response to emotional words, for example, could reflect active versus passive processing of the stimuli. One would expect emotional words to be highly accessible because of their affective quality and salience, which should increase their identifiability. Repressors, however, have a set to avoid negatively arousing stimuli (Bell & Byrne, 1977), and, as discussed previously, an active set can inhibit passive-accessibility effects (Posner, 1978). Thus, sensitizers should show the expected facilitation effect of increased construct accessibility (i.e., perceptual vigilance), whereas repressors should show the interference effect of the active, inhibitory set (i.e., perceptual defense), an analysis that is consistent with the evidence (Erdelyi, 1974). To take another example, the negative frame of mind associated with depressives has recently been interpreted in terms of the inaccessibility of positive constructs (Isen et al., 1978) and the accessibility of negative constructs (Kuiper & Derry, 1980).

Consideration of personality differences in terms of differences in construct accessibility could also help explain behavioral phenomena associated with personality differences that are not easily interpreted as resulting from the hypothesized source of the personality difference. If the source of a personality type tends to increase the accessibility of certain constructs, the increased construct accessibility itself could have effects on processing information about events and people (both self and others) that is functionally autonomous of the source; that is, increased construct accessibility can have implications for subsequent behavior that are independent of the original source of the increased accessibility. If so, then modifying the source of the personality type without modifying the increased accessibility could be ineffective in changing those behaviors influenced by the increased accessibility, whereas modifying the increased accessibility could change the behaviors associated with the personality type even though the original source of the increased accessibility was not modified.

Individual differences in construct accessibility may also have an important effect on interpersonal relations. As exemplified in the story of Michael and Minnie, individual differences in accessible constructs can lead to different judgments and memory of other people, which, in turn, can lead to conflict. It is well-known that agreement or disagreement in judging others can cause people to like or dislike each other, respectively (Heider, 1958; Newcomb, 1961). Similarity of accessible constructs could be an important determinant of agreement in judgment as well as an important determinant of agreement in recollection. In fact, interpersonal conflict may be especially acute when two people cannot even agree about the facts of an event they observed together. It is also possible that the classic relation between similarity and attraction described in the interpersonal attraction literature (Berscheid & Walster, 1978; Byrne, 1971) could be mediated, at least in part, by similarity of accessible constructs. After all, similar activities, demographic characteristics, opinions, and so on should lead to similarity of accessible constructs. It would be interesting to obtain separate measures of similarity of accessible constructs and similarity of opinions or activities and test the importance of similarity of accessible constructs for the classic similarity-attraction relation.

The aforementioned interpretation of repressors' and sensitizers' differential response to emotional words reflects another important feature of our construct accessibility model—the distinction between active and passive processing. This distinction also suggests that certain judgmental phenomena that have been interpreted in terms of active processing may instead, at least under certain circumstances, involve passive processing. For example, the tendency for a person's judgments of self and others to be similar (Hastorf, Richardson, & Dornbusch, 1958; Kuiper & Rogers, 1979; Shrauger & Patterson, 1974; Tagiuri, 1969) has been interpreted in terms of relatively active processes, such as *comparative appraisal, social comparison, assumed similarity,* and *self-reference* (Higgins, 1980; Kuiper & Rogers, 1979; Shrauger & Patterson, 1974). This phenomenon, however, need not involve an inferential process, nor even the use of the self as a comparison or reference point (as in *projection* or *egocentrism*). Instead, there could simply be a tendency for a person's accessible constructs to be passively utilized in processing his/her own behavior as well as the behavior of others. An active process is likely to be involved, however, when a person makes different judgments for similar and dissimilar others, with only the judgments of similar others matching the judgments of self (Higgins, in press).

The potential for passive processing effects of construct accessibility also has methodological implications. If a theoretical model proposes construct utilization as a mediating variable, then the model could be tested by observing the effects of direct and unobtrusive manipulation of the proposed mediating constructs in the absence of demand effects. For example, the attribution model of motivation (Weiner, Frieze, Kukla, Reed, Rest, & Rosenbaum, 1971) could be tested, with respect to the proposed effects of mediating attributions on expectations and subsequent performance, by increasing the likelihood of a particular attribution (e.g., ability, luck) through unobtrusive activation of the construct in a previous "unrelated" task. The potential biasing effects of exposure to specific labels in questionnaires, as demonstrated in Study 4, also suggests that researchers must be careful in their selection of labels when constructing scales or questions for their assessment materials.

Another processing distinction introduced by our model is that between identifying a stimulus *as* a construct instance and identifying a stimulus *with* a construct. There are a number of implications of the latter process that need to be explored. One interesting implication is that people may try to take advantage of this process to influence others' impressions of them. For example, people may wear clothes or hairstyles characteristic of admired movie or television stars in order to be identified with the star, hoping that others will then attribute to them additional characteristic attributes of the star (e.g., exciting, stylish, energetic, witty).

A final feature of our account of construct accessibility is the tendency for accessibility effects to increase over time. This feature can be conceptualized as a type of "sleeper effect" (Higgins et al., 1977) and is relevant to the general issue of persistence in judgments (Cook & Flay, 1978). The increased effects of construct accessibility over time is, perhaps, one reason why first impressions are so important in interpersonal relations. When people first meet another person, they store both the details of the behaviors observed and their initial impressions. They may feel that their first impressions are tentative and expect to reevaluate them when more information becomes available. The initial impressions, however, will tend to be supported by their later recollections of the target's behavior during the first meeting, because these impressions will be readily accessed when the target is later reconsidered and will form a basis for reconstructing the target's previous behavior. Defending against advertising appeals may also be difficult, because even though the discrepancy between the characteristics of the product and the persuasive labeling of the product may be evident at the time of the appeal, the characteristics of the product will gradually be distorted to agree with the labels, thus making the labels appear accurate.

The evidence of construct accessibility effects on information processing, as well as the implications of such effects for personality and interpersonal relations, suggest that construct accessibility is an important variable. On the one hand, there is the rather unsettling implication that a momentary or even accidental event can automatically and unconsciously influence the processing of a social stimulus such that subsequent memory and judgments of the stimulus are substantially, and increasingly, altered. On the other hand, there is the hopeful and comforting implication that a person's chronic tendency to characterize his/her own behavior or the behavior of others in a distorted, negative manner can be reduced through a variety of accessibility-modification techniques that would not require specific knowledge or intervention with respect to the original source of the tendency. These and other implications of construct accessibility need to be examined in future research.

ACKNOWLEDGMENTS

The research by the authors and their collaborators reported in this chapter was supported by Grant R01 MH 31427 from the National Institute of Mental Health to the senior author. We are very grateful to John Kihlstrom, Dick Nisbett, Jim Olson, Clive Seligman, and Bob Wyer for helpful comments and suggestions.

REFERENCES

Abelson, R. P. Concepts for representing mundane reality in plans. In D. G. Bobrow & A. Collins (Eds.), *Representation and understanding: Studies in cognitive science*. New York: Academic Press, 1975.

Abelson, R. P. Script processing in attitude formation and decision-making. In J. S. Carroll & J. W. Payne (Eds.), *Cognition and social behavior*. Hillsdale, N.J.: Lawrence Erlbaum Associates, 1976.

Allport, F. H. *Theories of perception and the concept of structure*. New York: Wiley, 1955.

Anderson, R. C., & Pichert, J. W. Recall of previously unrecallable information following a shift in perspective. *Journal of Verbal Learning and Verbal Behavior*, 1978, *17*, 1–12.

Bartlett, F. C. *Remembering*. Cambridge, Mass.: Cambridge University Press, 1932.

Bayton, J., & McAllister, H. Race–class stereotypes. In P. F. Secord & C. W. Backman (Eds.), *Problems in social psychology*. New York: McGraw-Hill, 1964.

Beach, L., & Wertheimer, M. A free response approach to the study of person cognition. *Journal of Abnormal and Social Psychology*, 1961, *62*, 367–374.

Becker, H. S. Becoming a marihuana user. In D. Solomon (Ed.), *The marihuana papers*. New York: Signet Books, 1966.

Bem, D. J. Self-perception theory. In L. Berkowitz (Ed.), *Advances in experimental social psychology* (Vol. 6). New York: Academic Press, 1972.

Bell, P. A., & Byrne, D. Repression-sensitization. In A. London & J. E. Exner, Jr. (Eds.), *Dimensions of personality*. New York: Wiley, 1977.

Berne, E. *Principles of group treatment*. New York: Oxford University Press, 1964.

Berscheid, E., & Walster, E. *Interpersonal attraction*. Reading, Mass.: Addison-Wesley, 1978.

Brigham, J. Views of black and white children concerning the distribution of personality characteristics. *Journal of Personality and Social Psychology*, 1973, *42*, 145–148.

Brown, R. *Words and things*. Glencoe, Ill.: The Free Press, 1958.

Bruner, J. S. On perceptual readiness. *Psychological Review*, 1957, *64*, 123–152.

Bruner, J. S. Social psychology and perception. In E. Maccoby, T. Newcomb, & E. Hartley (Eds.), *Readings in social psychology*. New York: Holt, Rinehart & Winston, 1958.

Bruner, J. S., & Tagiuri, R. The perception of people. In G. Lindzey (Ed.), *Handbook of social psychology* (Vol. 2). Cambridge, Mass.: Addison-Wesley, 1954.

Byrne, D. *The attraction paradigm*. New York: Academic Press, 1971.

Carlston, D. E. The recall and use of observed behavioral episodes and inferred traits in social inference processes. *Journal of Experimental Social Psychology*, in press.

Carmichael, L., Hogan, H. P., & Walter, A. A. An experimental study of the effect of language on the reproduction of visually perceived form. *Journal of Experimental Psychology*, 1932, *15*, 73–86.

Cantor, N., & Mischel, W. Traits as prototypes: Effects on recognition memory. *Journal of Personality and Social Psychology*, 1977, *35*, 38–48.

Cantor, N., & Mischel, W. Prototypes in person perception. In L. Berkowitz (Ed.), *Advances in experimental social psychology* (Vol. 12). New York: Academic Press, in press.

Chaires, W. M. *The effect of unobtrusive verbal exposure on creative problem solving*. Senior thesis, Department of Psychology, Princeton University, 1975.

Chapman, L. J., & Chapman, J. P. Illusory correlation as an obstacle to the use of valid psychodiagnostic signs. *Journal of Abnormal Psychology*, 1969, *74*, 271–280.

Cohen, C. E. *Cognitive basis of stereotyping*. Paper presented at the American Psychological Association Annual Meeting, San Francisco, September 1977.

Cohen, C. E., & Ebbesen, E. B. Observational goals and schema activation: A theoretical framework for behavior perception. *Journal of Experimental Social Psychology*, 1979, *15*, 305–329.

Collins, A. M., & Loftus, E. F. A spreading-activation theory of semantic processing. *Psychological Review*, 1975, *82*, 407–428.

Collins, A. M., & Quillian, M. R. Retrieval time from semantic memory. *Journal of Verbal Learning and Verbal Behavior*, 1969, *8*, 240–247.

Cook, T. D., & Flay, B. R. The persistence of experimentally induced attitude change. In L. Berkowitz (Ed.), *Advances in experimental social psychology* (Vol. 11). New York: Academic Press, 1978.

Dornbusch, S., Hastorf, A., Richardson, S. A., Muzzy, R., & Vreeland, R. S. The perceiver and the perceived: Their relative influence on the categories of interpersonal perception. *Journal of Personality and Social Psychology*, 1965, *1*, 434–440.

Duncker, K. On problem solving. *Psychological Monographs*, 1945, *58*, 5 (Whole No. 270).

Ebbesen, E. B., & Allen, R. B. Cognitive processes in implicit personality trait inferences. *Journal of Personality and Social Psychology*, 1979, *37*, 471–488.

Erdelyi, M. H. A new look at the new look: Perceptual defense and vigilance. *Psychological Review*, 1974, *81*, 1–25.

Fjeld, S. P., & Landfield, A. W. Personal construct consistency. *Psychological Reports*, 1961, *8*, 127–129.

Forbach, G. B., Stanners, R. F., & Hochhaus, L. Repetition and practice effects in a lexical decision task. *Memory & Cognition*, 1974, *2*, 337–339.

Geller, V., & Shaver, P. Cognitive consequences of self-awareness. *Journal of Experimental Social Psychology*, 1976, *12*, 99–108.

Glucksberg, S., & Weisberg, R. W. Verbal behavior and problem solving: Some effects of labeling in a functional fixedness problem. *Journal of Experimental Psychology*, 1966, *71*, 659–664.

Hamilton, D. L. Cognitive representations of persons. In E. T.Higgins, C. P. Herman, & M. P. Zanna (Eds.), *Social Cognition: The Ontario Symposium*. Hillsdale, N.J.: Lawrence Erlbaum Associates, 1981.

Hamilton, D. L., & Gifford, R. K. Illusory correlation in interpersonal perception: A cognitive basis of stereotypic judgments. *Journal of Experimental Social Psychology*, 1976, *12*, 392–407.

Hamilton, D. L., Katz, L., & Leirer, V. Organizational processes in impression formation. In R. Hastie, T. M. Ostrom, D. L. Hamilton, E. Ebbesen, R. S. Wyer, & D. Carlston (Eds.), *Person memory: The cognitive basis of social perception*. Hillsdale, N.J.: Lawrence Erlbaum Associates, 1980.

Hanawalt, N. G., & Demarest, I. H. The effect of verbal suggestion in the recall period upon the reproduction of visually perceived forms. *Journal of Experimental Psychology*, 1939, *25*, 159–174.

Hastie, R. Schematic principles in human memory. In E. T. Higgins, C. P. Herman, & M. P. Zanna (Eds.), *Social Cognition: The Ontario Symposium*. Hillsdale, N.J.: Lawrence Erlbaum Associates, 1981.

Hastorf, A. H., Richardson, S. A., & Dornbusch, S. M. The problem of relevance in the study of person perception. In R. Tagiuri & L. Petrullo (Eds.), *Person perception and interpersonal behavior*. Stanford, Calif.: Stanford University Press, 1958.

Heider, F. *The psychology of interpersonal relations*. New York: Wiley, 1958.

Higgins, E. T. The "communication game": Implications for social cognition and persuasion. In E. T. Higgins, C. P. Herman, & M. P. Zanna (Eds.), *Social Cognition: The Ontario Symposium*. Hillsdale, N.J.: Lawrence Erlbaum Associates, 1981.

Higgins, E. T. Role-taking and social judgment: Alternative developmental perspectives and processes. In J. H. Flavell & L. Ross (Eds.), *New directions in the study of social-cognitive development*. New York: Cambridge University Press, in press.

Higgins, E. T., & Chaires, W. M. Accessibility of interrelational constructs: Implications for stimulus encoding and creativity. *Journal of Experimental Social Psychology*, 1980, *16*, 348–361.

Higgins, E. T., Feldman, N. S., & Ruble, D. N. Accuracy and differentiation in social prediction: A developmental perspective. *Journal of Personality*, December, 1980.

Higgins, E. T., Kuiper, N. A., & Olson, J. M. Social cognition: A need to get personal. In E. T. Higgins, C. P. Herman, & M. P. Zanna (Eds.), *Social cognition: the Ontario symposium*. Hillsdale, N.J.: Lawrence Erlbaum Associates, 1981.

Higgins, E. T., & Rholes, W. S. "Saying is believing": Effects of message modification on memory and liking for the person described. *Journal of Experimental Social Psychology*, 1978, *14*, 363–378.

Higgins, E. T., Rholes, W. S., & Jones, C. R. Category accessibility and impression formation. *Journal of Experimental Social Psychology*, 1977, *13*, 141–154.

Howes, D. H. On the interpretation of word frequency as a variable affecting spread of recognition. *Journal of Experimental Psychology*, 1954, *48*, 106–112.

Huttenlocher, J., & Higgins, E. T. Adjectives, comparatives, and syllogisms. *Psychological Review*, 1971, *78*, 487–504.

Isen, A. M., Shalker, T. E., Clark, M., & Karp, L. Affect, accessibility of material in memory, and behavior: A cognitive loop? *Journal of Personality and Social Psychology*, 1978, *36*, 1–12.

Jeffery, K. M., & Mischel, W. Effects of purpose on the organization and recall of information in person perception. *Journal of Personality*, 1979, *47*, 397–419.

Jones, E. E., & Davis, K. E. From acts to dispositions: The attribution process in person perception. In L. Berkowitz (Ed.), *Advances in experimental social psychology* (Vol. 2). New York: Academic Press, 1965.

Jones, E. E., & Gerard, H. B. *Foundations of social psychology*. New York: Wiley, 1967.

Kahneman, D., & Tversky, A. On the psychology of prediction. *Psychological Review*, 1973, *80*, 237–251.

Kelly, G. A. *The psychology of personal constructs*. New York: W. W. Norton, 1955.

Kelley, H. H. The warm-cold variable in first impressions of persons. *Journal of Personality*, 1950, *18*, 431–439.

Kelley, H. H. Attribution theory in social psychology. In D. Levine (Ed.), *Nebraska Symposium on Motivation*, 1967. Lincoln: University of Nebraska Press, 1967.

Kelman, H. C. Compliance, identification, and internalization: Three processes of attitude change. *Journal of Conflict Resolution*, 1958, *2*, 51–60.

Kravetz, D. F. Sex role concepts of women. *Journal of Consulting and Clinical Psychology*, 1976, *44*, 437–443.

Kuiper, N. A., & Rogers, T. B. Encoding of personal information: Self-other differences. *Journal of Personality and Social Psychology,* 1979, *37,* 499–514.

Langer, E. J., & Abelson, R. P. A patient by any other name . . . : Clinician group difference in labeling bias. *Journal of Consulting and Clinical Psychology,* 1974, *42,* 4–9.

Levine, R., Chein, I., & Murphy, G. The relation of the intensity of a need to the amount of perceptual distortion: A preliminary report. *Journal of Psychology,* 1942, *13,* 283–293.

Lingle, J. H., & Ostrom, T. M. Retrieval selectivity in memory-based judgments. *Journal of Personality and Social Psychology,* 1979, *37,* 180–194.

Loftus, E. F. Activation of semantic memory. *American Journal of Psychology,* 1973, *86,* 331–337.

Loftus, E. F., Miller, D. G., & Burns, H. J. Semantic integration of verbal information into a visual memory. *Journal of Experimental Psychology: Human Learning and Memory,* 1978, *4,* 19–31.

Markus, H. Self-schemata and processing information about the self. *Journal of Personality and Social Psychology,* 1977, *35,* 63–78.

Mavin, G. H. *Memory effects of category accessibility in impression formation.* Honors thesis, Department of Psychology, University of Western Ontario, 1978.

McArthur, L. Z. What grabs you: The role of attention in impression formation and causal attributions. In E. T. Higgins, C. P. Herman, & M. P. Zanna (Eds.), *Social Cognition: The Ontario Symposium.* Hillsdale, N.J.: Lawrence Erlbaum Associates, 1981.

McGuire, W. J., McGuire, C. V., Child, P., & Fujioka, T. Salience of ethnicity in the spontaneous self-concept as a function of one's ethnic distinctiveness in the social environment. *Journal of Personality and Social Psychology,* 1978, *36,* 511–520.

McGuire, W. J., McGuire, C. V., & Winton, W. Effects of household sex composition on the salience of one's gender in the spontaneous self-concept. *Journal of Experimental Social Psychology,* 1979, *15,* 77–90.

McGuire, W. J., & Padawer-Singer, A. Trait salience in the spontaneous self-concept. *Journal of Personality and Social Psychology,* 1976, *33,* 743–754.

McKee, J. P., & Sherriffs, A. C. Men's and women's beliefs, ideas, and self-concepts. *American Journal of Sociology,* 1959, *64,* 356–363.

Meyer, D. E., Schvaneveldt, R. W., & Ruddy, M. G. Loci of contextual effects on visual word recognition. In P. M. A. Rabbit & S. Dornic (Eds.), *Attention and performance V.* London: Academic Press, 1975.

Miller, G. A. Practical and lexical knowledge. In E. Rosch & B. B. Lloyd (Eds.), *Cognition and categorization,* Hillsdale, N.J.: Lawrence Erlbaum Associates, 1978.

Mitsos, S. B. Personal constructs and the semantic differential. *Journal of Abnormal Social Psychology,* 1961, *62,* 433–434.

Neely, J. H. Semantic priming and retrieval from lexical memory: Roles of inhibitionless spreading activation and limited-capacity attention. *Journal of Experimental Psychology: General,* 1977, *106,* 226–254.

Neisser, U. *Cognitive psychology.* New York: Appleton-Century-Crofts, 1967.

Neisser, U. *Cognition and reality: Principles and implications of cognitive psychology.* San Francisco: Freeman, 1976.

Newcomb, T. M. *The acquaintance process.* New York: Holt, Rinehart & Winston, 1961.

Nisbett, R. E., & Ross, L. D. *Human inference: Strategies and shortcomings of informal judgment.* Century Series in Psychology. Englewood Cliffs, N.J.: Prentice-Hall, 1980.

O'Keefe, B. J., Delia, J. G., & O'Keefe, D. J. Construct individuality, cognitive complexity, and the formation and remembering of interpersonal impressions. *Social Behavior and Personality,* 1977, *5,* 229–240.

Paivio, A. *Imagery and verbal processes.* New York: Holt, Rinehart & Winston, 1971.

Petty, C. *The saga of Barbara and Bob: Effects of group sex composition on impression formation.* Senior thesis, Department of Psychology, Princeton University, 1977.

Pleck, J. H. The male sex role: Definitions, problems, and sources of change. *Journal of Social Issues*, 1976, *32*, 155–164.

Posner, M. I. *Chronometric explorations of the mind*. Hillsdale, N.J.: Lawrence Erlbaum Associates, 1978.

Posner, M. I., & Warren, R. E. Traces, concepts, and conscious constructions. In A. W. Melton & E. Martin (Eds.), *Coding processes in human memory*. Washington, D.C.: V. H. Winston & Sons, 1972.

Postman, L., & Brown, D. R. The perceptual consequences of success and failure. *Journal of Abnormal and Social Psychology*, 1952, *47*, 213–221.

Postman, L., Bruner, J. S., & McGinnies, E. Personal values as selective factors in perception. *Journal of Abnormal and Social Psychology*, 1948, *43*, 142–154.

Reed, S. K. Pattern recognition and categorization. *Cognitive Psychology*, 1972, *3*, 382–407.

Rosch, E. Principles of categorization. In E. Rosch & B. B. Lloyd (Eds.), *Cognition and categorization*, Hillsdale, N.J.: Lawrence Erlbaum Associates, 1978.

Rosch, E., & Mervis, C. B. Family resemblances: Studies in the internal structure of categories. *Cognitive Psychology*, 1975, *7*, 573–605.

Rosenberg, S., & Sedlak, A. Structural representations of implicit personality theory. In L. Berkowitz (Ed.), *Advances in experimental social psychology* (Vol. 6). New York: Academic Press, 1972.

Rosenkrantz, P., Vogel, S., Bee, H., Broverman, I., & Broverman, D. M. Sex-role stereotypes and self-concepts in college students. *Journal of Consulting and Clinical Psychology*, 1968, *32*, 287–295.

Ross, J. A. *Effects of exposure to social category terms on memory for stereotype descriptions of another person*. Masters thesis, Department of Psychology, Princeton University, 1977.

Ross, L. The intuitive psychologist and his shortcomings: Distortions in the attribution process. In L. Berkowitz (Ed.), *Advances in experimental social Psychology* (Vol. 10). New York: Academic Press, 1977.

Ross, L., Lepper, M. R., Strack, R., & Steinmetz, J. Social explanation and social expectation: Effects of real and hypothetical explanations on subjective likelihood. *Journal of Personality and Social Psychology*, 1977, *35*, 817–829.

Ross, M., & Olson, J. M. An expectancy-attribution model of placebo effects. *Psychological Review*, in press.

Ross, M., & Sicoly, F. Egocentric biases in availability and attribution. *Journal of Personality and Social Psychology*, 1979, *37*, 322–336.

Rothbart, M., Fulero, S., Jensen, C., Howard, J., & Birrell, P. From individual to group impressions: Availability heuristics in stereotype formation. *Journal of Experimental Social Psychology*, 1978, *14*, 235–255.

Ruble, D. N., & Higgins, E. T. Effects of group sex composition on self-presentation and sex-typing. *Journal of Social Issues*, 1976, *32*, 125–132.

Salancik, G. R. Inference of one's attitude from behavior recalled under linguistically manipulated cognitive sets. *Journal of Experimental Social Psychology*, 1974, *10*, 415–427.

Salancik, G. R., & Conway, M. Attitude inferences from salient and relevant cognitive content about behavior. *Journal of Personality and Social Psychology*, 1975, *32*, 829–840.

Sarbin, T. R., Taft, R., & Bailey, D. E. *Clinical inference and cognitive theory*. New York: Holt, Rinehart & Winston, 1960.

Schneider, D. J. Implicit personality theory: A review. *Psychological Bulletin*, 1973, *79*, 294–309.

Sherman, S. J., Ahlm, K., Berman, L., & Lynn, S. Contrast effects and their relationship to subsequent behavior. *Journal of Experimental Social Psychology*, 1978, *14*, 340–350.

Shiffrin, R. M., & Schneider, W. Controlled and automatic human information processing: II. Perceptual learning, automatic attending, and a general theory. *Psychological Review*, 1977, *84*, 127–190.

Shomer, R. W., & Centers, R. Differences in attitudinal responses under conditions of implicitly manipulated group salience. *Journal of Personality and Social Psychology,* 1970, *15,* 125-132.

Shrauger, J. S., & Patterson, M. B. Self-evaluation and the selection of dimensions for evaluating others. *Journal of Personality,* 1974, *42,* 569-585.

Sigal, H., & Page, R. Current stereotypes: A little fading, a little faking. *Journal of Personality and Social Psychology,* 1971, *18,* 247-255.

Smith, E. E., Shoben, E. J., & Rips, L. J. Structure and process in semantic memory: A feature model for semantic decisions. *Psychological Review,* 1974, *81,* 214-241.

Smith, J. C. *A study of the effect of sex-primed social context on self-concept and sex role.* Junior thesis, Department of Psychology, Princeton University, 1974.

Snyder, M., & Uranowitz, S. W. Reconstructing the past: Some cognitive consequences of person perception. *Journal of Personality and Social Psychology,* 1978, *38,* 941-950.

Spiro, R. J. Remembering information from text: The "state of schema" approach. In R. C. Anderson, R. J. Spiro, & W. E. Montague (Eds.), *Schooling and the acquisition of knowledge.* Hillsdale, N.J.: Lawrence Erlbaum Associates, 1977.

Taft, R. Selective recall and memory distortion of favourable and unfavourable material. *Journal of Abnormal and Social Psychology,* 1954, *49,* 23-28.

Tagiuri, R. Person perception. In G. Lindzey, & E. Aronson (Eds.), *The handbook of social psychology* (Vol. 3). Reading, Mass.: Addison-Wesley, 1969.

Taylor, S. E., & Crocker, J. Schematic bases of social information processing. In E. T. Higgins, C. P. Herman, & M. P. Zanna (Eds.), *Social cognition: The Ontario symposium.* Hillsdale, N.J.: Lawrence Erlbaum Associates, 1981.

Taylor, S. E., & Fiske, S. T. Salience, attention, and attribution: Top of the head phenomena. In L. Berkowitz (Ed.), *Advances in experimental social psychology* (Vol. 11). New York: Academic Press, 1978.

Taylor, S. E., Fiske, S. T., Close, M., Anderson, C., & Ruderman, A. *Solo status as a psychological variable: The power of being distinctive.* Unpublished manuscript, 1977.

Tsujimoto, R. N. Memory bias toward normative and novel trait prototypes. *Journal of Personality and Social Psychology,* 1978, *36,* 1391-1401.

Tulving, E., & Pearlstone, Z. Availability versus accessibility of information in memory for words. *Journal of Verbal Learning and Verbal Behavior,* 1966, *5,* 381-391.

Tversky, A., & Gati, I. Studies of similarity. In E. Rosch, & B. B. Lloyd (Eds.), *Cognition and categorization,* Hillsdale, N.J.: Lawrence Erlbaum Associates, 1978.

Tversky, A., & Kahneman, D. Availability: A heuristic for judging frequency and probability. *Cognitive Psychology,* 1973, *5,* 207-232.

Warren, R. E. Stimulus encoding and memory. *Journal of Experimental Psychology,* 1972, *94,* 90-100.

Weiner, B., Frieze, I., Kukla, A., Reed, L., Rest, S., & Rosenbaum, R. M. Perceiving the causes of success and failure. In E. E. Jones, D. E. Kanouse, H. H. Kelley, R. E. Nisbett, S. Valins, & B. Weiner (Eds.), *Attribution: Perceiving the causes of behavior.* Morristown, N.J.: General Learning Press, 1971.

Weisberg, R., & Suls, J. M. An information-processing model of Duncker's candle problem. *Cognitive Psychology,* 1973, *4,* 255-276.

Wickens, D. D. Characteristics of word encoding. In A. W. Melton & E. Martin (Eds.), *Coding processes in human memory.* Washington, D.C.: Winston and Sons, 1972.

Wispe, L. G., & Drambarean, N. C. Physiological need, word frequency and visual duration thresholds. *Journal of Experimental Psychology,* 1953, *46,* 25-31.

Wyer, R. S., & Carlston, D. E. *Social influence and attribution.* Hillsdale, N.J.: Lawrence Erlbaum Associates, 1979.

Wyer, R. S., & Srull, T. K. Category accessibility: Some theoretical and empirical issues concerning the processing of social stimulus information. In E. T. Higgins, C. P. Herman, & M. P.

Zanna (Eds.), *Social Cognition: The Ontario Symposium*. Hillsdale, N.J.: Lawrence Erlbaum Associates, 1981.

Yarrow, M. R., & Campbell, J. D. Person perception in children. *Merrill-Palmer Quarterly,* 1963, *9,* 57–72.

Zadny, J., & Gerard, H. B. Attributed intentions and informational selectivity. *Journal of Experimental Social Psychology,* 1974, *10,* 34–52.

Zajonc, R. B. The process of cognitive tuning and communication. *Journal of Abnormal and Social Psychology,* 1960, *61,* 159–167.

5 On Personality and Memory

John F. Kihlstrom
Harvard University

ON PERSONALITY AND MEMORY

Recent years have witnessed a dramatic increase in interest among both experimental and clinical psychologists in the relations between personality and cognitive processes. Within the domain of personality theory, for example, there has been a general disenchantment with earlier dynamic, trait, and situationist approaches to personality, accompanied by the emergence of an interactionist view that places principal stress on the individual's memories of the past, organization and perception of the present, and expectations for the future (Bowers, 1973; Kelly, 1955; Mischel, 1973, 1979). Cognitive interactionism in personality theory, once somewhat iconoclastic, is now thoroughly couched in the language of cognitive psychology. Thus it forms the conceptual basis for a new dynamic psychology that investigates the relations between personality and cognition. At the same time, the evolution of cognitive psychology from classical associationist learning theory to more recent accounts that underscore control processes and schema formation has led to a new emphasis on the importance of motivation, plans, and other characteristics of the individual perceiver, thinker, or rememberer (Mandler, 1975; Miller, Galanter, & Pribram, 1960; Neisser, 1967, 1976). Corresponding developments can be observed in clinical psychology, where strictly dynamic or behaviorist formulations have given way to a new cognitive therapy that stresses the influence of the patient's percepts, ideas, and memories on his or her clinical state (Beck, 1970; Mahoney, 1977; Meichenbaum, 1977).

In the past, most investigators of personality and cognition have emphasized individual differences in cognitive style, the "New Look" in perception, fantasy in thematic apperception and daydreaming, the organization of personal constructs, and the development and utilization of self-control strategies. Except for the psychoanalytic tradition, however, relatively little systematic attention has been devoted to aspects of personality and the recollection of the past. The major objective of this essay is to review previous efforts to explore the relation between personality and memory, particularly episodic memory.

A PERSPECTIVE ON PERSONALITY
AND MEMORY

At the outset, it seems important to spell out some assumptions that might guide empirical inquiry in this area. This is a little difficult because the place of personality within psychology is far from clear, and because cognitive interactionism within personality has not yet coalesced into a unified framework with a set of consensual constructs. Furthermore, memory theory is not a monolith, and there are many conceptual and methodological choices that an investigator must make. Finally, with few exceptions cognitive psychologists who study memory have not been centrally concerned with personality processes. Nevertheless, our research program, just beginning, is set against a backdrop of broad principles pertaining to personality, memory, and the relation between them.

The Domain of Personality

The field of personality is concerned with the distinctive patterns of thought, behavior, and experience that characterize a person's unique adjustment to his or her life situation. In principle, any personality theory must be a general psychological theory in which the knowledge gained from the study of physiological, cognitive, social, and developmental processes is synthesized into a comprehensive view of individual behavior and experience. The psychology of personality seeks to understand the joint operation of these processes from the point of view of the person involved, as he or she acts to understand, respond to, and change the physical and social world in which he or she lives. As noted earlier, the dominant theme in contemporary personality theory emphasizes the interaction of persons and situations. This chapter embraces a version of interactionism that emphasizes cognitive processes (Mischel, 1973, 1979) and reciprocal determinism (Bandura, 1974).

Traditionally, empirical inquiry within personality has focused on individual differences: their assessment, development, and impact on behavior and experience. This has led not only to the development of a sophisticated body of test theory (Cronbach & Meehl, 1955; Jackson, 1971; Wiggins, 1974) but also to a preoccupation with determining the number and nature of the dimensions that comprise personality (Eysenck, 1977; Guilford, 1975) and to a running debate concerning the temporal stability of personality features and the relations between generalized dispositions and actual behavior in specific situations (Block, 1977; Epstein, 1979). However, personality has never been confined to the study of individual differences. Freud, for example, was much more interested in general constructs such as sexuality, aggression, anxiety, and defense than in population variance on the dimensions implied by these constructs. Recently, the domain of personality has expanded to include the study of a number of broad constructs including consciousness, emotional behavior, self-awareness and self-regulation, intrinsic motivation, impression formation, attributional processes, and implicit personality theory. In most of this work there has been little or no explicit concern with individual differences—yet these topics clearly belong in the domain of personality.

Throughout its history, personality has been divided into two content areas concerned, respectively, with structure and dynamics. These distinctions can still be valuable within the framework of cognitive interactionism. For example, rather than conceptualizing the structure of personality in terms of some exhaustive list of abilities and predispositions, it may be useful to identify it with the cognitive structures (schemata) that organize our knowledge of ourselves and the physical and social world within which we live. Similarly, rather than construing the dynamics of personality in terms of the opposing forces that drive and direct behavior, they should be identified with the cognitive processes by which we perceive and remember information pertaining to ourselves, other people, and the social world. Of course, a firm distinction between structural and dynamic factors in personality is untenable. Personality structures, like cognitive structures generally, are constantly subject to development and change through the processes of assimilation and accommodation. There may be nothing static in personality except our awareness of ourselves as the same individual from one moment and situation to another—and even self-consciousness seems subject to division (Hilgard, 1977).

Given this framework, we need not confine ourselves to the study of individual differences in memory functioning and their correlates. The study of general processes involved in social and personal memory is itself a prime topic within the psychology of personality. Of particular interest is the nature of generalized mental representations concerning the self, others, and social situations; the processes involved in encoding and retrieving memories for social events and personal experiences; and the manner in which these episodes are represented in the cognitive system. Indeed, even the general processes involved in attribution and impression, part of the procedural knowledge represented in the memory system (Hastie & Carlston, 1980), belong as much to the domain of personality as to social or cognitive psychology.

At some point, however, the personality psychologist must confront individual differences in social and personal memory and relate these to other features of the person and his or her life situation. Adopting a functionalist approach to this problem, a good starting place is the taxonomy of cognitive–social learning person variables offered by Mischel (1973). The set of cognitive competencies, for example, includes individual differences in attentional capacity and cognitive style that are closely related to memory. Also important are the encoding and retrieval strategies by which social and personal information is processed in the memory system. These strategies, in turn, are influenced by the individual's system of personal constructs, values, interests, and needs, and also by his or her response to perceived situational demands, as reflected in expectations and plans. It should be noted that these kinds of person variables include both relatively enduring and relatively transient features of the person. These features need not be represented in the individual's phenomenal awareness, although it is recognized that the documentation of unconscious mental contents is fraught with difficulty.

Principles of Memory Functioning

Within the domain of relatively permanent memories, Tulving (1972) has distinguished between those that are episodic and those that are semantic in character. Episodic memories have to do with personal experience and carry as essential components some reference to the self and to the spatiotemporal context in which the events occurred; semantic memories, by contrast, have to do with the facts of the world, the meanings of words, rules of language and inference, logical and mathematical operations, and highly overlearned skills. Contrary to Tulving's intentions, there is a tendency to think of these as separate memory systems, but careful consideration confirms that they are in fact closely related (Reed, 1979; Schonfield & Stones, 1979). The formation of episodic memories is based on information provided by the knowledge structures of semantic memory, in that perceptual representations are constructed and interpreted on the basis of what the person already knows. Semantic memories, in turn, emerge as related individual episodic memories accumulate: The spatiotemporal features that distinguish the episodes become blurred, yielding a highly generalized representation of them as a whole. Thus new knowledge structures evolve that can more easily absorb and interpret later, similar experiences. Some of this organized knowledge is highly relevant to personality: This is especially so for the knowledge structures pertaining to ourselves, others, and social situations (Epstein, 1973; Schneider, 1973).

In contemporary cognitive theory, episodic memory traces are commonly conceptualized as bundles of features or attributes that describe perceptual events (Bower, 1967; Tulving & Watkins, 1975; Underwood, 1969; Wickens, 1972). The list of potential memory attributes is very long; it includes modality of experience, acoustic and visual recodings, frequency of occurrence, spatial and temporal relations with other stimuli, dictionary meaning, associative and categorical relationships with concepts in semantic memory, connotative meanings, and affective quality. In addition, stimuli are interpreted in the context of other distal and internal stimulus events, whose features are also encoded in this manner. In the present context, attributes such as connotative meaning, pleasantness, emotional valence, and aspects of the experiential context deserve particular attention. It should be clear that features of personality, including personal constructs, intentions, goals, motives, and emotions, can influence the interpretations given to perceptual events and that these aspects of the individual's state are themselves features of the experiential context in which the events took place. Thus, aspects of personality, by coloring the meaning given to an event and the context in which it takes place, help determine which features are available for encoding at the time of perception.

Equally important in current theory is the emphasis on control processes that guide the encoding and retrieval of memories (Anderson & Bower, 1972; Atkinson & Shiffrin, 1968; Craik & Lockhart, 1972; Tulving & Thomson, 1973). The exact nature of the memorial representation of an event is affected by random fluctuations and developmental changes in encoding processes, as well as by task demands on individual encoding strategies (Bach & Underwood, 1970; Bower, 1970; Underwood, 1965; Wickens, 1972). Additionally, the fate of the material over the retention interval will be a function of the extent to which it is elaborated within existing cognitive structures (Jacoby & Craik, 1979). Finally, the retrievability of an available memory trace will depend on the extent to which the cognitive structures that guide the retrieval attempt match the attributes that were encoded as features of the memory trace (Tulving & Thomson, 1973; Watkins & Tulving, 1975). Again, it should be clear that these control strategies can be biased to emphasize or avoid certain elements in the perceptual field or attributes of memories, depending on the relevance of features of the events and memories for the individual involved.

Although there is a tendency to talk about the processes involved in encoding and retrieval as if they entailed extracting information from the environment and recapturing memory traces, respectively, there is now some consensus that perceptual and memorial operations are better characterized as constructive and reconstructive activities, respectively (Bartlett, 1932; Jacoby & Craik, 1979; Jenkins, 1974; Neisser, 1967, 1976). It seems clear that the final product of memory operation is actively created on the basis of quite fragmentary trace information and is strongly influenced by the cognitive schemata that are active at the time. As a natural outcome of the subject's "effort after meaning," certain details may be omitted, transformed, or added in order to make the event fit with currently active schemata. Thus, again, salient features of personality have the opportunity to influence not only what is remembered, in the sense of encoding and retrieval, but also what shape the reconstructed memory will finally take.

APPROACHES TO THE STUDY OF PERSONALITY AND MEMORY

Interest in personality–memory interactions antedates the formal emergence of cognitive interactionism in personality. Ebbinghaus (1884), for example, invented the nonsense syllable precisely because he recognized that memory in the real world was affected by individual moods, motives, and interests. He wanted to begin by studying memory "in the raw," without having to account for these factors; it is unfortunate that succeeding generations of cognitive psychologists followed this program well past World War II, without going on to the second part of Ebbinghaus' agenda. Historically, of course, the first to concern themselves with the influence of personality processes on memory were those investigators allied with psychoanalysis especially Freud himself (1900, 1901, 1915) and Rapaport (1942). With the Gestalt psychologists the psychoanalysts rejected Ebbinghaus' notion that forgetting resulted from the decay or erosion of memory traces and asserted instead that memory was organized by, and expressive of, certain motives of the organism. In a different vein, Bartlett (1932) held that an important factor guiding the person's reconstruction of past experience was his or her attitude toward that experience. "Attitude" was construed quite broadly to include individual differences in motivation, affect, and interest patterns: "Here is the significance of the fact ... that when a subject is being asked to remember, very often the first thing that emerges is something of the nature of attitude. The recall is then a construction, made largely on the basis of this attitude, and its general effect is that of a justification of the attitude [Bartlett, 1932, p. 207]." Adler (1937; Ansbacher, 1947), like Bartlett, emphasized the mutuality of personality and memory. In his view, personal recollections are selected to correspond with, and to express, the style of life adopted by the individual; furthermore, they served to maintain that life-style in the face of threat or pressure for change.

The major efforts to study personality and memory may be categorized into four approaches, which are to be thought of as fuzzy sets: studies of repression, individual differences related to verbal learning, person memory, and autobiographical memory. The following review is necessarily selective: There are many individual efforts within each approach that have been excluded from consideration for reasons of economy and clarity of presentation.

Repression

The key concept in the psychoanalytic view of forgetting is the notion of repression. Certain instinctual wishes related to sexuality and aggression, which conflict with the demands of the external physical and social world, give rise to the experience of anxiety. Ideas and memories associated with these instinctual strivings are rendered unconscious by repression, thus relieving anxiety, and are allowed conscious expression again only after other defense mechanisms disguise their relation to the primitive instinct. The repression of memories, and their emergence into consciousness, is construed as a shift in "cathexis," or attention, away from or toward certain traces of past experience. Thus the psychoanalytic theory of memory anticipated contemporary information-processing theories by giving control processes a central role in memory function. By emphasizing the important influence of emotions on these control processes, it laid a foundation for the later study of interactions between personality and memory.

Within the domain of personality and memory, work on repression has the longest history (Erdelyi & Goldberg, 1979; Holmes, 1974; MacKinnon & Dukes, 1962; Rapaport, 1942; Zeller, 1950). It is also the least satisfactory, because of both conceptual ambiguities and methodological shortcomings. For Freud, repression acted upon percepts, ideas, and memories associated with primitive sexual and aggressive instincts and the primary source of evidence for it came from the analyst's interpretation of the free associations of individual patients. When the concept was operationalized for laboratory investigation, however, the target of repression was redefined to include almost anything threatening or unpleasant, especially unsuccessful or interrupted tasks (Holmes, 1974; Zeller, 1950). This line of research has been reviewed and rejected as evidence of repression by reviewers early and late, friendly and hostile: by Rapaport (1942) because it misinterpreted Freud's meaning of conflict, threat, and defense and by Holmes (1974) because the effects obtained could be interpreted in terms of *nondefensive* cognitive factors. At present, research on repression is caught in a double bind: Most members of the psychoanalytic community reject the experimental work as ill-conceived, irrelevant, and unnecessary; and most experimentalists are skeptical of psychosexual theory, clinical observation, and the interpretive method.

Recent restatements of the concept of repression, however, show how the selective processing of stimulus and trace attributes can be brought into the service of personality. For example, Mandler's (1975) interpretation of network theories of semantic memory holds that the attributes associated with conceptual nodes include personal and contextual meaning as well as dictionary meaning. When new information enters the cognitive system, it undergoes a meaning analysis in which its relation with concepts already present is established. Thus, by a process of generalization and discrimination a hierarchy of related nodes is developed in which each concept shares the meaning, including personal and contextual meaning, of some others. In Mandler's view of repression, a meaning analysis may operate so as to avoid concepts that are associated with conflict or anxiety; or a highly salient personal experience may sensitize the person to related information and color the meanings attached to it. Erdelyi and Goldberg

(1979) have recently proposed a similar information-processing account of repression. They begin with the assumption that information processing is selective and then assert that this selectivity, operative at all stages of processing, can be brought into the service of personality. Individuals can therefore limit the extent to which unpleasant or threatening new information is processed, so that the resulting memory traces are not encoded in easily accessible form, or individuals can limit search processes so as to circumvent the retrieval of this kind of information.

Thus, the presence of emotional and other connotative attributes of memory, coupled with the controlled selectivity of information processing, creates a theoretical context where a modified concept of repression is viable. A plausible redefinition of repression liberates it from Freudian psychosexual theory and holds that individuals are capable of defensively biasing information-processing functions so that threatening material available in both the perceptual field and memory is not represented in phenomenal awareness.

Memory for success and failure experiences has also been studied outside the psychoanalytic context (Butterfield, 1964; Weiner, 1966). An important source of this work is Gestalt theory, which held that memorial processes operated to distort trace information toward "good form": symmetry, regularity, simplicity, completeness and the like (Riley, 1962). The theory led to the prediction that traces of poor-form stimuli would be more memorable, at least over short intervals, because of the persisting mental activity involved in transforming them to good form. Interest in the role of personality in this process was stimulated by Zeigarnik's (1927) observation of individual differences in memory for interrupted or failed versus completed or successful tasks. In most subjects, retention favored the interrupted or uncompleted tasks, as predicted by the theory; for those subjects who perceived the task outcome as personally threatening, however, retention favored the completed or successful ones.

Discovery of the Zeigarnik effect and its reverse stimulated the interrupted-task research on repression discussed earlier, but selective memory in this paradigm has also been related to a number of other personality variables. For example, Atkinson (1953) found that subjects high in achievement motivation favored the recall of incompleted tasks, provided that the tasks were attempted in a context in which achievement motivation was aroused; Eriksen (1954) showed that subjects with high ego strength selectively recalled interrupted tasks under task-oriented conditions and completed tasks under self-oriented conditions. The measurement of selective recall in the task-interruption/failure paradigm is problematic (Pettinati & Evans, 1978), but the best evidence clearly indicates a general tendency for subjects to favor the recall of completed tasks or successful experiences. Recently, Matlin and Stang (1978) have compiled a number of demonstrations of the "Polyanna Principle" in cognition generally and memory in particular. Perhaps the most interesting contribution of the work is the suggestion that selectivity in recall varies as a function of both the personality characteristics of the subject and the situational context in which the critical events occurred.

Individual Differences and Verbal Learning

A large number of studies relevant to personality and memory employ methods that are quite familiar because of their association with the conventional study of human learning and memory in the experimental laboratory. In principle, of course, one could take any garden-variety experimental task employed in human learning (memory span, memory for designs, paired-associate learning, free recall, story memory) and correlate task performance with individual differences in personality. Such a strategy has been explicitly proposed by Johnson (1974), and the large body of relevant research has been thoroughly reviewed (H. Eysenck, 1973; M. Eysenck, 1977; Goodenough, 1976; Johnson, 1974). Two independent lines of research are especially noteworthy: These have to do with cognitive style and arousal, respectively.

Cognitive styles represent characteristic ways of handling information that govern perception, memory, and the organization of thought. A large number of such styles have been suggested by various investigators, but only a few have been studied within the context of memory paradigms: changing–condensing (Gomulicki, 1956), importing–skeletonizing (Paul, 1959), leveling–sharpening (Holzman & Gardner, 1960), broad–narrow categorizing (Messick & Damarin, 1964; Messick & Fritzky, 1963), and field independence–dependence (Goodenough, 1976). Only field independence has been subject to more than occassional inquiry, and Goodenough's review reveals a complex set of findings. Field independence should lead subjects to impose organization on stimulus material, but there does not appear to be any consistent relation between this dimension and either paired-associate learning or free recall. In a similar manner, field independence should permit the subject to make finer discriminations among stimuli arrayed along a dimension, but there is no relation to transfer of training or stimulus generalization. Goodenough has summarized this literature as follows: "field-dependent and field-independent people differ more consistently in how the learning or memory process occurs than in how effective that process is [p. 688]."

Hullian learning theory asserted that high arousal could facilitate or inhibit the learning or reproduction of associations, depending on the level of response competition. A later development in arousal theory was Walker's (1958) concept of action decrement, which held that high levels of arousal at the time of input would produce a longer lasting memory trace, but at the expense of a stronger inhibition on immediate utilization. The relevance of personality lies in the attempt to induce arousal by means of an experimental manipulation of emotional state or by relying on preexisting individual differences in characteristic levels of arousal. Many investigators have followed H. Eysenck in assuming that high scores on scales of introversion and neuroticism are associated, respectively, with high chronic levels of central and autonomic arousal. A large number of such studies (reviewed in H. Eysenck, 1973; M. Eysenck, 1977) appear to support the central predictions of Hull's and Walker's theories. M. Eysenck (1977) has recently provided a reinterpretation of the arousal-memory literature in terms more congruent with contemporary information-processing theories of cognition. He holds that high arousal restricts the number of attributes encoded as part of the memory trace and biases retrieval efforts toward the material most readily accessible in storage. The new theory accounts for the classic effects of arousal on learning and memory and also for some new findings: poor incidental learning among introverts and slower recall by introverts of items from difficult lists, for example.

There is a scattering of studies conducted in a similar vein relating other features of personality to memory-task performance (see Johnson, 1974, for a selective review). For example, curious subjects show better incidental memory than noncurious ones (Maw & Maw, 1961), but anal retentives have no better memories than anal expulsives (Fisher & Keen, 1972). Interestingly, there is relatively little work relating performance on memory tasks to individual differences in repression-sensitization (Bell & Byrne, 1978).

There are, however, several problems with this literature. The positive effects obtained are typically weak and unreliable, casting doubt on the whole enterprise, and there is little attempt to relate the laboratory findings to behavior. Johnson (1974) has pointed out another difficulty: These studies have only rarely been informed by the conceptual advances of contemporary cognitive psychology. He advocates that personality psychologists follow their cognitive colleagues in dividing memory storage into its sensory, primary, and secondary structures; subdividing secondary memory into episodic and semantic components; and distinguishing among the specific control processes involved in encoding memories, transferring them from one storage structure to another, and retrieving them. With this model of memory in mind, the investigator can go about the task of investigating the correlates of individual differences in the capacity of memory structures and in the operation of control processes within each stage of information processing. M. Eysenck (1977) has offered a similar program, emphasizing the effects of momentary arousal, introversion-extraversion, neuroticism, and intelligence on performance in primary and secondary, episodic, and semantic memory tasks.

Such an approach is certainly systematic, but the strategy presents certain difficulties from the point of view of both cognitive and personality psychology. For example, it has never been entirely clear how fruitful it is to compartmentalize memory into some number of storage structures (Craik & Lockhart, 1972; Melton, 1963; Tulving, 1968; Wickelgren, 1973), nor may it be as easy to separate the encoding and retrieval phases (Jacoby & Craik, 1979; Tulving & Thomson, 1973) or their substages (McClelland, 1979) as was once thought.

These ambiguities within cognitive psychology itself suggest that a task-oriented strategy may not, in the final analysis, fulfill its promise of theoretical richness. From the point of view of personality psychology, moreover, it is even clearer that this approach is fundamentally misguided. The goal is admirable enough: to study the influence of personality on memory, employing tasks that allow rigorous control over the conditions of acquisition, retention, and retrieval and that permit precise specification of the locus of the effects observed. However, the material involved is relatively inert, rarely ranging beyond the usual run of digits and nonsense syllables, word lists and banal prose passages, and geometric forms and unfamiliar faces. Equally important, the typical laboratory setting is quite sterile, not appreciably different from that employed in conventional studies of human learning and memory. There is no reason to think that personality processes will be particularly visible or influential under these circumstances.

Structural concepts, stage analysis, and an emphasis on control processes have undeniable heuristic value in the study of memory (Crowder, 1976) and have been very valuable in the investigation of individual differences in cognition (Hunt, Frost, & Lunneborg, 1973) or psychological dificit (Koh, 1978). However, it should be clear that, as far as personality and memory go, the topic of central interest should not be the relations between person variables and task variables in the abstract but rather those between person variables and the content of what is remembered and forgotten. Some of the approaches referred to in the foregoing implicitly recognize this, but on the whole the point is not often acted upon. A number of different kinds of experiments show how meaningful personality–memory interactions can be revealed within the context of conventional verbal-learning procedures, provided that the investigator selects appropriate stimulus materials or structures an appropriately involving context for encoding and retrieval.

For example, Wickens (1972) and his associates, examining release from proactive inhibition (RPI) in the Brown–Peterson paradigm, have found that subjects encode connotative meanings of words such as pleasantness, evaluation, and masculinity–femininity as well as denotative meanings such as category membership. There are substantial individual differences in the amount of RPI observed with shifts in connotative features. This suggests that some individuals are more sensitive to particular connotative meanings than others; alternatively, there may not be complete consensus as to the connotations of the words. Interestingly, a study by Kail and Levine (1976) showed that the extent of RPI observed when there is a shift between masculine and feminine attributes is related to the degree to which children identify with culturally prescribed sex-role stereotypes. Similarly, category clustering and subjective organization permit observation of the subject's encoding of stimulus attributes and his/her use of them to guide the retrieval and reconstruction of memories (Bower, 1970). In a study by Bousfield and Cohen (1956), women showed greater clustering of "feminine" words and men showed greater clustering of "masculine" words, suggesting that sex-role orientation might influence the encoding and/or retrieval of relevant information. More recently, S. Bem (1980) has reported that clustering of "masculine" and "feminine" words is related to individual differences in sex-role orientation, at least for men. Thus, features of personality can exert an influence on the encoding and retrieval of relevant memories.

Another direction for this kind of research is exemplified by the work of Rogers, Kuiper, and their colleagues on self-reference in memory (see Rogers, this volume; Kuiper & Derry, this volume). These experiments involve conventional procedures for the study of verbal learning, with the exception that the critical material is a list of adjectives varying in the degree to which they describe individual subjects. When subjects were presented with a set of trait adjectives to study, Rogers (1977) found that those who were asked to decide if each item were self-descriptive showed better recognition than uninstructed subjects; a subsequent comparative study involving incidental learning indicated that items for which self-reference decisions were made were retained better than items processed in conventional orthographic, phonemic, and semantic conditions (Rogers, Kuiper, & Kirker, 1977). In another experiment, subjects who had previously studied a list of adjectives under conditions of a self-referent orienting task and who later received a surprise test of recognition memory gave more false positive decisions for self-descriptive distractors than for nondescriptive ones (Rogers, Rogers, & Kuiper, 1979). A later study (Kuiper & Rogers, 1979) compared self- and other-reference to orthographic, phonemic, and semantic orienting tasks, consistently finding superior recall under the person-oriented conditions. Although self- and other-reference did not consistently yield different levels of recall (Bower & Gilligan, 1979), there was evidence of a differential relation between recall and processing time in the two conditions. The results indicate that encoding information with respect to oneself or a familiar other yields a rich and elaborate memory trace. This approach is especially interesting because it does not classify subjects on nomothetic trait dimensions but rather employs idiographic techniques for the assessment of self-descriptions, thereby reducing the risk that individuals have been forced into slots where they do not fit.

A rather different paradigm for the study of personality and memory involves state-dependent retention (SDR), in which performance of a response is contingent on the presence of the same organismic state as that in which acquisition originally took place. Although most studies of human SDR have entailed drug-induced states (Eich, 1977), there is some suggestion in the literature of SDR effects due to changes in emotional state (Isen, Shalker, Clark, & Karp, 1978; Weingartner, Miller, & Murphy, 1977). Bower, Monteiro, and Gilligan (1978, Experiment 3) adapted the SDR paradigm to study the effects of emotional state on retroactive inhibition. Emotional state was manipulated by means of hypnotic suggestion. Memory for the original list was best when there was congruence between the states present at encoding and retrieval, especially when the interpolated list was studied in the different state. Research by Nasby (1980), conducted entirely in the normal waking state, failed to find an effect of congruence between encoding and retrieval moods in a simple list-learning procedure. However, both encoding and retrieval were better for material whose affective connotations were consonant with the individual's mood at the time the operation was performed. These results indicate that mood is a contextual feature encoded as part of an episodic memory trace and that variations in emotional state at the time of processing can influence the accessibility of memories. Emotion-based SDR and similar effects are important because they should lead to a richer understanding of how affect is represented in the cognitive system (Zajonc, 1980).

Person Memory

The study of social cognition has enriched the literature of cognitive psychology by employing stimulus materials that bear a closer resemblance to "real-world" memory than the kinds of items that have been conventionally used in verbal-learning studies. In this way, it has helped address the issue of ecological validity by showing that the principles developed in the verbal-learning laboratory are generalizable to the encoding, organization, and retrieval of information about individuals and their actions in the social world. The work—whether or not it involves recognizable memory procedures—is highly relevant to the topic of this chapter because it reveals aspects of the nature and function of the knowledge structures that guide the encoding and retrieval of information about people (Hastie, Ostrom, Ebbesen, Wyer, Hamilton, & Carlston, 1980).

A large body of research has shown that information in semantic memory, including the declarative knowledge represented by implicit personality theory and the procedural knowledge represented by algorithms for impression formation, influence the way in which individuals are perceived and later remembered (Schneider, 1973; Schneider, Hastorf, & Ellsworth, 1979). Following Bartlett's (1932) emphasis on the role of prior knowledge and inference in perception and memory, these findings have often been summarized in terms of schematic principles (Taylor & Crocker, 1980). Much recent research has attempted to investigate the details of the structure and function of schemata in social cognition. For example, Cantor (1980; Cantor, Chap. 2, this volume; Cantor & Mischel, 1979) has argued that mental representations of social categories (persons and situations) are defined by prototypes with high convergent and discriminant cue validity. Hastie (1980a) has examined the effects of a prior personality impression in memory for specific behavioral information about a person, finding that both highly congruent and highly incongruent items are remembered better than irrelevant items. Elsewhere (Hastie, 1980b), he has argued that these findings are consistent with those in other domains of a curvilinear relation between schema congruence and memory.

Just as semantic memory contains generic information about the facts of the world, the meanings of words, the properties of common objects, and the attributes of specific individuals and wider social categories, so it must contain generalized representations of oneself. Accordingly, a major effort has been devoted to the analysis of the structure and function of the self-concept as an aspect of semantic memory. The self has variously been construed as a node in a memory network with links to other nodes representing specific behavioral episodes and summary trait information (Bower & Gilligan, 1979; Markus & Smith, this volume) or as a prototype representing the characteristic attributes of the individual (see Chap. 8 by Rogers and Chap. 9 by Kuiper & Derry, this volume). What is clear is that the self is a cognitive structure that guides the processing of information in memory: New information is examined for self-reference and coded accordingly, and the self-schema can interact with the encoded attribute of self-reference (and other more specific attributes) to guide subsequent retrieval attempts. It remains to be seen if the schema for self is qualitatively different from schemata for others; and the details of the structure of the self-schema need to be specified more clearly. For example, assuming that the self is structured as a prototype, does that prototype represent the statistical average of the person's standings on all the dimensions in the personality space (Rosenberg & Sedlak, 1972; Wiggins, 1979) or the list of only those traits that are most representative of him or her (Markus, 1977)? Moreover, it is possible that the self is not a monolithic cognitive structure but that there are many "selves," and thus many self-schemata, corresponding to different roles or social situations, represented in the cognitive system.

To date, most investigations of person memory have been more concerned with the discovery of general principles than with the study of individual differences. However, a straightforward extension of this research examines the influence of personality factors—whether enduring or transient—on memory for the characteristics and actions of other people. Some indication of the possibilities here is given by recent studies of memory for information with direct self-relevance. For example, Mischel, Ebbesen, and Zeiss (1976) examined selective memory for the results of a battery of personality tests, as affected by individual differences in repression–sensitization, immediate past experiences, and expectations about the future. There was a general bias toward selective memory for personal assets as opposed to liabilities, but this effect was strongest when the subjects expected to succeed on a subsequent cognitive task. When there was no prior experience or expectation of the future, memory for assets and liabilities was related to characteristic tendencies toward repression or sensitization. The results of another experiment employing a similar procedure suggest that the effect is due to factors operating at the encoding rather than the retrieval stage of information processing (Mischel, Ebbesen, & Zeiss, 1973).

Other studies have investigated the influence of personality variables on memory for others. A series of studies by Bower and his colleagues, for example, has examined the effects of mood and expectations on person memory. Monteiro and Bower (1979) asked subjects to read a short narrative about two characters while in a state of hypnotically induced happiness or sadness; one of the characters in the story was portrayed as happy, the other as sad. One day later, the subjects recalled the story in the normal waking state, with no attempted mood manipulation. Those who read the story while happy remembered more about the happy character, and those who read the story while sad remembered more about the sad one. In another study, Owens, Bower, and Black (1979) asked subjects to read an ambiguous text describing the events of a day in the life of a fictional character. Prior to this, some subjects read a short passage intended to bias their interpretations of the protagonist's motives. On a later memory test, recall favored the motive-relevant passage and showed intrusions and distortions consistent with the attributed motive.

Although these studies examined the influence of relatively transient variables, ongoing research by Kuiper, Markus, and their colleagues (Kuiper & Derry and Markus & Smith, this volume) has begun to study the influence of more stable features of personality (as represented by the self-concept) on the encoding and retrieval of information about others. These efforts foreshadow a renewed interest in the impact of personal constructs on person perception and person memory.

Autobiographical Memory

Concern for ecological validity in the study of memory, including personality–memory interactions, eventually must lead the investigator away from the laboratory and into the real world, exploring the individual's recollections of events and experiences that have transpired outside the laboratory. Although, in the past, cognitive psychologists have not been particularly concerned with direct inquiry into "real-world" memory (Bartlett, 1932; Meltzer, 1930; Neisser, 1978), there are presently definite trends in that direction—as witnessed by studies of memory for pleasure reading and prose or verse committed to memory in the course of everyday life (Neisser & Hupcey, 1974; Rubin, 1977), school classmates (Bahrick, Bahrick, & Wittlinger, 1975), public events (Squire & Slater, 1975; Warrington & Sanders, 1971), and eyewitness testimony (Hastie, Loftus, Penrod, & Winkler, 1980; Loftus, 1975). There is also an emerging literature on autobiographical memory (Linton, 1975, 1978; Robinson, 1976). This last topic is particularly interesting because even casual observations of ourselves and others suggest that autobiographical recollections are important aspects of personality. Indeed, what a person can and cannot remember, and the way in which personal experiences are reconstructed, may be more revealing of the individual's personality than the most sophisticated trait measure. Because so little is known about the remembering and forgetting of personal experiences, the topic provides a rare opportunity for cognitive and personality psychologists to make common cause.

Recently, Crovitz (Crovitz & Quina-Holland, 1976; Crovitz & Schiffman, 1974) and Robinson (1976) have introduced a method for the sampling of autobiographical memory based on observations by Sir Francis Galton. In the paradigm, a word serves as a cue for the retrieval of a discrete personal experience related to it. The task is a very engaging one for subjects and yields memories spanning a wide range of ages, content, salience, detail, and emotional valence. The technique also reveals individual differences in response to particular cues, the content and salience of the memories so recovered, and the handling of emotion; these may be related to other personality variables. Suppose, for example, that a particular person is strongly disposed to behave in a certain way, has certain goals or expectations paramount at the moment, is in a particular emotional state, or routinely thinks about him/herself and others in particular terms. One might reasonably expect to see these individual differences reflected in the ease with which the person can gain access to memories of relevant personal experiences and in the manner in which these events are reconstructed in detail.

More than half a century ago, Washburn and her colleagues studied such effects with a procedure much like that employed by Crovitz and by Robinson (Baxter, Yamada, & Washburn, 1917; Morgan, Mull, & Washburn, 1919; Washburn, Giang, Ives, & Pollock, 1925; Washburn, Harding, Simmons, & Tomlinson, 1925). In some of these experiments the subjects were presented with a stimulus word and instructed to recall either a pleasant or an unpleasant experience associated with it; in other cases the subjects were asked to recall experiences in which specific emotional states were aroused; in other experiments, the subjects were uninstructed about what to recall but were asked to rate the pleasantness of the memories that emerged. Individual differences in the qualities of the memories obtained, and in the latencies between presentation of the probe and recovery of memories of various types, were found to be related to self-ratings and peer ratings of the subjects on such dimensions as optimism-pessimism, cheerfulness, and emotionality.

In a similar manner, Lloyd and Lishman (1975) found that clinically depressed patients retrieved memories of unpleasant experiences faster than those of pleasant experiences, whereas normals showed the opposite pattern. Teasdale and Fogarty (1979) confirmed these results with normals subjected to an experimental induction of depressed mood. A questionnaire study by Markus (1977, Experiment 1) indicates that individuals who define independence–dependence as an important part of their self-concepts are able to gain access to more memories of specific past experiences where they behaved in an independent or dependent manner than subjects who did not possess such self-schemata. These kinds of effects deserve further and more detailed exploration.

In the past, most research on autobiographical memory has focused on individuals' earliest recollection from childhood. There are, of course, good reasons for cognitive psychologists to be interested in early memories, inasmuch as the alleged "childhood amnesia" occurring around 5 to 7 years of age raises questions concerning the course of cognitive development (White & Pillemer, 1979). Interestingly, there is no convincing evidence from studies of humans that childhood amnesia is distinct from the ordinary forgetting that would occur in adults over a comparable period of time. An analogous phenomenon has been studied intensively in infrahuman species, however (Campbell & Spear, 1972; Spear, 1979), and this should serve to sustain our interest until the necessary research has been performed. But is there any reason for personality psychologists to be interested in this phenomenon?

Historically, the answer is "yes." Freud (1901) held that the poverty of childhood memories was due to the repression of preoedipal experiences and that the surface memories could be analyzed to reveal the latent primitive contents underlying them; Adler (1937; Ansbacher, 1947) held that the manifest content of early recollections represented the life-style (personality) of the individual. In addition to descriptive studies of early recollections (Dudycha & Dudycha, 1933a, 1933b, 1941; Waldfogel, 1948), there have been several attempts to investigate their personality correlates. Many of these research efforts have been hampered by the use of cumbersome coding schemes that attempt to cover the minutiae of psychoanalytic theory (Kramer, Ornstein, Whitman, & Baldridge, 1967; Langs, Rothenberg, Fishman, & Reiser, 1960; Mayman, 1968; Saul, Snyder, & Shepard, 1956). Somewhat more tractable have been the Adlerian attempts to relate surface features of these memories to general constructs such as anxiety and psychological security (Ansbacher, 1947; Mosak, 1969; Purcell, 1952).

New research on early recollections can proceed along a number of different lines. For example, the development of autobiographical memory would seem to be an important aspect of the emergence of the self-concept. Thus, cross-sectional and longitudinal studies are needed to document more convincingly the alleged poverty of childhood memory. Some measure of childhood amnesia would be expected on the basis of what is already known about memory development in childhood (Brown, 1975; Hagen, Jongeward, & Kail, 1975). However, Schachtel (1947) and Neisser (1962) have also suggested that the disruption in memory may be functionally tied to aspects of personality and social development, which entail radical changes in the schemata which guide cognitive activity. While viewing the problem from rather different vantage points, they both propose that the amnesia occurs because the adult schemata that provide the framework for retrieval and reconstruction efforts are incompatible with the encodings produced by the childlike schemata applied to the original episode. Thus we are led to view the phenomenon in a context encompassing both personality and cognitive change.

There are also individual differences in the quality of early memories that may repay examination. Some people have richly detailed, vivid, and involving memories; others have early recollections that are rather fragmentary, vague, and inert. Those of the latter type are strongly reminiscent of the "screen memories" described by Freud, and it would be interesting to relate them to neuroticism, anxiety, and other aspects of personality. Finally, a series of early recollections can be treated as fantasy material, much like a story written to a TAT card, which can be coded objectively and then examined for thematic continuities within the corpus of the individual's early recollections or related to other person variables and individual behavioral styles.

Within the wider field of autobiographical memories, two further types seem particularly relevant to personality psychologists: "flashbulb" and "involuntary" memories. Flashbulb memories are particularly vivid, detailed memories of some personal experience: widely shared examples include one's memory for first hearing of the assassinations of John F. Kennedy and Martin Luther King, but it is also clear that each individual possesses some flashbulb memories that are quite idiosyncratic. Brown and Kulik (1977) conducted a survey of personal memory for salient news events and found that the occurrence of a flashbulb memory for any particular event was correlated with the "consequentiality" of that event for the person. One extension of this research would be to conduct a survey of individuals' flashbulb memories, for public or private events, and relate these to such personality factors as plans, goals, and interests. Involuntary memories, as described by Proust in *The Remembrance of Things Past* (see also Salaman, 1970), seem to come to the person unbidden. Often he or she can recognize the environmental cue involved, but what is interesting about these memories is that they occur spontaneously, without requiring deliberate attempts at retrieval and reconstruction on his or her part. These, then, are memories that are "waiting to happen." The events involved must have been particularly important at the time and may continue to be related to the person's life and self-concept.

SOME QUESTIONS ABOUT PERSONALITY AND MEMORY

Each of the approaches previously outlined is particularly suited for answering certain questions, and at this point it seems more appropriate to practice methodological pluralism than to become method-bound. With a set of methods in hand, then, it is time to turn to some broad issues that require attention.

Some of these issues have to do with the general processes by which social and personal information is represented and handled within the cognitive system. This includes "semantic memory" questions concerning the structure and organization of schemata pertaining to the self, other people, and social situations; of equal importance are "episodic memory" questions pertaining to the way in which recollections about particular people and experiences are encoded and retrieved. Both kinds of questions can be addressed by methods that are extensions of procedures already established in the study of cognition and memory. My laboratory has been particularly interested in memories for specific personal experiences, including events transpiring during hypnosis (Kihlstrom & Evans,

1979), the features of adults' earliest recollections of childhood (Kihlstrom & Harackiewicz, 1980), and the retrieval of autobiographical memories in general (Chew & Kihlstrom, 1980). We are also increasingly interested in exploring the phenomenon of childhood amnesia and the nature of generalized memory representations concerning the self.

Individual differences are a prominent feature of the material encountered in these experiments—in the ability to dissociate memories or otherwise control retrieval, in the availability of different types of memories, the amount of detail and vividness characteristic of them, and in their content and emotional valence. Memories related to certain topics, or associated with particular emotions, may be more salient to some individuals than to others. What is accessible in memory, and the manner in which these recollections are reconstructed, may be related to the individual's self-concept or other personal constructs, as well as to his or her emotional state, expecbations, and goals. It is not necessary to adopt a static, traitlike conception of personality in these studies. It is probably more rewarding to examine features of memory for personal experiences and other people as they are affected by changes in the individual's situation as he or she perceives it. Of particular interest are those changes in social and autobiographical memory that accompany personality development and therapeutic change. From a cognitive-interactionist point of view, both entail the emergence of fundamentally new ways of construing oneself and the social world; these changes in schemata should have consequences for the encoding, retrieval, and reconstruction of relevant memories. In any event, it is of course insufficient simply to show that some feature of memory is related to some feature of personality. It is crucial to attempt at least some inquiry into the details of the underlying process.

It also seems important to determine if the effect is to be conceptualized as a change in memory proper—in the accessibility of memories, or in the character of their reconstruction—or in terms of what the person is willing to bring to mind and report and how he or she is willing to think about it. There are at least two separate issues here—one having to do with the possibility of changes in conscious awareness of particular memories, the other having to do with the consequences of biased reconstruction. The first issue is related to the encoding specificity principle and the distinction between availability and accessibility, both familiar in the memory literature. Research on hypnotic amnesia and hyperamnesia is relevant here because it dramatically illustrates a division in consciousness affecting the ability of the person to recall voluntarily something that is available in the memory system (Hilgard, 1962, 1977; Kihlstrom, 1980). The dissociative processes so revealed may also be placed in the service of personality. Similarly, the phenomena of childhood amnesia and state-dependent retention suggest that the social categories and emotional states active at the time of recall may determine what a person is able to remember.

The second issue is closely related to the questions raised by Bartlett (1932) in his studies of repeated reproduction and by Loftus (1975) in her studies of eyewitness testimony. Memories may remain accessible despite changes in particular personality variables, but their reconstruction may be altered markedly by the changed schemata. The consequences of reconstructive activity for later remembering are largely unknown. The reconstructed episode may not be preserved in the store of permanent memories or it may be encoded independent of the original trace; yet, again, the reconstruction may supplant the old trace entirely. Whether one or both (or more) versions of an event are available and accessible to recall will be an important factor in subsequent personality–memory interactions.

Finally, from the point of view of the personality psychologist, social and personal memory are mostly interesting for the contribution they make to the individual's ongoing behavior in the world. Clearly, one's perception of oneself, others, and social situations, as well as one's expectations concerning the outcomes of particular events and actions, will be determined in large part by his or her specific autobiographical memories and the generic social and personal knowledge that develops from them. In this way, the interaction of personality and memory will affect the individual's planning and execution of interpersonal behavior. Similarly, the availability of specific memories of particular events and acts may affect the person's response to role and situational demands on behavior, or evaluation of information that is apparently inconsistent with his or her expectations and self-concept. Of course, the person's emotional state, active schemata, cognitive style, and other personality characteristics themselves control the availability and accessibility of particular memories and the manner in which they are reconstructed at the time of their retrieval. And in the process of cognitive–behavioral therapeutic endeavors, memories that are consistent with the newly developed schemata may become more salient while inconsistent ones become less available. Finally, the percepts, corresponding behaviors, and their effects on the environment are encoded as new episodes in the cognitive system. Although their fate is ultimately determined by the vicissitudes of assimilation and accommodation, in principle they are available for reference in subsequent cognitive–behavioral episodes—thus completing the cycle of transactions that lie at the core of reciprocal determinism.

We do not possess answers to any of these questions yet, but we are now trying to go about the business of finding some answers. If most of these problems strike the reader as relevant to anyone interested in cognitive psychology, and not just cognitively oriented personality psychologists, this is intentional. The study of personality and memory draws on concepts and methods familiar in the study of cognition and memory generally. However, it is our firm hope that the questions raised from the point of view of personality, and the answers forthcoming from the research, will prove interesting and useful to cognitive psychologists as well. From our point of view, the goal of the enterprise is a comprehensive account of human behavior and experience, to which both cognitive and personality psychologists, as well as others, must make contributions.

ACKNOWLEDGMENTS

Preparation of this chapter was supported in part by Grants #MH 29951 and 33737 from the National Institute of Mental Health, United States Public Health Service. I thank Nancy Cantor, Reid Hastie, and Susan Jo Russell for their comments during the preparation of this chapter. A special note of appreciation goes to the members of my research seminar—Clinton Anderson, Heather Brenneman, Beverly Chew, Judy Harackiewicz, and Bill Nasby—whose ideas, criticisms, and research have helped me greatly in beginning to understand this topic.

REFERENCES

Adler, A. The significance of early recollections. *International Journal of Individual Psychology,* 1937, *3,* 283–287.

Anderson, J. R., & Bower, G. H. Recognition and retrieval processes in free recall. *Psychological Review,* 1972, *79,* 97–123.

Ansbacher, H. L. Adler's place today in the psychology of memory. *Journal of Personality,* 1947, *3,* 197–207.

Atkinson, J. W. The achievement motive and recall of interrupted and completed tasks. *Journal of Experimental Psychology,* 1953, *46,* 381–390.

Atkinson, R. C., & Shiffrin, R. M. Human memory: A proposed system and its control processes. In K. C. Spence & J. T. Spence (Eds.), *The psychology of learning and motivation* (Vol. 2). New York: Academic Press, 1968.

Bach, M. J., & Underwood, B. J. Developmental changes in memory attributes. *Journal of Educational Psychology,* 1970, *61,* 292–296.

Bahrick, H. P., Bahrick, P. O., & Wittlinger, R. P. Fifty years of memory for names and faces: A cross-sectional approach. *Journal of Experimental Psychology: General,* 1975, *1,* 54–75.

Bandura, A. Behavior theory and the models of man. *American Psychologist,* 1974, *29,* 859–869.

Bartlett, F. C. *Remembering: A study in experimental and social psychology.* Cambridge, England: Cambridge University Press, 1932.

Baxter, M. F., Yamada, K., & Washburn, M. F. Directed recall of pleasant and unpleasant experiences. *American Journal of Psychology,* 1917, *28,* 155–157.

Beck, A. Cognitive therapy: Nature and relation to behavior therapy. *Behavior Therapy,* 1970, *1,* 184–200.

Bell, P. A., & Byrne, D. Repression-sensitization. In H. London & J. E. Exner (Eds.), *Dimensions of personality.* New York: Wiley-Interscience, 1978.

Bem, S. L. *Gender-schema theory: A cognitive account of sex-typing.* Paper presented at the 88th annual meeting of the American Psychological Association, Montreal, September 1980.

Block, J. Advancing the psychology of personality: Paradigmatic shift or improving the quality of research. In D. Magnusson & N. S. Endler (Eds.), *Personality at the crossroads: Current issues in interactional psychology.* Hillsdale, N.J.: Lawrence Erlbaum Associates, 1977.

Bousfield, W. A., & Cohen, B. H. Masculinity–femininity in the free recall of a categorized stimulus word list. *Perceptual and Motor Skills,* 1956, *6,* 159–165.

Bower, G. H. A multicomponent theory of the memory trace. In K. W. Spence & J. T. Spence (Eds.), *The psychology of learning and motivation* (Vol. 1). New York: Academic Press, 1967.

Bower, G. H. Organizational factors in memory. *Cognitive Psychology,* 1970, *1,* 18–46.

Bower, G. H., & Gilligan, S. G. Remembering information related to one's self. *Journal of Research in Personality,* 1979, *13,* 404–419.

Bower, G. H., Monteiro, K. P., & Gilligan, S. G. Emotional mood as a context for learning and recall. *Journal of Verbal Learning and Verbal Behavior*, 1978, *17*, 573-585.

Bowers, K. S. Situationism in psychology: An analysis and a critique. *Psychological Review*, 1973, *80*, 307-336.

Brown, A. L. The development of memory: Knowing, knowing about knowing, and knowing how to know. In H. W. Reese (Ed.), *Advances in child development and behavior* (Vol. 10). New York: Academic Press, 1975.

Brown, R., & Kulik, J. Flashbulb memories. *Cognition*, 1977, *5*, 73-99.

Butterfield, E. C. The interruption of tasks: Methodological, factual, and theoretical issues. *Psychological Bulletin*, 1964, *62*, 309-322.

Campbell, B. A., & Spear, N. E. Ontogeny of memory. *Psychological Review*, 1972, *79*, 215-236.

Cantor, N. Perceptions of situations: Situation prototypes and person–situation prototypes. In D. Magnusson (Ed.), *The situation: An interactional perspective*. Hillsdale, N.J.: Lawrence Erlbaum Associates, 1980.

Cantor, N., & Mischel, W. Prototypes in person perception. In L. Berkowitz (Ed.), *Advances in experimental social psychology* (Vol. 12). New York: Academic Press, 1979.

Chew, B. R., & Kihlstrom, J. F. *Retrieval of remote and recent autobiographical memories.* Manuscript in preparation, 1980.

Craik, F. I. M., & Lockhart, R. S. Levels of processing: A framework for memory research. *Journal of Verbal Learning and Verbal Behavior*, 1972, *11*, 671-684.

Cronbach, L. J., & Meehl, P. E. Construct validity in psychological tests. *Psychological Bulletin*, 1955, *52*, 281-308.

Crovitz, H. F., & Quina-Holland, L. Proportion of episodic memories from early childhood by years of age. *Bulletin of the Psychonomic Society*, 1976, *7*, 61-62.

Crovitz, H. F., & Schiffman, H. Frequency of episodic memories as a function of their age. *Bulletin of the Psychonomic Society*, 1974, *4*, 517-518.

Crowder, R. B. *Principles of learning and memory*. Hillsdale, N.J.: Lawrence Erlbaum Associates, 1976.

Dudycha, G. J., & Dudycha, M. M. Adolescents' memories of preschool experiences. *Journal of Genetic Psychology*, 1933, *42*, 468-480. (a)

Dudycha, G. J., & Dudycha, M. M. Some factors and characteristics in childhood memories. *Child Development*, 1933, *4*, 265-278. (b)

Dudycha, G. J., & Dudycha, M. M. Childhood memories: A review of the literature. *Psychological Bulletin*, 1941, *38*, 668-682.

Ebbinghaus, H. E. *Memory: A contribution to experimental psychology*. New York: Dover, 1964. (Originally published, 1884.)

Eich, J. E. State-dependent retrieval of information in human episodic memory. In I. M. Birnbaum & E. S. Parker (Eds.), *Alcohol and human memory*. Hillsdale, N.J.: Lawrence Erlbaum Associates, 1977.

Epstein, S. The self-concept revisited, or, a theory of a theory. *American Psychologist*, 1973, *28*, 404-416.

Epstein, S. The stability of behavior: I. On predicting most of the people much of the time. *Journal of Personality and Social Psychology*, 1979, *37*, 1097-1126.

Erdelyi, M. H., & Goldberg, B. Let's not sweep repression under the rug: Toward a cognitive psychology of repression. In J. F. Kihlstrom & F. J. Evans (Eds.), *Functional disorders of memory*. Hillsdale, N.J.: Lawrence Erlbaum Associates, 1979.

Eriksen, C. W. Psychological defenses and "ego strength" in recall of completed and incomplete tasks. *Journal of Abnormal and Social Psychology*, 1954, *49*, 45-50.

Eysenck, H. J. Personality, learning and "anxiety." In H. J. Eysenck (Ed.), *Handbook of abnormal psychology*. London: Pitman, 1973.

Eysenck, H. J. Personality and factor analysis: A reply to Guilford. *Psychological Bulletin*, 1977, *84*, 405-411.

Eysenck, M. W. *Human memory: Theory, research, and individual differences*. London Pergamon Press, 1977.

Fisher, D. F., & Keen, S. L. Verbal recall as a function of personality characteristics. *Journal of Genetic Psychology*, 1972, *120*, 83-92.

Freud, S. *The psychopathology of everyday life*. In J. Strachey (Ed.), *The standard edition of the psychological works of Sigmund Freud* (Vol. 4-5). London: Hogarth, 1953. (Originally published, 1900.)

Freud, S. *The psychopathology of everyday life*. In J. Strachey (Ed.), *The stan dard edition of the complete psychological works of Sigmund Freud* (Vol. 6). London: Hogarth, 1960. (Originally published, 1901.)

Freud, S. Repression. In J. Strachey (Ed.), *The standard edition of the complete psychological works of Sigmund Freud* (Vol. 14). London: Hogarth, 1957. (Originally published, 1915.)

Gomulicki, B. R. Individual differences in recall. *Journal of Personality*, 1956, *24*, 781-813.

Goodenough, D. R. The role of individual differences in field dependence as a factor in learning and memory. *Psychological Bulletin*, 1976, *83*, 675-694.

Guilford, J. P. Factors and factors of personality. *Psychological Bulletin*, 1975, *82*, 802-814.

Hagen, J. W., Jongeward, R. H., & Kail, R. V. Cognitive perspectives on the development of memory. In H. W. Reese (Ed.), *Advances in child development and behavior* (Vol. 10). New York: Academic Press, 1975.

Hastie, R. Memory for behavioral information that confirms or contradicts a personality impression. In R. Hastie, T. F. Ostrom, E. Ebbesen, R. Wyer, D. L. Hamilton, & D. Carlston (Eds.), *Person memory: The cognitive basis of social perception*. Hillsdale, N.J.: Lawrence Erlbaum Associates, 1980. (a)

Hastie, R. Schematic principles in human memory. In E. T. Higgins, P. Hermann, & M. P. Zanna (Eds.), *Social cognition: The Ontario symposium*. Hillsdale, N.J.: Lawrence Erlbaum Associates, 1980. (b)

Hastie, R., & Carlston, D. Theoretical issues in person memory. In R. Hastie, T. F. Ostrom, E. Ebesen, R. Hyer, D. L. Hamilton, & D. Carlston (Eds.), *Person memory: The cognitive basis of social perception*. Hillsdale, N.J.: Lawrence Erlbaum Associates, 1980.

Hastie, R., Loftus, E. F., Penrod, S., & Winkler, J. D. *The reliability of eyewitness testimony: Review of the psychological literature*. Manuscript in preparation, 1980.

Hastie, R., Ostrom, T. F., Ebbesen, E., Wyer, R., Hamilton, D. L., & Carlston, D. (Eds.), *Person memory: The cognitive basis of social perception*. Hillsdale, N.J.: Lawrence Erlbaum Associates, 1980.

Hilgard, E. R. What becomes of the input from the stimulus? In C. W. Eriksen (Ed.), *Behavior and awareness: A symposium of research and interpretation*. Durham, N.C.: Duke University Press, 1962.

Hilgard, E. R. *Divided consciousness: Multiple controls in human thought and action*. New York: Wiley-Interscience, 1977.

Holmes, D. S. Investigations of repression: Differential recall of material experimentally or naturally associated with ego threat. *Psychological Bulletin*, 1974, *81*, 632-653.

Holzman, P. S., & Gardner, R. W. Leveling-sharpening and memory organization. *Journal of Abnormal and Social Psychology*, 1960, *61*, 176-180.

Hunt, E., Frost, N., & Lunneborg,C. Individual differences in cognition: A new approach to intelligence. In G. H. Bower (Ed.), *Advances in learning and motivation* (Vol. 7). New York: Academic Press, 1973.

Isen, A. M., Shalker, T. E., Clark, M., & Karp, L. Affect, accessibility of material in memory, and behavior: A cognitive loop? *Journal of Personality and Social Psychology*, 1978, *36*, 1-12.

Jackson, D. N. The dynamics of structured personality tests: 1971. *Psychological Review*, 1971, *78*, 229-248.

Jacoby, L. L., & Craik, F. I. M. Effects of elaboration of processing at encoding and retrieval: Trace distinctiveness and recovery of initial context. In L. S. Cermak, & F. I. M. Craik (Eds.), *Levels of processing and human memory*. Hillsdale, N.J.: Lawrence Erlbaum Associates, 1979.

Jenkins, J. J. Remember that old theory of memory? Well, forget it! *American Psychologist*, 1974, *29*, 785-795.

Johnson, J. H. Memory and personality: An information processing approach. *Journal of Research in Personality*, 1974, *8*, 1-32.

Kail, R. V., & Levine, L. E. Encoding processes and sex-role preferences. *Journal of Experimental Child Psychology*, 1976, *21*, 256-263.

Kelly, G. A. *The psychology of personal constructs*. New York: Norton, 1955.

Kihlstrom, J. F. Posthypnotic amnesia for recently learned material: Interactions with "episodic" and "semantic" memory. *Cognitive Psychology*, 1980, *12*, 227-251.

Kihlstrom, J. F., & Evans, F. J. Memory retrieval processes during posthypnotic amnesia. Ir. J. F. Kihlstrom & F. J. Evans (Eds.), *Functional disorders of memory*. Hillsdale, N.J.: Lawrence Erlbaum Associates, 1979.

Kihlstrom, J. F., & Harackiewicz, J. *The earliest recollection of childhood: A new survey*. Manuscript in preparation, 1980.

Koh, S. D. Remembering of verbal materials by schizophrenic young adults. In S. Schwartz (Ed.), *Language and cognition in schizophrenia*. Hillsdale, N.J.: Lawrence Erlbaum Associates, 1978.

Kramer, M., Ornstein, P. H., Whitman, R. M., & Baldridge, B. J. The contribution of early memories and dreams to the diagnostic process. *Comprehensive Psychiatry*, 1967, *8*, 344-374.

Kuiper, N. A., & Rogers, T. B. Encoding of personal information: Self-other differences. *Journal of Personality and Social Psychology*, 1979, *37*, 499-514.

Langs, R. J., Rothenberg, M. B., Fishman, J. R., & Reiser, M. F. A method for the clinical and theoretical study of the earliest memory. *Archives of General Psychiatry*, 1960, *3*, 523-534.

Linton, M. Memory for real-world events. In D. A. Norman, D. E. Rummelhart, & the LNR Research Group. *Explorations in cognition*. San Francisco, Freeman, 1975.

Linton, M. Real world memory after six years: An *in vivo* study of very long term memory. In M. M. Gruneberg, P. E. Morris, & R. N. Sykes (Eds.), *Practical aspects of memory*. New York: Academic Press, 1978.

Lloyd, G. G., & Lishman, W. A. Effect of depression on the speed of recall of pleasant and unpleasant experiences. *Psychological Medicine*, 1975, *5*, 173-180.

Loftus, E. F. Leading questions and the eyewitness report. *Cognitive Psychology*, 1975, *7*, 560-572.

MacKinnon, D., & Dukes, W. Repression. In L. Postman (Ed.), *Psychology in the making*. New York: Knopf, 1962.

Mahoney, M. Reflections of the cognitive-learning trend in psychotherapy. *American Psychologist*, 1977, *32*, 5-13.

Mandler, G. *Mind and emotion*. New York: Wiley, 1975.

Markus, H. Self-schemata and processing information about the self. *Journal of Personality and Social Psychology*, 1977, *35*, 63-78.

Matlin, M., & Stang, D. *The Polyanna principle: Selectivity in language, memory, and thought*. Cambridge, Mass.: Schenckman, 1978.

Maw, W. H., & Maw, E. W. Information recognition by children with high and low curiosity. *Education Research Bulletin*, 1961, *40*, 197-201.

Mayman, M. Early memories and character structure. *Journal of Projective Techniques*, 1968, *32*, 303-316.

McClelland, J. L. On the time relations of mental processes: A framework for analyzing processes in cascade. *Psychological Review*, 1979, *86*, 287-330.

Meichenbaum, D. *Cognitive-behavior modification: An integrative approach.* New York: Plenum, 1977.

Melton, A. W. Implications of short-term memory for a general theory of memory. *Journal of Verbal Learning and Verbal Behavior,* 1963, *2,* 1–21.

Meltzer, H. The present status of experimental studies on the relationship of feeling to memory. *Psychological Review,* 1930, *37,* 124–139.

Messick, S., & Damarin, R. Cognitive style and memory for faces. *Journal of Abnormal and Social Psychology,* 1964, *69,* 313–318.

Messick, S., & Fritzky, F. J. Dimensions of analytic attitude in cognition and personality. *Journal of Personality,* 1963, *31,* 347–370.

Miller, G. A., Galanter, E., & Pribram, K. H. *Plans and the structure of behavior.* New York: Holt, Rinehart & Winston, 1960.

Mischel, W. Towards a cognitive-social learning reconceptualization of personality. *Psychological Review,* 1973, *80,* 252–283.

Mischel, W. On the interface of cognition and personality: Beyond the person–situation debate. *American Psychologist,* 1979, *34,* 740–754.

Mischel, W., Ebbesen, E. B., & Zeiss, A. R. Selective attention to the self: Situational and dispositional determinants. *Journal of Personality and Social Psychology,* 1973, *27,* 129–142.

Mischel, W., Ebbesen, E. B., & Zeiss, A. R. Determinants of selective memory about the self. *Journal of Consulting and Clinical Psychology,* 1976, *44,* 92–103.

Monteiro, K. P., & Bower, G. H. *Using hypnotic mood induction to study the effect of mood on memory.* (Hypnosis Research Memorandum No. 155.) Stanford, Calif.: Laboratory of Hypnosis Research, Department of Psychology, Stanford University, 1979.

Morgan, E., Mull, H. K., & Washburn, M. F. An attempt to test moods or temperaments of cheerfulness and depression by directed recall of emotionally toned experiences. *American Journal of Psychology,* 1919, *30,* 302–304.

Mosak, H. H. Early recollections: Evaluation of some recent research. *Journal of Individual Psychology,* 1969, *25,* 56–63.

Nasby, W. *An experimental approach to the study of affect and memory in children.* Unpublished doctoral dissertation, Harvard University, 1980.

Neisser, U. Cultural and cognitive discontinuity. In T. E. Gladwin & W. Sturtevant (Eds.), *Anthropology and human behavior.* Washington, D.C.: Anthropological Society of Washington, 1962.

Neisser, U. *Cognitive psychology.* New York: Appleton-Century-Crofts, 1967.

Neisser, U. *Cognition and reality: Principles and implications of cognitive psychology.* San Francisco: Freeman, 1976.

Neisser, U. Memory: What are the important questions? In M. M. Gruneberg, P. E. Morris, & R. N. Sykes (Eds.), *Practical aspects of memory.* New York: Academic Press, 1978.

Neisser, U., & Hupcey, J. A Sherlockian experiment. *Cognition,* 1974, *3,* 307–311.

Paul, I. H. Studies in remembering: The reproduction of connected and extended verbal material. *Psychological Issues,* 1959, *1,* Whole No. 2.

Owens, J., Bower, G. H., & Black, J. B. The "soap opera" effect in story recall. *Memory and Cognition,* 1979, *7,* 185–191.

Pettinati, H. M., & Evans, F. J. Posthypnotic amnesia: Evaluation of selective recall of successful experiences. *International Journal of Clinical and Experimental Hypnosis,* 1978, *26,* 317–329.

Purcell, K. Memory and psychological security. *Journal of Abnormal and Social Psychology,* 1952, *47,* 433–440.

Rapaport, D. *Emotions and memory.* Baltimore: Williams & Wilkins, 1942.

Reed, G. Everyday anomalies of recall and recognition. In J. F. Kihlstrom & F. J. Evans (Eds.), *Functional disorders of memory.* Hillsdale, N.J.: Lawrence Erlbaum Associates, 1979.

Riley, D. A. Memory for form. In L. Postman (Ed.), *Psychology in the making.* New York: Knopf, 1962.

Robinson, J. A. Sampling autobiographical memory. *Cognitive Psychology*, 1976, *8*, 578–595.

Rogers, R. B. Self-reference in memory: Recognition of personality items. *Journal of Research in Personality*, 1977, *11*, 295–305.

Rogers, T. B., Kuiper, N. A., & Kirker, W. S. Self-reference and the encoding of personal information. *Journal of Personality and Social Psychology*, 1977, *35*, 677–688.

Rogers, T. B., Rogers, P. J., & Kuiper, N. A. Evidence for the self as a cognitive prototype: The "false alarms effect." *Personality and Social Psychology Bulletin*, 1979, *5*, 53–56.

Rosenberg, S., & Sedlak, A. Structural representations of implicit personality theory. In L. Berkowitz (Ed.), *Advances in experimental social psychology* (Vol. 6). New York: Academic Press, 1972.

Rubin, D. C. Very long-term memory for prose and verse. *Journal of Verbal Learning and Verbal Behavior*, 1977, *16*, 611–622.

Salaman, E. *A collection of moments.* London: Longman, 1970.

Saul, L., Snyder, T., & Sheppard, E. On earliest memories. *Psychoanalytic Quarterly*, 1956, *25*, 228–237.

Schachtel, E. G. On memory and childhood amnesia. *Psychiatry*, 1947, *10*, 1–26.

Schneider, D. J. Implicit personality theory: A review. *Psychological Bulletin*, 1973, *79*, 294–309.

Schneider, D. J., Hastorf, A. H., & Ellsworth, P. C. *Person perception* (2nd ed.). Reading, Mass.: Addison–Wesley, 1979.

Schonfield, D., & Stones, M. J. Remembering and aging. In J. F. Kihlstrom & F. J. Evans (Eds.), *Functional disorders of memory.* Hillsdale, N.J.: Lawrence Erlbaum Associates, 1979.

Spear, N. E. Experimental analysis of infantile amnesia. In J. F. Kihlstrom & F. J. Evans (Eds.), *Functional disorders of memory.* Hillsdale, N.J.: Lawrence Erlbaum Associates, 1979.

Squire, L. R., & Slater, P. C. Forgetting in very long-term memory as assessed by an improved questionnaire technique. *Journal of Experimental Psychology: Human Learning and Memory*, 1975, *104*, 50–54.

Taylor, S. E., & Crocker, J. Schematic bases of social information processing. In E. T. Higgins, P. Hermann, & M. P. Zanna (Eds.), *Social cognition: The Ontario symposium.* Hillsdale, N.J.: Lawrence Erlbaum Associates, 1980.

Teasdale, J. D., & Fogarty, S. J. Differential effects of induced mood on retrieval of pleasant and unpleasant events from episodic memory. *Journal of Abnormal Psychology*, 1979, *88*, 248–257.

Tulving, E. Theoretical issues in free recall. In T. R. Dixon & D. L. Horton (Eds.), *Verbal behavior and general behavior theory.* Englewood Cliffs, N.J.: Prentice-Hall, 1968.

Tulving, E. Episodic and semantic memory. In E. Tulving & W. Donaldson (Eds.), *Organization of memory.* New York: Academic Press, 1972.

Tulving, E., & Thomson, D. M. Encoding specificity and retrieval processes in episodic memory. *Psychological Review*, 1973, *80*, 352–373.

Tulving, E., & Watkins, M. J. Structure of memory traces. *Psychological Review*, 1975, *82*, 261–275.

Underwood, B. J. False recognition produced by implicit verbal responses. *Journal of Experimental Psychology*, 1965, *70*, 122–129.

Underwood, B. J. Attributes of memory. *Psychological Review*, 1969, *76*, 559–573.

Underwood, B. J. Individual differences as a crucible in theory construction. *American Psychologist*, 1975, *30*, 128–134.

Waldfogel, S. The frequency and affective character of childhood memories. *Psychological Monographs.* 1948, *62* (Whole No. 291).

Walker, E. L. Action decrement and its relation to learning. *Psychological Review*, 1958, *65*, 417–429.

Warrington, E. K., & Sanders, H. I. The fate of old memories. *Quarterly Journal of Experimental Psychology*, 1971, *23*, 432–442.

Washburn, M. F., Giang, F., Ives, M., & Pollock, M. Memory revival of emotions as a test of emotional and phlegmatic temperaments. *American Journal of Psychology*, 1925, *36*, 456–459.

Washburn, M. F., Harding, L., Simmons, H., & Tomlinson, D. Further experiments on directed recall as a test of cheerful and depressed temperaments. *American Journal of Psychology*, 1925, *36*, 454–456.

Watkins, M. J., & Tulving, E. Episodic memory: When recognition fails. *Journal of Experimental Psychology: General*, 1975, *1*, 5–29.

Weiner, B. The effects of motivation on the availability and retrieval of memory traces. *Psychological Bulletin*, 1966, *65*, 24–37.

Weingartner, H., Miller, H., & Murphy, D. L. Mood-state dependent retrieval of word associations. *Journal of Abnormal Psychology*, 1977, *86*, 276–284.

White, S. H., & Pillemer, D. B. Childhood amnesia and the development of a socially accessible memory system. In J. F. Kihlstrom & F. J. Evans (Eds.), *Functional disorders of memory*. Hillsdale, N.J.: Lawrence Erlbaum Associates, 1979.

Wickelgren, W. A. The long and short of memory. *Psychological Bulletin*, 1973, *80*, 425–438.

Wickens, D. D. Characteristics of word encoding. In A. W. Melton & E. Martin (Eds.), *Coding processes in human memory*. Washington, D.C.: Winston, 1972.

Wiggins, J. S. *Personality and prediction: Principles of personality assessment*. Reading, Mass.: Addison-Wesley, 1974.

Wiggins, J. S. A psychological taxonomy of trait-descriptive terms: The interpersonal domain. *Journal of Personality and Social Psychology*, 1979, *37*, 395–412.

Zajonc, R. B. *Feeling and thinking: Preferences need no inferences. American Psychologist*, 1980, *35*, 151–175.

Zeigarnik, B. Das Behalten von erledigten und unerledigten Handlugen. *Psychologische Forschungen*, 1927, *9*, 1–85.

Zeller, A. An experimental analogue of repression: I. Historical summary. *Psychological Bulletin*, 1950, *47*, 39–51.

SOCIAL JUDGMENT

6 Social Stereotypes and Social Judgment

Eugene Borgida
University of Minnesota

Anne Locksley
New York University

Nancy Brekke
University of Minnesota

Psychological theories of social stereotypes emphasized their possible motivational and affective determinants for years (Adorno, Frenkel-Brunswick, Levinson, & Sanford, 1950; Allport, 1954; Sherif, 1956). This emphasis led to research on personality and situational variables that would be predictive of extreme and aberrant social attitudes and behavior. Much of this research, however, has proven to be either empirically invalid or limited in explanatory power (Brown, 1965; Christie & Jahoda, 1954; Hamilton, 1976; Tajfel, 1970). More recently, social stereotypes have been investigated within the general theoretical framework of social cognition (Ashmore & Del Boca, 1979; Hamilton, 1980; McCauley & Stitt, 1978; Ruble & Ruble, 1980; Snyder & Uranowitz, 1978; Taylor, Fiske, Etcoff, & Ruderman, 1978). From this perspective, social stereotypes are viewed as products of normal everyday cognitive processes of social categorization, social inference, and social judgment and so may be studied in terms of general principles of human cognitive activity.

To date, social-cognitive research on stereotypes has concentrated primarily on two basic problems: (1) how social stereotypes are formed; and (2) why social stereotypes persist even though they are more often than not objectively erroneous. Current studies of these problems have attempted to determine the nature of the cognitive processes involved in each of these phenomena.

153

With respect to the first problem, Taylor (in press), for example, suggests that social stereotypes are, in effect, categories for sorting people according to their membership in social groups and therefore have functional utility for simplifying and organizing complex social information. Taylor and her colleagues (Taylor et al., 1978) demonstrated that people spontaneously use social categories when processing information about individuals. Other studies have found that similarly categorized stimuli, whether social or nonsocial, are judged to be similar on other conceptually unrelated dimensions as well (Brewer, 1979; Hamilton & Gifford, 1976; Locksley, Ortiz, & Hepburn, in press; Tajfel & Wilkes, 1963). The results of these studies suggest that the effects of categorization on perceived similarity of group members may contribute to the tendency to generalize attributes across group members characteristic of social stereotyping. Hamilton (1976; Hamilton & Gifford, 1976) demonstrated a related effect of social categorization on the formation of stereotypic impressions of social groups. He found that subjects overestimate the correlation between social categories and categories of behavior and personality traits that share some feature or quality with the social category. An example of this effect is the stereotypic overestimation of the proportion of black persons engaging in criminal behavior. Black persons are distinctive by virtue of their minority status, and criminal behavior is distinctive by virtue of its socially deviant status.

Other social-cognitive studies have addressed the question of why, once formed, social stereotypes persist. Why don't people gradually realize that stereotypes represent erroneous generalizations? Snyder (in press) suggests several reasons why people can continue to believe in stereotypes of social groups even when those stereotypes are objectively invalid. One reason is that a person's stereotypes can guide his or her social interaction with a member of the stereotyped group in such a way as to induce the member to behave in ways consistent with the stereotype (Snyder & Swann, 1978; Snyder, Tanke, & Berscheid, 1977; Word, Zanna, & Cooper, 1974). Thus stereotypes can create their own apparent behavioral confirmation. Other factors contributing to the persistence of social stereotypes are general cognitive biases in memory processes. Hepburn (1979) demonstrated that stereotypic behavior is more cognitively available or easier to recall than neutral behavior. To the extent that people rely on availability or ease of recall to estimate the frequency of observed behavior (Tversky & Kahneman, 1973), the actual occurrence of stereotypic behavior will be overestimated in retrospect. Thus people will have the subjective experience of remembering more confirmatory instances of social stereotypes than actually occurred. In a related vein, Snyder and Uranowitz (1978) found that previously encountered information about a person can be selectively "reconstructed" in memory to enhance or confirm current stereotypic impressions of the person.

These studies indicate that ordinary human cognitive processes of organizing and comprehending the social world are implicated in the formation and persistence of social stereotypes. Along with a shift in emphasis from motivational and affective determinants to cognitive or information-processing determinants, the social-cognitive approach has shifted our conceptualization of stereotypes from examples of irrational, unusual social beliefs to examples of normal, everyday social beliefs. From this perspective, social stereotypes are regarded as cognitive products of human social interaction.

A third problem that has not yet been investigated from the social-cognitive perspective is the determination of conditions under which social stereotypes actively influence social judgments. That people form beliefs about characteristics of social groups has been amply documented by years of stereotype assessment research (Brigham, 1971; Katz & Braly, 1933). The question is, under what conditions do these stereotypic beliefs affect judgments about individual members of stereotyped groups? This problem is crucial to understanding social–cognitive processes of stereotyping, and constitutes the focus of this chapter.

Prevalent notions about the power of stereotypes and expectancy effects have contributed to the assumption that people who have stereotypic beliefs use them, consciously, intentionally, or otherwise, in encounters with members of stereotyped groups. Social behavior is often sufficiently ambiguous to permit a wide latitude of interpretation and, thus, may be easily assimilated to stereotypic expectations. Given these assumptions, research on the problem of determining conditions under which social stereotypes affect social judgments may seem either unnecessary or theoretically uninteresting. After all, studies have demonstrated effects of social stereotypes on social judgments (Snyder, Tanke, & Berscheid, 1977; Snyder & Uranowitz, 1978). There are, however, a number of studies in which predicted effects of stereotypes have *not* been obtained. Although such null effects are difficult to evaluate theoretically, we argue in this chapter that sufficient evidence has accumulated to preclude experimental error as a plausible explanation. We argue further that there are systematic differences between those studies that report stereotypic effects on social judgment and those that report null results. Furthermore, we present a theoretical framework that yields predictions about the conditions under which social stereotypes affect judgments about individual members of stereotyped groups. We begin with an example of two social judgment studies of a well-documented stereotype that did not obtain predicted effects of stereotypes.

A Social Judgment Study of Sex Stereotypes

Consider the robustness of sex stereotypes. Sex stereotypes have been measured off and on for almost thirty years, and the results have been fairly consistent. Different studies of sex stereotypes have all used a similar assessment format. In general, subjects have been presented with a list of personality attributes and asked to rate the extent to which each attribute is characteristic of the typical man and the typical woman. The attributes receiving significantly different mean ratings have been conceptually similar across time and across studies. In essence, the typical man is described as more assertive, active, objective, rational, and competent than the typical woman; and the typical woman is described as more passive, emotional, submissive, compassionate, and irrational than the typical man (Bem, 1974; Broverman, Vogel, Broverman, Clarkson, & Rosenkrantz, 1972; McKee & Sherriffs, 1957; Sherriffs & McKee, 1957; Spence & Helm-reich, 1978). Thus stereotypic beliefs about sex differences have been well documented and appear to be relatively stable.

The results of these studies suggest that people treat an individual's sex as a source of probabilistic information about his or her personality characteristics. Given prevalent assumptions about the power of stereotypes and expectancy effects, one would predict that knowledge of an individual's sex as well as information about his or her behavior would affect sex-associated trait attributions to that person. For example, assertive behavior on the part of a man is consistent with sex stereotypic expectations, and so should be attributed to his enduring personality characteristics. Assertive behavior on the part of a woman is inconsistent with sex stereotypic expectations (or less probable), and thus would be less likely to elicit assertive trait attributions than a man's assertive behavior.

Locksley, Borgida, Brekke, and Hepburn (in press) conducted an experiment that provided a sensitive test of this hypothesis. Subjects read a purportedly real, first-person account of a college student's behavior in three ordinary problem situations. The trait characteristic of the behavior was systematically varied along a dimension that is a salient, central, and stable component of sex stereotypes: assertiveness/passivity. Information about the target's behavior was fully crossed with information about the target's sex, so that in two versions of the account the target's behavior was sex-stereotypically consistent (a male whose behavior was consistently assertive or a female whose behavior was consistently passive) and in two other versions of the account the target's behavior was sex-stereotypically inconsistent (a male whose behavior was consistently passive or a female whose behavior was consistently assertive).

After reading through the account once, subjects returned a full 24 hours later to fill out a questionnaire assessing their predictions of the target's behavior in four novel problem situations (which subjects were led to believe had actually occurred), and their impressions of the target's personality in terms of a set of sex stereotype trait dimensions. The delay between stimulus presentation and assessment of subjects' predictions and impressions of the target was intended to allow the immediate impact of the behavioral information to fade in memory.

An independent panel of judges from the same subject population rated the responses to the behavior prediction task for the degree of attributed masculinity and attributed femininity on a six-point scale. Subjects' ratings of the target were averaged across the 20 stereotypic masculine traits and also across the 20 stereotypic feminine traits from the Bem Sex Role Inventory (BSRI) (Bem,

TABLE 6.1
Effects of Target's Sex and Behavior on Subjects' Impressions
of the Target's Personality[a]

	Source of Effect		
	Sex	Behavior	Sex by Behavior
Attributed masculinity	3.51(1,173)	21.87(1,173)[b]	83(1,173)
Attributed femininity	.66(1,140)	19.07(1,140)[b]	.00(1,140)
Rated masculinity	2.01(1,179)	115.13(1,179)[b]	.03(1,179)
Rated femininity	2.25(1,177)	27.62(1,177)[b]	.03(1,177)

[a] F-tests are presented in cells with accompanying degrees of freedom in parentheses.
[b] $p < .001$.

1974). The possible range of these scores was one to seven. Table 6.1 presents the results of analyses of variance on these dependent measures.

The second column of Table 6.1 shows that subjects did use information about the target's behavior to form impressions of his or her personality and to predict his or her behavior in novel situations. When predicting and explaining the target's behavior, subjects in the assertive target conditions characterized the target as less feminine ($M = 3.47$) and as more masculine ($M = 3.80$) than subjects in the passive target conditions ($M = 3.76$, $M = 3.45$, respectively). Furthermore, assertive targets received more masculine ratings on the BSRI masculinity scale ($M = 4.02$) than passive targets ($M = 2.42$).[1] Also, the assertive target was rated in a less feminine direction on the BSRI femininity scale ($M = 2.62$) than the passive target ($M = 3.22$). Thus information about the target's behavior had considerable impact on subjects' inferences about the target's unobserved behavior and personality characteristics.

In contrast, the first column of Table 6.1 shows that information about the target's sex had no effect on subjects' predictions or on subjects' ratings of the target's personality characteristics. The third column of Table 6.1 shows that information about the target's sex did not affect subjects' reliance on behavioral information for the prediction and rating tasks. Regardless of whether the target's behavior was consistent or inconsistent with sex stereotypic expectations, subjects' inferences about his or her personality were apparently based entirely on behavioral information.

It could be argued that the trait manipulation overwhelmed effects of sex because the target was so behaviorally consistent across three situations. In

___

[1]The size of this effect [$F(1, 179) = 115.23$, $p < .001$] may be attributed to the fact that many of the trait items on the scale are practically synonymous with the term "assertiveness" (e.g., aggressive, assertive, dominant, forceful, strong personality, willing to take a stand, willing to take risks).

reality, of course, behavior is not so trait-consistent, and sex stereotypes may lead people to infer more consistency in sex-associated traits than they actually observe. A second experiment conducted by, but not reported in, Locksley et al. (in press) tested this possibility, using stimulus materials from the previous study with two modifications: (1) Only the female stimulus person versions of the transcript were used. (2) Transcripts were altered to reduce the cross-situational consistency of the assertive and passive stimulus persons. There were two versions of the account. In one version the female target behaved assertively in one situation and passively in the other two situations; in the second version the female target behaved passively in one situation and assertively in the other two problem situations. The order of the inconsistent behavior was fully counterbalanced. The procedures and dependent measures were identical to those used in the previous study.

To estimate the effects of consistency, data from the comparison conditions in the first experiment (i.e., from subjects in the female assertive and female passive target conditions) were used. If sex stereotypes affect social judgments under conditions of behavioral variability, this experiment should find a significant interaction effect between the consistency of the target's behavior and the trait characteristic of her behavior. For example, the consistently assertive female target may be judged as unlikely to be passive. The female target who behaves passively in one situation, however, may be judged as likely to be passive as the female target who behaves passively in two situations, given that passivity is considered to be a likely characteristic of women.

Table 6.2 presents the results of 2 (behavior) by 2 (consistency) analyses of variance on the dependent measures. It can be seen in the second and third columns of Table 6.2 that decreasing the behavioral consistency of the target did

TABLE 6.2
Effects of Consistency of Behavioral Information on Subjects' Impressions
of the Target's Personality[a]

| | Source of Effect | | |
	Behavior	Consistency	Behavior by Consistency
Attributed masculinity	$9.92(1,101)^c$	$1.26(1,101)$	$1.25(1,101)$
Attributed feminity	$14.70(1,80)^d$	$1.42(1,80)$	$.29(1,80)$
Rated masculinity	$33.75(1,102)^d$	$2.03(1,102)$	$2.93(1,102)$
Rated femininity	$4.99(1,101)^b$	$.17(1,101)$	$1.87(1,101)$

[a] F-tests are presented in cells with accompanying degrees of freedom in parentheses.
[b] $p < .05$
[c] $p < .01$
[d] $p < .001$

not affect the probability of attribution of sex stereotypic traits. None of the behavior-by-consistency interaction effects were significant, nor were any of the main effects of the consistency factor significant. As in the previous experiment, subjects relied on the available behavioral information about the target, regardless of the degree of behavioral consistency. The first column of Table 6.2 shows that the effects of the behavior manipulation on attributed masculinity, attributed femininity, and ratings on the BSRI masculinity and femininity scales were all significant. These effects were in the expected directions. The assertive female was characterized as more masculine ($M = 3.96$) and less feminine ($M = 3.54$) than the passive female ($M = 3.64$, $M = 3.67$, respectively). The assertive female was also rated in a more masculine direction on the BSRI masculinity scale ($M = 4.17$) than the passive female ($M = 2.92$), and rated in a less feminine direction on the BSRI femininity scale ($M = 2.67$) than the passive female ($M = 3.02$). It should be emphasized that this pattern of effects was obtained regardless of the degree of consistency of the target's behavior.

The stability and consistency of sex–stereotype assessment results sharply contrast with the failure of these experiments to obtain effects of sex stereotypes on social judgments. If certain traits are strongly associated with sex, why doesn't information about sex increase the probability of attributing sex-associated traits to the target?

We suggest that the absence of sex–stereotype effects in these experiments is indeed theoretically meaningful and that the problem of determining the conditions under which social stereotypes do or do not affect social judgments deserves serious consideration. The remainder of this chapter presents a theoretical framework that, it is hoped, will permit the systematic derivation of predictions for effects of social stereotypes on judgments about individual members of stereotyped groups. We begin with a closer examination of the characteristics of stereotypic beliefs.

Social Stereotypes as Distributional Beliefs. Traditionally, social stereotypes have been assessed by providing subjects with a list of traits and asking them to rate the extent to which each trait is characteristic of members of particular social groups (Brigham, 1971; Katz & Braly, 1933). Though problematic in certain respects (McCauley & Stitt, 1978; McCauley, Stitt, & Segal, 1980), this assessment format does produce comparatively reliable results, indicating that people do believe that pertinent traits are *distributed* differently across social groups. We emphasize the term *distributed* because, as McCauley and Stitt (1978) observe, social stereotypes essentially reflect the extent to which group membership is regarded as a source of *probabilistic*, rather than perfect, information about any given individual's personality traits. For example, sex stereotypes may be viewed as equivalent to a set of statements like "On the average, women are less assertive than men," or "More men are assertive than women.'' Thus social stereotypes may be formally viewed as popular beliefs about distributions of traits within social groups.[2]

Given this recognition of stereotypic beliefs as distributional in nature, research on utilization of distributional or base rate information in prediction and judgment tasks becomes a relevant source for deriving predictions that specify the conditions under which social stereotypes will or will not influence social judgments.

Social Stereotypes and the Psychology of Prediction.   Two types of information are normatively relevant for making predictions or judgments about a target individual. One is *base rate information,* or knowledge about the distribution of the criterion in a relevant population.   Another is *target case information,* or knowledge about the particular individual who is to be judged with respect to the criterion. Furthermore, target case information can be of two sorts: *nondiagnostic,* or information that is uncorrelated with the criterion, and *diagnostic,* or information that is correlated with the criterion. Research in the psychology of prediction has relied heavily on Bayes' rule for a normative description of the appropriate use of data for predictions and judgments. Given two events, A and B, Bayes' rule states that $p(A/B) = p(A) \cdot p(B/A)/p(B)$. Thus Bayes' rule states that predictions of A given B should be affected both by the prior probability of A and the probability of B given A. Rephrased in the terminology previously noted, Bayes' rule states that predictions should be affected both by the prior probability or base rate distribution of the criterion $[p(A)]$ and the strength of the relationship between the target case information and the criterion $[p(B/A)/p(B)]$.

---

[2]McCauley and Stitt (1978; McCauley, Stitt, & Segal, 1980) have proposed a formal quantification of stereotypes in terms of the diagnostic ratio $p(\text{trait/category})/p(\text{trait})$, or the ratio of the probability of a trait given social category information over the probability of the trait in general. This ratio exceeds 1 for any trait that is believed to be more probable for members of a given social category than for people in general, and thus aptly represents a stereotypic belief. Because McCauley and Stitt are concerned with the effect of social-category information on the probability of traits, they use the term *base rate* to refer to the value $p(\text{trait})$, or the distribution of the trait in general. In this chapter, however, we are primarily concerned with: (1) the fact that stereotypic beliefs are distributional in nature; and (2) determining the conditions under which stereotypes affect judgments about particular members of stereotyped groups. Thus we use the term *base rate* to refer to the value $p(\text{trait/category})$, with the assumption that the argument pertains to stereotypic beliefs for which the diagnostic ratio deviates from 1. Furthermore, the diagnostic ratio itself is not strictly appropriate for the type of judgment problem that constitutes the focus of this chapter. Consider the problem in which a person has both social category information (C) and other types of information (I) about an individual and is asked to make a judgment about whether or not the individual has a trait (T) that is stereotypically associated with C. The Bayesian description for this problem would be: $p(T/I) = p(T) \cdot p(I/T)/p(I)$, where $p(T) = P(T/C) = p(C/T) \cdot p(T)/p(C)$. Thus C serves only to identify the relevant population for which $p(T)$ is known (or believed to be known) and for which $p(T/C)$ differs from $p(T)$ in general. McCauley and Stitt are exclusively concerned with the revision of trait probabilities given only social category information, and thus with problems of the normative form $p(T/C) = p(C/T) \cdot p(T)/p(C)$, from which the diagnostic ratio $p(T/C)/p(T)$ is derived.

Normatively, when target case information is nondiagnostic or uncorrelatzd with the criterion $[p(B/A)/p(B) = 1]$, or when target case information is unavailable, people should rely solely on the prior probability of the criterion. When target case information is diagnostic $[|p(B/A)/p(B)| > 1]$, people should revise the prior probability of the criterion according to the predictive value of the target case information.

The problem with which we are concerned is: Given information about a member of a stereotyped group, what is the probability that stereotypically associated traits will be attributed to that individual? This problem may be cast in the terms of research in the psychology of prediction. Thus, stereotypes may be regarded as beliefs about the distributions of traits within social groups; information about an individual's membership in a stereotyped social group may be regarded as nothing other than sampling information (i.e., that the individual belongs to a population for which a trait distribution is "known" or believed to be true); and target case information consists of any individuating knowledge about the particular characteristics of the individual, which may or may not be subjectively diagnostic of the stereotypically associated trait. Suppose people behave like Bayesian statisticians. If we consider the problem in which all that is known about an individual is his or her membership in a stereotyped social group, then the prediction that they would have a stereotypically associated trait (T) is simply $p(T)$ for that social group (G), so that $p(T) = p(T/G) = p(T) \cdot p(G/T)/p(G)$. If we consider the problem in which target–case information (I) about the individual is known in addition to social group membership, then $p(T/I) = p(T) \cdot p(I/T)/p(I)$, where $p(T) = p(T/G) = p(T) \cdot p(G/T)/p(G)$. Thus, if people behave like Bayesian statisticians, one unfortunate consequence would be pervasive effects of social stereotypes on social judgments! If they do not, then one benign consequence would be limited effects of social stereotypes on social judgments.

It should be emphasized that these formulas are normative descriptions of the effects of stereotypes on social judgments. For although base rate information or prior probabilities are normatively appropriate (from a statistical perspective) for predictions about individuals, according to Bayes' theorem, a number of studies have shown that people often fail to take sufficient account of base rates when making predictions (Ajzen, 1977; Hammerton, 1973; Kahneman & Tversky, 1973; Lyon & Slovic, 1976; Nisbett & Borgida, 1975; Nisbett, Borgida, Crandall, & Reed, 1976; Slovic, Fischhoff & Lichtenstein, 1977; Tversky & Kahneman, 1974, 1980). In particular, people appear to be excessively swayed by the presence of target–case information, whether it is nondiagnostic *or* diagnostic (Kahneman & Tversky, 1973; Nisbett, Zukier & Lemley, 1980)! For example, in one study, Kahneman and Tversky (1973) instructed subjects that a panel of psychologists had administered personality tests to 30 engineers and 70 lawyers. Subjects were asked to estimate the probability that a specific respondent was one of the engineers. In one condition, subjects were told only that the target had been randomly selected from the sample of respondents. In a second condition, subjects were provided with a description of the target which was written so as to be entirely uninformative or nondiagnostic of the target's choice of profession. In a third condition, subjects were provided with a description of the target that was written so as to be informative or diagnostic of the target's choice of profession. Kahneman and Tversky (1973) found that subjects who had no information about the target appropriately used the base rate when judging the probability that the target was an engineer or lawyer. However both subjects in the nondiagnostic information condition and subjects in the diagnostic information condition significantly underutilized the base rate distribution of engineers and lawyers from which the target had presumably been sampled. Indeed, the median probability estimate of subjects in the nondiagnostic condition was .50.

Several studies on the effects of social stereotypes on social judgments have designs which are similar to those characteristic of research on base rate utilization.[3] For example, in the studies conducted by Locksley, Borgida, Brekke and Hepburn (in press), subjects were presented with a description of a target that contained an ample amount of both nondiagnostic and diagnostic target–case information, in addition to social category information. In these studies, no effects of sex of the target were obtained on sex stereotypically associated trait ratings of the target, indicating that sex stereotypes were not influencing subjects' judgments. Similarly, Taylor et al. (1978) had subjects witness discussions among groups of public–school teachers varying in sex composition. This procedure would provide subjects with a considerable amount of nondiagnostic and possibly diagnostic target case information, and indeed the study obtained either weak or no effects of sex stereotypes on subjects' attributions of sex stereotypically associated traits to the target individuals.

The results of studies on effects of sex stereotypes on clinical judgments also fit the base rate utilization pattern. Broverman et al. (1972) found that clinicians presented only with the social category information, "female adult" or "male adult," rated men as significantly more likely to have psychologically healthy traits than women. In contrast, a number of other clinical judgment studies that

---

[3]As noted in Footnote 2, McCauley and Stitt (1978; McCauley, Stitt, & Segal, 1980) have assessed social stereotypes within a Bayesian framework. They have found that subjects are "behaving like Bayesian statisticians"; that is, subjects appear to be appropriately using prior probabilities when estimating stereotypic trait probabilities. However it was also noted in Footnote 2 that McCauley and Stitt are exclusively concerned with the problem of revising trait probabilities in the presence of social category information only. From our perspective, this problem is anlogous to the Kahneman and Tversky (1973) condition in which no target case information is available and in which subjects were found to be appropriately using prior probabilities. This problem is also analogous to stereotype studies in which subjects are presented only with social category information and in which effects of social stereotypes on subjects' judgments are typically obtained. In other words, McCauley and Stitt (1978) have not yet investigated prediction problems in which target case information is available in addition to social-category information, and their conclusions are limited accordingly.

have presented clinicians with individuating target case information in addition to social category information have obtained only weak or no effects of sex stereotypes (Abramowitz & Dokecki, 1977; Stricker, 1977).

An elegant series of studies by Nisbett, Zukier, and Lemley (1980) provides a dramatic illustration of the impact of target case information on judgments about members of stereotyped groups. Their studies used stereotypic beliefs about college majors. Engineer majors, by virtue of their presumed masculinity and familiarity with machines, are believed to be able to tolerate more shock in a psychology experiment than music majors. English majors, by virtue of their presumed general cultural and literary interests, are believed to attend more movies than premedical students. In one set of conditions, subjects were informed that a target was either an engineer or a music major and were asked to estimate the amount of shock he tolerated in a psychology experiment. Other subjects were informed that a target was either an English major or a premedical student and asked to estimate the number of movies he attended. In a second set of conditions, subjects were presented both with information about the target's college major and with manifestly nondiagnostic target case information, such as information about the target's place of birth, grade point average, and parents' occupations. Nisbett, Zukier, and Lemley (1980) found that the presence of nondiagnostic target case information significantly and substantially reduced the impact of information about the target's college major on subjects' predictions. Moreover, when Nisbett, Zukier, and Lemley (1980) replicated the study using stereotypic beliefs about college majors that were less extreme than those used in the previous study, they found that the presence of nondiagnostic target case information completely eradicated the effects of the college major information on subjects' predictions.

Considering that the majority of social judgment studies of stereotypes have not been designed with a base rate utilization framework in mind, the conceptual and empirical parallels between the two are quite striking. Social stereotypes, after all, are distributional beliefs. In any study of the effects of social stereotypes on judgments about a target, they have the logical status of prior probabilities. And the results of both base rate utilization research and the social judgment studies discussed in the foregoing, suggest that the effects of social stereotypes on judgments of individuals may not be as pervasive or as powerful as psychologists have traditionally assumed. Social stereotypes may affect judgments of individuals about whom little else is known but their social category. But as soon as individuating particular characteristics of a person are known, stereotypes may have minimal, if any, impact on judgments of that person. Anecdotal accounts of the bigots who claim that "some of my best friends are . . ." may have a kernel of truth. People may sustain general prejudices while simultaneously treating individuals with whom they frequently interact in a nonprejudicial manner.

Just as research on the psychology of prediction can provide a useful source for explaining the absence of stereotype effects in a number of social judgment studies, it can suggest conditions under which stereotypes might still exert effects even when target case information is available. Several studies on base rate utilization have found that the more extreme the base rate, the more likely it is to affect subjects' judgments (Wells & Harvey, 1977). Thus distributions of extremely rare or extremely common events are more likely to affect predictions than less radically skewed distributions, possibly because of the novelty associated with rare events (Taylor & Fiske, 1978). This finding suggests an interesting interpretation of the variable results of studies investigating effects of sex of target on performance attributions (Chabot, Goldberg, Abramson, & Abramson, 1974; Deaux, 1976; Deaux & Emswiller, 1974; Etaugh & Brown, 1975; Feather & Simon, 1975; Feldman-Summers & Kiesler, 1974; Fidell, 1970; Goldberg, 1968; Hesselbart, 1977; Pheterson, Kiesler, & Goldberg, 1971; Taynor & Deaux, 1975). One general finding of these studies is that sex of target effects are highly sensitive to characteristics of the task at which the target succeeds or fails. Indeed, the most reliable effects of sex are obtained when the task in question is distinctively masculine, involving objects like wrenches or occupations like surgeon (Deaux & Emswiller, 1974; Feather & Simon, 1975; Feldman-Summers & Kiesler, 1974; Taynor & Deaux, 1975). When the tasks are less strongly sex-associated, like writing or painting, effects of sex become either less reliable or are entirely absent (Chabot et al., 1974; Goldberg, 1968; Levenson, Burford, Bonna, & Davis, 1975; Pheterson et al., 1971). Of course, more distinctively sex-associated tasks parallel more extreme base rate distributions. Comparatively few women become proficient with tools like wrenches, and even fewer women become surgeons. The consequential role of task characteristics in performance attribution studies of sex stereotypes may be a function of their implications for distributional characteristics of pertinent stereotypic beliefs.

Distributional characteristics of stereotypic beliefs may also explain temporal instability in the results of social judgment studies of stereotypes. For example, Goldberg's (1968) finding that an article was evaluated differently, depending on whether it was believed to be written by a man or a woman, has failed to replicate (Chabot et al., 1974; Levenson et al., 1975). This could be a consequence of temporal changes in the extremity of popular beliefs about sex differences in competence at this task. In this connection, it should be noted that traditional methods of assessing social stereotypes are not particularly sensitive to changes of this sort. For example, people may still believe that men are significantly more likely to be good writers than women, but to a lesser extent than was believed 10 or 20 years ago. Until we adopt more sensitive methods of assessing social stereotypes (McCauley & Stitt, 1978) it will be impossible to evaluate empirically considerations of the sort advanced here.

One final implication of distributional characteristics of stereotypic beliefs should be mentioned. Recall at this point that the Bayesian description of the problem with which we are concerned is $p(T/I) = p(T) \cdot p(I/T)/p(I)$, where $p(T) = p(T/G) = p(T) \cdot p(G/T)/p(G)$, and T = stereotypically associated trait,

I = target case information, and G = social group to which the target belongs. As just noted, when $p(T/G)$ is extreme (1 or 99%), it is more likely to affect social judgments and predictions than when it is less extreme. There are a number of determinants of the popular perception of $p(T/G)$, or the extremity of a stereotypic belief, but one worth noting is the sheer size of the social group. Other things being equal, the smaller the social group, the more infrequent will be social interaction between group and nongroup members. Thus the less likely it is that either nondiagnostic or diagnostic information about any given member of the group will be encountered by nongroup members. Any stereotypic belief about traits that are distinctively associated with the group, therefore, on the average, will be less likely to have been "diluted" (Nisbett, Zukier, and Lemley, 1980) by target case information. Over time, then, such beliefs may be more likely to remain extreme than stereotypic beliefs about larger groups. Furthermore, the smaller the social group, the less likely it is that any given group member will be observed behaving in ways that are diagnostic of traits characteristic of people in general. Given that people appear to be insufficiently sensitive to proportionate frequencies and overly sensitive to absolute frequencies (Estes, 1976), stereotypes of smaller groups should be more extreme than stereotypes of larger groups and thus should be more likely to affect judgments of individual members of small groups than individual members of larger groups. Any other factor, such as economic, occupational, or geographical segregation, that decreases the frequency of interaction between groups should have a similar impact on the extremity of stereotypic beliefs about social groups and thus on the effects of those beliefs on social judgments.

Besides extremity, another variable which affects use of base rate information in judgment or prediction tasks is whether or not it appears to be *causally relevant* with respect to the criterion (Ajzen, 1977; Tversky & Kahneman, 1980). Ajzen (1977) argues that:

> [when] asked to make a prediction, people look for factors that would cause the behavior or event under consideration. Information that provides evidence concerning the presence or absence of causal factors is therefore likely to influence predictions. Other items of information, even though important by the normative principles of statistical prediction, will tend to be neglected if they have no apparent causal significance [p. 304].

Thus, if the base rate information enables the judge to infer a probable cause of the criterion, it will be more likely to affect predictions than if it does not appear to be causally relevant.

Social stereotypes are essentially noncausal distributional beliefs. Even though people may have diverse theories about why social groups are characterized by different trait distributions, social category membership in and of itself does not represent a cause of traits. Thus, for the type of judgment problem with which we have been concerned so far, social stereotypes represent non-causal base rate information. For a different type of social judgment problem, however, stereotypes may acquire more apparent causal relevance. Suppose a judgment problem involves predicting a person's value on a criterion that is not in and of itself stereotypically associated with a social group but that is subjectively regarded as a *direct* effect of stereotypically associated traits. For example, suppose you were presented with the problem of predicting the probability that an Irishman beats his wife. Heavy drinking is stereotypically associated with being Irish, and is also considered to be a cause of wife beating. For such a judgment problem, stereotypes may still affect predictions even when nondiagnostic or diagnostic information is provided in addition to the social category information, "Irishman." Because there are no social judgment studies of stereotypes that cleanly fit the parameters of this problem, the hypothesis cannot be evaluated even on a retrospective basis, although studies that have obtained discriminatory employment decisions in the presence of diagnostic target case information (Fidell, 1970) may be examples of this effect.

SUMMARY

This chapter attempts to delineate a theoretical framework within which the problem of determining the conditions under which social stereotypes affect judgments may be systematically investigated. The basic premise of the argument is that social stereotypes may be viewed as popular beliefs about base rate distributions of characteristics within social groups. Once social stereotypes are defined in this way, research on effects of social stereotypes can be integrated into the more general area of the psychology of prediction and judgment. There are several advantages to adopting this theoretical framework. The primary advantage of the proposed theoretical framework is that it permits the systematic derivation of hypotheses concerning effects of social stereotypes on social judgments. A second advantage is that it would require the development of stereotype assessment methods (McCauley & Stitt, 1978) that would be much more sensitive to the magnitude of stereotypic beliefs than traditional stereotype assessment procedures. Besides enabling an empirical test of the theory presented here, more sensitive assessment procedures would enable the investigator to control more effectively for temporal changes as well as for individual differences in stereotypic beliefs. And, to the extent that discriminatory behavior is a manifestation of stereotypic judgments, this framework may permit a more systematic investigation of the effects of social stereotypes on social behavior.

Of course, the utility of this theoretical perspective will ultimately be determined on an empirical basis. However, this chapter attempts to demonstrate that the variable results of existing social judgment studies of social stereotypes are at least consistent with the major predictions that are derived from a base rate utilization framework. Research in the psychology of prediction has demonstrated that both characteristics of target case and base rate information affect the probability that people will use base rate data for prediction or judgment tasks. Perhaps the most counterintuitive finding of base rate utilization research is that target case data often dominate the effects of base rate data. This finding suggests, in turn, that social stereotypes may not exert as pervasive or powerful an effect on social judgment as has been traditionally assumed. Social stereotypes may affect judgments of individuals about whom little else is known besides their social category. But as soon as individuating, particular characteristics of a person are known, social stereotypes may have minimal, if any, impact on judgments about that person.

ACKNOWLEDGMENTS

The authors are grateful to Leon Festinger, Richard Nisbett, Mark Snyder, Nancy Cantor, James Uleman, and Susan Fiske for their comments on an earlier draft of this manuscript. Preparation of this manuscript was supported in part by a grant from the Graduate School of the University of Minnesota to Eugene Borgida, and by NSF Grant BNS-7912940 to Anne Locksley.

REFERENCES

Abramowitz, C. V., & Dokecki, P. The politics of clinical judgment: Early empirical returns. *Psychological Bulletin*, 1977, *84*, 460–476.

Adorno, T., Frenkel-Brunswick, E., Levinson, D., & Sanford, N. *The authoritarian personality*. New York: Harper, 1950.

Ajzen, I. Intuitive theories of events and effects of base-rate information on prediction. *Journal of Personality and Social Psychology*, 1977, *35*, 303–314.

Allport, G. *The nature of prejudice*. New York: Doubleday & Company, 1954.

Ashmore, R. D., & Del Boca, F. K. Sex stereotypes and implicit personality theory: Toward a cognitive–social psychological conceptualization. *Sex Roles*, 1979, *5*(2), 219–248.

Bem, S. L. The measurement of psychological androgyny. *Journal of Consulting and Clinical Psychology*, 1974, *42*, 155–162.

Brewer, M. B. In-group bias in the minimal intergroup situation: A cognitive–motivational analysis. *Psychological Bulletin*, 1979, *86*, 307–324.

Brigham, J. C. Ethnic stereotypes. *Psychological Bulletin*, 1971, *76*, 15–38.

Broverman, I., Vogel, S., Broverman, D., Clarkson, F., & Rosenkrantz, P. Sex-role stereotypes: A current appraisal. *Journal of Social Issues*, 1972, *28*, 59–78.

Brown, R. *Social psychology*. New York: Free Press, 1965.

Chabot, D., Goldberg, P., Abramson, L., & Abramson, P. Prejudice against women: A replication and extension. *Psychological Reports*, 1974, *35*, 478.

Christie, R., & Jahoda, M. (Eds.), *Studies in the scope and method of "The Authoritarian Personality."* New York: Free Press, 1954.

Deaux, K. Sex: A perspective on the attribution process. In J. H. Harvey, W. J. Ickes, & R. F. Kidd

(Eds.), *New directions in attribution research* (Vol. 1). Hillsdale, N.J.: Lawrence Erlbaum Associates, 1976.

Deaux, K., & Emswiller, T. Explanations of successful performance on sex-linked tasks: What is skill for the male is luck for the female. *Journal of Personality and Social Psychology*, 1974, *29*, 80–85.

Estes, W. K. The cognitive side of probability learning. *Psychological Review*, 1976, *83*, 37–64.

Etaugh, C., & Brown, B. Perceiving the causes of success and failure of male and female performers. *Developmental Psychology*, 1975, *11*, 103.

Feather, N. T., & Simon, J. G. Reactions to male and female success and failure in sex-linked occupations: Impressions of personality, causal attributions, and perceived likelihood of different consequences. *Journal of Personality and Social Psychology*, 1975, *31*, 20–31.

Feldman-Summers, S., & Kiesler, S. B. Those who are number two try harder: The effects of sex on attributions of causality. *Journal of Personality and Social Psychology*, 1974, *30*, 846–855.

Fidell, I. Empirical verification of sex discrimination in hiring practices in psychology. *American Psychologist*, 1970, *25*, 1094–1098.

Goldberg, P. Are women prejudiced against women? *Trans-action*, 1968, *5*, 28–30.

Hamilton, D. L. (Ed.). *Cognitive processes in stereotyping and intergroup behavior*. Hillsdale, N.J.: Lawrence Erlbaum Associates, in press.

Hamilton, D. L. Cognitive biases in the perception of social groups. In J. S. Carroll & J. W. Payne (Eds.), *Cognition and social behavior*. Hillsdale, N.J.: Lawrence Erlbaum Associates, 1976.

Hamilton, D. L., & Gifford, R. K. Illusory correlation in interpersonal perception: A cognitive basis of stereotypic judgments. *Journal of Experimental Social Psychology*, 1976, *12*, 392–407.

Hammerton, M. A case of radical probability estimation. *Journal of Experimental Psychology*, 1973, *101*, 252–254.

Hepburn, C. *Availability as a function of sex association: Implications for the maintenance of sex stereotypes*. Unpublished manuscript, New York University, 1979.

Hesselbart, S. Sex role and occupational stereotypes: Three studies of impression formation. *Sex Roles*, 1977, *3*, 409–422.

Kahneman, D., & Tversky, A. On the psychology of prediction. *Psychological Review*, 1973, *80*, 237–251.

Katz, D., & Braly, K. W. Racial stereotypes of one hundred college students. *Journal of Abnormal and Social Psychology*, 1933, *28*, 280–290.

Levenson, H., Burford, B., Bonno, B., & Davis, L. Are women still prejudiced against women? A replication and extension of Goldberg's study. *Journal of Psychology*, 1975, *89*, 67–71.

Locksley, A., Borgida, E., Brekke, N., & Hepburn, C. Sex stereotypes and social judgment. *Journal of Personality and Social Psychology*, in press.

Locksley, A., Ortiz, V., & Hepburn, C. Social categorization and discriminatory behavior: Extinguishing the minimal intergroup discrimination effect. *Journal of Personality and Social Psychology*, in press.

Lyon, D., & Slovic, P. Dominance of accuracy information and neglect of base rates in probability estimation. *Acta Psychologica*, 1976, *40*, 287–298.

McCauley, C., & Stitt, C. L. An individual and quantitative measure of stereotypes. *Journal of Personality and Social Psychology*, 1978, *36*, 929–940.

McCauley, C., Stitt, C. L., & Segal, M. Stereotyping: From prejudice to prediction. *Psychological Bulletin*, 1980, *87*, 195–208.

McKee, J. P., & Sherriffs, A. C. The differential evaluation of males and females. *Journal of Personality*, 1957, *25*, 356–371.

Nisbett, R. E., & Borgida, E. Attribution and the psychology of prediction. *Journal of Personality and Social Psychology*, 1975, *32*, 932–943.

Nisbett, R. E., Borgida, E., Crandall, R., & Reed, H. Popular induction: Information is not necessarily informative. In J. S. Carroll & J. W. Payne (Eds.), *Cognition and social behavior.* Hillsdale, N.J.: Lawrence Erlbaum Associates, 1976.

Nisbett, R. E., Zukier, H., & Lemley, R. E. *The dilution effect: Nondiagnostic information weakens the implications of diagnostic information.* Unpublished manuscript, University of Michigan, 1980.

Pheterson, G. I., Kiesler, S. B., & Goldberg, P. A. Evaluation of the performance of women as a function of their sex, achievement, and personal history. *Journal of Personality and Social Psychology,* 1971, *19,* 114–118.

Ruble, D. N., & Ruble, T. L. Sex stereotypes. In A. G. Miller (Ed.), *In the eye of the beholder: Contemporary issues in stereotyping.* New York: Holt, Rinehart & Winston, 1980.

Sherif, M. Experiments in group conflict. *Scientific American,* 1956, *195,* 54–58.

Sherriffs, A. C., & McKee, J. P. Qualitative aspects of beliefs about men and women. *Journal of Personality,* 1957, *25,* 451–464.

Slovic, P., Fischhoff, B., & Lichtenstein, S. Behavioral decision theory. *Annual Review of Psychology,* 1977, *28,* 1–39.

Snyder, M. On the self-perpetuating nature of social stereotypes. In D. L. Hamilton (Ed.), *Cognitive processes in stereotyping and intergroup behavior.* Hillsdale, N.J.: Lawrence Erlbaum Associates, in press.

Snyder, M., & Swann, W. B., Jr. Behavioral confirmation in social interaction: From social perception to social reality. *Journal of Experimental Social Psychology,* 1978, *14,* 148–162.

Snyder, M., Tanke, E. D., & Berscheid, E. Social perception and interpersonal behavior: On the self-fulfilling nature of social stereotypes. *Journal of Personality and Social Psychology,* 1977, *35,* 656–666.

Snyder, M., & Uranowitz, S. Reconstructing the past: Some cognitive consequences of person perception. *Journal of Personality and Social Psychology,* 1978, *36,* 941–951.

Spence, J., & Helmreich, R. *Masculinity and femininity.* Austin: University of Texas Press, 1978.

Stricker, G. Implications of research for psychotherapeutic treatment of women. *American Psychologist,* 1977, *32,* 14–22.

Tajfel, H. Experiments in intergroup discrimination. *Scientific American,* 1970, *223,* 96–102.

Tajfel, H., & Wilkes, A. L. Classification and qualitative judgment. *British Journal of Psychology,* 1963, *54,* 101–114.

Taylor, S. E. A categorization approach to stereotyping. In D. L. Hamilton (Ed.), *Cognitive processes in stereotyping and intergroup behavior.* Hillsdale, N.J.: Lawrence Erlbaum Associates, in press.

Taylor, S. E., & Fiske, S. Salience, attention, and attribution: Top of the head phenomena. In L. Berkowitz (Ed.), *Advances in experimental social psychology.* New York: Academic Press, 1978.

Taylor, S. E., Fiske, S., Etcoff, N., & Ruderman, A. Categorical and contextual bases of person memory and stereotyping. *Journal of Personality and Social Psychology,* 1978, *36,* 778–793.

Taynor, J., & Deaux, K. Equity and perceived sex differences: Role behavior as defined by the task, the mode, and the actor. *Journal of Personality and Social Psychology,* 1975, *32,* 381–390.

Tversky, A., & Kahneman, D. Availability: A heuristic for judging frequency and probability. *Cognitive Psychology,* 1973, *5,* 207–232.

Tversky, A., & Kahneman, D. Judgment under uncertainty: Heuristics and biases. *Science,* 1974, *185,* 1124–1131.

Tversky, A., & Kahneman, D. Causal schemata in judgments under uncertainty. In M. Fishbein (Ed.), *Progress in social psychology.* Hillsdale, N.J.: Lawrence Erlbaum Associates, 1977.

Wells, G. L., & Harvey, J. H. Do people use consensus information in making causal attributions? *Journal of Personality and Social Psychology,* 1977, *35,* 279–293.

Word, C. O., Zanna, M. P., & Cooper, J. The nonverbal mediation of self-fulfilling prophecies in interracial interaction. *Journal of Experimental Social Psychology,* 1974, *10,* 109–120.

7 INVOLVEMENT, EXPERTISE, AND SCHEMA USE: EVIDENCE FROM POLITICAL COGNITION

SUSAN T. FISKE
Carnegie-Mellon University

DONALD R. KINDER
Yale University

The interplay between new information and old endures as a fundamental problem in psychology. Social cognition research has recently extended this tradition by advancing our appreciation of how prior knowledge influences the processing of information about the social world. The elaboration and refinement of schema-driven models (as they are customarily known) is an exciting and propitious development. In the midst of all this activity, our own analysis should be construed as a gentle (and unfashionable) reminder concerning interindividual variation. Our central message is that people differ enormously both in schema availability and schema use. Our theoretical analysis and research concentrate on the interaction between individual differences in expertise and involvement, on the one hand, and the ease by which schemata are invoked and, once invoked, how sensitively they are put to use, on the other. The involved and the expert in a particular domain will more easily bring to mind applicable schemata; they will also employ such schemata in more sensitive ways. To develop and illustrate these points is the central purpose of this chapter.

As do others in this volume, we draw on evidence from social cognition and lean heavily on theoretical advances in cognitive psychology. Our work departs from the mainstream in its explorations of *political* information processing. A secondary purpose, then, is to investigate parallels between the burgeoning social cognition literature and research on political cognition (Kinder, Fiske, & Wagner, 1979). In so doing we shall sermonize for a schematic approach to understanding political information processing. We shall also suggest that politics represents a rich though currently underutilized domain for cognitive research.

The remainder of the chapter is divided into four sections. It begins, as chapters often do, with answers to definitional questions: What is meant by a schematic approach to information processing? What are schemata and what functions do they serve? The first section also presents representative examples of research from the social cognition literature. We do this partly in order to position our own theoretical analysis, which derives substantially from contemporary work in social cognition and partly to make the point that social cognition research has so far paid little attention to the interplay between individual differences and schema use, a neglect we hope to redress. Section 2 then develops an analysis of *political* information processing, the conceptual centerpiece of which is the activation and use of political schemata. Here we argue that understanding of the political world may be best appreciated in theoretical terms as an interaction between schemata imposed on political information and the information itself. Moreover, and this is our central point, political schema activation and use are affected by chronic individual differences, in particular by differences in political involvement and expertise. This conceptual analysis is then illustrated in Section 3, with evidence taken from our recent experiments on political cognition. The final section of the chapter then draws out the implications of our analysis for social cognition research. Our own research is confined to political information processing, but it has implications for the social cognition literature more generally, as we try to show. We would not make the foray into politics unless we expected to bring back more widely applicable social and cognitive principles.

SCHEMA-BASED INFORMATION PROCESSING:
DEFINITIONS, PRINCIPLES,
AND ILLUSTRATIONS

The social cognition literature has yet to settle finally on a single definition, but there does appear to be consensus on some fundamentals. According to Rumelhart and Ortony (1977), schemata are cognitive representations of generic concepts. They include the attributes that constitute the concept and relationships among the attributes. Social schemata are then abstract conceptions people hold about the social world—about persons, roles, and events (Taylor & Crocker, in press). As we see shortly from illustrative research in this emerging tradition, schemata serve as the layperson's social theories: People form hypotheses and develop expectations about extroverts, about college professors, about what events are likely to unfold when they enter a restaurant, and so forth.

In functional terms, schemata provide cognitive economy. We are all cognitive misers (Taylor, in press), making the best of our limited mental capacities. If we have available ready-made and well-structured information elicited by a single cue, then our scarce mental resources do not have to be squandered constructing and organizing afresh at each encounter with new information. Schemata, then, enable an efficient understanding of the environment. Current discussions in cognitive psychology center around the nature of knowledge representations that make complex information processing possible (Anderson, 1977; Bobrow & Norman, 1975; Rumelhart & Ortony, 1977). Underlying this discussion is the more basic point that enormous efficiency (and sometimes confusion) accrues to the processing of information that is thematically organized (Bower, Black, & Turner, 1979; Smith, Adams, & Schorr, 1978). Thus, schemata constitute serviceable although imperfect devices for coping with complexity. They direct attention to relevant information, guide its interpretation and evaluation, provide inferences when information is missing or ambiguous, and facilitate its retention. Evidence on each of these points is assembled by Taylor and Crocker (in press); their review testifies to the promise of a schematic approach to social information processing.

How people develop these useful devices has been addressed in cognitive psychology. That work focuses on mechanisms by which specific encounters are gradually abstracted into general rules on the basis of experience, that is, through repeated exposure to varied examples (Reed, 1972). The research suggests one process by which people form social generalizations; prolonged exposure to a particular domain creates memory for exemplars, which themselves may never have been seen, but which may be remembered better than actually experienced instances (Bransford & Franks, 1971; Hayes-Roth & Hayes-Roth, 1977). Although one never sees the perfect extrovert or the ideal restaurant, experience enables one to create vivid conceptions of each. Without such experience, one can have no such conceptions. This hints that a person with more exposure to a particular domain (a restaurant critic) would have more developed schemata available for that domain than would someone less practiced—a point that we develop shortly.

Schema research (or better, research that can be interpreted in schema terms) has so far showed an understandable preference for testing and refining general principles of information processing. Research and theory both have depended on shared knowledge structures, on consensual schemata. This is illustrated nicely, even prototypically, by Cantor and Mischel's research on social categorization (Cantor & Mischel, 1979). Drawing on Rosch's (1978) work in object perception, they focus on the cognitive role played by shared social categories such as *extrovert* or *cultured person*. Cantor and Mischel find that when an individual is described in terms that exemplify such a category, memory for behavioral details improves, and attributes associated with the category are confidently remembered, whether actually presented or not (Tsujimoto, 1978; Tsujimoto, Wilde, & Robertson, 1978).

Complementing this work on categorization driven by shared dispositional categories is research on demographic-based categorization. Taylor, Fiske, Etcoff, and Ruderman (1978) have shown that people encode information about others according to their race and sex: Perceivers minimize within-group differences and exaggerate between-group differences and accordingly ascribe stereotyped attributes both to people and to groups. Not only do perceivers confuse category members with each other, but they also attribute stereotype-consistent information that was, in fact, never provided (Cohen, 1977). Snyder and Uranowitz (1978) provide further evidence that such role-based memory confusions can occur in retrospect, that is, when a label such as lesbian is provided post hoc. (See Hamilton, 1979, for a review of the cognitive bases of stereotyping.) These studies show that culturally shared knowledge about social roles and groups structures people's inferences and memory about newly encountered persons.

Cognitive categories may also encompass knowledge about familiar social events. Bower, Black, and Turner (1979) have collected evidence for Schank and Abelson's (1977) normative social scripts that describe routine activities such as going to a restaurant or a doctor's office. Two studies elicited consensus on likely types of characters, props, and actions and on the ordering and segmenting of actions into sequential "scenes." As in other research, subjects presented with stories describing such routine activities misremembered expected events that were, in fact, unstated, and misrecalled scrambled events into the expected sequence. Moreover, inferences from the stored generic concept were more likely to be confused with actually encountered instances the more often the generic concept was invoked. Anderson and Pichert (1978); Smith, Adams, and Schorr (1978), and Zadny and Gerard (1974) present related evidence that abstract goals and intentions influence memory for specific event details. All these studies rely on consensual notions about goal-directed social events.

As a final illustration of the effects of shared generic knowledge on memory and inferences, perspective-taking experiments show that imagined visual point-of-view influences recall. Fiske, Taylor, Etcoff, and Laufer (1979) found that subjects who imaged a story from a particular character's visual perspective (e.g., the motorcycle driver involved in a motocycle–taxi collision) best remembered details uniquely available from that vantage point. Bower (1977) and Abelson (1976) have obtained similar results. These findings all are explained nicely by Minsky's (1975) conception of visual frames, defined as common knowledge about the rules for visual perspective. Social perceivers' memory is guided by such expectations about visual perception, although at a verbal level, the information perceivers neglect is equally available.[1] Again, this research depends on substantial agreement across subjects—this time on the rules of visual perspective.

---

[1]Related experiments that manipulate actual visual perspective obtain uneven results on recall for details best seen from differing points of view (Taylor & Fiske, 1978). However, such studies do show recall and inferences driven by other sorts of schemata, specifically perceivers' theories about what constitutes appropriate evidence for social causality (Fiske, Kenny, & Taylor, 1979).

As this illustrative summary suggests, the social cognition literature has dealt with a wide range of consensual schemata: shared knowledge about extroverts, blacks and whites, men and women, librarians, lesbians, going into a restaurant, visiting the doctor, rules underlying visual perspective, and more. Although diverse in content, such schemata share certain structural properties: Each includes (usually) a label, along with a set of presumed (or default) values for key attributes and relationships among those attributes. The restaurant script, for example, incorporates assumptions about event sequence: that first one enters, then sits, orders, eats, pays, and departs. The central point here is that each of the experiments we have referred to assumes that the knowledge represented by such schemata is shared: that most people have mastered the restaurant script, know what sort of a person a librarian is, share a set of rules about visual vantage points, and so forth. The stimulus materials then manipulate the pertinent consensual schema. Such schemata are invoked by salient triggering cues—such as "John walked into the restaurant and ordered lobster" or "Laura is energetic, spirited, outgoing, and vivacious." Individual differences, to the extent they exist, are relegated by these investigations to the error term.

Thus, in its attention to general processes and consensual schemata, research in social cognition has tended to slight individual differences. An interest in individual variation surfaces really only in Markus's research on "self-schemata."[2] Markus has shown in a series of convergent studies that people for whom a particular domain is salient ("schematics") differ in their processing of domain-relevant information from those for whom the domain is not salient ("aschematics"). Individuals differ according to what domains are salient: one person focusing on autonomy, another on femininity, another on obesity, and so forth. Whatever the domain, schematics differ in predictable ways from aschematics in their handling of domain-relevant information. In particular, self-schemata enable more efficient processing of information in the relevant domain, ease retrieval of evidence, and provide a basis for confident predictions (Markus, 1977; Markus, Sentis, & Hamill, 1978).

Schema research has thus concentrated largely on the elicitation of consensual knowledge structures, as in the first set of examples, and rather little on individual variation in the availability of particular schemata, as in Markus's research. Moreover, no attention at all has been paid to the interplay between individual differences and schema *use:* that people might not only differ in schema availability (as shown by Markus) but also differ in how schemata are

---

[2]In a pair of investigations that are another exception to this general rule, Tesser and Leone (1977) have argued that better-developed schemata lead to more polarized evaluations over time. In a separate series of studies, Linville (1979) has predicted and found the opposite in the short run—that more complex schemata lead to more moderate immediate evaluations. Both sets of experiments are relevant in their focus on individual differences in schema content; however, both focus on evaluative judgments rather than memory and inference, so they are tangential in this particular context.

employed in information processing. The next section of the chapter does attend to this interplay as part of a more general argument on behalf of schema-based political information processing.

SCHEMATIC UNDERSTANDING OF POLITICS

It hardly seems reckless to move from the social cognition literature to political information processing. Consider Chicago's late Mayor Daley: He was perhaps the prototype Machine Pol, a kind of political Godfather, looking after "his" city with an overzealous paternalism. Daley can be assimilated easily into a particular schema for politician that is widely shared. Now consider Jimmy Carter. A wide variety of consensual schemata may be brought to bear, but his characteristics and actions do not seem to fit any of them particularly well. Yet each of us manages to settle on some general rubric by which to understand the President.

As is the social world, so too is the political world (and its actors) complex, ambiguous, objectively overwhelming. Each day most of us are bombarded by political news of all kinds. Yet, most Americans remain indifferent to and generally poorly informed about much of what transpires in the political world (Converse, 1975; Sears, 1969). The average citizen is thus enormously selective when it comes to political information. This suggests that people may grapple with the massive amounts of political information available to them in ways that are described in the social cognition literature (i.e., by invoking generic knowledge structures, or what we shall call political schemata). Such schemata represent stored structural information about politics, including conceptions of politicians, policies, rules, events, and institutions. Political schemata presumably guide political information processing: Their elicitation affects the selection, interpretation, use, and remembrance of information about the political world. In the face of considerable complexity, ambiguity, and downright confusion, political schemata provide cognitive economy. This service seems particularly relevant in a sphere such as politics, where the potential information levels are so high but the typical person's investment in the information appears relatively low (Converse, 1975; Downs, 1957; Lippman, 1922; Popkin, Gorman, Phillips, & Smith, 1976).

This argument regarding political information processing finds its parallel in cognitive psychologists' recent work on expert–novice differences. According to this literature, differences between the two in particular domains can be traced to the effects of prolonged practice. Chase and Simon (1973), for example, contrasted chess masters with beginners, concluding that skill depended on "a vast, organized long-term memory of specific information about chessboard patterns [p. 279]," based on thousands of hours of experience, and further that expertise was specific to that one highly practiced domain. Turning from chess to

dinosaurs, Chi (1979) drew on an intensive case study of a four-year-old preco-
cious paleontologist to argue that the knowledge of experts is denser than that of
novices. Not only is there more information, but it is organized more complexly.
Experts know more, but they also make more connections. In other problem-
solving domains (e.g., algebra: Hinsley, Hayes, & Simon, 1977; and physics:
Larkin, McDermott, Simon, & Simon, 1980), expertise appears as the capacity to categorize problems so as to elicit a set of heuristics especially useful to
their solution.[3] The development of integrated knowledge structures is one way
to explain the paradox of the expert; that is, why knowing a lot in a particular
domain does not necessarily make it harder to remember any one thing. The
escalation of information need not interfere with rapid retrieval, if the information is organized (Smith, Adams, & Schorr, 1978; but see also Reder & Anderson, 1979).

Thus, through practice, experts acquire more—and more complexly
organized—knowledge, which includes strategies for dealing with particular
domains. These knowledge structures—in our theoretical vocabulary,
schemata—encompass both declarative knowledge (descriptions of attributes)
and procedural knowledge (rules or strategies for the use of that knowledge)
(Anderson, 1976; Taylor & Crocker, 1980; Taylor, Crocker, & D'Agostino,
1978). Chi and Glaser (in press) discuss the procedural knowledge of experts as
involving larger numbers of more finely discriminated procedures organized in
different ways. This more elaborate and efficient procedural knowledge may
provide experts with more effective problem-solving strategies (Chi & Glaser,
1979; Simon & Simon, 1978). Furthermore, in their approach to problems,
experts employ more abstract, sophisticated strategies (Chi & Glaser, 1979;
Larkin, McDermott, Simon & Simon, 1980). They are diverted less by superficial
characteristics and identify more readily the problem's fundamental structures.

The implications of this literature for our analysis of political information
processing—and for social cognition more generally—seem obvious. The first is
that political understanding should depend vitally on prior knowledge that is
itself an organized and abstracted version of previous experience. Such
schemata—or sets of schemata—will include both declarative and procedural
knowledge. The second is that individuals will vary enormously, first, in the
availability of schemata and, second, in how they are put to use. Both schema
availability and schema use are shaped by practice in the domain, be it chess,
dinosaurs, or politicians. Just as some of us are chess masters and some of us
paleontologists, so too are some of us expert in the political domain. Political

---

[3]In social and political settings, the "problem" to be solved is less explicit than an algebra word
problem. Yet hiring a research assistant, compiling a list of dinner party guests that will get along
together, or attributing motives to a person who behaves strangely all may be seen as examples of the
social problem solver at work. Similarly, choosing a President and attributing motives to an impeach-
able one are examples of the political problem solver.

experts should be set off from the rest of us by the nature of the schemata available to them, and by the ease by which such schemata are employed in the various tasks set by political cognition.

Though evidently innocent of social cognition research, Philip Converse (1975) makes essentially the same point in his review of public opinion research. His discussion of citizens' understanding of politics emphasizes the interplay between new information and old:

> If an informed observer hears a surprising policy statement in the news by the secretary of defense, he may prick up his ears and pay close attention. He relates this information to what he knows of recent policy, what he knows of the secretary's relationship to the president, what he knows of past positions the secretary may have taken, and the like, since he is intensely interested to detect even small reorientations of national policy. In short, he automatically imports enormous amounts of prior information that lends the new statement high interest. The poorly informed person, hearing the same statement, finds it as dull as the rest of the political news. He only dimly understands the role of secretary of defense and has no vivid image grounded in past information as to the inclinations of the current incumbent. His awareness of current policy is sufficiently gross that he has no expectation of detecting nuances of change. So the whole statement is confronted with next to no past information at all, hence is just more political blather: in five minutes he probably will not remember that he heard such a statement, much less be able to reconstruct what was said [p. 97].

All we need add to Converse's analysis is that it is useful to think about the "automatic importation of prior information" in schematic terms.[4]

In politics, what form do such schemata take? With what types of cognitive structure do people approach information about the political world? Suggestive evidence on these points can be found in Converse's (1964) qualitative analysis of responses to open-ended questions included in a national survey. Respondents were asked to report what they liked, and in a separate question, what they disliked, about each of the major parties and about each of the major party presidential candidates. Converse classified respondents as "ideologues" to the degree they gave indications of a relatively general and abstract basis for their

---

[4]Explanations for expert–novice differences are strikingly parallel in politics and psychology, although the vocabulary differs. From political scientist Converse (1964), "The more highly constrained [inter-correlated] a system of multiple elements, the more economically it may be described and understood. From the point of view of the actor, the idea organization that leads to constraint [coherence] permits him to locate and make sense of a wider range of information from a particular domain than he would find possible without such organization [p. 214]." From Chi and Glaser (in press) compare: "The network of an expert's knowledge base . . . is dense, containing clusters of related information, whereas the network for the novice is sparse, with relatively few highly interrelated clusters [p. 4]." The general point common to both is made: The more experience one has, the more—and more organized—prior knowledge can be brought to bear on new information.

political evaluations (almost invariably liberalism—conservatism). Respondents who referred to general and abstract dimensions in their evaluations, but appeared neither to rely upon them heavily nor to understand them very well, were classified as "near-ideologues." Converse's most striking result was the scarcity of ideologues: Within the national sample, only 2½% of the respondents achieved ideologue status, with another 9% falling into the near-ideologue category. Evidently, political schemata seldom are constituted by highly abstract, ideological concepts.

Even Converse's critics concur with this conclusion. For example, Robert Lane, who has been his most persistent antagonist on questions of ideology, reached a similar conclusion on this particular point. In interpreting his in-depth interviews with a small number of working-class men, Lane distinguished between two modes of thought: "contextualizing," or thinking that places political events in topical, temporal, and historical perspective; and "morselizing," or thinking that considers events in isolation. Lane argued that for his respondents, on most political topics, morselizing was by far the more common:

> This treatment of an instance in isolation happens time and again and on matters close to home: a union demand is a single incident, not part of a more general labor-management conflict; a purchase on the installment plan is a specific debt, not part of a budgetary pattern—either one's own or society's. The items and fragments of life remain itemized and fragmented. . . . [Lane, 1962, p. 353].

The concepts used by the working-class men in their analysis of political events and problems were typically close to home: specific, concrete, and usually related to their own personal experiences—just as Converse would predict (Field & Anderson, 1969; Lane, 1973; Nie, Verba, & Petrocik, 1976; Putnam, 1971).

For most of us, then, the schemata imposed to order and lend meaning to political information are not abstract concepts like *liberalism* or *conservatism*. Few of us are ideologues. What forms do schemata take, then, if not an abstract, ideological one? According to Converse's evidence, most people seemed to rely on schemata tied to group identifications: for example, that the Democrats are for the working people; that Eisenhower is the kind of president who caters to the interests of big business.

One particular brand of group identification that plays a paramount role in political information processing is partisanship. Introduced by Angus Campbell and his colleagues in their suvey-based studies of voting (Campbell et al., 1960), partisanship was conceived of as a psychological identification with a political party that lends order—particularly evaluative order—to the complicated and confusing world of politics:

> Our interest here centers primarily on the role of party as a supplier of cues by which the individual may evaluate the elements of politics. The fact that most

elements of national politics are far removed from the world of the common citizen forces the individual to depend on sources of information from which he may learn indirectly what he cannot know as a matter of direct experience. Moreover, the complexities of politics and government increase the importance of having relatively simple cues to evaluate what cannot be matters of personal knowledge. In the competition of voices reaching the individual, the political party is an opinion-forming agency of great importance [p. 128].

The power of partisanship for the individual citizen resides, in part, in cognitive service: in its considerable ability to make sense of politics. Party identification is an enormously efficient schematic device in the organization of beliefs, evaluations, and feelings toward the political world (Popkin et al., 1976).

Some people, of course, *do* approach political information with more abstract concepts: Converse's ideologues. Who are such people? According to Converse's (1964) analysis, they are the well educated and the politically involved. Abstract, ideological perspectives on politics are found with any regularity only within a rather narrow slice of the general public. Thus, as one proceeds from the political beliefs of political elites to those of the general public: "... what is held to be central changes systematically: from the remote, generic, and abstract to the increasingly simple, concrete, or close to home; from abstract, ideological principles to the more obviously recognizable social groupings or charismatic leaders, and finally to such objects of immediate experience as family, job, and immediate associates [p. 213]."

So far we have argued that a schematic approach to political information processing makes eminently good sense in theory. In practice, there has been less attention paid to identifying political schemata than one could hope for. From Converse's and Lane's research, we do know that wide-ranging, abstract conceptions of politics are hard to find in the general public. Perhaps more importantly, we also know that there is enormous variation in this: Across the American public, politics is understood in vastly different terms. For some, characterized especially by their intense involvement in politics, new information of a political kind is greeted by the activation of well-organized, wide-ranging, highly abstract prior knowledge. For others, the processing of new information—its selection, interpretation, evaluation, and remembrance—is guided by narrower, less abstract concepts, such as party affiliations and group identifications.

Our analysis of political information processing must, therefore, be sensitive to the range and multiplicity of available schemata. It is at this point that the role of political involvement joins our analysis. Consider, for one moment, your thoughts about President Carter. After more than a few years in office, Carter continues to provoke puzzlement—in the popular press and in the general public. Some think him honest and well-intentioned but inept, crippled by an intransigent Congress: Carter as an ineffective outsider. Others see him in cahoots with the oil companies to jack up energy prices: as a typical conniving politician. Some emphasize Carter's background in the nuclear navy and see in him the prototypic technocrat: icy under fire, overcontrolled, technically sophisticated. Still others think instead about Carter as a Southern Baptist preacher: his occasional emotional outbursts, his apparent passion for human rights, his frequent moral appeals. Carter is a good example of schema–based understanding because he is such a complicated, enigmatic figure. Information about Carter is sufficiently diverse and ambiguous to elicit one of several schemata people might entertain about a President (or about this particular President).

Now there are certainly those among us who wonder about the fascinating qualities of Carter's personality, and often. But there are others who, out of cynicism, apathy, or a preoccupation with other activities, could hardly care less. Such differences are reflections of individual variation in political involvement.

More precisely, involvement in any realm—but here we consider politics in particular—comprises several interlocking aspects. By political involvement, we mean first of all cognitive engagement. The politically involved are interested in and attentive to information about the political world (Nie & Verba, 1975). Involvement in politics is also characterized by intensity of affective reaction. People distinguished by their greater involvement in politics will have more, and more intense, affective reactions to a wide range of political stimuli (Key, 1961; McClosky, 1964; Milbraith & Goel, 1977). Finally, political involvement includes an overt behavioral component. The politically involved are set off partly by their greater participation in politics, be it proselytizing for a favorite candidate, firing off angry letters to the local newspaper, or (more exotically) plotting the revolution (Nie & Verba, 1975). The three components of involvement—cognitive, affective, and behavioral—are conceptually separable but causally entangled. Greater attention to politics encourages sharper affective reactions and greater behavioral involvement. These, in turn, enhance interest in politics, and so the cycle continues.

Our special interest in involvement here hinges on its role in understanding political information processing. Political involvement provides a conceptual handle on interindividual variation in the availability and use of political schemata. Thus, for example, political information processing is likely to be facilitated (or at least affected) by comparatively abstract schemata only among the politically involved—those who possess the most sophisticated and elaborate schemata. Or, less extremely, it is the politically involved who can put abstract schemata to the most sophisticated use. Information packaged in highly abstract, ideological terms will be processed at roughly that level by ideologues but not by the rest of us who, lacking that level of schema, may miss the point altogether. Ideologues, in turn, may be cognitively frustrated by campaign coverage that emphasizes a candidate's charismatic ability to stir a crowd. Concrete or group-oriented information is more likely to satisfy the nonideologues among us.

INVOLVEMENT AND POLITICAL COGNITION

The most straightforward prediction from our analysis is that the politically involved should differ from the uninvolved in their processing of information about politics: in the nature of schemata available to them, in the ease by which such schemata are invoked, and the facility with which such schemata are employed in information processing. We did not come to our investigations of political cognition knowing this. Rather, these predictions emerged gradually from a series of experiments on political cognition (Fiske, Kinder, & Larter, 1979).

Our first study was designed to examine the role of schemata in processing information about third-world countries. It was based on our presumption that information about such countries is most commonly understood by invoking one of two schemata: a military government schema, which emphasizes Army coups d'etat, suspension of civil liberties, and assassination as prototypic features; and a (Marxist) exploitation schema, emphasizing enormous disparities in wealth, power, and prestige; a privileged, well-educated ruling class; and a vast impoverished illiterate mass. In order to make these schemata differentially salient, student subjects were presented with two descriptions of third world countries, roughly similar to special news reports. One group of subjects listened to accounts of Togo and Indonesia, depicted as exemplars of the military-government schema; another group heard descriptions of Senegal and Venezuela, described as fine examples of the exploitation schema. A third group listened to accounts of Ghana and Nepal, selected so as to invoke no particular schema at all. Then all subjects were presented with a third description, this time of an obscure West African country, Upper Volta. (Not even Harvard undergraduates knew anything about Upper Volta.) One-half the subjects heard Upper Volta portrayed largely as a military dictatorship; the other half listened to an account that emphasized the exploitation of Upper Volta's poor by unscrupulous business and political leaders. We predicted that making the military and exploitation schemata differentially available would shape subjects' subsequent understanding of Upper Volta, in directions consistent with the invoked schema.

Our dependent measures in this first study included subjects' recall, their organization of recall, the quality of their understanding of Upper Volta, their predictions regarding Upper Volta's future (e.g., the likelihood that Major-General Lamizana would be ousted from politics in the coming year), and their confidence in such predictions. We also included, almost as an afterthought, a battery of questions to assess subjects' political involvement, taken from standard measures developed by the University of Michigan's Center for Political Studies for use in their national surveys (Campbell et al., 1960). These questions included measures of the subjects' behavioral participation in politics, their attention to sources of political news, and their interest in public affairs and government.

The results of this first experiment, and those of a variant that immediately followed, were annoyingly uneven. We did find effects due to invoking different political schemata to be sure, but they showed little consistency. In one study, for example, subjects recalled schema-relevant information first (i.e., schema-relevant information is seemingly more available, Kahneman & Tversky, 1973), but in another subjects tended to remember schema-irrelevant information first.[5] Differences between the two groups of subjects seemed to explain this inconsistency. Specifically, the sample that remembered schema-relevant information first was composed of summer school students, many of them fresh out of high school. The second set of subjects, who showed the opposite effect, all were Harvard undergraduates and probably more politically sophisticated. Because the individual difference measures were only included for the latter group, no precise between-study comparisons were possible. But within the second study, the more politically involved subjects showed bigger availability effects than did the uninvolved. One general finding emerged from this empirical clutter, then: Politically involved subjects behaved differently from their less involved counterparts.

Now alerted to the importance of political involvement, we launched a second series of experiments. These investigations continued our interest in the schematic basis of political information processing. This time, however, we relied upon the network of assumptions people hold about *Democratic* and about *Communist* nations. We did so because when we asked undergraduate subjects to name types of political systems, these two were mentioned most frequently (with Socialist, Fascist, and dictatorship trailing behind.) Perhaps, not surprisingly, Communist and Democratic were also the "richest" categories. Subjects associated with each a distinctive set of attributes, touching upon, for example, ease of emigration, freedom of religion, standard of living, as well as elections and their corruption. Such associations extended even to assumptions about national character: Citizens of Democratic countries are driven by greed; under Communist systems, citizens are motivated by the common good—at least according to Carnegie-Mellon undergraduates.

Based on these data, we drew up a description of Mauritius (as far as our subjects were concerned, a hypothetical country), containing information of two kinds: Democratic and Communist. The mixed description was then presented to a second group of subjects, who were told that the country was, in fact, Democratic, that it was Communist, or were told nothing at all. As before, our interest here was in schema-based understanding of political information, but with spe-

---

[5]The distinction between schema relevance and schema consistency eluded us at that stage. Our subjects apparently did not consider the two alternative schemata to contradict each other, as we discovered in subsequent ratings of our stimuli by independent judges. Thus, strictly speaking, the information concerning each alternative schema was irrelevant to the other (Hastie, in press). Our next experiments explicitly constructed alternative schemata that were considered inconsistent with rather than irrelevant to each other, providing a stronger test of schematic processing.

cial attention paid to individual differences in schema use as captured by political involvement.

Our first dependent measure was intended to assess availability (i.e., ease of recall; Tversky & Kahneman, 1973). In a timed recall task, information *consistent* with the manipulated schema tended to be mentioned in the first minute. Thus, subjects told that the description portrayed a Democratic country tended to remember first those details consistent with that label—that the country held fair and aboveboard elections, for example. Similarly, information concordant with a Communist schema—for example, restrictions on emigration—were more available when the country was described as Communist. These differences were unaffected by subjects' level of political involvement, an indication of the consensual nature of the Democratic and Communist schemata.

Elsewhere, however, political involvement did influence information processing. That the politically involved follow different processing strategies—use schemata differently—is implied by three kinds of evidence. The first comes from an analysis of total recall. The basic schema prediction here is an interaction between schema label and information type, such that subjects best remember either schema-consistent or schema-inconsistent information; that is, schema theory predicts that once elicited, a consensually understood schematic label (such as Democratic or Communist) directs attention to schema-relevant information, but whether perceivers should focus on schema-consistent or schema-inconsistent information is less clear (Fiske, Kenny, & Taylor, 1979; Hastie, in press; Taylor & Crocker, in press). But regardless of which form it takes, an interaction of label and information relevance is indicative of schematic processing. Such an interaction did emerge in our experiment but qualified by subjects' involvement in politics. Low-involvement subjects remembered more schema-consistent information overall, whereas the politically involved showed no such tendency. Providing low-involvement subjects with a schema evidently helped them to organize information and, as a consequence, they selectively remembered information consistent with the schema. The highly involved subjects, however, were not limited to remembering consistent information: They remembered consistent and inconsistent details equally. This is so, we suggest, because they were particularly sensitive to the schema label but were not limited by it, as were low-involvement subjects.

Our second point is that although providing low-involvement subjects with a schematic label evidently helped them to remember information, they did not organize the information in as sophisticated a fashion as did the highly involved. Our measure of organization was the degree to which Democratic and Communist attributes were clustered in a free-recall task, controlling for total recall of that type (an index used, for example, by Hamilton, Katz, & Leirer, 1980). In their organization of information, low-involvement subjects seemed to rely on the schema label in a rather mechanical way, clustering together information consistent with the schema. Given the Communist label, for example, low-involvement subjects tended to recall in sequence several prototypically Communist attributes. Highly involved subjects appeared to follow a more complicated procedure, using *inconsistency* as a criterion. Thus, subjects distinguished by their greater involvement in politics, when given the Communist label, tended to cluster attributes in their recall that were prototypically Democratic. Such differences may reflect processing rules of differing complexity. One strategy would be to proceed through a description noticing schema-consistent information and ignoring the rest, but another—and more sophisticated—would be to notice each separately, collecting details that violate the schema. Note, however, that this, perhaps, more sensitive use of the schema label did not pay off in total recall, because, as mentioned previously, involvement was unrelated to total recall of schema-relevant information.

The final bit of evidence pointing to differential sophistication in schematic processing is derived from the predictions subjects advanced about the future of Mauritius. Low-involvement subjects made predictions consistent with the schema labels, whereas high-involvement subjects made more cautious predictions. That is, when asked "how organized would you expect the government to be?" or "how high would you expect the population density to be?", the less involved subjects made predictions in line with the label they had been given (i.e., for Communist, extremely much; for Democratic, not at all). Highly involved subjects, on the other hand, made predictions closer to the scale midpoint, less influenced by the label they were given. This makes good sense: High-involvement subjects seemed particularly aware of the ambiguities of the description itself and did not rely so blindly on the schematic label.

Thus the politically involved seem to make more sensitive use of consensual political schemata than do the uninvolved. Our involved subjects made more cautious inferences from ambiguous materials, organized information by a more complex criterion (inconsistency), and were not limited to recalling only schema-consistent information. In contrast, low-involvement subjects relied heavily on consensual schemata when they were explicitly invoked, remembered only schema-consistent information, organized information mechanically (i.e., by consistency), and made stronger schema-relevant inferences. In these various ways, political involvement seems to influence schema-based processing of political information.

IMPLICATIONS

Our central argument has been a simple one: that in a particular domain—be it personality analysis, chess, or politics—people may differ substantially from one another in the nature of the schemata available to them, in the ease by which such schemata are invoked, and by the facility with which such schemata are employed in information processing. The argument seemed worth making in large part because it cuts against the contemporary grain. Most social cognition research investigates, and in a sense capitalizes upon, consensual schemata, that is, *shared* knowledge about a particular domain. Our complaint here is only that such preoccupations should not (and need not) preclude analysis of individual variation. As we have seen, our argument on behalf of individual differences is supported both by developments in cognitive psychology contrasting experts with novices and by strikingly parallel though psychologically innocent interpretations of political reasoning advanced by political scientists. More pointedly, our argument is supported by evidence taken from several of our recent experiments on political information processing. Individual differences do matter—differences in involvement and expertise, in particular.

Although our analysis and results have been directed to political information processing, they hold implications for the social cognition literature more generally. The clearest prescription is that social cognition researchers should integrate individual differences in schema availability and use into their practice and into their theories. In particular, people's involvement in the invoked consensual schema will matter, and we have argued that three kinds of involvement merit consideration: cognitive, affective, and behavioral. Together, these facets of involvement form an interwoven continuum, from the completely uninterested, unconcerned, and inexperienced—the *uninitiated*—through those who are some of each—*novices*—up to those who are *experts*—fully involved cognitively, affectively, and behaviorally. In any realm, the uninitiated, the novice, and the expert will differ in the complexity and richness of schemata available and in the schema-driven processing strategies employed.

Consider the continuum applied to problems in social cognition. As we have seen, schema research has typically examined the processing effects of such shared social categories as extrovert, librarian, blacks, women, and so forth. In applying this involvement continuum, the most basic question is whether people understand the category at all. For the *uninitiated,* who fail this first and most elementary test, a schema trigger (i.e., a salient cue designed to invoke a relatively consensual schema) simply would not register. Presumably such complete ignorance is not an issue for most social schemata—at least for those that have been investigated so far. This is one respect in which political cognition differs from social cognition: The uninitiated are much more in evidence when it comes to politics.

Yet social situations do arise in which perceivers should properly be considered uninitiated. Consider the plight of a poor freshman who naively expresses an interest in becoming a psychologist. Such a person may have a vague conception that psychologists study people (more likely that they help them) but essentially no idea of the role at all, and no affective investment either. To explore individual variation in the availability and use of schemata about such social roles, we must appreciate that some—perhaps many—have only the barest appreciation of the label itself.

Consider again the freshman would-be major, but as a graduating senior with a dozen or so psychology courses behind her. Our senior is now a good example of the novice: without direct experience of the psychologist's role; in possession of a modicum of official psychological knowledge; emotionally ambivalent about the value of such knowledge. This intermediate level of involvement may roughly characterize our typical relationship to the categories that guide social information processing.

Finally, now imagine the student in graduate school, participating directly in the role of psychologist, becoming increasingly sophisticated and committed to it. Our student now possesses highly available and complex schemata for the role of psychologist: in this domain, she has become an expert (even if she can't find a job).

The fundamental point here is that schema availability and schema use depend importantly on individual differences—especially, we have argued, on expertise and involvement: The uninitiated do not have appropriate schemata available; novices possess concrete versions of consensual schemata and use them in simpleminded ways; and experts possess abstract schemata that they use in sophisticated ways. Our search for general principles of social information processing will be facilitated as we recognize that such principles are themselves contingent upon cognitive, affective, and behavioral involvement.

ACKNOWLEDGMENTS

We would like to thank various people who suffered through and improved previous drafts: Richard Ashmore, Michelene Chi, Reid Hastie, John Kihlstrom, Jill Larkin, and Shelley Taylor. The writing of this chapter was supported in part by a subcontract from the Center for Political Studies, University of Michigan.

REFERENCES

Abelson, R. P. Script processing in attitude formation and decision-making. In J. S. Carroll & J. W. Payne (Eds.), *Cognition and social behavior*. Hillsdale, N.J.: Lawrence Erlbaum Associates, 1976.

Anderson, J. R. *Language, thought, and memory*. Hillsdale, N.J.: Lawrence Erlbaum Associates, 1976.

Anderson, R. C. The notion of schemata and the educational enterprise. In R. C. Anderson, R. J. Spiro, & W. E. Montague (Eds.), *Schooling and the acquisition of knowledge*. Hillsdale, N.J.: Lawrence Erlbaum Associates, 1977.

Anderson, R. C., & Pichert, J. W. Recall of previously unrecallable information following a shift in perspective. *Journal of Verbal Learning and Verbal Behavior*, 1978, *17*, 1–12.

Bobrow, D. G., & Norman, D. A. Some principles of memory schemata. In D. G. Bobrow & A. Collins (Eds.), *Representation and understanding: Studies in cognitive science*. New York: Academic Press, 1975.

Bower, G. H. *"On injecting life into deadly prose"*: Studies in explanation-seeking. Paper presented to Western Psychological Association, Seattle, 1977.

Bower, G. H., Black, J. B., & Turner, T. J. Scripts in memory for text. *Cognitive Psychology,* 1979, *11,* 177-220.

Bransford, J. D., & Franks, J. J. The abstraction of linguistic ideas. *Cognitive Psychology,* 1971, *2,* 331-350.

Campbell, A., Converse, P. E., Miller, W. E., & Stokes, D. E. *The American voter.* New York: Wiley, 1960.

Cantor, N., & Mischel, W. Prototypes in person perception. In L. Berkowitz (Ed.), *Advances in experimental social psychology* (Vol. 12), New York: Academic Press, 1979.

Chase, W. G., & Simon, H. A. The mind's eye in chess. In W. G. Chase (Ed.), *Visual information processing.* New York: Academic Press, 1973.

Chi, M. T. H. *Exploring a child's knowledge of dinosaurs: A case study.* Society for Research in Child Development, March, 1979.

Chi, M. T. H., & Glaser, R. *Encoding process characteristics of experts and novices in physics.* Paper presented to American Educational Research Association, San Francisco, 1979.

Chi, M. T. H., & Glaser, R. The measurement of expertise: Analysis of the development of knowledge and skill as a basis for assessing achievement. In E. L. Baker & E. S. Quellmalz (Eds.), *Design, analysis, and policy in testing and evaluation.* Beverly Hills, Calif.: Sage Publications, in press.

Cohen, C. E. *Cognitive bases of stereotyping.* Paper presented to American Psychological Association, San Francisco, 1977.

Converse, P. E. The nature of belief systems in mass publics. In D. E. Apter (Ed.), *Ideology and discontent.* New York: Free Press, 1964.

Converse, P. E. Public opinion and voting behavior. In F. I. Greenstein & N. W. Polsby (Eds.), *Handbook of political science* (Vol. 4), Reading, Mass.: Addison-Wesley, 1975.

Downs, A. *An economic theory of democracy.* New York: Harper, 1957.

Field, J., & Anderson, R. Ideology in the public's conceptualization of the 1964 election. *Public Opinion Quarterly,* 1969, *33,* 380-398.

Fiske, S. T., Kenny, D. A., & Taylor, S. E. *Structural models for the mediation of salience effects on attribution.* Unpublished manuscript, Carnegie-Mellon University, Pittsburgh, Pa., 1979.

Fiske, S. T., Kinder, D. R., & Larter, W. M. *The novice and the expert: Schematic strategies in political cognition.* Unpublished manuscript, Carnegie-Mellon University, Pittsburgh, Pa., 1979.

Fiske, S. T., Taylor, S. E., Etcoff, N. L., & Laufer, J. K. Imaging, empathy, and causal attribution. *Journal of Experimental Social Psychology,* 1979, *15,* 356-377.

Hamilton, D. L. A cognitive-attributional analysis of stereotyping. In L. Berkowitz (Ed.), *Advances in experimental social psychology* (Vol. 12), New York: Academic Press, 1979.

Hamilton, D. L., Katz, L. B., & Leirer, V. O. Organizational processes in impression formation. In R. Hastie, T. Ostrom, E. Ebbesen, R. Wyer, D. Hamilton, & D. Carlston (Eds.), *Person memory: The cognitive basis of social perception.* Hillsdale, N.J.: Lawrence Erlbaum Associates, 1980.

Hastie, R. Schematic principles in human memory. In E. T. Higgins, C. P. Herman, & M. P. Zanna (Eds.), *Social Cognition: The Ontario Symposium.* Hillsdale, N.J.: Lawrence Erlbaum Associates, in press.

Hayes-Roth, B., & Hayes-Roth, F. Concept learning and the recognition and classification of exemplars. *Journal of Verbal Learning and Verbal Behavior,* 1977, *16,* 321-338.

Hinsley, D. A., Hayes, J. R., & Simon, H. A. From words to equations: Meaning and representation in algebra word problems. In M. A. Just & P. A. Carpenter (Eds.), *Cognitive processes in comprehension.* Hillsdale, N.J.: Lawrence Erlbaum Associates, 1977.

Kahneman, D., & Tversky, A. On the psychology of prediction. *Psychological Review,* 1973, *80,* 237-251.

Key, V. O. *Public opinion and American democracy*. New York: Knopf, 1961.

Kinder, D. R., Fiske, S. T., & Wagner, R. G. *Social psychological perspectives on political leadership*. Unpublished manuscript, Yale University, 1979.

Lane, R. E. Patterns of political belief. In J. Knutson (Ed.), *Handbook of political psychology*. San Francisco: Jossey-Bass, 1973.

Lane, R. E. *Political ideology: Why the American common man believes what he does*. New York: Free Press, 1962.

Larkin, J. H., McDermott, J., Simon, D. P., & Simon, H. A. Models of competence in solving physics problems. *Science*, 1980, *208*, 1335-1342.

Lippmann, W. *Public opinion*. New York: Harcourt, 1922.

Linville, P. *Dimensional complexity and evaluative extremity: A cognitive model predicting polarized evaluations of outgroup members*. Unpublished doctoral dissertation, Duke University, 1979.

Markus, H. Self-schemata and processing information about the self. *Journal of Personality and Social Psychology*, 1977, *35*, 63-78.

Markus, H., Sentis, L., & Hamill, R. *On thinking you are fat: Consequences for information processing*. Paper presented at the American Psychological Association Meeting, Toronto, August 1978.

McClosky, H. Consensus and ideology in American politics. *American Political Science Review*, 1964, *58*, 361-382.

Milbraith, L. W., & Goel, M. L. *Political participation*. Chicago: Rand-McNally, 1977.

Minsky, M. A framework for representing knowledge. In P. H. Winston (Ed.), *The psychology of computer vision*. New York: McGraw-Hill, 1975.

Nie, N. H., & Verba, S. Political participation. In F. I. Greenstein & N. Polsby (Eds.), *Handbook of political science*. Reading, Mass.: Addison-Wesley, 1975.

Nie, N. H., Verba, S., & Petrocik, J. R. *The changing American voter*. Cambridge, Mass.: Harvard University Press, 1976.

Popkin, S., Gorman, J. W., Phillips, C., & Smith, J. A. Comment: What have you done for me lately? Toward an investment theory of voting. *American Political Science Review*, 1976, *70*, 779-805.

Putnam, R. Studying elite culture: The case of ideology. *American Political Science Review*, 1971, *65*, 651-681.

Reder, L. M., & Anderson, J. R. *Use of thematic information to speed search of semantic nets*. Paper presented at International Joint Conference on Artificial Intelligence. Tokyo, 1979.

Reed, S. K. Pattern recognition and categorization. *Cognitive Psychology*, 1972, *3*, 382-407.

Rosch, E. Principles of categorization. In E. Rosch & B. B. Lloyd (Eds.), *Cognition and categorization*. Hillsdale, N.J.: Lawrence Erlbaum Associates, 1978.

Rumelhart, D. E., & Ortony, A. The representation of knowledge in memory. In R. C. Anderson, R. J. Spiro, & W. E. Montague (Eds.), *Schooling and the acquisition of knowledge*. Hillsdale, N.J.: Lawrence Erlbaum Associates, 1977.

Schank, R., & Abelson, R. *Scripts, plans, goals, and understanding: An inquiry into human knowledge structures*. Hillsdale, N.J.: Lawrence Erlbaum Associates, 1977.

Sears, D. O. Political behavior. In G. Lindzey & E. Aronson (Eds.), *Handbook of social psychology* (Vol. 5) (2nd ed.). Reading, Mass.: Addison-Wesley, 1969.

Simon, D. P., & Simon, H. A. Individual differences in solving physics problems. In R. S. Siegler (Ed.), *Children's thinking: What develops?* Hillsdale, N.J.: Lawrence Erlbaum Associates, 1978.

Smith, E. E., Adams, N., & Schorr, D. Fact retrieval and the paradox of interference. *Cognitive Psychology*, 1978, *10*, 438-464.

Snyder, M. *When believing means doing: A cognitive social psychology of action*. Paper presented to the American Psychological Association, San Francisco, 1977.

Snyder, M., & Uranowitz, S. W. Reconstructing the past: Some cognitive consequences of person perception. *Journal of Personality and Social Psychology,* 1978, *36,* 941–950.

Taylor, S. E. The interface of cognitive and social psychology. To appear in J. Harvey (Ed.), *Cognition, social behavior, and the environment.* Hillsdale, N.J.: Lawrence Erlbaum Associates, in press.

Taylor, S. E., & Crocker, J. Schematic bases of social information processing. In E. T. Higgins, C. A. Herman, & M. P. Zanna (Eds.), *Social Cognition: The Ontario Symposium.* Hillsdale, N.J.: Lawrence Erlbaum Associates, in press.

Taylor, S. E., Crocker, J., & D'Agostino, J. Schematic bases of social problem solving. *Personality and Social Psychology Bulletin,* 1978, *4,* 447–451.

Taylor, S. E., & Fiske, S. T. Salience, attention, and attribution: Top of the head phenomena. In L. Berkowitz (Ed.), *Advances in experimental social psychology* (Vol. 11). New York: Academic Press, 1978.

Taylor, S. E., Fiske, S. T., Etcoff, N. L., & Ruderman, A. J. Categorical and contextual bases of person memory and stereotyping. *Journal of Personality and Social Psychology,* 1978, *36,* 778–793.

Tesser, A., & Leone, C. Cognitive schemas and thought as determinants of attitude change. *Journal of Experimental Social Psychology,* 1977, *13,* 340–356.

Tsujimoto, R. N. Memory bias toward normative and novel trait prototypes. *Journal of Personality and Social Psychology,* 1978, *36,* 1391–1401.

Tsujimoto, R. N., Wilde, J., & Robertson, D. R. Distorted memory for exemplars of a social structure: Evidence for schematic memory processes. *Journal of Personality and Social Psychology,* 1978, *36,* 1402–1414.

Tversky, A., & Kahneman, D. Availability: A heuristic for judging frequency and probability. *Cognitive Psychology,* 1973, *5,* 207–232.

Zadny, J., & Gerard, H. B. Attributed intentions and informational selectivity. *Journal of Experimental Social Psychology,* 1974, *10,* 34–52.

IV THE SELF: STRUCTURE AND PROCESS

8 A Model of the Self as an Aspect of the Human Information Processing System

T. B. Rogers
The University of Calgary

It is commonly held that a major feature that distinguishes the human from other animals is our capacity for self-awareness. The puzzlement and wonder attending this capacity has been fodder for religion, myth, and art—and only relatively recently, in an historical time frame, become the subject of intensive scientific inquiry. Our capacity for self-awareness is most strongly reflected in our day-to-day experience of continuity of identity. I know that I am the same person now as I was in graduate school. Maybe some aspects of my personality have changed, but I am the same organism—the same self—as I was 8 years ago. This continuity of identity has become a critical construct of most self-theories. From James (1890) and his conception of the "I" through to Brewster Smith's (1978) recent analysis of selfhood as encompassing "the feeling of identity over a lifetime" we find this theme interwoven throughout our attempts to understand ourselves.

As the research begins to unfold in the cognitive domain, and social and personality psychologists begin to interact with cognitive psychologists (witness this volume), it becomes increasingly appropriate to ask if we can analyze these "feelings of identity" from a cognitive perspective. Can we, in the tradition of our colleagues studying the processes of pattern recognition or semantic memory, begin to unravel some of the mysteries attending selfhood? Perhaps an understanding of the processes involved in the interpretation of social and personal information will provide insight into this age-old problem of identity. Is it possible to extract information from the "blooming, buzzing confusion" of our mental lives that allows us to pinpoint critical features of the processes by which we interpret and remember information about ourselves? Can we use this knowledge to construct a model of how we retain continuity in our "feelings of selfhood"?

The concerns underlying these questions are not new—dating back through the history of civilized man—but the style of analysis and approach is. It is this new, neomentalistic approach (Paivio, 1975) to the classical problems of selfhood that is the focal concern of this paper.

In an effort to outline our approach to this problem, this chapter is divided into several sections. First, data demonstrating that the self is involved in cognitive processing will be reviewed. A discussion of the structure of the self follows. The final section introduces discussion of the processes involved when the self becomes active in the information processing system. The overall goal is to offer an accounting of how the self functions as an aspect of the human cognitive system.

A COGNITIVE VIEW OF THE SELF

The cognitive system can be construed as a series of "black boxes" that become involved in the information transformations occurring between the distal, external stimulus world and behavior. Each black box can impact on these transformations in any number of ways—it can guide us to interpret an ambiguous stimulus in a certain manner; direct our focus of attention on certain aspects of the environment, ignoring others; embellish input information to make it more easily retrieved; offer us a warning of potential threat; enter into our choice of responses in a difficult decision process—and many others. As a start, we wished to see if the self could be construed as one of these black boxes—as a cognitive structure which influences the processing of information.

Preliminary Data

An early manifestation of these concerns involved the use of the incidental learning paradigm popularized by Craik (Craik & Lockhart, 1972; Craik & Tulving, 1975). In an experiment by Rogers, Kuiper, and Kirker (1977), subjects made a series of ratings on a list of adjectives. For some adjectives the subjects made the familiar structural, phonemic, and semantic ratings; they made self-reference ratings (i.e., "Does this word describe you?") for still others. When faced with the task of remembering the words they had rated, subjects showed superior recall for the words rated under self-reference, relative to semantic, phonemic, and structural encoding tasks. The data suggest that involvement of the self during the encoding of semantic information produces a strong and rich memory trace.

Since that time there have been a number of replications (e.g., Hull & Levy, 1979) and extensions of this "self-reference memory enhancement" effect. Older persons show enhanced incidental memory facilitation under self-referent encoding compared to younger subjects (Rogers & Rogers, 1979), whereas clinical depressives show no such facilitation (Davis, 1979). In other experiments involving incidental memory for faces (Mueller, Courtois, & Bailis, 1979) and situations (Kendzierski, 1980), self-reference again emerges as a very powerful encoding task as reflected in the memory data. In addition, a number of papers have compared other-referent judgments (e.g., "Does this word describe your best friend?") with self-referent judgments (Bower & Gilligan, 1979; Keenan & Baillet, 1980; Kuiper, 1978; Kuiper & Rogers, 1979). In general, the self has been found to produce exceptionally "deep" encodings reflected in superior incidental memory, promoting Keenan and Baillet (1980) to suggest that "the self is the richest schema in memory [p. 5]."

Other research directions begin to converge on the importance of the self in the human information processing system. Memory for self-initiated acts appears to be superior to that for behaviors initiated by another person. For example, Brenner (1973) found superior memory for subjects' own verbal output protocols compared to what other subjects had said (also Jarvella & Collas, 1974). Markus (1977) found that subjects for whom dependence or independence were important to their self-concepts provided more exemplars of relevant behaviours than did other subjects. Furthermore, they were more resistant to data ostensibly conflicting with their self-ratings of independence–dependence than were other subjects. These data suggest that the self imposes some influence on the availability of personal data as well as the interpretation of and response to relevant information.

In our laboratory, current work continues to explore the kinds of experimental tasks that reveal the effects of the self on information processing. For example, we have found that highly self-descriptive terms are prone to a "false alarms effect" which shows that self-reference imparts a bias to perceive novel, self-descriptive terms as familiar (Rogers, Rogers, & Kuiper, 1979). The time required to make paired-comparison judgments of degree of self-reference of two adjectives is a linear function of the distance between the adjectives in self-referent space (Rogers, Kuiper, & Rogers, 1979), which indicates that the self is a powerful and consistent cognitive structure. Times required to make self-descriptive judgments show an inverted U-shaped function with degree of self-reference suggesting that the extremes of the self-referent continuum (items that really do *or* do not describe the subject) are being processed using a highly efficient cognitive structure (Kuiper, this volume; Kuiper & Rogers, 1979). Self-referent judgments show indication of being more efficient than judgments of other persons be they relative strangers (Kuiper & Rogers, 1979) or better-known acquaintances (Kuiper, 1978).

Each of the findings outlined earlier offers a demonstration that the self is involved in the processing of certain kinds of information. Stimuli ranging from adjectives through prose passages and personality items have been involved in paradigms involving experimental, instructional, idiographic and individual difference manipulations. Dependent variables of correct performance in various memory tasks, reaction times, free responses and subjective ratings have been used in these demonstrations. These indicate that the self *can* impact on the information processing system. In effect, this evidence allows us to think of the self as a viable candidate for the list of possible "black boxes" involved in human information processing.

The Self as a Prototype

With these demonstrations of the self as an active cognitive structure in hand, the question now becomes: *How and when does the self become involved in processing information?* Further, can we document the extent to which it exerts significant effects on the overall system? Beyond this, can we explore the self in systematic ways that allow us to comprehend it as an important part of our mental lives?

Our starting point here is to postulate that the self is a prototype that contains a collection of features the person sees as describing him or her. Its organization is probably not unlike those considered to underlie semantic memory. Cantor and Mischel (1979) offer a detailed description of such a structure as it relates to categories of people. In our case the elements of the prototype are self-descriptive terms such as traits, values, and possibly even memories of specific behaviors and events. These terms are ordered hierarchically, becoming more concrete, distinctive, specific, and less inclusive, with increasing depth into the hierarchy. Making a self-referent decision involves comparing the stimulus item with the prototype to determine if it "fits" into the structure. Presumably the self-prototype is a fuzzy set in that no feature is necessary or sufficient for category membership. Moreover, the self-referent decision is probabilistic in nature, in that positive and negative decisions will not always correspond perfectly with the presence or absence of the category in the self-prototype. The level of inclusiveness reached in the hierarchy while making a self-referent decision will be determined by the type of stimulus (e.g., global descriptor or questionnaire item) and the context in which it is presented.

The involvement of the self in a "prototypic" manner can occur in a number of ways. For example, a person having to remember considerable amounts of personal information (e.g., in a lecture about obsessive-compulsive neuroses) may be forced to self-reference these in order to encode them adequately. During retrieval, the "medical student syndrome" may emerge wherein the student is convinced he possesses the described characteristics. When dealing with other people the self may anchor relativistic appraisals of others (e.g., he's taller than I am—hence he's really tall; Snygg & Coombs, 1959), or a person may project his self-descriptive qualities onto other people (e.g., everyone is as honest as I am; Koltuv, 1962). These few examples serve to indicate the flavor of how the self may be involved in the processing of personal information. The fundamental thesis is that the concept of prototype—as considered in the cognitive literature—offers a good preliminary model of how the self works.

Empirical Evidence for a Self-Prototype

One advantage of the concept of prototype is that there are some clear-cut things that should happen if the self really is structured as a prototype. Three of these empirical expectations are outlined here.

False alarms effect.   When a prototype is involved in a processing sequence, it has been demonstrated that the probability of committing a false alarm in a recognition memory task (saying a previously unseen item was seen before) increases with the similarity of the item to the prototype (Cantor & Mischel, 1977; Pompi & Lachman, 1967; Posner & Keele, 1970; Reed, 1972; Tsujimoto, 1978). For example, Cantor and Mischel showed subjects a series of statements describing an extrovert (among other characters). They were then shown a second series of statements that included (among other things) the original statements and some new extravert items, with instructions to indicate which items they had seen in the initial test. Although the subjects accurately identified the original extravert items, they also tended to indicate they had seen the new items before. In other words, these subjects showed false alarms to the new extravert statements. These data indicate that the concept of extravert was involved in the subjects' processing of the original items. During the recognition task, this concept interfered with accuracy by virtue of inducing a bias to perceive new items as old. This finding can be used to infer that the prototype of extraversion was involved during the recognition memory task.

To determine if the self can produce a "false alarms effect" thereby supporting the prototype model, Rogers, Rogers and Kuiper (1979) gathered self-ratings for a series of 84 adjectives from a group of university students. Three-and-one-half months later, these same subjects were run in a recognition-memory study using these same adjectives. It was found that subjects tended to commit more false alarms with the highly self-referent adjectives. This "false alarms effect" provides evidence that the self functions as a prototype.

The prototype effect.   A second way of assessing the presence of a prototype involves analyzing decision times to decide if an item is a member of the category. Items that are very close to the prototype (highly prototypical) show fast decision times, as do those that are extremely distant from it (highly unprototypical); items in the mid-range of degree of prototypicality show relatively long decision times (Rosch, 1973, 1975; Schnur, 1977; Smith, 1976). As such, the documentation of an inverted-U-shaped function relating decision time to degree of prototypicality would be evidence in support of the presence of a prototype.

In our case, dealing with the self prototype, highly self-descriptive stimuli (and highly non-self-descriptive ones) should show faster RT's when compared to moderately self-descriptive items. This pattern of results had emerged in earlier research using personality items as stimuli. Rogers (1974a, 1974b, 1978) documented an inverted-U function between probability of a "True" response (p) to a personality item and response time to it suggesting that a prototype— presumably the self (Rogers, 1974b)—mediates personality item responding. However, this finding was based on normative data (using group determined p values) and cannot be used in exclusive support of the self-as-prototype view— although it is certainly compatible with this formulation. A more direct test is offered by Kuiper (this volume, 1978; Kuiper & Rogers, 1978). Here self-ratings were gathered after subjects had made self-referent decisions to items and had their response times recorded. When response times were sorted into low, medium and high degrees of self-reference, an inverted-U-shaped function was obtained. This documentation of the prototype effect for the self serves as a second piece of evidence in favor of the self as a prototype.

Enhanced memory for self-descriptive words.   Because prototypes are one form of cognitive schema, items that are easily accommodated into the prototype should be recalled relatively easily and well compared to less prototypical items. Such findings have been familiar in the literature on schemas since Bartlett (1932).

The most direct test of this deduction is in Perry (1979). She gathered self-ratings from a group of students and several weeks later performed a free-recall study on these subjects using some of these adjectives as items. She found that the self-ratings predicted recall performance, with subjects recalling mostly self-descriptive words. More support for this proposition comes from inspection of the incidental recall studies (Kuiper & Rogers, 1979; Rogers et al., 1977; Rogers & Rogers, 1979). In this paradigm, subjects make dichotomous self-referent decisions to some of the items and then attempt to recall them. A self-as-prototype position predicts that those items receiving a YES response (indicating it describes them) should be better recalled than those given a NO response. In all possible cases (23 separate studies) YES-rated words were better recalled than NO-rated words, indicating substantial support for the prediction. Interestingly, the YES/NO recall difference for self-reference tasks seldom reaches significance in a single study (see Rogers et al., 1977, p. 686 for a discussion of this). However, the constant emergence of this effect across studies argues that it is a meaningful effect. The one case where the YES/NO difference did emerge as significant was in the older sample (mean age = 55 years) in the Rogers and Rogers (1979) study. Possibly these older subjects have "more developed" self-concepts which function as stronger prototypes, thereby enhancing the size of the YES/NO recall difference.

The documentation of the "false alarm" and "prototypicality" effects for the self, in combination with the recall data, argue very strongly for the proposition that the self is a prototype. Although further research is necessary to uncover the boundary conditions of its involvement in information processing, these data present a strong case in support of the primary hypothesis.

The Self as a Fixed Reference Point

Another aspect of the self is that it is thought to function as a fixed reference point for the interpretation of personal and social information. The self appears to serve as an anchor point or immobile point of reference for deciphering and interpreting personal information. This follows directly from our definition of the self as a cognitive structure, when we consider that all information we have gathered about ourself *and* other people has been obtained in the presence of the processor's self. Thus the self, and its attending impacts on the information-processing system, is inevitably present when encoding personal and social information.

Empirical investigation of this aspect of the self can be addressed by means of a paired-comparisons task. Such a task typically reveals a symbolic distance effect, in which response latencies parallel the distance on the continuum between the items being compared, and a congruity effect, in which "greater than" judgements are faster for pairs lying at the high end of the dimension, and "less than" judgements are faster for pairs at the low end. These paired-comparisons judgements can be modeled by assuming that the subject places an internal pointer at some place along the continuum being evaluated (Holyoak, 1978). For example, if a subject is required to judge which of two digits is larger, he will place the pointer at the large end of an internalized size continuum. The paired comparisons judgements of "larger than" will be made in reference to this pointer. This model can account for both the symbolic distance and congruity effects. More generally, a strong symbolic distance effect seems to be indicative of a stable underlying cognitive structure, whereas the congruity effect shows that the subject is able to move his internal pointer from one end of the continuum to the other. The lack of congruity effect would suggest an inability to move the internal pointer, or in other words, that the judgments are made in relation to a fixed, nonmobile, reference point.

To test this proposition, Rogers, Kuiper, and Rogers (1979) performed two experiments where response time (RT) to choose which of two adjectives was most self-descriptive was measured. In Experiment 1 subjects first made self-ratings on 14 trait adjectives. They then examined all possible pairs of these adjectives and indicated which one they felt described them best. RTs for these judgements were then sorted into inter-item distances using the self-ratings. Inter-item distances and RTs showed a near-perfect negative correlation ($r =$

−.97), indicating a clear "symbolic distance effect." This result, combined with some secondary analyses, indicates that self-reference is a robust and consistent process.

Experiment 2 in Rogers et al. (1979) attempted to demonstrate a congruity effect for self-reference by having subjects indicate which adjective of a pair described them BEST for some pairs and which member of the pair described them LEAST for others. The emergence of a congruity effect would suggest that subjects could move their internal reference point. The results indicated a clear failure to demonstrate a congruity effect. A number of secondary analyses continued to support the conclusion that subjects appear unable to move the internal pointer away from the "describes you BEST" end of the self-reference continuum. This is tantamount to stating that the self functions as a fixed reference point. In combination with Experiment 1, this finding indicates that subjects were unable to judge in reference to anything other than the self in this paired comparisons task.

Thus, far, empirical data have been reviewed to indicate that the self is active during the processing of personal information. Evidence in support of the self as a prototype has been offered and further research suggesting that it functions as a fixed reference point has also been presented. These discussions sketch the bare bones for a theory of the self. Having documented aspects of its structure and function permits movement to a finer-grained theoretical analysis.

PROCESSES INVOLVING ACCESSING THE SELF: SOME POSSIBLE MODELS

The next major question that begs an answer relates to the cognitive processes involved with the self. What kinds of processes or mechanisms can be formulated to account for the data reviewed thus far? The fundamental concern here is with *how* the self—as a prototype—can be seen to interact with incoming information. It is reasonably well established that the self does influence encoding—but so far the mechanisms responsible have not been identified or modeled. This section of the chapter offers a start at these considerations.

An analysis of the sort offered below has relevance beyond the cognitive approach outlined thus far. One feature of personality research over the past few decades has been its reliance on self-report measures of personality. Indeed, the use of the personality item as a means of measuring personality has gained both in popularity and technological sophistication (Jackson, 1971). One of the troubling aspects of the personality assessment area is lack of knowledge about the psychological antecedents of an obtained True or False answer to a personality item. The researcher (or the practitioner) can never be certain of exactly what a given response means for a specific person. To be certain the accumulation of a series of responses converging on a given hypothesis can be useful. However, the processes and structures underlying the responding to such items are still relatively unexplored. In personality assessment the history has been to ignore the antecedents by suggesting they are not important (Meehl, 1945) or to adopt a rather restrictive view focussing on either content or stylistic variables.

The present attempts to model the processes of self-reference can be seen to offer an accounting of the psychological antecedents of personality item responding. Knowing the structure of the self, and how it is accessed or referenced, will provide information of use in understanding personality item responding. At the present, our knowledge about the self-structure is not sufficient to build a strong bridge between our work and personality assessment. Much more research is needed. Considered over the long term, however, the potential of the current work for being useful in analysing personality assessment should be noted.

The personality item, which is typically a first person singular sentence, is one of a series of stimuli designed to force access of the self-concept. Rogers (1974b) suggested that the processes attending this access consist of four stages. The first two stages (Stimulus Encoding and Stimulus Comprehension) relate to the linguistic processes involved in deciphering the item. The third stage, involves the comparison of the encoded item input with the Self structure. This Self-Referent Decision stage if of central concern in the present context. The fourth stage in the Rogers' formulation involves Response Selection. In a series of experiments Rogers (1974a, 1974b, 1978) was able to show that these four stages were modular or independent using Sternberg's (1969) reaction time paradigm. These results prompted the conclusion that personality item responding can be seen as very similar to other forms of psycholinguistic processing. In fact, the Rogers model converged on the Clark and Chase (1972) formulation which modeled the popular sentence verification task in the psycholinguistic domain.

The critical next step in the item responding model was to come to grips with the Self-Referent decision. This need spawned the post-1974 research in our lab. There are several families of models that can be used to describe the self-referent processes. These alternative formulations present themselves fairly readily. These are: a strictly associationistic model in the tradition of Anderson and Bower's (1973) Human Associative Memory (HAM) algorithm, a computational model that focuses on the availability of information, and a model of incorporating affect as an aspect of the self-referent process. These three types of models of the self-referent decision are discussed in the following sections.

HAM-Type Models

Bower and Gilligan (1979) suggest that the self-reference process can be characterized as an example of the general rule that "any well differentiated cognitive structure can serve as a 'hitching post' for evaluation and attaching to the items to be remembered [p. 429]." They go on to suggest that the self-referent memory effects outlined earlier can be understood in the framework provided by models such as HAM (Anderson & Bower, 1973). In this model the self is thought of as part of a network of concepts joined by specific types of logical relationships. The fundamental relation would be a subject-predicate construction (e.g., Anderson, 1976). Bower and Gilligan provide data that indicate that recalling episodes related to the self or to one's mother produced comparable levels of incidental memory.[1] These results led them to suggest that the general form of the semantic memory models can accommodate the self-reference effects.

If the self is a network of the HAM variety several things follow. Certainly it must be a very large net as the entirety of self-relevant experience must be incorporated into it. If this is the case, the "look-up operation" should be exceedingly complex and therefore time consuming. Even a directory telling where to begin the search (e.g., the equivalent of a card catalogue in a library) would be of a tremendous size, given the amount of information that is accommodated in the self-concept. This leads to the prediction of a "fanning effect" (Anderson & Bower, 1973), where look-up times increase with the amount of information in the concept. If the self is a HAM-type network, a "fanning effect" should be observed and the performance of self-referent judgments should require more time than other-referent judgments. Several recent experiments provide data to permit assessment of this prediction of a fanning effect in the self-concept. These relate to studies concerned with the time required to make self-referent and other-referent decisions and judgements about whether a word describes another target person in the incidental memory paradigm.

Some available data permit determination of the times required to make self- and other-referent judgements. Kuiper and Rogers (1979) had subjects decide whether adjectives described themselves or the experimenter. In Experiment 2, the self-referent decisions required a mean time (RT) of 2605 msec compared to 2846 msec for the other-referent judgements. In Experiment 3, self-referent RTs were again shorter than for the other-referent task (3191 compared to 3784 msec, $p < .01$). These data do not support a simplistic network model. Rather they suggest that there must be some feature of the self-referent process that is not presently postulated in the Bower and Gilligan formulation.

One weakness of the Kuiper and Rogers (1979) data is the use of a relatively unknown person (the experimenter) for the other-referent task. Perhaps the curious inversion of RTs relative to the HAM formulation does not occur for more familiar or well-known targets. Keenan and Baillet (1980) have presented data that speak directly to this possibility. In their Experiment 1, they used six other targets, self-reference and a semantic task—resulting in a total of eight encoding

---

[1] Discussion of the Bower and Gilligan data is restricted to the episode retrieval task because of their failure to include an evaluative task for the other target (e.g., Describes Mother?). Further, their use of constant stimulus exposure times and a between subjects design makes comparisons between this study and others in the area very difficult.

tasks. The other targets used were a best friend, a parent, a friend, a teacher or boss, a favorite TV character, and Jimmy Carter. These are in decreasing degree of familiarity. After making one of the eight encoding judgements on 48 adjectives, subjects were subjected to a recognition task. Memory performance was found to be a linear function of degree of familiarity, with Jimmy Carter showing the poorest and self-reference the best recognition data. These results were obtained using both normative and idiographic ratings of how well the target was known. Consonant with the Kuiper and Rogers (1979) data, the self-reference task showed the shortest RTs of all the encoding tasks used. These data further underscore the conclusion that a simple model of the HAM variety is not an adequate representation of the self-concept.

Important Self-Other Differences

One thing that should be kept in mind regarding the self as a cognitive structure, and attempts to model it, is that the self is clearly a unique cognitive structure, different in nature from those structures representing others. This uniqueness emerges from four special properties of the self-concept. Firstly, our self is the one person from whom we cannot escape. Like it or not, there are aspects of our self that will not change, and this differentiates it from most other cognitive structures. Secondly, as mentioned previously, the self may well be the largest and most rich prototype we have in our cognitive aresenal. A third property worth mentioning is that the self has a strong affective component. The blushing and giggling that accompany self-description exercises attest to this. Fourthly, evidence is beginning to accumulate to suggest that the self spills over into the encoding of information about other persons (Kuiper, 1978; Kuiper & Rogers, 1979). Possibly the self-prototype frames the dimensions along which a person categorizes other people, thereby inducing a subtle bias to seek out specific types of information during the processes of "coming to know someone." Each of these considerations cautions us against thinking of the self-concept as identical to constructs concerning other people. The self is unique and, as such, deserves sensitive analysis that treats it in an appropriate context, from a proper perspective.

One area of apparent difference between the self and other structures comes from comparisons of self- and other-referent encoding tasks. Kuiper and Rogers (1979) suggested that one of the differences between self- and other-referent encoding relates to the degree of organization of the cognitive structure accessed during the task. The "other" representation would appear to be less organized and integrated than the self. Possibly the increased organization of the self can explain the fast look-up times for self-referent decisions. The data speaking to such possible organizational differences involved an interaction in the RTs for self- and other-referent judgements and the probability of recall of an adjective. Specifically, words recalled under the other-referent task were those upon which the subject expended more effort as witnessed by the inflated RTs (M = 3223 msec), compared to words which were not recalled (M = 2714 msec). The opposite pattern of results was obtained for the self-rating task, with recalled words showing faster RTs (M = 2375 msec) compared to those that were not recalled (M = 2558 msec). Thus, recall under the other-referent condition is "effort tied," whereas self-reference recall is not.

These data suggest that there are different types of cognitive processes involved in the self- and other-referent tasks. The other-referent task appears to be a rehearsal or frequency process, while self-reference involves a highly organized and efficient mechanism. These particular data were based on an other-referent target person that was relatively unknown to the person doing the rating. Several other studies in Kuiper and Rogers (1979) allowed for a more detailed analysis of this "two process" interpretation and verified it for better known rating targets.

Some other data also speak to the potential uniqueness of the self-concept. As part of a larger study (reported in part by Rogers, 1977), subjects were instructed to use imagery as a mnemonic for a recognition task involving personality items. A group told to "form a mental picture of yourself interacting with the content of the item" did not show enhanced memory performance relative to subjects given no instructions. This surprised us as such interactive instructions involving two potent mnemonic devices in this paradigm (imagery and self-reference) *should* have produced spectacular levels of recognition. Lord (1980) has also documented the poor imagery qualities of the self using the incidental recall paradigm, while Mueller et al. (1979) have shown that self-reference instructions do not combine additively with other deep encoding tasks in an incidental facial recognition situation, again suggesting some differential characteristics for the self. These and other failures to document predicted self-referent memory enhancements (Mueller, Bailis & Goldstein, in press; Perry, 1979; Hansen, 1978) can be interpreted as indicating that the effects of the self are not simple and straightforward as would be expected from a "typical" cognitive structure. However, the research reported in this paragraph does not make the necessary comparisons with cognitive structures related to specific people other than the self. Hence, alternative interpretations that these effects are a function of social-cognitive structures in general—rather than the unique self-concept—are still tenable (Hamilton, 1979, articulates this argument quite well).

An Availability/Computational Model of Self-Reference

In contrast to a HAM-type model, it is possible to view self-reference as consisting of availability and computational processes. On the one hand, items that are part of the self-concept may be processed using the readily available dimensions that make up the processors' self-concept. These self-descriptive terms would be processed fast because the relevant dimensions would be "ready for action" in the Tversky and Kahneman (1973) availability sense. On the other hand, words that are not associated with the self-concept might require a series of intelligent guesses—or computations—to determine a response. This computed response would not be as fast as a self-referent dimensional response, thereby predicting the fast RTs for self-referent judgements documented by Keenan and Baillet (1980) and Kuiper and Rogers (1979).

Keenan and Baillet (1980) offered this model to account for the observed negative correlation between RT for encoding and person familiarity. When deciding if one's best friend is kind or honest it is very likely that specific behavioural instances are stored in memory that help formulate a response. Because of this availability the obtained response will be fast and leave a rich memory trace. However, with a person less familiar (e.g., Jimmy Carter) specific instances may not be available, and the person is forced to "guess" or "compute" a probable response. These guesses or computations will take time, *and* be more frequent with less familiar people. This suggests that judgments about the personality of unfamiliar persons should be relatively slow and produce weak memory traces, when compared to familiar persons. This is indeed what has been found by both Kuiper and Rogers (1979) and Keenan and Baillet (1980).

One expectation from the computation hypothesis is that words with fast RTs should be well remembered, as the faster words should be related to developed cognitive structures—therefore providing more elaborate encodings. A reanalysis of data from Rogers et al. (1977) allowed a test of this expectation. For each encoding task the 10 available RTs were subdivided into a fast and a slow subset (five RTs in each) separately for each subject. The computation hypothesis predicts superior memory for the fast subset, particularly in the self-reference condition. The critical main effect and interaction were not significant in the analysis, failing to support the computation hypothesis. The available data do not yet permit a definitive evaluation of the computation hypothesis. Further research is clearly necessary to fully explore this model and any number of hybrids that can be generated from combinations of the HAM-type formulations, availability versions and some of the schema positions currently emerging.

Affect as an Aspect of Self-Reference

While both HAM-type and the availability/computational model have some reasonableness, there is one major item missing. As currently formulated, these models do not really permit statements about the emotional quality of the self-referencing processes. It is possible that the inability of these models to completely handle the data is due to their lack of consideration of the role of affect. In their conclusions, Keenan and Baillet (1980) acknowledge that emotions may be a critical aspect of memory; "the crucial dimension underlying memory is not what the subject knows or the amount of knowledge that is used in encoding the item, but rather what the subject feels about what he knows [p. 25]." They also indicate that their data do not permit differentiation between their computational formulation and an account using affect as a central explanatory device.

A review of the classic self theories shows that affect has been accorded a key role in almost all cases. James (1890) argued that the spiritual self (this is similar to our prototype) is "the most felt and at the same time the most objectively obscure." Cooley (1902) indicates that things labeled as self produce stronger emotions than those not so labeled. Snygg and Coombs (1959), viewing emotion as a state of readiness to act, suggest that affect is determined by the relevance of the initial perception to the self. Carl Rogers (1951) sees emotional intensity as related to degree of involvement of the self. In a very elaborated cognitive model of self, Epstein (1973) suggests that cognitions that produce intense emotions are indicative of major components of the self. Not only does affect help to organize past experience, but it also primes the individual to act. As well, self-related affect is seen as an important component of day-to-day phenomenological experience.

Our model of the self—defining it as a cognitive prototype—is, at present, clearly deficient in its handling of affective phenomena. This position makes a start at integrating cognition and behavior by explaining what information we may accept or reject when perceiving stimuli in our environment, but it does not explain the particular feeling of self spoken of in earlier theories. Nor does it link the self directly to behaviour. Earlier theories proposed a motivational link between the self and behaviour, whereas the present theory has not yet developed past the stage of positing a self-related cognitive structure. It is clear then that if our model of self is to see itself as historically and realistically adequate, it must integrate emotion. As the basis of the present theory is largely related to memory performance, it may be fruitful to look briefly at what is known about emotion and memory.

Bartlett (1932) was one of the earliest researchers to postulate emotion as a component of memory. After a series of studies he introduced the concept of schema, a hierarchical ordering of information from general to specific. He also proposed that attitudes served as the basis for the organization of this information, and that the schema functions to justify this attitude or feeling. The function of the schema was an orientation of the organism towards the stimulus and in this fashion the schema affected behavior.

More recently, Dutta and Kanungo (1975) have produced a similar theory of the relation of affect and memory. For them it is the perceived intensity of affect which determines memory. That is, it is the degree to which a subject perceives that a stimulus is personally relevant that determines his—her recall for stimuli. To test this, subjects were exposed to descriptions of two groups of people. One group was the subject's own social group, while another was an out-group. After reading these descriptions, the subjects were asked to rate a list of adjectives, all of which had appeared in the descriptions. After this task, subjects were asked to recall the adjectives. Analysis showed that: (1) adjectives used in the story about one's own group produced superior recall; (2) adjectives ascribed to one's own group were rated as more intense on emotional scales and finally; (3) recalled words were rated as more intense than nonrecalled words. It appears, thus, that there is reasonable evidence for the relation of perceived self-relevance and emotion—the more self-relevant a stimulus, the greater the emotion associated with it.

Some recent data speak to this issue using the incidental memory paradigm. Keenan and Baillet (1980) examined recognition following evaluative and factual types of encoding tasks. Their results indicated the usual superiority for self-reference *for the evaluative questions only;* self-reference questions of fact did not produce a memory enhancement. When this is combined with Bower and Gilligan's (1979) finding that episode retrieval does not produce self-referent memory enhancement as well, a case can be made for the memory effects documented by us (e.g., Rogers et al., 1977; Kuiper & Rogers, 1979) being specific to evaluative types of encoding tasks. In other words, the self impacts on the memory system only when evaluative types of judgements are involved. This conclusion not only offers some reasonable boundary conditions for this area of research, but also gives us a place to start exploring affect.

Before developing a model of affect and self-reference, it is necessary to demonstrate that the self-reference memory effects are not simply due to the evaluative nature of this encoding task. If self-reference is redundant with other types of evaluations (e.g., good/bad, pleasantness and desirability), a better approach would be to study processes of evaluation in general, rather than focus on self-reference. Kirker and Rogers (1978) conducted a series of incidental recall studies using the group procedure (Rogers et al., 1977, Experiment 2). These studies involved using the evaluative tasks of good/bad, pleasantness and desirability in various combinations, as well as self-reference and the standard incidental recall paradigm. Each study involved at least 23 university undergraduate volunteers. The experiments are summarized in Table 8.1. In all cases, the affective tasks produced higher recall than the semantic task and lower performance than the self-reference encoding task. Although these figures may be partially affected by context, they seem to indicate that the affective rating tasks are not identical to the self-reference task. These data establish self-reference as different from standard evaluative ratings. These data, in combination with some other experiments (e.g., Experiment 3 in Rogers, 1977), indicate that self-reference is not just another evaluative task. Rather, it shows properties that differentiate it from standard evaluative judgements. Although finer-grained analyses are necessary before substantive documentation of the actual differences between self-reference and evaluative tasks can be made, these open the door to modelling how affect may become involved in self-reference. A preliminary model follows.

A model of affect in self-reference.   We assume that affect exerts its major effects during the encoding of personal information. Essentially, highly self-

TABLE 8.1
Mean Proportion Correct Scores as a Function of
Encoding Tasks for the Incidental Recall Studies
in Kirker & Rogers (1978)

Tasks	Number of Studies	YES	NO	Mean
Long?	5	.07	.17	.12
Rhythmic?	5	.13	.11	.12
Specific?	6	.14	.11	.12
Pleasant?	2	.16	.13	.14
Good?	1	.19	.15	.17
Desirable?	2	.21	.17	.19
Describes You?	3	.33	.25	.29

descriptive terms—those highly accessible in the subject's self prototype—are though to be involved in the determination of which aspects of the environment are personally relevant. Thus, a highly independent person will be monitoring his environment for indicators of independence both in other people and in terms of feedback about his own self-concept. This person has ready access to behavioral exemplars relating to highly self-descriptive terms (Markus, 1977), making these kinds of evaluations easy to execute. The person can be thought of as "maintaining a watching brief" for indicators of self-relevant events. When such an indicator is encountered, the person's attention is directed toward it. In this way *the self becomes involved in encoding personal information by directing attention to certain aspects of the current environment.* This attention direction is toward information that is personally relevant *and* also toward information that the person is already an "expert" at analyzing. Affect, then, is thought to direct the person's attention toward a specific environmental occurrence. An event indicative of kindness may not be signaled for a person whose self-concept is centered on independence, but for a person with kindness in his self-prototype, it would evoke an affective response, thereby drawing the person's attention to it. The affective response can be seen to act as an "early warning system" to signal the importance of currently available information and to direct attention toward salient aspects of the current processing environment.

This model suggests that the encoding of a unit of personal information will be a combination of the actual cognition plus an affective signal or tag. Encodings with this tag will be self-relevant and probably embellished because of the comparison with the self-descriptive terms. The strength of the signal will vary directly as the degree of self-relevance—and will effect the strength of the memory trace left by the encoding operation. The affective signal here will act as a kind of amplifier, increasing embellishment and interpretation of the input along the dimensions framed by the person's self-concept.

The resulting model is a two-factor account of the encoding trace. One factor derives from the cognitive procesisng system in the tradition of Craik and Lockhart (1972), in which availability/computational processes are active. The second factor relates to the affective signal, which also becomes part of the memory trace. It is conceivable that these two components are very different in terms of neural or cognitive representation and in the rules or laws that govern how they are processed prior to becoming part of the memory trace. For example, the affective signal may be fast and undifferentiated relative to the cognitive component. Further, it is also possible that these two components interact in complex ways. For example, a strong affective signal could serve to inject more effort into cognitive processing, causing an even more embellished cognitive component in the memory trace. Possibly a strong, but negative, affective response moderates the cognitive processing by diverting attention elsewhere or overloading the system.

In a post-hoc fashion, this formulation can accommodate most of the data reviewed thus far. The faster RTs for self-reference judgements (e.g., Keenan & Baillet, 1980) derive from the "watching brief" concept plus the affective signal, which implies an enhanced readiness to process self-referent information. The superiority of self-referent memory performance for evaluative tasks (e.g., Rogers et al., 1977) results from the rich and strong two-factor trace left by a self-referent judgement. The failure to document self-referent memory enhancement for nonevaluative tasks (e.g., Bower & Gilligan, 1979; Keenan & Baillet, 1980; Mueller et al., in press) results from the affective component being less salient to the processing task, thereby not augmenting the cognitive component of the trace. The superiority of self-reference encoding over other evaluative tasks (e.g., Kirker &Rogers, 1978) is due to the relative lack of structure in the cognitive system. For the evaluative tasks, affect is there, but the nonstructured cognitive trace cannot incorporate it effectively. If recognition memory involves comparing the processed input of the test item with memory traces from the study phase of the experiment, the "false alarm effect" documented in Rogers et al., (1979) is also explained. Self-referent adjectives will produce strong affective signals during the test stage of the study. It is reasonable to assume that the test/study item memory comparison will sometimes be influenced by the affective component of the trace—predicting increased confusions with increased degree of self-reference, which was found in Rogers et al., (1979).

To date, we have only one study that speaks directly to this model-incorporating affect. Kirker (in preparation) conducted an incidental recall study using words rated as either "very emotional" or neutral. The attempt here was to isolate the emotionality component in order to determine if it interacted appropriately with the self-reference task. The emotionality ratings required the subjects to indicate "the feeling of arousal or excitement conveyed in the words." If emotionality acts as an amplifier for the self-referent task, incidental self-referent recall should be greatest for the highly emotional words. Using idiographic emotionality ratings, this prediction was confirmed in the Kirker data. Normative emotionality ratings did not show this effect, suggesting substantial individual difference variance.

This one study in no way validates the two-factor model outlined earlier. Psychometric research is necessary to establish the construct validity of the emotionality ratings and a number of other derivations should be put to empirical test before considering this a viable formulation. Furthermore, additional theorizing regarding the interaction of the embellishment and affective components of the trace will be necessary to flush out this model. For now, the main thing is that affect has been added to the cognitive models available for the self-referent process. As the strictly cognitive models (i.e., HAM-type and the computation hypothesis) have some difficulty handling both the data and the phenomenological experience of selfhood, the insertion of an affective component seems necessary. Whether the particular version proffered here will stand the test of time remains to be seen.

SOME CONCLUDING REMARKS

One of the strongest temptations in working with the self is to move into theorizing before the data is fully supportive. This is a very real temptation given the contemporary cries of "relevance" and "community interest" that are echoing throughout academia. However, as far as the self is concerned, this temptation should be resisted. The history of self-theory is rife with examples of formulations without sufficient empirical documentation. As such, the self has earned, in empirically oriented circles at least, a very poor reputation.

Our current work ascribes to the need for a strong interaction between data and theory in an effort to bring some aspects of self-theory into focus. To this end, some of our empirical demonstrations may appear insignificant. But the critical thing is to explore all avenues of theoretical expectation through data. Only then can we uncover the hidden assumptions and value judgements that creep into our science. Ours is a commitment to a *neomentalistic* approach to the self, as outlined by Paivio (1975). This emergent approach embraces:

> mental phenomena as its subject matter and behavioural approaches as the method of study. It aims to understand both the form and function of ideas, images, meanings, and anything else that can be conceptualized as cognitive information by studying their behavioural manifestations and relating these to a theory of mind [p. 264].

The major characteristic of a neomentalistic approach to self is its commitment to thoroughgoing empirical analysis of any theoretical propositions that are advanced. This is a fundamental divergence between previous self-theory and research and the current work. While nonempirical speculation is clearly necessary in the initial stages of experimental planning, the final verdict of the admissability of a proposition must be based on the behavioral evidence that has been gathered. The need for this "hardheaded" stance is underlined by Paivio (1975):

> Mentalistic ideas are so seductive that one is in danger of being led by them down the garden path of introspection and mysticism forever. For that reason, perhaps only a tough-mined behaviourist can afford to entertain the seductress [p. 287].

This adoption of a "hard-line" on the admissability of theoretical propositions is an important feature of current research in that it differentiates it from previous research efforts involving the self (see Wylie, 1974 for a detailed critique of the previous work).

This "hardheaded" stance is especially important in dealing with the self. It is clear that our current culture values a highly individualized view of man (e.g., Kanfer, 1979; Smith, 1978). A part of this is a tendency to reify the self and accord it status beyond what it merits. It is a short leap before such cultural factors become injected into our science (Sampson, 1977) and hidden assumptions begin to colour our understanding even more than they already do. An awareness of this possibility, in combination with a firm commitment to the canons of empirical investigation, offers promise of new and meaningful developments in understanding the self. With this in mind, it becomes possible to forge a theory of self that will speak to the issues of human identity and selfhood. If we keep our guard up, an understanding of the self as mental structure and a series of operations involving this structure *can* offer insights into the psychological reality of the experience of human identity and its continuity over time.

ACKNOWLEDGMENT

Preparation of this report and the research carried out in our laboratory was supported by grants from the Social Sciences and Humanities Research Council of Canada.

REFERENCES

Anderson, J. R. *Language, memory and thought*. Hillsdale, N.J.: Lawrence Erlbaum Assoc., 1976.
Anderson, J. R., & Bower, G. H. *Human associative memory*. Hillsdale, N.J.: Lawrence Erlbaum Assoc., 1973.
Bartlett, F. C. *Remembering*. Cambridge, G. B.: Cambridge University Press, 1932.
Bower, G. H., & Gilligan, S. G. Remembering information related to one's self. *Journal of Research in Personality*, 1979, *13*, 420–432.

Brenner, M. The next-in-line effect. *Journal of Verbal Learning and Verbal Behavior,* 1973, *12,* 320–323.

Cantor, N., & Mischel, W. Traits as prototypes: Effects on recognition memory. *Journal of Personality and Social Psychology,* 1977, *35*(1), 38–48.

Cantor, N., & Mischel, W. Prototypes in person perception. In L. Berkowitz (Ed.), *Advances in Experimental Social Psychology.* New York: Academic Press, 1979.

Clark, H. H., & Chase, W. G. On the process of comparing sentences against pictures. *Cognitive Psychology,* 1972, *3,* 472–517.

Cooley, C. H. *Human nature and the social order.* New York: Scribner, 1902.

Craik, F. I. M., & Lockart, R. S. Levels of processing: A framework for memory research. *Journal of Verbal Learning and Verbal Behavior,* 1972, *11,* 671–684.

Craik, F. I. M., & Tulving, E. Depth of processing and the retention of words in episodic memory. *Journal of Experimental Psychology: General,* 1975, *104*(3), 268–294.

Davis, H. Self-reference and the encoding of personal information in depression. *Cognitive Therapy and Research,* 1979, *3,* 97–110.

Dutta, S., & Kanungo, R. N. *Affect and memory: A reformulation.* Oxford: Pergamon Press, 1975.

Epstein, S. The self-concept revisited: Or a theory of a theory. *American Psychologists,* 1973, *28,* 404–416.

Hamilton, D. L. *Cognitive representations of others.* Unpublished manuscript, University of California, Santa Barbara, 1979.

Hansen, E. *Self-reference and identity status.* Master's thesis, The University of Calgary, 1978.

Holyoak, K. J. Cognitive reference points in comparative judgement. *Cognitive Psychology,* 1978, *10,* 203–243.

Hull, J. G., & Levy, A. S. The organizational functions of the self: An alternative to the Duval and Wicklund model of self-awareness. *Journal of Personality and Social Psychology,* 1979, *37,* 756–768.

Jackson, D. N. The dynamics of structured personality tests: 1971. *Psychological Review,* 1971, *78*(3), 229–248.

James, W. *Principles of psychology.* New York: Holt, 1890.

Jarvella, R. J., & Collas, J. G. Memory for the intentions of sentences. *Memory and Cognition,* 1974, *2,* 185–188.

Kanfer, F. H. Personal control, social control, and altruism: Can society survive the age of Individualism? *American Psychologist,* 1979, *3,* 231–239.

Keenan, J. M., & Baillet, S. D. Memory for personally and socially significant events. In R. S. Nickerson (Ed.), *Attention and performance VIII.* Hillsdale, N.J.: Lawrence Erlbaum Assoc., 1980.

Kendzierski, D. Self-schemata and scripts: The recall of self-referent and scriptal information. *Personality and Social Psychology Bulletin,* 1980, *6,* 23–29.

Kirker, W. S. *Emotionality and self-reference in the encoding of personal information.* Master's thesis, The University of Calgary, in preparation.

Kirker, W. S., & Rogers, T. B. *Self-reference and affect.* Unpublished manuscript, The University of Calgary, 1978.

Koltuv, B. Some characteristics of intrajudge trait intercorrelations. *Psychological Monographs,* 1962, *76* (33, Whole No. 552).

Kuiper, N. A. *The self as an agent in the processing of personal information about others.* Unpublished doctoral dissertation, The University of Calgary, 1978.

Kuiper, N. A., & Rogers, T. B. *Convergent evidence for the self as a cognitive prototype.* Paper presented at Canadian Psychological Association meetings, Ottawa, 1978.

Kuiper, N. A., & Rogers, T. B. The encoding of personal information: Self-other differences. *Journal of Personality and Social Psychology,* 1979, *37,* 449–514.

Lord, C. G. *Schemas and images as memory aids: Two modes of processing social information.* *Journal of Personality and Social Psychology,* 1980, *38,* 257–269.

Markus, H. Self-schemata and processing information about the self. *Journal of Personality and Social Psychology,* 1977, *35,* 63–78.

Meehl, P. E. The dynamics of "structured" personality tests. *Journal of Clinical Psychology,* 1945, *1,* 296–303.

Moyer, R. S. Comparing objects in memory. *Perception and Psychophysics,* 1973, *13*(2), 180–184.

Mueller, J. H., Bailis, K. L., & Goldstein, A. G. Depth of processing and anxiety in facial recognition. *British Journal of Psychology,* in press.

Mueller, J. H., Courtois, M. R., & Bailis, K. L. *Self-reference in facial recognition.* Unpublished manuscript, University of Missouri, Columbia, 1979.

Paivio, A. Neomentalism. *Canadian Journal of Psychology,* 1975, *29,* 263–291.

Perry, D. *Self-reference as an aspect of memory for connected discourse.* Master's thesis, The University of Calgary, 1979.

Pompi, K. F., & Lachman, R. Surrogate processes in the short term retention of connected discourse. *Journal of Experimental Psychology,* 1967, *75,* 143–150.

Posner, M. I., & Keele, S. W. Retention of abstract ideas. *Journal of Experimental Psychology,* 1970, *83,* 304–308.

Reed, S. K. Pattern recognition and categorization. *Cognitive Psychology,* 1972, *3,* 382–407.

Rogers, C. R. *Client-centered therapy.* New York: Houghton Mifflin, 1951.

Rogers, P. J., & Rogers, T. B. *Self-referent encoding in a middle aged group.* Unpublished manuscript, The University of Calgary, 1979.

Rogers, T. B. An analysis of the stages underlying the process of responding to personality items. *Acta Psychologica,* 1974, *38*(3), 204–214. (a)

Rogers, T. B. An analysis of two central stages underlying responding to personality items: The self-referent decision and response selection. *Journal of Research in Personality,* 1974, *8,* 128–138. (b)

Rogers, T. B. Self-reference in memory: Recognition of personality items. *Journal of Research in Personality,* 1977, *11,* 295–305.

Rogers, T. B. Experimental evidence for the similarity of personality and attitude item responding. *Acta Psychologica,* 1978, *42,* 21–28.

Rogers, T. B., Kuiper, N. A., & Kirker, W. S. Self-reference and the encoding of personal information. *Journal of Personality and Social Psychology,* 1977, *35*(9), 677–688.

Rogers, T. B., Rogers, P. J., & Kuiper, N. A. Evidence for the self as a cognitive prototype: The "false alarms effect." *Personality and Social Psychology Bulletin,* 1979, *5,* 53–56.

Rogers, T. B., Kuiper, N. A., & Rogers, P. J. Symbolic distance and congruity effects for paired-comparison judgements of degree of self-reference. *Journal of Research in Personality,* 1979, *13,* 433–449.

Rosch, E. On the internal structure of perceptual and semantic categories. In T. E. More (Ed.), *Cognitive development and acquisition of language.* New York: Academic Press, 1973.

Rosch, E. Cognitive representations of semantic categories. *Journal of Experimental Psychology: General,* 1975, *104,* 192–233.

Sampson, E. E. Psychology and the American ideal. *Journal of Personality and Social Psychology,* 1977, *35*(11), 767–782.

Schnur, P. Testing the encoding elaboration hypothesis: The effects of exemplar ranking on recognition and recall. *Memory and Cognition,* 1977, *5,* 666–672.

Smith, E. E. Theories of semantic memory. In W. K. Estes (Ed.), *Handbook of learning and cognitive processes* (Vol. 5). Hillsdale, N.J.: Lawrence Erlbaum Assoc., 1976.

Smith, M. B. Perspectives on selfhood, *American Psychologist,* 1978, *33*(12), 1053–1063.

Snygg, D., & Coombs, A. W. *Individual behavior: A new frame of reference for psychology.* New York: Harper, 1959.

Sternberg, S. The discovery of processing stages: Extensions of Donder's methods. *Acta Psychologica*, 1969, *30*, 276–315.

Tsujimoto, R. N. Memory bias toward normative and novel trait prototypes. *Journal of Personality and Social Psychology*, 1978, *36*, 1391–1401.

Tversky, A., & Kahneman, D. Availability: A heuristic for judging frequency and probability. *Cognitive Psychology*, 1973, *5*, 207–232.

9

The Self as a Cognitive Prototype: An Application to Person Perception and Depression

Nicholas A. Kuiper
Paul A. Derry
The University of Western Ontario

The concept of self has provided a topic of considerable interest to philosophers and psychologists alike (Diggory, 1966; Epstein, 1980; Gergen, 1971; Rosenberg, 1979). The early fascination evident in William James' (1890) treatment of this topic can be traced through to the more modern phenomenological approaches of the 1950s (Rogers, 1951; Snygg & Coombs, 1959). Even more recently, this interest in self has reemerged in a social-cognition perspective. Drawing heavily from the information-processing models of cognitive psychology, several investigators of social cognition have proposed that the self functions as a cognitive schema or prototype (Kuiper & Rogers, 1979; Markus, 1977; Rogers, Rogers, & Kuiper, 1979). In this role, it both facilitates and biases the processing of any personally relevant information encountered by an individual in his or her social environment.

The present chapter employs this social-cognition perspective as a theoretical framework for delineating the role of the self in two widely diverging areas. First, it extends and elaborates the self-as-prototype model by documenting the nature of cognitive self-involvement in the processing of information about other people. In doing so, it maps out some of the important elements in person perception and memory, particularly the dimension of familiarity. Second, the present chapter illustrates the application of a cognitive model of the self to research and theorizing in the domain of psychopathology. Specifically, we suggest that the self-concept displayed by depressives differs in several respects from the cognitive view of self typically held by normals or nondepressives.

THE SELF AS A COGNITIVE PROTOTYPE[1]

The origins for both of the preceding aims can be traced back to a cognitive perspective that views the self as a schema (Bartlett, 1932) or prototype (Posner & Keele, 1968). The self is considered to be part of the information-processing system available to an individual, and becomes activated according to Rogers, Kuiper, and Kirker (1977) "when a person encounters a situation involving personal information [p. 678]." As a prototype or schema, the self consists of both a structural and functional component. Structurally, the self has been defined by Rogers et al. (1977) as a "list of terms or features that have been derived from a lifetime of experience with personal data [p. 677]." This list of features includes both general and specific terms. The general terms in the self might be conceived of as being similar to personality traits. The specific terms, on the other hand, according to Rogers et al., may relate to "less salient and more situation-specific aspects of self-perception as well as specific behaviours [p. 678]." Overall, these terms are thought to be organized in a hierarchical fashion, going from the general to specific (Jones, Sensenig, & Haley, 1974). At a functional level, this cognitive model has proposed that the self (Rogers et al., 1977), "acts as a background or setting against which incoming data are interpreted or coded [p. 678]." The self-schema or prototype may function both to enhance and to distort the personal information-processing sequence.

This cognitive approach to the self has received considerable empirical support. For example, Ross and Sicoly (1979) have demonstrated that people tend to overestimate their own contributions to a joint venture and have more accurate recall for self-referent statements. Similarly, other research has indicated that self-referent traits yield an increased number of specific behavioral examples on a free-recall task and are more resistant to incongruent information (Markus, 1977). Self-referent decisions or instructions have also been found to result in enhanced recall (Kuiper & Rogers, 1979; Rogers et al., 1977) and recognition performance (Rogers, 1977) when compared to other rating tasks or instructions. Finally, it has been shown that self-referent judgments are extremely orderly and consistent in terms of rating times for paired-comparisons judgments (Rogers, Kuiper, & Rogers, 1979). All of these findings are consistent with the notion that the self functions as a schema or prototype.

When considered in combination, these studies have incorporated numerous dependent measures and various empirical operations to document the effects of the self as an integral aspect of the human information-processing system. As such, this research program embodies a *neomentalistic* perspective (Paivio, 1975). Just as some social and personality psychologists have offered overall strategies or frameworks for pursuing research in the personality and social

---

[1]For additional information concerning the theoretical model underlying the present work, see Rogers (this volume).

domains (Campbell & Fiske, 1959; Crowne & Marlow, 1964), so too have cognitive psychologists advanced broad conceptual frames or plans for conducting cognitive research. Neomentalism attempts to strengthen the data-theory bridge by using overt behavioral data (e.g., memory performance and response times) to make inferences about covert cognitive processes and structures. Furthermore, *multiple* and *converging* empirical operations or indicators are specified (e.g., instructional and experimental manipulations, stimulus attributes, individual differences) for each major theoretical construct in a proposed cognitive model. This systematic overlap and convergence is designed to provide a strong empirical foundation for any hypothesized constructs.

To illustrate the neomentalistic approach to the self, the concept of a self-prototype has been inferred from both a "false-alarms effect" in recognition memory and an "inverted-U effect" for rating times concerning self-referent personality judgments. In the first of these demonstrations, Rogers et al. (1979) found that the number of adjectives falsely identified as being presented during the study phase of a recognition memory test increased as these adjectives became more self-referent. In other words, more false alarms occurred for previously unseen adjectives that were highly self-descriptive or prototypical. This pattern is identical to the false-alarms effect that has traditionally been associated in the cognitive literature with the involvement of a prototype (Posner & Keele, 1968). In a similar fashion, Kuiper and Rogers (1978) have found faster rating times for self-referent judgments concerning adjectives extremely like or unlike the self, when compared to adjectives only moderately self-descriptive. This schematic inverted-U effect has also been documented for decision times concerning social attitudes (Judd & Kulik, 1980). Its extension to include self-referent judgments thus offers further converging evidence for the self-as-prototype model. Furthermore, it suggests that extremely self-referent terms (either high or low) are more accessible in memory (Higgins & King, this volume). This differential accessibility then facilitates self-referent judgments along dimensions or traits that are extremely prototypical or self-descriptive.

PERSON PERCEPTION AND SELF-INVOLVEMENT

An individual's self-concept may play a key role in forming descriptions, evaluations, or judgments about another person. For example, person-perception findings have indicated that the observer's view of self is critical in the choice of categories or dimensions selected for describing others (Dornbusch, Hastorf, Richardson, Muzzy, & Vreeland, 1965; Shrauger & Patterson, 1974). Specifically, highly self-referent dimensions emerge more frequently and earlier in descriptions of others (Lemon & Warren, 1974). Similarly, the attribution literature indicates that the self may function as a cognitive reference point for interpreting information about others (Hansen & Donoghue, 1976). Research on the "self-based" consensus bias has shown that individuals base population estimates and their causal attributions about others on their *own* behavioral choices, while ignoring sample-based information (Ross, 1977). Theoretically, Snygg and Coombs (1959) have proposed that the self functions as a fixed cognitive reference point for the processing of *all* information. Their argument that "people are not really fat, unless they are fatter than we are [p. 145]" also forms the basis for the social comparison theories of Jones and Gerard (1967) and Festinger (1954). Even more recently, it has been suggested that the self-prototype may function to organize personal information about others in memory (Hamilton, 1980; Ostrom, Pryor, & Simpson, 1980). In this respect, the self (Kuiper & Rogers, 1979) may "guide the abstraction process that allows us to summarize the available information about the other person [p. 513]."

The exploration of this type of self-involvement necessitates a neomentalistic research strategy, in which various stages in the information-processing sequence are tapped by different dependent measures. For instance, perhaps the effects of self-reference are most pronounced in earlier encoding stages rather than during retrieval. Combined with the possibility that extremely self-referent traits may be more "accessible" in memory, there may be a facilitation effect for social judgments about others along these dimensions. In this case, rating times for making various personality decisions about another might serve as the dependent measure, with faster rating times evident for the *perceiver's* most self-relevant traits or characteristics.

Rogers and Kuiper (1980) tested this notion by requesting subjects to make decisions regarding the applicability of adjectives either to themselves (self-referent condition) or to an actual person they were meeting for the first time (unknown other-referent condition). When rating times for decisions were idiographically categorized according to their degree of self-reference (low, low middle, high middle, high) for each *perceiver* a prototypical inverted-U effect was obtained for self-referent judgments. The effect also obtained for personality judgments concerning the unknown other: Subjects were found to make reliably quicker judgments about a *stranger* along dimensions or traits that were extreme in *self*-reference (either low or high) when compared to traits that were only moderately self-descriptive. This inverted-U effect for unknown other-referent processing replicated across two independent studies, in which a variety of strangers were judged.

One explanation for this pattern is that the self-prototype serves an "embellishing" function when the actual amount of information known about another is extremely limited. When required to make personality judgments about a stranger, a perceiver is faced with a fairly complex and difficult task. This is compounded by the scarcity of potentially relevant information to assist in the decision-making process. Under these circumstances, available input such as physical appearance, exhibited behaviors, and socioeconomic demographic data may be supplemented and bolstered by the use of stereotyped information pertaining to this unknown other (Schneider, Hastorf, & Ellsworth, 1979; Secord &

Backman, 1974). The use of such a stereotyping strategy allows the perceiver to embellish an incomplete memory representation resulting from an inadequate opportunity to observe the target (Kuiper & Rogers, 1979). The perceiver may also use his or her own view of self to serve this embellishing function. Because of their increased accessibility, these self-referent terms might be used more often and more quickly to embellish an otherwise insufficient data pool. The end result of this strategy would be a rating-time pattern that closely matches the pattern for self-referent judgments. Thus, the inverted-U effect obtained for self-referent decisions would also obtain for unknown other-referent judgments, as witnessed in Rogers and Kuiper (1980).

Although considerable research is required to explore adequately the preceding proposal, the embellishing function of the self is not inconsistent with current views in the attributional and implicit personality domains. As described earlier, work on the "self-based consensus" in causal attributions has determined that individuals often use their own view of self as a reference point for interpreting information about others (Hansen & Donoghue, 1976; Heider, 1958). Furthermore, the "projectivist" hypothesis (Koltuv, 1962) has suggested that this type of self-involvement may be maximal for decisions or evaluations concerning ambiguous or unknown others.

Familiarity and a Model of Other-Processing

Although the self-prototype may operate as just described when processing information about unknown others, its function may change as the other person becomes more familiar. This view is supported by several reports in the social and personality literature that hint at the potent effects of familiarity on the processing and organization of information about others. For example, one line of research has demonstrated that the willingness to ascribe traits to another person varies with familiarity level (Fiske & Cox, 1979; Nisbett, Caputo, Legant, & Marecek, 1974); another has revealed more complex factorial structures for implicit personality theories concerning personal acquaintances as compared to strangers (Koltuv, 1962). In general accord with these findings, Kuiper and Rogers (1979) have recently proposed a model of other-processing that incorporates familiarity as a key dimension.

Personality judgments about a stranger are based on a combination of several input factors including physical appearance, exhibited behaviors, social relationships, the context of the interaction, and various demographic characteristics (Beach & Wertheimer, 1961; Jones & Gerard, 1967; Secord & Backman, 1974). Cognitive structures such as stereotypes or implicit personality theories may assist in the interpretation of this input information. In any case, this judgmental process is relatively ineffectual and time-consuming due to the absence of a well-integrated and highly organized cognitive structure for the efficient representation, interpretation, and storage of personal information about this particular person.

However, as a person becomes more familiar, two critical aspects may change. First, there is much more information available about that particular person. The perceiver is often exposed to the other person across a number of occasions or settings. This permits a sampling of behavior to occur, with the amount of information pertaining to the other accumulating rapidly. Second, with the increase in familiarity also comes the additional time required to formulate a specific cognitive structure or organization for that person. This structure functions to reduce the increasing amounts of information about that person to a more manageable level. Multiple, redundant data about another are categorized via this structure in order to facilitate economy in the cognitive system. The final result is the development of a reasonably accurate and organized cognitive structure pertaining specifically to a particular known other. This structure then facilitates the processing of information about that person.

Some empirical support for this model comes from a series of experiments reported by Kuiper and Rogers (1979), using the incidental-recall paradigm employed in earlier work. In these studies the subject made various types of ratings on a set of personal adjectives (e.g., rational, outgoing). After completing the orienting tasks, recall was tested for the adjectives. Experiment 1 was conducted in a group setting during a classroom period and compared self-ratings with ratings of the course instructor, who at the time was a relatively unknown other. Under these circumstances, adjectives rated in the other-referent condition were more poorly recalled than those rated in the self-referent condition. Experiment 4, conducted in the same class later in the school term, when the instructor had become a more familiar other to the students, found that recall performance was equivalent in the self- and other-referent conditions. This facilitation in recall hints at the use of a specific cognitive structure for a familiar other. Decisions based on this structure would then produce reasonably elaborate memory encodings and subsequent enhanced recall. Experiment 2 in this series employed an individual testing method that permitted an examination of the response latencies during the rating task for items subsequently recalled. The orienting tasks involved rating adjectives with respect to oneself and an unknown other. For the self-referent task the recalled adjectives had very short rating times, suggesting the involvement of a highly organized and efficient schema that readily integrated new input. In contrast, only adjectives with very long rating times were recalled for the unknown other-referent task, suggesting the importance of effort or rehearsal.

A further series of experiments compared response latencies during the rating task with subsequent recall for personality judgments about the self and various types of others, including complete strangers, casual acquaintances, close relatives, and best friends (Rogers & Kuiper, 1980). In the case of a well-known other (i.e., best friend or close relative), recalled words had shorter judgment latencies than nonrecalled words. This pattern is similar to that found for self-referent judgments and indicated that efficient and well-integrated cognitive structures are implicated in processing of information about both the self and highly familiar others.[2] Again, in the stranger condition the rating times for recalled words were consistently longer than times for nonrecalled words.

Overall, this pattern offers evidence in support of a "two-process" interpretation of self- and other-referent processing. Processing of information about the self and familiar others appears to be schema-based, whereas processing of information about strangers does not. Instead, *effort* appears to be the critical variable, in lieu of an efficient cognitive structure for interpreting and storing information about a person. Such structures probably develop via an abstraction and consolidation process in which specific information relating to a person is summarized into more general and economical trait labels.

Further support for this proposed developmental sequence comes from an examination of results for persons at an intermediate level of familiarity (i.e., casual acquaintances) in the Rogers and Kuiper (1980) experiment. It was only at this particular level that recalled words, rated both "yes" *and* "no" (i.e., descriptive and nondescriptive), had longer rating times than nonrecalled words. This pattern may reflect the acquisition and retention of both positive and negative information in memory about that person, ranging from sociodemographic background material to individual behavioral exemplars and displayed attitudes and interests. When required to make a personality judgment about a casual acquaintance, the perceiver may first search through this specific information and then abstract it into a more general trait form. This search and conversion process would require extensive cognitive analysis and thus account for the longer rating times for both yes and no ratings in this condition. Rogers and Kuiper (1980) have suggested that this search and conversion strategy would apply only to individuals at a moderate level of familiarity (i.e., casual acquaintances). These people would be in a "preconsolidation" phase, where stored information had not yet been summarized. However, as a person becomes better known, the specific information is consolidated or abstracted. This "postconsolidation" phase would be marked by efficient schema-based processing, as demonstrated in the well-known–other conditions of the experiment.

Familiar Others and Self-Involvement

Although the experiments just outlined trace the development of a specific cognitive structure for organizing, representing, and interpreting information about well-known others, they do not address the potential role of the self-prototype in guiding or assisting this developmental process. As suggested earlier, one means of investigating this issue is to classify idiographically rating times for various

---

[2]Further data analyses of recall patterns for both tasks hinted at substantial differences in the cognitive structures involved in each type of rating. Specifically, the extremely poor recall performance for the well-known other-referent condition suggested that the facilitative effects associated with a "familiar other" cognitive structure are most pronounced during early encoding stages. In contrast, the higher recall levels for the self-referent task suggested that the self-prototype facilitates both encoding and retrieval phases for personal information.

personality judgments (i.e., self and others) into their degree of self-reference (low, low-middle, high-middle, high) for the perceiver. Using this strategy, Rogers and Kuiper (1980) found "inverted-U" rating-time (RT) effects in the processing of information about the self, close family members, best friends, and strangers but not for casual acquaintances. In other words, a rating-time "savings" related to extreme degrees of perceiver self-reference was not evident for personality judgments concerning casual acquaintances.

In an attempt to explain this pattern, Rogers and Kuiper (1980) postulated that the self-prototype may play a critical role in selecting and abstracting pertinent information about familiar others. For a casual acquaintance or moderately familiar other, the perceiver may be desirous of acquiring more information about that person. One possible means of searching for and organizing this material might be in terms of its personal relevance to the perceiver. Thus, the perceiver might invoke his or her self-schema as an agent to guide this search and accumulation process. Because it has been demonstrated also that extremely prototypical terms in the self-schema are more accessible in memory (Kuiper & Rogers, 1978), it is quite possible that these particular terms play a dominant role in determining what is selected and retained. Ultimately, this differential accessibility would result in the acqustion of a great deal of specific information relating to the more available traits in the self-prototype. Because this information had not been summarized, there would be no RT savings evidenced for personality judgments concerning these traits. However, as the individual becomes better known, a summarization process would occur. Again, differential accessibility of the terms in the self-prototype may have an important bearing on the exact nature of the development of this other-referent cognitive structure. Because more extreme terms are more accessible, it is possible that a summarization or abstraction process would be limited primarily to these terms. This restriction would reflect an attempt to develop a more succinct and economical cognitive representation, that, at the same time, would provide the perceiver with the kind of information that would be the most personally useful and relevant. To satisfy these criteria, abstraction may relate primarily to the more accessible self-referent terms, because these would probably be employed more often in the processing of personal information. This would ultimately produce a "savings" in RTs for these more extreme traits.

PSYCHOPATHOLOGY
AND A COGNITIVE MODEL OF SELF

Although the utility of the neomentalistic approach to the self has been repeatedly demonstrated in normal subjects, it may also extend to include the self-concept in various pathological groups. The remainder of this chapter applies the cognitive model of the self-as-prototype to account for information-processing biases and their sequelae in psychopathology, particularly depression.

Social and personality psychologists have long had a direct interest in clinical problems and their amelioration (Strong, 1978). For example, laboratory work on causal attributions and the conditions under which attributions may change (Jones, Kanouse, Kelley, Nisbett, Valins, & Weiner, 1971) led to the development of attribution therapies (Kopel & Arkowitz, 1975). Similarly, Ross and his colleagues (Ross, Lepper, & Hubbard, 1975) have documented the perseverance of beliefs, attitudes, and implicit social theories in the face of discrediting evidence. It is tempting to extend these notions to psychopathological disorders such as depression, paranoia, hypochondriasis, and obsessive–compulsive neurosis, where the patient cannot be swayed from a fixed irrational idea. In the case of depression, the patient may continually reiterate that he or she is a dismal and absolute failure and is personally responsible for all the wrongdoings and sins in the world. These statements are usually made in light of totally discrediting evidence and are extremely resistant to therapeutic intervention and change (Beck, Rush, Shaw, & Emery, 1979). Finally, Taylor and Crocker (1980) have suggested several ways in which schema-based information processing may place limitations on social cognition. One such limitation is that the perceiver may utilize the wrong schema. In psychopathology, parallel limitations can be noted in depressives' use of inappropriately negative schemata to encode, organize, and retrieve data. Beck et al. (1979) have proposed that the depressive has a negative perspective on himself, the world, and the future (i.e., the cognitive triad). These negative, self-defeating evaluations influence reflections about the self that tend toward overcontrol of the environment. Personal responsibility is then unnecessarily assumed for most unpleasant life events (Kuiper, 1978). Moreover, depressed individuals seem to believe themselves to be qualitatively inferior, tending to misinterpret or exaggerate losses and/or overgeneralize the meaning of self-relevant information. In schematic terms, one would expect the depressive to confront a given situation with a "wrong" schema, one that is organized to process data in a negative, unflattering, and self-depreciating manner, regardless of its objective or "true" nature. Overall, these parallels suggest that work in a social cognition that includes an emphasis on schematic information processing (Bower, 1978), and the various factors that influence category accessibility (Higgins & King, this volume) has a clear and logical extension to contemporary theoretical perspectives on depression.

The Self in Psychopathology and Depression: Cognitive and Interpersonal Aspects

Recent theorizing in psychopathology has placed an increased emphasis on conceptualizing disorders in terms of particular attitudes or views toward one's self. Bandura's (1980) work on self-efficacy and the self-system is a major example of this type of approach. Employing social-learning terms, Bandura has defined the self-system as a series of cognitive structures for perceiving, evaluating, and regulating one's own behavior. An important aspect of this view is the regulatory function of this system. If the self-system is faulty or error-based, then inappropriate self-regulation might presumably lead to psychological discomfort and psychopathology.

Indirect support for such a position can be found in studies of interpersonal relationships in depression. Some of this work (Lewinsohn, Mischel, Chaplin, & Barton, 1980) stems from an interest in the self-encoding of personal competencies. Lewinsohn et al. (1980) investigated whether depressives have an unrealistically negative view of self or whether their lowered personal estimates reflect actual social deficits, which are accurately perceived by the depressive. Self-ratings and observer ratings of social interaction were collected on groups of depressives, psychiatric controls, and normals several times in the course of treatment. Consistent with previous literature, self-ratings and observer ratings of social competence for depressives were lower than for the other groups. Moreover, depressives' self-perceptions improved over time. Less expected, however, were data suggesting the depressed were more realistic regarding their self-perceptions (i.e., yielded ratings that were closer to observer ratings) than either control group. Nondepressives saw themselves more positively than they were judged by observers, whereas depressives' self-estimates were closer to the way they were actually seen. Lewinsohn et al. (1980) posited an "illusory glow" to account for their results, suggesting nondepressives are characterized by a somewhat unrealistic self-enhancement bias; namely, we see ourselves more positively and less negatively than others see us. This suggestion received indirect support from supplementary data. Over time and improvement from treatment, depressives became less realistic in their self-appraisals, adopting the "illusory glow" of nondepressives. Overall, this study clearly supports the fundamental involvement of self-perception in how depressives and nondepressives feel and think about themselves.

Other lines of research have also examined interpersonal aspects of depression, and find, in general, that depressives elicit negative reactions from others. For example, Coyne (1976) recorded evaluations of students to depressed and nondepressed female patients using a telephone interaction paradigm. He found that depressives were evaluated most negatively. Moreover, subjects who had interacted with the depressed patients reported feeling more depressed, anxious, and hostile than did subjects who conversed with nondepressives. In general, this work highlights one role that negative self-evaluations may assume in depression. Depressives view themselves in negative terms, a phenomenon that would seem to extend itself into lower perceptions of themselves by others.

The Self as a Cognitive Prototype and Depression

The poor self-concept displayed by depressives may have important implications for the manner in which they process personal and/or social information. The emphasis on the self in depression (and its subsequent effects on information processing) suggests that the application of a cognitive model of self may reward us with an increased understanding of this disorder. This exploration might proceed along the lines described earlier. The neomentalistic strategy has been incorporated in a research program currently underway in our laboratory (Derry & Kuiper, 1980; Kuiper & Derry, 1980; Kuiper & MacDonald, 1980).

In one study attempting to evaluate the self-schema of depressives, Davis (1979) employed the orienting-task paradigm heretofore used with normal individuals. Clinically depressed [mean Beck Depression Inventory Rating = 28 Beck, Ward, Mendelson, Mock, and Erbaugh (1961)] and normal subjects made structural, phonemic, and semantic judgments on some words and self-referent judgments on others. These ratings were made on the same set of nonpathological personal adjectives used in Rogers et al. (1977). The depressives failed to show the usual enhanced recall for adjectives rated under the self-referent task, when compared to recall levels for semantically rated adjectives. Noting that this finding did occur for a nondepressed control group, Davis (1979) concluded that "a self-schema is not an active agent in the encoding of personal information in depression as it is with normals [p. 107]" and that "depression involved non-schema-based responding [p. 108]."

That "non-schema-based responding" should characterize this group seems somewhat surprising, in view of the previously outlined self-research and theorizing. Davis' conclusions are also puzzling in that they stand in marked contrast to the majority of cognitive distortion literature documented earlier for depressives (Beck et al., 1979; Nelson & Craighead, 1977). This literature would suggest that depressives also employ a self-prototype, but one that primarily incorporates material of a negative valence. A clue to this inconsistency may lie in the choice of personal adjectives employed in the Davis (1979) study. These adjectives had been previously selected *precisely* because of their nonpathological nature (Rogers et al., 1977, p. 680). This suggests that the "normal" target stimuli in Davis (1979) may be inappropriate for assessing the potential existence of a self-prototype in depressives. The possibility would therefore remain that depressives have an integrated self-prototype but that it is organized for the processing of different personal information than nondepressives. By incorporating depressive content in the personal adjectives, evidence for a self-prototype might emerge. In view of this, we have initiated a series of experiments designed to clarify the content component of depressives' self-schema (Derry & Kuiper, 1980; Kuiper & Derry, 1980). This work has manipulated the content (depressed versus nondepressed) of target adjectives presented to depressed and nondepressed subjects. Using the orienting-task paradigm, independently normed depressed and nondepressed personal adjectives (Derry & Kuiper, 1979) were rated under structural, semantic, and self-referent conditions, followed by an incidental recall test.

In contrast to Davis' (1979) conclusions, predictions for the Kuiper and Derry (1980) depressed students sample focused on a "content-specificity" hypothesis.

If depressives were to possess an integrated self-prototype that is specific for depressively toned adjectives, then the traditional recall superiority of self-referent encodings would obtain only for *depressive content* adjectives for the depressed group. Consistent with this notion, one would also expect content-specificity for the nondepressives' self-prototype. If such were the case, self-reference enhancement would be observed only for recall of nondepressed content adjectives (i.e., schema-consistent information). A slightly different pattern of results for the depressives could still offer support for a self-schema interpretation. In this less robust version of the content-specificity hypothesis, only nondepressives would distinguish between depressed and nondepressed content. Depressives, on the other hand, might display enhanced self-reference recall for *both* depressed and nondepressed content adjectives. If this pattern were to obtain, it would indicate that medium depressed individuals incorporated both pathological and nonpathological terms in their view of self, whereas nondepressives are restricted only to nonpathological content.

The results for nondepressives were clear. Their self-reference enhancement was limited *only* to nondepressive content. This pattern corroborates earlier findings for nonpathological personal adjectives (Rogers et al., 1977) and lends strong support to the content-specificity hypothesis for nondepressives. Essentially, it indicates that the self-prototype of nondepressives revolves primarily around normal or nonpathological content. Overall, the obtained recall patterns for depressives argued against the "non-schema-based" interpretation advanced by Davis (1979). Instead, the findings suggested that depressives also employ a self-schema in personal information processing, but one that differs in a variety of ways from a nondepressive's. Specifically, an analysis of recall patterns according to depth or severity of depression revealed that "mild" depressives (mean Beck Depression Inventory Rating = 11.05) did not benefit significantly from self-referent instructions under either content condition. In contrast, "medium" depressives (mean Beck Depression Inventory Rating = 19.86) showed enhanced self-referent recall for both depressed and nondepressed terms. This latter finding supported the less robust version of the content-specificity hypothesis for this group of student depressives.

To accommodate and explain this data, Kuiper and Derry (1980) outlined a self-schema model for depression in which severity level is a critical determinant of both the content and cohesiveness of the depressive's self-prototype.[3] As severity level progresses, the ratio of depressed to nondepressed content increases systematically. At moderate or medium levels this would produce approximately equivalent pathological and nonpathological content. At more extreme levels there would be an overrepresentation of depressive content (i.e., the level tapped by Davis, 1979). The precise nature of this composition would then be a key determinant in delimiting the type of personal information that might be

[3]Thanks are due to Joan Olinger for her invaluable assistance in conceptualizing this model.

suitably self-referenced. For example, medium depressives might process both nondepressed and depressed content in terms of their self-schema (Kuiper & Derry, 1980), whereas more severe depressives may only be capable of self-referencing pathologically oriented material (as witnessed by Davis' failure to find a self-reference effect for *non*pathological content with this group).

This latter possibility was empirically tested by Derry and Kuiper (1980). Clinical depressives, nondepressed psychiatric controls, and normal nondepressives made structural (Small letters?), semantic (Means same as a given word?), and self-referent (Describes you?) ratings on depressed and nondepressed content adjectives. Consistent with predictions generated from the content-specificity hypothesis, both normals and nondepressed psychiatric controls displayed superior recall *only* for self-referenced, nondepressed content adjectives. In contrast, clinical depressives displayed significantly enhanced recall *only* for depressed content adjectives, rated under the self-referent task. This finding supports the most robust form of the content-specificity hypothesis for severe depressives. In turn, this suggests the existence of a well organized negative self-schema, specific and unique to clinical depressives.

The model also acknowledges the importance of cohesiveness of the self-schema in facilitating self-reference processing. For nonpathological samples, considerable research has supported the view that the self-schema is an integrated, well-organized, and highly stable cognitive structure (Rogers et al., 1979). However, the degree of cohesiveness or organization of the self-schema may change with differing degrees of psychopathology. In this respect, degree of organization may play a particularly salient role at very mild levels of depression. Here, the initial onset of mild depressive symptoms may contribute to a state of flux within the individual's self-schema. This initial phase of depression might be marked by a period of confusion surrounding the self-prototype. Although this person already may have begun to experience some of the symptoms relating to depression, the very mild nature of the symptoms may prohibit positive and precise identification at this stage. This potential difficulty in labeling nonsevere depression-related experiences and phenomena may then contribute to a state of uncertainty and disorganization concerning one's self-concept (Rosenberg, 1979). This diffuse state may even generalize to include formerly stable nonpathological content in the person's self-schema. Overall, this lack of organization and uncertainty would reduce the effectiveness of the self-schema. It would no longer function as a reliable cognitive structure for processing and retaining personally relevant information. For mildly depressed individuals, this would then result in the observed failure in the Kuiper and Derry (1980) study to obtain significant self-reference enhancement effects for mildly depressed persons. Only after reconsolidation of the self-schema to accommodate the new depressed content would the prior efficiency of this cognitive structure return. This reconsolidation would occur only at more severe levels of depression, as witnessed by Derry and Kuiper (1980).

The issue of efficiency has been directly assessed by the inclusion of a rating time measure in two of our studies (Derry & Kuiper, 1980; Kuiper & MacDonald, 1980). Whereas incidental recall data may reveal a bias toward retention of schema-consistent information, it does not indicate how efficiently this information may have been processed. As such, the amount of time taken for self-referent personality judgments might be used as an index or measure of processing efficiency. Rating time findings for clinical depressives indicated they were no less efficient than normals in processing personal information (Derry & Kuiper, 1980). In contrast, university students at a medium level of depression were significantly less efficient than normal controls (Kuiper & MacDonald, 1980). However, consistent with Kuiper and Derry (1980), these medium depressives recalled equal amounts of positive and negative information about themselves. Normals, on the other hand, were heavily biased towards positive self-referent material. Overall, these findings suggest an efficient depressively-toned self-schema for clinical depressives, and a relatively inefficient combined content self-schema for less severe forms of this disorder.

The utility of the model proposed by Kuiper and Derry may lie in its ability to serve as an organizing framework for drawing together and clarifying some of the cognitive literature pertaining to depression. In addition to providing an explanation for the rather complex pattern of results obtained by our research, an extrapolation of the theoretical components of the model to more severe levels of depression can also account for the nonschema results reported by Davis (1979).

A second illustration of this explanatory power comes from a reassessment of results documented by Lloyd and Lishman (1975). They found that increasing depression was associated with a progressively diminishing ratio between the speed of recall for pleasant versus unpleasant events. For the least depressed, pleasant memories were recalled faster. This relationship then reversed for the most depressed subjects. Short response latencies in this paradigm may indicate possibly the use of a well-organized and efficient cognitive schema to assist in the output of information (Kuiper & Rogers, 1979). As such, the Lloyd and Lishman ratio is quite consistent with the proposed depressive self-schema model. Reinterpreted in this framework, the diminishing ratio traces the evolution of the depressive self-structure from a secondary to primary emphasis on depressed content.

CONCLUDING REMARKS

This chapter has examined the role of the self-as-prototype in person perception and depression. A number of studies were outlined in which subjects made personality judgments about themselves and various others. Overall, the major findings from these experiments point to three aspects of theoretical importance in the personal information-processing sequence. First, they suggest that familiarity is a fundamental component in determining the exact nature of other-referent processing. This is reflected in the formulation of a model of other processing. It is proposed that as a person becomes more familiar, we develop a specific and efficient cognitive structure to assist in the interpretation and retention of information about that person. Second, the findings argue strongly for prototypical self-involvement in the making of personality judgments about unknown others or strangers. The facilitation in rating times for terms extremely like or unlike the perceiver hint that the self-prototype may embellish an otherwise insufficient data source, as in the case of someone being met for the first time. Finally, the results of these studies also suggest that the self-prototype may play a role in familiar other processing. Here, the self-prototype may guide the abstraction and consolidation process whereby we develop a specific cognitive structure or schema for a well-known other. Overall, these findings argue strongly for the proposal that both familiarity level and personal relevance impact heavily on the perceiver's judgments or evaluation of those about him or her.

The present chapter has also proposed that the self-as-prototype model may prove of some value in advancing our knowledge of cognitive processes and structure in depression. However, considerable research is still required to elucidate more fully some of the theoretical concepts incorporated in the model (i.e., degree of cohesiveness and efficiency). More generally, this approach represents a strategy of amalgamating work in social cognition with research and theorizing in the domain of psychopathology. Hopefully this strategy ultimately may result in the accumulation of knowledge that can then be applied to the prevention or treatment of depression and other debilitating disorders.

ACKNOWLEDGMENTS

The authors are grateful to John Kihlstrom for his detailed comments and suggestions. Preparation of this manuscript was supported by a University of Western Ontario Dean's Grant to the first author.

REFERENCES

Bandura, A. The self and mechanisms of agency. In J. Suls (Ed.), *Social psychological perspectives on the self*. Hillsdale, N.J.: Lawrence Erlbaum Associates, in press.

Bartlett, F. C. *Remembering*. Cambridge, England: Cambridge University Press, 1932.

Beach, L., & Wertheimer, M. A free-response approach to the study of person cognition. *Journal of Abnormal and Social Psychology*, 1961, *62*, 367–374.

Beck, A. T., Rush, A. J., Shaw, B. F., & Emery, G. *Cognitive therapy of depression*. New York: The Guilford Press, 1979.

Beck, A. T., Ward, C. H., Mendelson, M., Mock, J., & Erbaugh, J. An inventory for measuring depression. *Archives of General Psychiatry*, 1961, *4*, 561–571.

Bower, G. H. Contacts of cognitive psychology with social learning theory. *Cognitive Therapy & Research*, 1978, *2*, 123–146.

Campbell, D. T., & Fiske, D. W. Convergent and discriminant validation by the multitrait-multimethod matrix. *Psychological Bulletin*, 1959, *56*, 81–105.

Coyne, J. C. Depression and the response of others. *Journal of Abnormal Psychology*, 1976, *85*, 186–193.

Crowne, D. P., & Marlow, D. *The approval motive: Studies in evaluative dependence.* New York: Wiley, 1964.

Davis, H. Self-reference and the encoding of personal information in depression. *Cognitive Therapy & Research*, 1979, *3*(1), 97–110.

Derry, P. A., & Kuiper, N. A. *Content, imagery, social desirability, and emotionality ratings for depressed and nondepressed personal adjectives.* Unpublished manuscript, University of Western Ontario, 1979.

Derry, P. A., & Kuiper, N. A. *Schematic processing and self-reference in clinical depression.* Unpublished manuscript, University of Western Ontario, 1980.

Diggory, J. C. *Self-evaluation: Concepts and studies.* New York: Wiley, 1966.

Dornbusch, S. M., Hastorf, A. H., Richardson, S. A., Muzzy, R. E., & Vreeland, R. S. The perceiver and the perceived: Their relative influence on categories of interpersonal perception. *Journal of Personality and Social Psychology*, 1965, *1*, 434–440.

Epstein, S. The self-concept: A review and the proposal of an integrated theory of personality. In E. Staub (Ed.), *Personality: Basic issues and current research.* Englewood Cliffs, N.J.: Prentice-Hall, 1980.

Festinger, L. A theory of social comparison processes. *Human Relations*, 1954, *7*, 117–140.

Fiske, S. T., & Cox, M. G. The effect of target familiarity and descriptive purpose on the process of describing others. *Journal of Personality*, 1979, *47*, 136–161.

Gergen, K. J. *The concept of self.* New York: Holt, Rinehart & Winston, 1971.

Hamilton, D. L. Cognitive representations of others. In E. T. Higgins, C. P. Herman, & M. P. Zanna (Eds.), *Social Cognition: The Ontario Symposium.* Hillsdale, N.J.: Lawrence Erlbaum Associates, in press.

Hansen, R. D., & Donaghue, J. M. The power of consensus: Information derived from one's own and other's behavior. *Journal of Personality and Social Psychology*, 1976, *35*, 294–302.

Heider, F. *The psychology of interpersonal relations.* New York: Wiley, 1958.

James, W. *The principles of psychology.* New York: Holt, 1890.

Jones, E. E., & Gerard, H. B. *Foundations of social psychology.* New York: Wiley, 1967.

Jones, E. E., Kanouse, D. E., Kelley, H. H., Nisbett, R. E., Valins, S., & Weiner, B. (Eds.), *Attribution: Perceiving the causes of behavior.* Morristown: General Learning Press, 1971.

Jones, R. A., Sensenig, J., & Haley, J. V. Self-descriptions: Configurations of content and order effects. *Journal of Personality and Social Psychology*, 1974, *30*, 36–45.

Judd, C. M., & Kulik, J. A. Schematic effects of social attitudes on information processing and recall. *Journal of Personality and Social Psychology*, 1980, *38*, 569–578.

Koltuv, B. Some characteristics of intrajudge trait intercorrelations. *Psychological Monographs*, 1962, *76*(33, Whole No. 552).

Kopel, S., & Arkowitz, H. The role of attribution and self-perception in behavior change: Implications for behavior therapy. *Genetic Psychology Monographs*, 1975, *92*, 175–212.

Kuiper, N. A. Depression and causal attributions for success and failure. *Journal of Personality and Social Psychology*, 1978, *36*, 236–246.

Kuiper, N. A., & Derry, P. A. *Encoding personal adjectives: The effects of depression on self-reference.* Unpublished manuscript, University of Western Ontario, 1980.

Kuiper, N. A., & MacDonald, M. R. *Self-reference and person perception in depression.* Unpublished manuscript, University of Western Ontario, 1980.

Kuiper, N. A., & Rogers, T. B. *Convergent evidence for the self as a cognitive prototype.* Paper presented at the Annual Meeting of the Canadian Psychological Association, Ottawa, Ontario, June, 1978.

Kuiper, N. A., & Rogers, T. B. Encoding of personal information: Self–other differences. *Journal of Personality and Social Psychology,* 1979, *37,* 499–514.

Lemon, N., & Warren, M. Salience, centrality, and self-relevance of traits in construing others. *British Journal of Social & Clinical Psychology,* 1974, *13,* 119–124.

Lewinsohn, P. M., Mischel, W., Chaplin, W., & Barton, R. Social competence and depression: The role of illusory self-perceptions. *Journal of Abnormal Psychology,* 1980, *89,* 203–212.

Lloyd, G. G., & Lishman, W. A. Effect of depression on the speed of recall of pleasant and unpleasant experiences. *Psychological Medicine,* 1975, *5,* 173–180.

Markus, H. Self-schemata and processing of information about the self. *Journal of Personality and Social Psychology,* 1977, *35,* 63–78.

Nelson, R. E., & Craighead, W. E. Selective recall of positive and negative feedback, self-control behaviors, and depression. *Journal of Abnormal Psychology,* 1977, *86,* 379–388.

Nisbett, R. E., Caputo, C., Legant, P., & Marecek, J. Behaviour as seen by the actor and as seen by the observer. *Journal of Personality and Social Psychology,* 1974, *27,* 154–164.

Ostrom, T. M., Pryor, T. B., & Simpson, D. D. The organization of social information. In E. T. Higgins, C. P. Herman, & M. P. Zanna (Eds.), *Social Cognition: The Ontario Symposium.* Hillsdale, N.J.: Lawrence Erlbaum Associates, in press.

Paivio, A. Neomentalism. *Canadian Journal of Psychology,* 1975, *29,* 263–291.

Posner, M., & Keele, S. W. On the genesis of abstract ideas. *Journal of Experimental Psychology,* 1968, *77,* 353–363.

Rogers, C. R. *Client-centered therapy.* Boston: Houghton Mifflin, 1951.

Rogers, T. B. Self-reference in memory: Recognition of personality items. *Journal of Research in Personality,* 1977, *11,* 295–305.

Rogers, T. B., & Kuiper, N. A. *Encoding of personal information about others: Effects of familiarity.* Unpublished manuscript. The University of Calgary and The University of Western Ontario, 1980.

Rogers, T. B., Kuiper, N. A., & Kirker, W. S. Self-reference and the encoding of personal information. *Journal of Personality and Social Psychology,* 1977, *35,* 677–688.

Rogers, T. B., Kuiper, N. A., & Rogers, P. J. Symbolic distance and congruity effects for paired-comparisons judgments of degree of self-reference. *Journal of Research in Personality,* 1979, *13,* 433–449.

Rogers, T. B., Rogers, P. J., & Kuiper, N. A. Evidence for the self as a cognitive prototype: The "false alarms effect." *Personality and Social Psychology Bulletin,* 1979, *5,* 53–56.

Rosenberg, M. *Conceiving the self.* New York: Basic Books, 1979.

Ross, L. The intuitive psychologist and his shortcomings: Distortions in the attribution process. In L. Berkowitz (Ed.), *Advances in Experimental Social Psychology* (Vol. 10). New York: Academic Press, 1977.

Ross, L., Lepper, M., & Hubbard, M. Perseverance in self perception and social perception: Biased attributional processes in the debriefing paradigm. *Journal of Personality and Social Psychology,* 1975, *32,* 880–892.

Ross, M., & Sicoly, F. Egocentric biases in availability and attribution. *Journal of Personality and Social Psychology,* 1979, *37*(4), 322–336.

Schneider, D. J., Hastorf, A. H., & Ellsworth, P. *Person perception* (2nd Ed.). Menlo Park, California: Addison-Wesley Publishing Company, 1979.

Secord, P. F., & Backman, C. W. *Social psychology.* New York: McGraw-Hill, 1974.

Shrauger, J. S., & Patterson, M. B. Self-evaluation and the selection of dimensions for evaluating others. *Journal of Personality,* 1974, 569–585.

Snygg, D., & Coombs, A. W. *Individual behavior: A perceptual approach to behavior* (Rev. ed.). New York: Harper, 1959.

Strong, S. R. Social psychological approach to psychotherapy research. In S. L. Garfield & A. E. Bergin (Eds.), *Handbook of psychotherapy and behavior change: An empirical analysis.* New York: Wiley, 1978.

Taylor, S. E., & Crocker, J. Schematic bases of social information processing. In E. T. Higgins, C. P. Herman, & M. P. Zanna (Eds.), *Social Cognition: The Ontario Symposium.* Hillsdale, N.J.: Lawrence Erlbaum Associates, in press.

10 The Influence of Self-Schemata on the Perception of Others

Hazel Markus
Jeanne Smith
The University of Michigan

It is not as ye judge that ye shall be judged, but as you judge yourself so shall you judge others.

—Sullivan, 1947

INTRODUCTION

The idea that the self provides a touchstone for all our perceptions about other people is an extremely prevalent assumption of much of clinical and personality psychology. Although direct empirical support is limited, corroborating evidence for this notion can be found in a surprising variety of areas. Across a range of psychological phenomena, investigators have noted that evaluations, judgments, predictions, and inferences about *other people* often depend on the individual's *own* position on the judged quality. Mintz (1956), for example, noted a strong positive relationship between children's own ages and what they estimated to be the age of Peter Pan. Goldings (1954) reported that perception of the happiness of others was positively related to one's own reported level of happiness. Similarly, Katz and Allport (1931) found that one's prediction of the number of other people who were likely to cheat was clearly related to one's own level of cheating. In the attitude literature, Sherif and Hovland (1961) repeatedly demonstrated that one's own stand on an important issue had a marked impact on how one interpreted the responses of others to that issue.

The relationship between the self and the perception of others is central to social comparison theory, attribution theory, and work on role-taking and identification. Whether one is forming an impression of others or seeking them out for purposes of information, comparison, or identification, there is a vast amount of information potentially available in the behavior of others, and this information cannot all be equally attended to and processed. It usually becomes necessary to focus on particular features of the behavior of others while ignoring other aspects. The perceiving organism is systematically selective, and thus the process of attending to specific aspects of behavior is not random. One highly accessible internal structure that influences these selective processes and that is used in organizing, categorizing, or interpreting information about others is one's *self-structure*. The self-structure—also called the self, the self-concept, or the self-system—has been broadly implicated in the study of person perception and cognition. Construed in the most general sense, the question of the impact of the self on the perception of others refers to how the individual's thoughts, feelings, attributes, attitudes, and cognitive structures influence the perception of others. The issue of concern here, however, is limited to the question of how the self-structure, which is comprised of thoughts and feelings *about the self* in particular domains, influences the individual's perception and cognition of others in those domains. More specifically, assuming that individuals differ in the ways they organize and interpret their own behavior or in the ways they represent themselves in thought and memory, what is the influence of the organization and evaluation of our own behavior on the organization and evaluation of the behavior of others? Or, to turn Sullivan's assertion into a question: What types of influence do judgments about ourselves in a given area have on our judgments about other people in these areas?

The Scope of the Self-Structure

An exploration of this question requires some assumptions about the specific role of the self-structure in the person-perception process and in the information-processing sequence generally. The issue is a matter of some controversy. There are those who have tried to downplay the role of the self and have regarded it as one of those irksome factors that prevent veridical perception. Others, such as From (1971), believed that a person's own attributes and qualities could indeed exert an influence over the processing of the traits and behaviors of others, but that this would occur primarily in ambiguous stimulus situations: "... when the stimulus is . . . sufficiently vague to permit several interpretations, then, to use Koffka's expression from the perception of figures, it becomes possible for the 'inner organizing forces' to exercise a dominating influence on the experiences of the acting persons, their actions, expressions, and stamp [p. 129].'' This type of view is most compatible with the idea, sketched in Fig. 10.1, that the self is a potentially important structure but only one of many possible structures available to process incoming information.

Others have assumed that the self is really the center of the perceptual or cognitive field and that it functions as an anchor for all other judgments. Combs

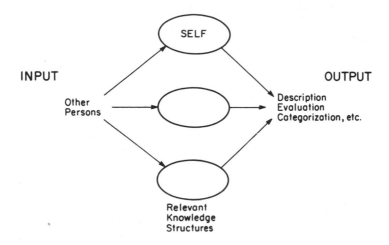

FIG 10.1.   The Self in information processing—View 1.

and Snygg (1949) noted, for example, that ''people are not really fat unless they are fatter than we [p. 145].'' Scriven's (1966) position is even more extreme. He assumed that our understanding of others is almost immediately available from the self-system and does not require any inferences. He claimed that ''when we understand a person's behavior in terms of his attitudes, goals and perceptions of the situation in which he finds himself, etc., in short in terms of the phenomenology of the situation—what we are doing is, so to speak, attaching the facts of the particular case to the terminals of our own response systems, i.e., our own personality [p. 60].'' These ideas, outlined in Fig. 10.2, imply a somewhat different view of the self—one in which the self is a central force, the main anchor, or the first structure through which all stimulus information is initially processed.

Further Definition of the Question

Beyond different viewpoints about the centrality of the self, there is a host of other issues that surrounds the question of the impact of the self-system on the perception of others. Most theories of person perception and impression formation either skirt the issue of the self-structure altogether or broach it very tentatively; it has been examined directly in only relatively few studies. An optimal answer to the self–other question requires first a fairly clear definition of the self-system and then some notion about what components or aspects of other-perception are likely to be influenced by the self-system. Typically, the empirical studies meet only one of these criteria. The relevant research has employed a mixture of definitions of the self and a wide array of person-perception tasks. The

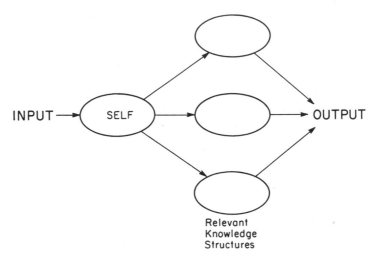

FIG. 10.2.   The Self in information processing—View 2.

self or the self-system has been defined as one's personality, traits or characteristics that describe the self, attitudes toward the self, attitudes toward objects or persons that are important to the self, motivation, construct systems, and response systems.

With respect to the products of the person-perception process, the focus has sometimes been on the description and evaluation of traits or characteristics of others and, other times, on the description and evaluation of the attitudes, motivations, and behavior of others. The issue is further complicated by the fact that the emphasis in this question can be on *products,* such that the concern is exclusively with the nature and content of the description and evaluation of others as a function of the self-system, or the focus can be on the *process* itself; that is, how does the self-system work to influence the processing of social information, or how do the "inner, organizing forces" comprising the self do their work on information from incoming stimuli?

The purpose of this chapter is to: (1) outline an approach to the self that will allow for a more concise formulation of the problem and that will generate a series of specific experimental questions relevant to both the process and outcome of person-perception; and (2) present the results from several studies designed to answer some of these questions.

BACKGROUND

The early self theorists (e.g. Combs & Snygg, 1949; Murphy, 1947; Rogers, 1951; Sullivan, 1947) viewed the self-structure as a key explanatory and causal factor in all interpersonal processes, including person perception and impression formation. Because the self was at the center of the perceptual or cognitive field, it was reasonable to assume that the self was deeply implicated in how one organized or understood other people in one's social world. Most of this theorizing, however, ignored the specifics of the person-perception process, and even the most relevant arguments tended to be quite general, such as Sullivan's (1947) statement that "if there is a valid and real attitude toward the self, that attitude will be manifest as valid and real toward others [p. 178]." There are, however, at least three areas of research that can provide some measure of support for the idea that the self has an important influence on the perception of others.

1. Person-Perception Research. This area has generated a number of studies that indicate that we tend to see others as we see ourselves (Crockett & Meidinger, 1956; Fiedler, 1958; Jones, 1954; Koltuv, 1962; Leary, 1957; Phares & Lamiell, 1975; Phares & Wilson, 1972; Rogers, 1951; Scodel & Friedman, 1956; Shrauger & Altrocchi, 1964; Sosis, 1974; Steiner & Johnson, 1963). Studies in this area also have found that traits known to be important for self-description are involved in the free description of others more often than traits that are not self-relevant (Dornbusch, Hastorf, Richardson, Muzzy, & Vreeland, 1965; Hastorf, Richardson, & Dornbusch, 1958; Lemon & Warren, 1974; O'Keefe, Delia, & O'Keefe, 1977; Shrauger & Patterson, 1976).

Recently, concern with the relationship between self- and other-perception has emerged in studies of the "false consensus" effect—the idea that laymen are likely to assume that their own behavioral choices and judgments are quite common and that alternative responses are inappropriate and even somewhat deviant. A number of studies by Ross and his colleagues (Ross, 1979; Ross, Greene, & House, 1977) have confirmed the idea that perceptions of social consensus and inferences about others are related to one's own behavioral choices. They found this self–other relationship to exist with respect to a variety of personal problems, preferences, and characteristics. Their pattern of findings is somewhat at odds, however, with results from similar studies showing that individuals like to assume that they are quite different from others, often despite compelling evidence to the contrary (Nisbett & Borgida, 1975; Nisbett, Borgida, Crandall, & Reed, 1976).

Overall, the person-perception research has unambiguously demonstrated only that self-relevant qualities (traits and behaviors) can figure in the description of others. It has not succeeded in specifying the nature, the direction, or the outcome of the influence of the self-structure on perceiving others. In fact, little has been added to the 20-year-old statement of Hastorf, Richardson, and Dornbusch (1958) that there is a strong positive relationship between "categories people use in describing other people and in describing themselves [p. 61]."

2. Clinical Research. In this area, the question of the impact of the self on the perception of others arises in investigations of projection—the tendency of individuals to endow others with those traits and feelings that are identical to their own (e.g., hostile persons seeing others as hostile). This view assumes that certain aspects of the self-structure are quite naturally and automatically invoked in perceiving and knowing others. Studies on projection (Bramel, 1962; 1963; Edlow & Kiesler, 1966; Holmes, 1968; Secord, Backman, & Eachus, 1964) indicate that when individuals are convinced they possess an undesirable trait, they will project that trait onto other persons who are desirable. In the Freudian view (Freud, 1924), this is done so that individuals can re-evaluate the characteristics as less negative and thereby alleviate some of the stress associated with possession of this trait. Alternatively, the fact that evauations of others are skewed in the direction of our own ratings may simply be the result of what Horney (1939) called the naive assumption that "others feel or react in the same manner as we ourselves do [p. 26]."

Explanations of the projection phenomenon are complicated by studies that show that under some circumstances individuals will attribute to others not the *same* trait they possess but rather a different trait or its complement; that is, subjects who are frightened will show an increased tendency to view others not as frightened but as frightening or threatening (Hornberger, 1960). This phenomenon has been labeled "complementary projection" and suggests that a simple stimulus-generalization interpretation of the relationship between self- and other-perception is inadequate and that a somewhat more complex model of the relationship may be needed.

3. Attitude Research.   In the area of attitudes, the assimilation-contrast model of social judgments (Sherif & Hovland, 1961) is particularly relevant to the question of how the self-structure influences one's evaluation of others. Sherif and Hovland were concerned with the influence that personal involvement with a social issue has on the judgment process and suggested that when an individual is very involved with a particular attitude issue (i.e., when such an issue is extremely self-relevant), his or her own stand will serve as the main anchor for judgments of information related to it. They hypothesized that the range of positions on an issue that an individual considers acceptable will comprise a *latitude of acceptance* and will be assimilated to his or her own stand. Attitude positions that the individual finds objectionable constitute a *latitude of rejection* and will be contrasted with his or her own position. Moreover, the more ego-involved the individual becomes, the more restricted the range of acceptable positions becomes. In Sherif and Hovland's terms, the ego-involved individual "is willing to tolerate only slight deviation from this [the individual's preferred] category and finds further deviation obnoxious [p. 13]." This type of effect has been confirmed repeatedly in empirical research on attitudes (Cartwright, 1941; Johnson, 1955; LaFave & Sherif, 1959).

This model of assimilation and contrast can be readily applied to the functioning of the self-structure (cf. Berkowitz, 1960). The individual has the most clearly defined attitude positions for behavior in those areas that have the most meaning to the individual (i.e., those areas that are self-relevant). The self is then viewed as a personal benchmark for behavior in these realms.

Across these three areas of literature the only idea that received some consistent support is that of stimulus generalization, or the notion that we tend to see others as we see ourselves. Although this explanation does account for some of the results, it is inadequate or inappropriate for a number of other studies. For example, some investigators have urged, in a manner similar to the projection theorists, that individuals only attribute to others those of their own characteristics that are problematic or dissonance-producing for them; that is, they will attribute some of their own qualities or motivations to others to avoid the dissonance associated with seeming to be different from others that are important to them. Still others have argued that only some types of people are likely to attribute their characteristics to others. For example, Bramel (1963) found that individuals with low self-esteem were more likely to attribute or generalize their own traits to others than were those with high self-esteem.

Even when a stimulus generalization explanation does appear to account for the findings in a relatively straightforward fashion, there are still many unanswered questions. How does the individual decide when the attributes of another cannot be generalized from one's own traits but instead must be differentiated? What is it that determines which aspects of another will be considered sufficiently like one's own that generalization from the self can be made?

Progress on understanding the relationship between self and other-perception seems dependent on attention to and clarification of a number of different issues. Some of these needs and concerns are outlined below. They are organized in terms of (1) the self-structure, (2) the stimuli (the to-be-perceived others), and (3) the process that relates the self to other perception.

1. The perceiver's self-structure, including:
   (a) A clearer definition of the self or the feature of self that is implicated in the particular aspect of person perception under investigation;
   (b) Consideration of the fact that aspects of the stimulus (the to-be-perceived others) may be differentially relevant to different perceivers;
   (c) Attention to variation in the perceiver's expectations or goals for the person perception situation
2. The stimuli (the to-be-perceived others), including:
   (a) Greater specification of the stimuli to determine how the perceived individuals stand relative to the perceiver on the trait, quality, motivation, or attitude in question;
   (b) Attention to the mode of presentation of stimuli (e.g., verbal, pictorial, free interaction).
3. The process involved in relating the self to the perception of others, including:

(a) When and how the self-structure will be implicated in the person perception process;

(b) How the self-structure will influence the processing of relevant information about others (e.g., what are the effects of the self-structure on attention, encoding, storage, retrieval from memory).

A COGNITIVE VIEW OF THE SELF

Self-Schemata

In the research to be described the self is conceptualized as a system of self-schemata which are knowledge structures developed to understand, explain, or integrate one's own behavior in particular domains. A schema integrates all the information known about the self in a given behavioral domain into a systematic framework used during processing (Neisser, 1976; Palmer, 1977).

In general, schemata are the basis of the selectivity that is operative in information processing. According to Neisser (1976) "perceivers pick up only what they have schemas for and willy-nilly ignore the rest [p. 80]." Similarly, self-schemata are the basis for the perception of our own behavior. We will attend to certain features of our behavior while disregarding others. We can, for example, attend to our physical selves and notice hair with split ends, bloodshot eyes, or clothes that are out of style. We also can focus on a variety of tastes and preferences, noting that we like to play paddleball, put in a respectable effort at computer Star Trek, and have a passionate love for disco. Self-schemata also include some more subtle and complex generalizations about our behavior: that we are pathologically late for appointments; that we are nervous in front of large groups; or that we are creative, cautious, or ambitious. Self-schemata are generalizations or theories about the self, developed from the repeated similar categorization and evaluation of behavior by oneself and others, that result in a clearly differentiated idea of the kind of person one is with respect to a particular domain of behavior. These types of structures enable individuals to understand their own social experiences and to integrate a wide range of stimulus information about the self into meaningful patterns. They also direct attention to behavior that is informative of these aspects of the self. It is assumed that an individual who has developed a schema about some aspect of the self (e.g., body weight) will have integrated a large number of independent cognitive representations, perceived as relevant to body weight, into a single, unified cognitive or knowledge structure that will be activated as a whole when the individual focuses on his or her body weight. The representations might include verbal summary labels such as chubby or thin, images about how one's body looks in comparison to others, or a variety of knowledge about food and its relationship to body weight. Someone without the schema (an *aschematic* with regard to body weight) will not delineate or evaluate stimuli with respect to their relevance for body weight and will handle weight-relevant information very differently from a *schematic*. These body-image aschematics may not attend to this information at all, or they may organize it with respect to some other self-structure.

A series of studies on how individuals describe and organize their own behavior (Markus, 1977; Markus, Crane, & Siladi, 1978; Markus, Sentis, & Hamill, 1979) have shown that self-schemata influence the processing of information about the self in a variety of domains (personality, sex-role, physical appearance). In one study (Sentis & Markus, 1979), designed to investigate the effect of self-schemata on processing time for judgments about the self and for recognition memory for self-relevant information, individuals with schemata in the domain of independence (schematics) were compared with individuals who were without schemata (aschematics) in this domain. Schematics were those individuals who rated themselves as extreme on several trait adjectives concerning independence and who also indicated that they viewed independence as important to their overall self-evaluation. Aschematics rated themselves in the middle of these trait scales and indicated that independence was not a very important aspect of their self-concept.

In a laboratory phase of this study, subjects were asked to indicate whether or not a series of trait adjectives described them by responding "ME" or "NOT ME" to each trait. The list of words contained both schema-relevant adjectives (i.e., those traits related to independence or dependence,) and a set of schema-irrelevant adjectives related to the dimension of creativity. After the "ME/NOT ME" segment of the experiment, subjects performed an intervening task which was followed by a standard recognition memory test. In the recognition phase, subjects judged whether or not a particular adjective was one of the set seen earlier in the "ME/NOT ME" task by responding "OLD" if they had seen the word earlier or "NEW" if they had not seen it.

Results from the "ME/NOT ME" task replicated earlier findings (Markus, 1977) showing that schematic subjects are faster to respond "ME" to schema-consistent adjectives than to inconsistent adjectives. The group of individuals who thought of themselves as "dependent" responded "ME" to a large proportion of dependent adjectives, and required a much shorter time to make their judgments of dependence than they did for judgments to the independent adjectives. The dependent schematics were presumably quite accustomed to thinking of themselves as "conforming" and "obliging", and could, therefore, make these judgments quite quickly. In contrast, they were probably not so accustomed to thinking about themselves as "assertive" and individualistic" (even though they might like to); it therefore took them longer to process those words that were inconsistent with the self-schema. The group of people who thought of themselves as "independent" showed the same pattern of results, responding much faster to the independent adjectives than they did to the dependent adjectives.

In clear contrast to the independent and dependent schematics were the aschematics, who did not differ at all in their processing times for independent and dependent words. Aschematics appeared not to have defined themselves with respect to independence and to be equally at ease labeling their behavior with independent or dependent adjectives. They apparently did not have a structure for independence and thus did not respond differentially. With respect to memory, the schematics showed superior recognition for schema-relevant material. Again, the aschematics did not exhibit a difference in recognition for schema-relevant or irrelevant material. In addition, schematics made fewer errors and were faster at recognizing schema-relevant material than were aschematics. Also, the schematic individuals were significantly faster at recognizing schema-relevant words they had endorsed than schema-relevant words not endorsed; that is, the prior "ME/NOT ME" judgment had an effect on the speed with which schematics were able to recognize traits they had seen before. Reaction times for aschematics did not differ according to whether the word had previously been judged as self-descriptive.

These findings have been replicated with respect to schemata about creativity, body weight, and sex role. In brief, these studies have shown that individuals having schemata in particular areas are readily able to: (1) evaluate new information with respect to its relevance for this domain; (2) process information about the self in the given domain (e.g., make judgments and decisions) with relative ease or certainty; (3) retrieve behavioral evidence in these areas; (4) predict future behavior in the area; and (5) resist information that is counter to the prevailing schema.

The Self as a System of Schemas

A cognitive view of the self has substantial theoretical precedent. There have been a number of theorists, including Sarbin (1954), Kelly (1955) and more recently Epstein (1973), who have explicitly considered the self as a cognitive structure or set of structures that organize, modify, and integrate functions of the person. Our definition of the self as a system of schemata builds on this work and allows us to be more specific about the possible content and function of the self.

What is the nature of the schemata that comprise the self? Are they special or different in any way from other schemata or structures about the social world? There is now a growing body of research that suggests that structures about the self may indeed be unique in some ways. Rogers, Kuiper, and Kirker (1977) found remarkably high rates of incidental recall of words encoded using a self-reference task ("Does this word describe you?") when compared to recall of semantically encoded words ("Does this word mean the same as another word?"). Moreover, words used to judge the self were recalled better than words used to judge the experimenter (Kuiper & Rogers, 1979) or Walter Cronkite (Lord, 1978). Other findings indicate that: (1) Self-relevant stimuli, both verbal and pictorial, are more quickly and confidently endorsed than other types of stimuli (Markus, 1977; Markus, et al., 1979) and (2) Self-referent decisions or instructions produce enhanced recall (Keenan & Baillet, 1980; Kuiper & Rogers, 1979; Lord, 1978; Rogers, et al., 1977; Turner, 1978) and enhanced recognition of verbal and pictorial material (Kendzierski, 1978; Mueller, Courtois, & Bailis, 1979; Rogers, 1977; Sentis & Markus, 1979).

Although research on the specific effects of self-reference is quite recent, the idea that making information self-relevant can produce unique effects has been heavily traded on by teachers, politicians, and lawyers. Advertisements in educational journals claim that to teach a child to read, or to help him or her learn faster, better, and with more enthusiasm, it is helpful to insert the child's name in the story. Although the assumption appears to be untested, the idea is that having the child imagine himself or herself in the thick of the action with Dick and Spot will have a number of important effects. Attorneys also seem to know the power of making events self-relevant. Jurors are asked to imagine themselves in the defendant's place, to imagine pain, to experience the fear, and to share the uncertainty. And advertisers unmercifully exploit the self-reference technique. The merchandisers of smoke alarms ask "If there is a fire in *your* home tonight, will *your* family awaken in time?"

Besides the anecdotal evidence, there is also other research, some of it much older and not done with reference to cognitive structures, that supports the idea that the self can have a profound influence on information processing. It has been found repeatedly, for example, that one's personal record of past accomplishments may not be a perfect match with an observer's record of the same behavior. When concerned with memory for events about the self, it seems that the good, the correct, the responsible, the consistent, and the successful aspects of one's activities are much more likely to be recalled than the bad, the incorrect, the irresponsible, the inconsistent, or the unsuccessful (Bradley, 1978; Cartwright, 1956; Mischel, Ebbesen, & Zeiss, 1973; Ross & Sicoly, 1979; Wallen, 1942; Wortman, 1976; Zeller, 1950).

This research indicates that, depending on its content, information about the self may be processed differentially, but it has not addressed the issue of the actual role of the self-structure in the information-processing sequence. A schema approach to the self can accommodate a variety of views about the nature of the self in the processing sequence. Our conceptualization assumes that the self is represented in memory just as other individuals and other aspects of the social environment are represented. A separate set of structures for the self is reasonable if for no other reason than that there is a strong linguistic pressure to develop a concept of "I" or "me". The simplest way to represent the cognitions—"I went to college," "I bought a sailboat," "I go jogging along the river," "I like Mary," "I can't bear Stan," and "I feel sick"—is to represent the self as a single node in memory that is associated with a large number of other nodes, such as college, sailboat, etc. Individuals are constantly required to code their social world in terms of the concepts of "I" or "me", and an "I" or "self" category or set of categories would seem to be a natural consequence of this process.

Our view of the self suggests that all general self-representations are stored together in one distinct self-system that is then linked with other concepts in

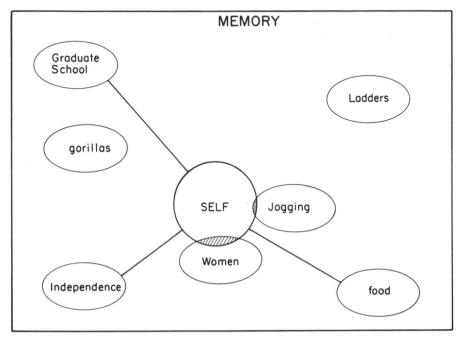

FIG. 10.3.   The Self in memory.

memory (Fig. 10.3). General sclf-representations include such identifying features of the self as one's own name, the representation of one's physical appearance, representations related to other key aspects of the self (age, sex, marital
status, kinship, and occupational role), overall evaluations of the self, etc. Most
concepts are linked with the self-concept because most things are experienced
with reference to the self. Other concepts in memory that are not very self-
relevant such as "ladders" and "gorillas" are not shown as connected to the
self, yet obviously they could be should the need arise. This view allows for
temporary intersections of the self with other objects as well as for more permanent and enduring connections. Repeated associations of the self with other
concepts and structures will lead to stronger and more certain links. Eventually
there may be a virtual overlapping of the self and some other concept. This
occurs when a large number of representations in a particular structure become
self-relevant and when an increasingly larger share of the representations comprising the self-sytem are associated with this structure. Once there is an overlapping of the self and another concept, a self-schema may be said to emerge or
develop. This structure is now part of the self and is automatically activated when
the self-structure is activated. These structures become the ones most salient,
central, or important in organizing information about the self and, perhaps, the
social world in general.

    As an example of this process, consider the intersection of the self with the
concept of jogging. For a given individual, the concept of jogging is initially a

very simple undifferentiated structure loaded with negative affect. It is not associated with the self at all, except when the individual drags the far reaches of memory and is confronted with an image of himself or herself as an overweight eighth-grader huffing and puffing through fifty laps, under the watchful eye of the cruel and heartless gym teacher. However, as this now much older individual is induced by his or her friends to try jogging and is given a fashionable new jogging suit, the connections between the concepts of the self and jogging are increased. When jogging is found to be enjoyable and this person begins to spend time reading *Runners World* to determine the best brand of shoes and attends with real enthusiasm to the results of the Boston Marathon, the intersection between the self and jogging begins. Not only has the knowledge structure associated with jogging become much more articulated, but also many of the representations in this structure now involve the self. Simultaneously, many more of the self-representations include cognitions about the self and some aspect of jogging. Finally, as this individual begins really to enjoy jogging, starts to think of himself or herself as a jogger, and feels that this is very important to his or her overall self-evaluation, he or she becomes *schematic* with respect to jogging or develops a *self-schema* in this domain. This will then become one of the structures that the individual will use in processing information about the self and others.

The Role of Self-Schemata in Person-Perception

This rudimentary model of the self falls under the general class of models described earlier, which see the self as a central set of structures that are at the focus of one's phenomenal world. All incoming stimuli are evaluated according to their relevance to the self. There are, of course, many types of stimuli that may not be seen as immediately self-relevant because thinking about them or evaluating them does not in any significant way implicate thoughts and feelings about the self. For example, under many circumstances a photograph of Tegucigalpa would not be perceived as self-relevant. However, if this stimulus *is* perceived as self-relevant for one reason or another and the self-structure is activated, it will be processed quite differently than when it is regarded as non–self-relevant.

The class of stimuli that are most likely to be perceived as having relevance for the self are those that have immediate consequences for the self. As such, other people are prime candidates for stimuli that will have automatic self-relevance. Even strangers often may be perceived as self-relevant because they have the power to engender powerful consequences for the self. They can provide information, serve as standards of comparison, be the focus of interaction, and, through their ability to evoke strong feelings, dramatically change an individual's phenomenal state.

Since all people are likely to be perceived as self-relevant, to one degree or another, the differences in how we perceive others will derive primarily from whether the person or some aspect of the person to-be-perceived is relevant to a and thinking about others in self-schema relevant domains should exhibit a about another person, the incoming information will be integrated with information already organized in the schema. The stimulus information may then take on a variety of meanings that would not be attached to it were it to be processed by someone who is aschematic in this domain. Thus the sight of someone laying waste to a hot fudge sundae is a very different stimulus for someone with a body-weight schema than for someone without one.

The schema provides a framework within which stimulus input can be interpreted. Without this framework, certain aspects of the stimulus may not be attended to at all unless they are very distinctive. Thus a person who is aschematic with respect to body weight may not notice the weight of another person unless the person is quite thin or quite fat, or unless the stimulus situation requires attention to body weight. In contrast, the schematic will automatically use the variety of representations that have been organized into the self-schema in responding to the stimulus. In fact, not to use a particular self-schema in thinking about others and/or in interpreting and understanding their behavior may necessitate concentrated attempts to suppress this aspect of the self-structure or deliberate efforts not to be "ego-involved" and is likely to meet with only limited success. In situations when an individual is perceiving others without well-specified goals or orientations, these others will be evaluated automatically, using one's schematic dimensions.

The judgments of others and the process of making these judgments about others in areas where one is schematic are likely to be distinctive for a number of reasons. First, the stimulus inputs provided by the to-be-perceived others may not be identical for schematics and aschematics; that is, the stimulus may be organized or encoded differently by the two groups. Second, the schematic has a great deal more information that can be immediately brought to bear on the stimulus and with which it can be integrated, such that many more inferences and potential elaborations of the stimulus will be possible. Third, schematic domains are those which involve affect. Individuals develop self-schemata in those areas that are important to them and about which they have strong preferences. Thus the new input is likely to take on those affective qualities and will be subject to the same forms of facilitation and interference that characterize affective material generally (Zajonc, 1978). For example, everyone has some structure associated with the idea of creativity and, when asked to think about another person in these terms, will invoke this structure as a framework. However, this task will be decidedly different for individuals who consider themselves to be creative artists than for those without such pretensions.

This view of the self suggests that Sullivan's statement should be paraphrased to read "*In schematic domains,* as you judge yourself so shall you judge others." In the process of person perception, the predictions that hold for attending to, interpreting, and reconstructing information about oneself should also hold for processing information about others in the relevant domains. Thus, feeling particular self-schema. If a self-schema is activated in processing information pattern of attention to data and a systematic discrimination and consistency in response that is characteristic of thoughts and feelings about the self in these domains. What the specific impact of this differential processing will be on the outcome or product of person perception (i.e., how an individual will be judged, what predictions will be made about behavior, whether response latency will be short or long) is still indeterminate, however. These more detailed hypotheses can be generated only with reference to the type of task required, the perceiver's expectations, and the nature of the relationship between the perceiver and to-be-perceived.

The goal of our present research is to explore further the nature of schematic processing and to begin to delineate the specific impact on self-schemata on the outcomes of person perception, including the description and evaluation of traits, attributes, and behaviors.

EMPIRICAL EVIDENCE

One of the first questions to be asked in systematically exploring the impact of self-schemata on the perception of others concerns the extent of their influence when there is only minimal information available. Hamill (1980) investigated the effects of self-schemata on recognition memory for unfamiliar faces. The study employed a relatively well-established methodology for studying face memory developed from the levels-of-processing model proposed by Craik and Lockhart (1972). This framework proposes that the perception and encoding of visual stimuli may occur at a number of stages or levels, ranging from very shallow processing (e.g., focused on physical features) to deep processing (involving the semantic or abstract attributes of the stimulus. It is assumed that deep processing involves more elaboration of the target stimulus; that is, the information in the stimulus makes contact with a network of past knowledge and thus can be enriched. This in turn produces a stronger memory trace and therefore better recognition. Although most of this work (e.g. Hyde & Jenkins, 1973), concerns the encoding of verbal material, Bower and Karlin (1974), Winograd (1976) and Strnad and Mueller (1977) found superior recognition memory for faces that had been judged along an abstract trait dimension (e.g., honesty) than for those involving decisions about physical features (e.g., the size of the nose). Mueller, Bailis and Goldstein (in press) reasoned that judgments about a face involved self-reference, and that this might explain the deeper processing and superior recognition performance. Although they replicated previous findings with respect to abstract and physical features, they failed to find a difference in recognition between faces judged for abstract features and those involving self-reference. Hamill proposed that the facilitative effects of self-reference would be evidenced only if the judgment involved a domain in which the subject had an extensive network of knowledge, such as a self-schema, that would facilitate "deeper" or richer encoding of the information available in the target faces.

To evaluate this idea, subjects who were either schematic or aschematic with respect to independence were shown a series of slides of faces. Subjects were asked to make a judgment about each face along either a physical dimension ("Does this person have wide-set eyes?") or a dimension related to independence ("Does this person look like the independent type?"). Following an intervening task, subjects participated in a standard recognition memory test involving a series of faces that included some they had viewed earlier. During the recognition test, subjects were to respond "OLD" if they had seen the face or "NEW" if they had not seen the face earlier. As shown in Table 10.1, the schematics had superior hit rates (correctly identifying "OLD" faces) when they previously had to make self-relevant decisions about the faces ("Does this person look like the independent type?") than when they had to make physical judgments about the faces.

Schematics also exhibited higher hit rates than aschematics. The performance of aschematics did not differ according to the type of prior judgment. They exhibited the same level of recognition memory performance whether their original judgments had been about eyes or about independence. This work provides initial evidence for the facilitative effects of a self-schema on processing information about other people in relevant domains. When making an independence judgment, the schematics were probably able to elaborate the stimulus with information from their own schema, which resulted in a rich encoding and enhanced memory for the stimulus. In this formulation, the schema functions as an anchor against which to compare the stimulus. This anchor may provide, for example, a set of criteria about what an independent person looks like, which allows for relatively finer resolution of the components of the stimulus face and thus makes it distinctive and easier to recognize. For the aschematics, the independence and the physical tasks had similar effects because these subjects do not possess an articulated schema for either domain. Further research using this task will attempt to explore other consequences of schematic processing besides those directly involved

TABLE 10.1
Percent Correct Face Recognition
by Subject Type and Judgment Type

Type of Subject	Type of Judgment	
	Physical	Independence
Independent schematics	58.2	75.6
Aschematics	61.5	66.9

with memory. An effort will be made to determine whether schema-relevant judgments are made more quickly and confidently than other types of judgments and how other people are evaluated on schema-relevant dimensions.

The emphasis in this study was on the effects of self-schemata on the perception of others in a minimal information situation. Although this study provides some information on the basic influence of the self on the memory and evaluation of others, it is rare that person-perception is so impoverished. Most often, there is a great deal of information available in the target person. What is the expected influence of the self-structure in these more complex situations?

To investigate these ideas directly (Markus & Fong, 1979), we asked individuals who were independent schematics and individuals who were aschematic with respect to independence to read one of three stories constructed about "Mary," an average University of Michigan student. In one story, Mary is portrayed as the independent woman's "independent woman"; that is, she tells the doctor she needs a second opinion when he gives her a diagnosis of her injured knee, she asks a man she meets in the bookstore if he would like to go to a concert with her, she fixes her flat tire, etc. In a second story, Mary is portrayed as half this independent. In the first story, there are 18 situations where she behaves independently; in the second story she behaves independently in only nine of these situations. In a third story, Mary does not behave independently in any of these situations. rather, she behaves in what was rated as a neutral manner. After subjects read one of three stories about Mary they are asked first to rate her on a large number of dimensions that relate to independence and dependence and then to make a number of inferences about the relative independence/dependence of Mary's future behavior.

TABLE 10.2
Ratings of the Actor on
Independent, Dependent, and Neutral Traits

Type of Ratings and Subjects	Proportion of Independent Actions in Story		
	0	.5	1.0
Mean ratings on independent traits			
Independent schematics	4.76	7.50	9.53
Aschematics	6.50	6.98	8.70
Mean ratings on dependent traits			
Independent schematics	8.60	6.84	4.50
Aschematics	7.16	6.99	4.56
Mean ratings on neutral traits			
Independent schematics	7.60	7.85	7.21
Aschematics	7.90	7.48	7.38

dent traits. It can be seen from the third panel that schematics and aschematics did not differ when rating Mary on the neutral traits, although they differed markedly in their ratings of her independence and dependence. The independent schematics thought Mary was much less independent and much more dependent than did the aschematics in the zero condition story. In the 100% independence story, the independent schematics thought Mary was much more independent than did the aschematics. The identical pattern held for behavioral inferences made about Mary. It appears that for the schematics, the self-schema provides an anchor or a framework that furnishes a baseline for independence and makes individuals sensitive to variations in independence. Without a self-schema in this domain the level or type of independence exhibited by Mary may not be at all salient. For the aschematics, various other aspects of Mary's behavior may be more distinctive and, when called upon to evaluate her level of independence, aschematics may rely on basic social schemata or views about the independence of people in general.

As suggested earlier in the section on judging the attitudes of others, an assimilation-contrast model of social judgments (Sherif & Hovland, 1961) may provide a framework for thinking about some aspects of this problem. In this study, for example, there is an indication that the 50% story does overlap with the schematics' latitude of acceptance; in this condition, Mary is given a mean rating on the 15 independence-trait terms that is similar to the schematics' own ratings of independence. To the extent that Mary's actions fall outside an individual's latitude of acceptance for independence, however, such that they are seen as very independent (as in the 100% condition) or very dependent (as in the 0% condition), they will be seen as distinctive and will be contrasted with the individual's own position.

In a third study, we were interested in looking more closely at what happens with information when it is integrated to a schema. Integration can be seen as the process by which new information is organized and interpreted. This is similar to Piaget's (1954) conceptualization of assimilation. Each component of the stimulus does not have to be thoroughly analyzed and evaluated because the existing structure provides a context and meaning for the incoming stimuli (Hayes-Roth, 1977; Sentis & Burnstein, 1979). What for an aschematic may seem an isolated or curious bit of behavior will, for the schematic, be integrated into the existing knowledge structure as a meaningful part of a larger whole. A self-schema allows one to integrate information that is conceptually relevant.

To explore this idea, we used a technique devised by Newtson (1973). Newtson has been concerned with how observers organize the stream of behavior into discrete chunks or units. He proposed that the perceiver actively organizes observed behavior into meaningful actions; it may be argued that the self-schema, by providing a framework within which actions can become meaningful to the observer, allows the observer to integrate those actions into an existing knowledge structure. This integration process may cause individuals with self-schemata in a particular domain to resemble gross-unit perceivers (i.e., those individuals who chunk the behavior into the largest possible units) in this domain. Schematics will chunk the behavior of others into larger units corresponding to and aligned with their conceptual framework and this, in turn, will influence processing of information about the target others, having effects on the recall of information and the attributions made.

In a study on sex role self-schemata (Markus, Crane, & Siladi 1978), individuals who had masculine self-schemata and individuals who had feminine self-schemata were compared with individuals classified as androgynous (aschematic with respect to sex-role stereotypes). The masculine schematics were much faster at endorsing masculine adjectives than they were at endorsing feminine adjectives, and were much more confident that these adjectives described them than they were about feminine words. Conversely, the feminine schematics were faster and more confident in their endorsements of feminine words. Among the androgynous subjects, there was no difference in processing time or the masculine and feminine adjectives.

For the present study, the masculinity schema was chosen because of the clear differentiation found between schematics and aschematics in processing schema-relevant information. Self-rating scales, identical to those used by Markus, Crane, & Siladi, 1979), were administered to several undergraduate psychology classes to identify people with a masculinity schema. From among those completing the scales, 46 males were selected to participate in the study.

Masculine Schematics. Twenty-four male participants who indicated that two out of three of the masculine adjectives—aggressive, dominant, leader—were self-descriptive (points 8-11 on an 11-point scale) *and* who indicated that two out of three of these adjectives were important *and* who rated the adjective "feminine" as not self-descriptive (points 1-4 on an 11-point scale) *and* who indicated that this dimension was unimportant were termed masculine schematics.

Aschematics. A second group of 22 males who rated themselves on the middle range (points 5-7 on an 11-point scale) on two out of three of the masculine adjectives *and* who rated two out of three of these adjectives as unimportant *and* who placed themselves on the middle or low range on the adjective "feminine" were considered aschematic subjects.

Both groups of subjects observed a film (schema-relevant) of a male college student in his dormitory room. Some of the actor's behaviors were stereotypically masculine (e.g., crushing a beer can, reading *Playboy*) and some were neutral with respect to sex type (doing school work, eating an apple). Another film (schema-irrelevant) that served as a control film showed the same actor performing routine activity (eating soup) in a room with almost no context or background. Subjects in this study were given the same instructions as in the Newtson study—to "divide the behavior into meaningful units."

Following the unitizing task, subjects were shown the 60 trait adjectives comprising the Bem Sex Role Inventory (BSRI) (1974), including 20 masculine words, 20 feminine words, and 20 neutral words, in random order. They were asked to judge whether the adjectives described the stimulus actor they saw in the film by pushing a button labelled "HIM" if the word was descriptive of the actor or a button labelled "NOT HIM" if it was not descriptive of the actor. Subjects then performed a series of tasks in which they were asked for recall of the actor's behavior. Following the recall task, subjects were asked to judge if the 60 trait adjectives from the BSRI described them by pushing a button labelled "ME" if the word was self-descriptive or "NOT ME" if the word was not self-descriptive. The words were presented in a random order different from that used in the "HIM/NOT HIM" task.

In analyzing the data from the unitizing task, schematics were compared with aschematics for the mean number of button presses for each minute of the film. If having a self-schema allows the individual to integrate information relevant to that schema, masculine schematic subjects should resemble gross-unit perceivers in a schema-relevant situation. Results provide support for this hypothesis. As shown in Table 10.3, masculine schematic subjects consistently divided the film displaying sterotypically masculine behavior into larger units than did aschematic subjects (a smaller number of responses indicates larger units), although the two groups did not differ in their unitizing of the control film.

These findings are consistent with the notion that the structure of the task allowed the schematics to use their self-structure as an interpretive framework that allowed for the integration of individual bits of behavior into larger conceptual chunks. Presumably, the masculine behavior portrayed in the schema-relevant film evoked the masculine self-schema for the schematics, which in turn led to larger chunking of the stream of behavior. Differences between schematics and aschematics did not occur in the schema-irrelevant film, however, because the actions portrayed (eating soup in a context-free setting) did not activate the masculinity self-schema.

TABLE 10.3
Mean Responses Per Minute in Film Unitizing Task

Type of Subject	Film Segment	
	Schema-irrelevant	Schema-relevant
Masculine schematics	11.86	7.26
Aschematics	11.97	9.70

In an attempt to understand something more about the nature of the difference between schematics and aschematics in other-perception, responses to the "HIM/NOT HIM" attribution task were analyzed. As shown in Table 10.4, schematic and aschematic subjects ascribed roughly the same number of feminine and neutral words to the target actor. Schematic subjects, however, ascribed more masculine attributes to the actor than did the aschematics. This follows the pattern found in earlier studies on self-description and suggests that the schematics see the actions of the actor as relatively more masculine, perhaps because of the similarity of these actions to their own behavior.

With respect to response latency for attributions to the actor, analysis revealed that schematics take longer to ascribe masculine words to the actor (make "HIM" judgments) than they do to feminine words. A similar difference occurred for "NOT HIM" responses. Neither of these differences occurred for aschematics. If the schematics are assumed to have an integrated network of information relevant to masculinity, the somewhat longer latencies for judgments about the actor may reflect the relatively longer time it takes schematics to search their larger array of information to determine whether the actions of the actor conform to their masculinity self-structure.

The response latency data exhibits several notable features. Both groups of subjects take longer to make judgments about others than about themselves. This is hardly surprising, given one's greater opportunities to observe, analyze, and make judgments about one's own behavior. Schematics and aschematics differ in their patterns of self and other processing times in at least one important respect, however. In previous studies on self attributions, masculine schematics typically have been faster to attribute masculine words to themselves and slower to attribute feminine words; this pattern is just the opposite for attributions to others. Aschematics do not differentiate masculine and feminine words with respect to latency for either self-or other-judgments. It seems, then, that the schema contributes to a relatively quick response with respect to judgments about the *self* because having a schema in a particular domain means that relevant information about the self has been summarized and organized for easy access. With respect to judgments about *others*, however, this same schema may lead to relatively

TABLE 10.4
Percentage of Masculine, Feminine, and Neutral Words
Endorsed in "Him/Not-Him" Attribution Task

Type of Subject	Masculine		Feminine		Neutral	
	Him	Not him	Him	Not him	Him	Not him
Schematics	58.2	41.8	58.4	41.6	54.7	45.3
Aschematics	48.4	51.6	55.6	44.1	52.3	47.7

longer judgment times because it must be compared with the information available in the actor's behavior. The longer latencies exhibited by the schematics when attributing masculine characteristics to others may be a function of trying to match aspects of the actor's behavior to aspects of their own. Additional inferences may be required to link the actor's behavior with particular masculine attributes, and these other inferences are likely to consume processing time. Aschematics, who have not encoded their own behavior with respect to masculinity, would not engage in this process, and thus would not exhibit differential latencies to masculine and feminine words.

There were, also, marked differences between schematics and aschematics in confidence for attributions to the actor. As shown in Table 10.5, schematic subjects were significantly more confident in making "NOT HIM" judgments than "HIM" judgments. In contrast, aschematic subjects showed no difference in confidence to these judgments. This finding suggests that the self-schema is operating to provide schematic subjects with a consistent frame of reference for judging the actor's behavior. Schematic subjects were significantly more confident in making "NOT HIM" judgments to all types of words than were aschematic subjects, indicating that having a schema on one dimension may allow them to develop a clearer image of the actor in general and reject possible attributes with some conviction. If a schema provides a clear set of criteria for what is masculine, it is reasonable that the limited information available in the film may not be sufficient as a basis for confident "HIM" judgments. Yet these same criteria could make it relatively easier to determine what is certainly *not* true of the actor.

Analysis of the responses to the "ME/NOT ME" task allowed us to look at some possible contingencies between self-judgments and other-judgments. Data from this last task cannot be compared uncritically with similar data from other studies because these self-judgments were obtained only *after* the judgments had been made about the actor ("HIM/NOT HIM") using the same stimulus words. Thus, these judgments are subject to a number of potential interpretations that do not constrain the data in previous studies. Yet the results are suggestive in a number of respects. As noted in the foregoing, schematic subjects ascribed more masculine traits to the actor than did aschematics. Further analysis reveals that this difference is only significant for those words that schematics do *not* endorse as self-descriptive, thus indicating that, although the actor is seen as

TABLE 10.5
Mean Confidence Rating for Characteristics Attributed to Actor

Type of Subject	Confidence	
	Him	*Not him*
Masculine schematics	3.82	4.06
Aschematics	3.58	3.51

relatively masculine compared to how he is seen by the aschematics, he is definitely *not* masculine in the same way that schematics see themselves. They are clearly sensitive to the actor's masculine behavior, but that masculine behavior is quite different from their own. Using Sherif and Hovland's terms (1961), schematics' self-involvement with the dimension of masculinity is causing them to restrict their latitude of acceptance for masculine behavior and thereby to reject a relatively larger number of characteristics related to that dimension as similar to their own.

With respect to the number of words endorsed, schematics, as expected, tend to endorse more masculine words. Further analysis reveals that this difference is due primarily to differences in endorsements of masculine words to which schematics responded "NOT HIM" (i.e., did not think described the actor), once again indicating that they see their own masculinity as somewhat different and more narrowly defined than do aschematics. As indicated by the "HIM/NOT HIM" data, schematics do see the actions of the actor as more masculine than do the aschematics. This does not mean, however, that they see the actor as similar to themselves. Simple stimulus generalization from self to other cannot explain these results. In the area in which schematics have a clear picture of themselves, they are quite careful to set themselves apart from others. No comparable pattern of relationships between "HIM/NOT HIM" and "ME/NOT ME" judgments exists for the aschematics and this type of self/other differentiation does not seem to occur.

Differences between groups in confidence of self-descriptions support this differentiation or contrast hypothesis. Schematics were more confident of "ME" responses to masculine words only when they had responded "NOT HIM" to those words. They were more confident of their "NOT ME" responses for these words only when they had previously responded "HIM" to those words for the actor. These differences did not occur for the aschematics. These data are consistent with the notion that the self has been used as an anchor for judgments about the actor in the "HIM/NOT HIM" judgment.

In the recall task at the end of the study, no differences were found between schematics and aschematics with respect to either the schema-relevant or schema-irrelevant behaviors. Both groups were quite accurate in their answers for both films. The amount of "crossover" (i.e., substituting details from one film segment to another) was negligible. Large differences were found in confidence for recall, however. Schematic subjects were consistently more confident than aschematic subjects. Moreover, these differences became greater as a film progressed, indicating that as the schema became more firmly entrenched, the schematics "filled in" from their schemata and became relatively more confident about the nature and meaning of the actor's behavior. A dummy variable multiple regression was performed to analyze these confidence data. There was a significant main effect for the relationship between confidence and percentage of correct answers, as well as for the relationship between confidence and percentage of wrong answers. In the case of the incorrect answers, there was a significant interaction with subject type. Aschematic subjects showed a significant negative correlation between percentage of incorrect responses and their confidence ratings; the correlation between percentage incorrect and confidence approached zero for schematics.

Thus schematics, whose self-concept gives them status as "experts" in the area of masculinity, are more confident of their responses, regardless of the correctness of those responses; their schema operates to make them quite confident of those details they have filled in or supplied. In contrast, aschematics do not possess a schema to fill in details they may have missed and are consequently less confident of their guesses and more aware of gaps in their knowledge of the film.

DISCUSSION AND CONCLUSIONS

Together, these studies indicate that the self-structure does function to provide an anchor or frame of reference for judgments and evaluations of others. When the self is conceptualized as a set of knowledge structures that explain and integrate one's own behavior in particular domains, it is evident that there is marked variation in the perception of others as a function of the content and scope of these self-structures. Consistent with earlier work on person-perception, it appears that an individual is likely to attend to variation in the behavior of others in those areas that are important to or salient to the self (areas in which one has a self-schema or is schematic). The research reported here has allowed us to go beyond the conclusions from earlier work, however, in suggesting that individuals will differentially process information about others that is relevant to their own schematic domains. Thus when some aspect of the stimulus (the person-to-be perceived) is relevant to an area that is important to the perceiver, this aspect is likely to be focused on and elaborated with information from the individual's own self-structure. This elaboration or articulation of stimuli has a diverse set of consequences. It may lead, as in Hamill's (1980) study where the stimuli were not initially schema-relevant, to more accurate recognition memory. When the stimulus material is rich and schema-relevant, schematics may fill in the stimulus with information from their own knowledge structure and this may actually impair some aspect of performance (thus schematics were quite confident about their memories even when incorrect). This "filling in" also may be related to more extreme evaluations and judgments of the behavior of the perceived other. Thus a schema-relevant target is seen as either more independent or more dependent by an individual with an independence self-schema than by one without this schema. The self-schema also has a range of consequences for the speed and confidence with which information about the task is processed. Results from unitizing the behavior of others suggest that a self-schema may provide an interpretive framework that allows an individual to organize the pertinent information into larger, more global conceptual chunks than would be the case without this structure. Overall these data suggest that the self is a structure that is invoked in the perception of others, and that it acts as an anchor or a set of criteria in organizaing our percpetions of others in self-relevant domains.

Based on the findings from these initial studies, several general hypotheses about the effects of self on other-perception can be suggested. It is now evident that the relationship is complex and cannot be adequately described by the statement that "as you judge yourself, so shall you judge others." The nature of these complexities stems from the fact that knowledge structure such as the self-structure can have different effects depending on the perceivers' expectations, the nature of the task, and the characteristics of the information. Generally the pattern of findings from these and other studies implies that if a perceived person's actions or behavior are relevant to one's own, in areas of behavior that are important to the self, then one is likely to evaluate or judge the target individual on *the same dimensions* or *within the same categories* one uses to judge one's self. Following this initial evaluation or categorization of the stimulus person, at least two other types of results are possible.

In cases where the perceiver is not given the time or the opportunity to make explicit self/other comparisons, some amount of stimulus generalization is likely to result. We can surmise that this may be especially true in those instances where one has minimal information about these stimulus others and/or when the behavior is quite similar to one's own (within a latitude of acceptance implied by the self-schema). Initially, the film study satisfied these criteria. When unitizing the actor's behavior, subjects were not asked to compare the actor with themselves. Nor did they know they would be expected to do so later in the study. The information provided about the actor was not extreme with respect to masculinity and was designed to be potentially similar to actions of the subject. In this task, schematic subjects responded as though the actor's behavior were familiar enough to be understood with one's self-schema. Given that a self-schema may be activated very early in the information processing sequence, such that stimuli perceived as schema-relevant will be encoded or organized differently (e.g., in larger chunks, or in categories that we use to organize our own behavior), then this tendency to see others as similar in schema-relevant domains may occur almost automatically and perhaps without conscious awareness. Perceived similarity may be a function of processing information about others with one's self-structures as though it were information about the self. In those instances of person perception that meet the conditions outlined above, we may be quite likely to judge others as we judge ourselves; that is, we will evaluate them on the *same dimensions* we use for our own behavior, and will assign them the *same values* on these dimensions. ("If I'm fairly happy, I think you're fairly happy." "If I cheat a little bit, you must cheat a little bit, too.")

However, given more time, a task that requires explicit comparison or evaluation of another person, or a very rich or articulated stimulus, then the stimulus person is not likely to be seen as similar to the self at all. In fact, this individual may be viewed as markedly different from the self. In these cases, the self-schema will operate to accentuate the differences between the perceiver and perceived. In the tasks that involved an explicit evaluation of the perceived other, the schematics exhibited much sharper differentiation in their judgments of others than did the aschematics. Thus the behavior of others may be evaluated in the domains of one's self-schema, but the outcome of the judgment may be quite different for the self than for others. We are quite likely to insist on a variety of differences between ourselves and others in areas that are important to one's self-definition. Overall, the evidence lends support to the idea of the self-structure as a baseline against which relevant information about others is compared and contrasted. This baseline shifts depending on the nature of the task and the type of stimulus material.

These are, of course, only initial investigations, and many other types of studies are needed to become more specific about how the self-structure is implicated in the perception of others and to understand the nature of its impact. These studies will allow us to become more specific about the criteria that determine when schema-relevant others will be seen as similar, when they will be seen as different, and what produces these differences. The studies reported have focused on variations in the self-structure and its impact on perception. They have not attended to variations in the characteristics of the stimulus (the to-be-perceived other) or to variations in the relationship between the perceiver and the perceived. However, as indicated in the beginning of the chapter, these issues also are central to defining the effects of the self on the understanding of others.

The approach outlined here, although exploratory, has implications for a potentially wide range of problems. Knowledge about the role of the self-structure in the perception of others will help us to understand the role of the self in behavioral interaction. It should be possible, for example, to explain why it may be difficult to change sterotypic ideas and attitudes about others. If individuals use the self-structure as a frame of reference within which they assimilate or differentiate information about others, it first may be necessary to change some elements of the self-structure to insure change in judgments of others. Examining individual variations in the impact of the self-structure on perception of others also may illuminate some commonplace assumptions about egocentrism or self-centeredness. Do people differ in the range of stimuli that are likely to be perceived as self-relevant or schema-relevant? Do some individuals have relatively greater difficulty in suppressing the self-structure when thinking about others and therefore more difficulty in being sensitive to the thoughts and feelings of others, or in displaying empathy, or in taking the role of another? Specifying the nature of the relationship between the self-structure and other-perception may also be useful in understanding some elements of interpersonal attraction. Might it be the case, for example, that we will like or be attracted to other people whose behavior can be easily organized and interpreted with our own self-structure?

Further research on these and other issues may reveal that self-relevance is not just one of many mediating variables in social perception and cognition, but instead, as the early self theorists implied, a key element in understanding the construction and interpretation of social behavior.

REFERENCES

Bem, S. L. The measurement of psychological androgyny. *Journal of Consulting and Clinical Psychology,* 1974, *42,* 155–162.

Berkowitz, L. The judgmental process in personality functioning. *Psychological Review,* 1960, *67,* 150–142.

Bower, G. H., & Karlin, M. B. Depth of processing: Pictures of faces and recognition memory. *Journal of Experimental Psychology,* 1974, *103,* 751–757.

Bradley, G. W. Self-serving biases in the attribution process: A reexamination of the fact or fiction question. *Journal of Personality and Social Psychology,* 1978, *36,* 56–71.

Bramel, D. A dissonance theory approach to defensive projection. *Journal of Abnormal and Social Psychology,* 1962, *64,* 121–129.

Bramel, D. Selection of a target for defensive projection. *Journal of Abnormal and Social Psychology,* 1963, *66,* 318–324.

Cartwright, D. Relation of decision time to the categories of response. *American Journal of Psychology,* 1941, *54,* 174–196.

Cartwright, D. Self-consistency as a factor affecting immediate recall. *Journal of Abnormal and Social Psychology,* 1956, *52,* 212–219.

Combs, A. W., & Snygg, D. *Individual behavior: A perceptual approach to behavior.* New York: Harper & Brothers, 1949.

Craik, F. I. M., & Lockhart, R. S. Levels of processing: A framework for memory research. *Journal of Verbal Learning and Verbal Behavior,* 1972, *11,* 671–684.

Crockett, W. H., & Meidinger, T. Authoritarianism and interpersonal perception. *Jounal of Abnormal and Social Psychology,* 1956, *53,* 378–380.

Dornbusch, S. M., Hastorf, A. H., Richardson, S. A., Muzzy, R. E., & Vreeland, R. S. The perceiver and the perceived: Their relative influence on the categories of interpersonal cognition. *Journal of Personality and Social Psychology,* 1965, *1,* 434–440.

Edlow, D., & Kiesler, C. Ease of denial and defensive projection. *Journal of Experimental Social Psychology,* 1966, *2,* 56–69.

Epstein, S. The self-concept revisted: Or a theory of a theory. *American Psychologist,* 1973, *28,* 404–416.

Fiedler, F. E. Interpersonal perceptions and group effectiveness. In R. Taguiri & L. Petrullo (Eds.), *Person perception and interpersonal behavior.* Stanford: Stanford University Press, 1958.

Freud, S. The dynamics of transference. In *Collected Papers* (Vol. 2). London: Hogarth, 1924.

From, F. *Perception of other people.* New York: Columbia University Press, 1971.

Goldings, H. J. On the avowal and projection of happiness. *Journal of Personality,* 1954, *25,* 50–47.

Hamill, R. Self-schemas and face recognition: Effects of cognitive structures on social perception and memory. Unpublished dissertation, University of Michigan, 1980.

Hastorf, A. H., Richardson, S. A., & Dornbusch, S. M. The problem of relevance in the study of person perception. In R. Tagiuri & L. Petrullo (Eds.), *Person perception and interpersonal behavior*. Stanford: Stanford University Press, 1958.

Hayes-Roth, B. Evolution of cognitive structures and processes. *Psychological Review*, 1977, *84*, 260–278.

Holmes, D. S. Projection as a defense mechanism. *Psychological Bulletin*, 1968, *69*, 248–268.

Hornberger, R. The projective effects of fear and sexual arousal on the rating of pictures. *Journal of Clinical Psychology*, 1960, *16*, 328–331.

Horney, K. *New ways in psychoanalysis*. New York: Norton, 1939.

Hyde, T. S., & Jenkins, J. J. Recall for words as function of semantic, graphic, and syntactic orienting tasks. *Journal of Verbal Learning and Verbal Behavior*, 1973, *12*, 471–480.

Johnson, D. M. *The psychology of thought and judgment*. New York: Harper, 1955.

Jones, E. E. Authoritarianism as a determinant of first impression formation. *Journal of Personality*, 1954, *25*, 107–127.

Katz, D., & Allport, F. *Students attitudes*. Syracuse: Craftsman Press, 1931.

Keenan, J. M., & Baillet, S. D. Memory for personally and socially significant events. In R. S. Nickerson (Ed.), *Attention and performance VIII*. Hillsdale, N.J.: Lawrence Erlbaum Associates, 1980.

Kelly, G. A. *The psychology of personal constructs* (Vol. I). New York: W. W. Norton & Co., 1955.

Kendzierski, D. Self-schema and scripts: The recall of self-referent and scriptal information. *Personality and Social Psychology Bulletin*, 1980, *6*, 23–29.

Koltuv, B. B. Some characteristics of intrajudge trait intercorrelations. *Psychological Monographs*, 1962, *76* (33, Whole No. 552).

Kuiper, N. A., & Rogers, T. B. The encoding of personal information: Self-other differences. *Journal of Personality and Social Psychology*, 1979, *37*, 499–514.

LaFave, L. & Sherif, M. *Placement of items on a controversial social issue*. Institute of Group Relations, University of Oklahoma, 1959.

Leary, T. *Interpersonal diagnosis of personality*. New York: Ronald Press, 1957.

Lemon, N., & Warren, N. Salience, centrality and self-relevence of traits in contruing others. *British Journal of Social and Clinical Psychology*, 1974, *13*, 119–124.

Lord, C. G. Schemas and images as memory aids: Two modes of processing social information. *Journal of Personality and Social Psychology*, 1980, *38*, 257–269.

Markus, H. Self-schemata and processing information about the self. *Journal of Personality and Social Psychology*, 1977, *35*, 63–78.

Markus, H., Crane, M., & Siladi, M. *Cognitive consequences of androgyny*. Paper presented at the annual meeting of the Midwestern Psychological Association, Chicago Illinios, May 1978.

Markus, H. & Fong, G. *The role of the self on other perception*. Unpublished manuscript, University of Michigan, 1979.

Markus, H., Sentis, K., & Hamill, R. *Thinking fat: Self-schema for body weight and the processing of weight relevant information*. Unpublished manuscript, University of Michigan, 1979.

Mintz, E. An example of assimlative projection. *Journal of Abnormal and Social Psychology*, 1956, *52*, 270–280.

Mischel, W., Ebbesen, E. B., & Zeiss, A. R. Selective attention to the self: Situational and dispositional determinants. *Journal of Personality and Social Psychology*, 1973, *27*, 129–142.

Mueller, J. H., Bailis, K. L., & Goldstein, A. G. Depth of processing and anxiety in facial recognition. *British Journal of Psychology*, in press.

Mueller, J. H., Courtois, M. R., & Bailis, K. L. *Self-reference in facial recognition*. Unpublished manuscript, 1979.

Murphy, G. *Personality: A biosocial approach to origin and structure*. New York: Harper, 1947.

Neisser, U. *Cognition and reality: Principles and implications of cognitive psychology*. San Franciso: Freeman, 1976.

Newtson, D. Attribution and the unit of perception of ongoing behavior. *Journal of Personality and Social Psychology*, 1973, *1*, 28–38.

Nisbett, R. F. & Borgida, E. Attribution and psychology of prediction. *Journal of Personality and Social Psychology*, 1975, *32*, 932–943.

Nisbett, R. F., Borgida, E., Crandall, R., & Reed, H. Popular induction: Information is not necessarily informative. In J. S. Carroll & J. W. Payne (Eds.), *Cognition and social behavior*. Hillsdale, N.J.: Lawrence Erlbaum Associates, 1976.

O'Keefe, B. J., Delia, J. G., & O'Keefe, D. J. Construct individuality, cognitive complexity, and the formation and remembering of interpersonal impressions. *Social Behavior and Personality*, 1977, *5*, 229–240.

Palmer, S. E. Hierarchical structure in perceptual representation. *Cognitive Psychology*, 1977, *9*, 441–474.

Phares, J. & Lamiell, J. T. Internal–external control, interpersonal judgments of others in need, and attribution of responsibility. *Journal of Personality*, 1975, *3*, 23–38.

Phares, E. J. & Wilson, K. G. Responsibility attribution: Role of outcome severity, situational ambiguity, and internal–external control. *Journal of Personality*, 1972, *40*, 392–406.

Piaget, J. *The construction of reality in the child*. New York: Basic Books, 1954.

Rogers, C. P. *Client-centered therapy*. Boston, Mass.: Houghton Mifflin, 1951.

Rogers, T. B. Self-reference in memory: Recognition of personality items. *Journal of Research in Personality*, 1977, *11*, 295–305.

Rogers, T. B., Kuiper, N. A., & Kirker, W. S. Self-reference and the encoding of personal information. *Journal of Personality and Social Psychology*, 1977, *35*, 677–688.

Ross, L. D. The intuitive psychologist and his shortcomings: Distortions in the attribution process. In L. Berkowitz (Ed.), *Advances in experimental social pscyhology* (Vol 10). New York: Academic Press, 1979.

Ross, L. D., Greene, D., & House, P. The "false consensus effect": An egocentric bias in social perception and attribution processes. *Journal of Experimental Social Psychology*, 1977, *13*, 279–301.

Ross, M. & Sicoly, F. Egocentric biases in recall and attribution. *Journal of Personality and Social Psychology*, 1979, *37*, 322–336.

Sarbin, T. R. Role theory. In G. Lindzey (Ed.), *Handbook of social psychology* (Vol. I). Cambridge, Mass: Addison-Wesley, 1954.

Scodel, A., & Friedman, M. L. Additional observations on the social perceptions of authoritarians and nonauthoritarians. *Journal of Abnormal and Social Psychology*, 1956, *52*, 92–95.

Scriven, M. The contribution of philosophy of the social sciences to educational development. In G. Barrett, (Ed.), *Philosophy and educational development*. London: G. Harrays & Co., 1966.

Secord, P. F., Backman, C. W., & Eachus, H. T. Effects of imbalance in the self-concept on the perception of persons. *Journal of Abnormal and Social Psychology*, 1964, *68*, 442–446.

Sentis, K., & Burnstein, E. Remembering schema-consistent information: Effects of a balance schema on recognition memory. *Journal of Personality and Social Psychology*, 1979, *37*, 2200–2211.

Sentis, K., & Markus, H. *Self-schemas and recognition memory*. Unpublished manuscript, University of Michigan, 1979.

Sherif, M., & Hovland, C. I. *Social judgment: Assimilation and contrast effects in communication and attitude change*. New Haven and London: Yale University Press, 1961.

Shrauger, S. J. & Altrocchi, J. The personality of the perceiver as a factor in person perception. *Psychological Bulletin*, 1964, *62*, 289–308.

Shrauger, S. J., & Patterson, M. B. Self-evaluation and the selection of dimensions for evaluating others. *Journal of Personality*, 1976, *42*, 569–585.

Sosis, R. H. Internal-external control and the perception of responsibility of another for an accident. *Journal of Personality and Social Psychology*, 1974, *30*, 393–399.

Steiner, I. D., & Johnson, H. H. Authoritarianism and "tolerance of trait inconsistency." *Journal of Abnormal and Social Psychology,* 1963, *67,* 388–391.

Strnad, B. R., & Mueller, J. H. Levels of processing in facial recognition memory. *Bulletin of the Psychonomic Society,* 1977, *9,* 17–18.

Sullivan, H. S. *Conceptions of modern psychiatry.* Washington, D.C.: William Alanson White Psychiatric Foundation, 1947.

Turner, R. G. Consistency, self-consciousness, and the predictive validity of typical and maximal personality measures. *Journal of Research in Personality,* 1978, *12,* 117–132.

Wallen, R. Ego-involvement as a determinant of selective forgetting. *Journal of Abnormal and Social Psychology,* 1942, *37,* 10–39.

Winograd F. Recognition memory for faces following nine different judgments. *Bulletin of the Psychonomic Society,* 1976, *8,* 419–421.

Wortman, C. B. Causal attributions and personal control. In J. H. Harvey, W. J. Ickes, & R. F. Kidd (Eds.), *New directions in attribution research* (Vol. 1). Hillsdale, N.J.: Lawrence Erlbaum Associates, 1976.

Zajonc, R. B. *Feeling and thinking: Preferences need no inferences.* Paper presented at the 87th Annual Convention, America Psychological Association, New York, 1978.

Zeller, A. F. An experimental analogue of repression: I. Historical summary. *Psychological Bulletin,* 1950, *47,* 39–51.

11 Considerations for a Theory of Self-Inference Processes

Anne Locksley
Michael Lenauer
New York University

That people form beliefs about their own personality traits and characteristics is both intuitively obvious and empirically demonstrable. A considerable amount of research indicates that people can be induced to make inferences about their attitudes, feelings, and traits, by experimental manipulations that are either unobtrusive or not intuitively plausible as sufficient causes of behavior (Bem, 1972; Festinger & Carlsmith, 1956; Lepper, Greene, & Nisbett, 1973; Nisbett & Valins, 1971; Ross, Lepper, & Hubbard, 1975). Recent studies of cognitive processing of self-related information have shown that people readily process dispositional terms with respect to their notions about themselves and their own behavior (Markus, 1977; Rogers, Kuiper, & Kirker, 1977), and McGuire and Padawer-singer (1976) have found that people spontaneously offer trait terms when asked to describe themselves. In general, individuals have a uniquely rich and diverse array of information about themselves and their behavior. How do they come to form specific beliefs about their own personality characteristics? What kinds of information do people use to form these beliefs? What sorts of reasoning processes are involved in self-inferences about traits? How reliable or accurate are people's inferences about their own personality characteristics?

Bem's (1972) theory of self-perception provides a useful point of departure for thinking about these issues. Although Bem was primarily concerned with explaining how people infer their attitudes toward a stimulus, his general point holds true for inferences about traits as well. He approached the problem of how people know what their attitudes are by considering how people learn to describe internal states or events. Because, by and large, children acquire the capacity for self-description by learning word usage rules from others (Quine, 1960), it follows that at least some of the criteria for self-description, namely overt behavior and its context, will be those used by observers. Thus, Bem (1972) argued that:

> Individuals come to "know" their own attitudes, emotions, and other internal states partially by inferring them from observations of their own overt behavior and/or the circumstances in which it occurs. Thus to the extent that internal cues are weak, ambiguous, or uninterpretable, the individual is functionally in the same position as an outside observer, an observer who must necessarily rely upon those same external cues to infer the individual's inner states [p. 3].

Like attitudes, some personality traits such as aggression, affiliation or sociability, and compassion or empathy do imply information about internal states of arousal. We assume that agressive people have frequent feelings of hostility or anger or that compassionate people are "moved by" or aroused by the problems of others. Other personality traits such as intelligence, extraversion, assertiveness, or dependency do not imply unambiguous information about internal states or events. In cases where people are making inferences about their own traits when internal cues are irrelevant or ambiguous, it is necessarily true that they are functionally in the same position of an outside observer. Their own overt behavior and the circumstances of their acts are the only sources of information about their traits. In cases where people are making inferences about their own traits when internal cues are relevant, then of course those internal cues constitute an additional source of information about their traits, though that information may be more ambiguous than ordinarily assumed (Bem, 1972). In any case, people do not have direct access to internal neuropsychic structures, and self-inferences about traits necessarily originate in some set of observations of one's own behavior and its context, and by accompanying internal states when implied by the trait term in question. The problem that a theory of self-inference must solve is to specify the characteristics of a set of behavioral observations necessary and sufficient to evoke the belief that one has a particular trait.

Attribution theorists have been concerned with the problem of trait or person attributions for some time (Heider, 1958; Jones & Davis, 1965; Kelley, 1967, 1971, 1973). However, the primary focus of attributional research has been on observers' attributions for a target's behavior, and there has been some hesitation about generalizing observers' attributional processes to actors. Self-inference or self-attributional processes have been treated as a special case within attribution theory for three basic reasons. First, actors have more extensive beliefs and memories about their own behavior than observers usually have about another person's behavior. Actors' knowledge of their prior behavioral history may affect their inferences about any particular instance of their behavior, whereas observers may rely more on proximate characteristics of another person's behavior when attributing causes of the behavior. Second, Jones and Nisbett (1971) demonstrated that actors and observers do not necessarily attribute the actor's behavior to the same cause. They proposed that actors are in general more likely to attribute their behavior to situational requirements, whereas observers tend to attribute the same behavior to personal dispositions on the part of the actor. They suggested that an actor's attention ordinarily is directed away from his or her own behavior, scanning aspects of the situation. In contrast, an observer's attention ordinarily is focused on the actor. Thus actor–observer differences in causal attribution may be accounted for by differences in the perceptual salience of possible causes.

The third reason for treating self-inference processes as a special case of attribution theory may be simply methodological. Observers' attributional processes may be explored systematically by manipulating characteristics of the information available about a target's behavior. The inability to manipulate systematically either characteristics of actors' prior behavioral history or actors' retrieval processes in any given experiment sets intrinsic limits on investigations of self-inference processes. For this same reason, whether or not to treat self-inferences as a special case within attribution theory must be viewed as an open question. There is no evidence as yet suggesting that actors' unique access to their own behavioral history necessarily implies that they *reason* about their own behavior any differently than observers reason about the behavior of other people. Jones and Nisbett (1971) have shown that actors and observers *can* have divergent perceptions of the causes of the actor's behavior, but there are other studies that have not obtained actor–observer differences in attributions of the actor's behavior (Bem 1965, 1967; Ross, Amabile, & Steinmetz, 1977; Ross, Lepper, & Hubbard, 1975) and still other studies that have obtained actor–observer differences in the opposite direction to those obtained by Jones and Nisbett (Monson & Snyder, 1977). For instance, Ross and Sicoly (1979) found that, for group tasks, each participant remembered more of his or her own contributions to the group activity and assumed greater responsibility for the outcome of the group activity than the other participants remembered or attributed to them. What factors account for this variability of results in comparisons of actors' and observers' attributional judgments remains to be determined by further research. It should be noted that differences in judgments do not necessarily imply differences in inferential logic and may eventually be explained fully either by differences in available information or by differences in encoding or retrieval processes (Ross & Sicoly, 1979).

At this point, the problem of applying attribution theory to the question of how people form beliefs about their own personality traits has less to do with the special status of actors than with the generality of existing attributional categories. The bulk of attributional theory to date has been concerned either with broad discriminations between situational and dispositional causes (Kelley, 1967, 1971, 1973) or with establishing preliminary criteria for dispositional attributions (Jones & Davis, 1965). Although these sorts of discriminations may be presupposed by trait inferences, they do not explain the ways in which people come to make specific inferences about particular traits. Consider the following example of a pattern of information that has been hypothesized to predict person versus situational attributions (Kelley, 1967; McArthur, 1972): (1) John likes the painting; (2) In the past, John has almost always liked this painting; (3) Hardly anyone who has seen this painting likes it; (4) John also likes almost every other painting he has seen. Presented with this information and asked to judge whether something about John or something about the painting caused John's response, one is likely to infer that something about John caused his response (McArthur, 1972). *What* it is about John that caused his response remains ambiguous. It could be that John has bad taste. Or it could be that John is anxious to appear cultured. Or it could be that John, having once tried his hand at painting, is aware of the difficulty of the task and is loath to criticize anyone else's artistic efforts. The point of the example is that general criteria for discriminating dispositional from situational causes of behavior do not always permit inferences about specific causes of behavior. Because beliefs about traits, in a sense, represent inferences about specific causes of behavior, it is necessary to consider what sorts of inferential processes might be involved in the identification of specific causes of behavior. Clearly, people believe that they have *particular* traits (Markus, 1977; Rogers et al., 1977). What leads them to infer that they have particular trait characteristics?

One way to view self-inferences about traits is as though they were answers to problems of self-classification. For example, the statement "I am an extravert" may be viewed as an answer to the question "What is the probability that I am an extravert?" Presumably, people use some set of observations of their own behavior and its circumstances to answer this type of question. What is the nature of this set of observations?

The cumulative results of personality-trait research are instructive with respect to this question. Typically, trait research involves obtaining correlations between dispositional self-descriptions and behavior in relevant settings. The generally poor predictive validity of self-report measures of traits (Mischel, 1968) suggests two conclusions. First, processes of self-inference probably do not correspond to the normative inductive criteria used by personality psychologists to infer traits. Indeed, on the basis of existing research on intuitive induction in general (Chapman & Chapman, 1967, 1969; Nisbett & Ross, 1980; Ross, 1977; Ward & Jenkins, 1965; Wason & Johnson-Laird, 1972), we have little reason to expect that self-inference processes involve assessments of behavioral consistency across situations in which traitlike behavior is *possible* or attempts to entertain and preclude at least nonobvious alternative explanations of traitlike behavior when it does occur (Ross, Amabile, & Steinmetz, 1977; Ross, Lepper, & Hubbard, 1975). Bem and Allen (1974) did find comparatively high correlations between self-report measures of traits and behavior, but *only* under the condition that the behavioral assessment remain restricted to the set of situations across which subjects knew their behavior was "trait-consistent." These results indicate that subjects are probably not using the same criterion of cross-situational consistency used by personality psychologists. In general, individuals may attend to the absolute frequency of actual occurrences of traitlike behavior instead of relative frequencies such as the ratio of actual occurrences to nonoccurrences across the domain of situations in which traitlike behavior is possible.

The second conclusion suggested by the generally poor predictive validity of self-report measures of traits is that actual regularities in behavior are neither necessarily noticed nor necessarily form the basis of trait inferences. It is interesting, for example, to consider the number of reliable behavioral correlates of extraversion–introversion (Wilson, 1977) that do not appear to be part of popular conceptions of extraverted and introverted behavior (Cantor & Mischel, 1977). Research on implicit personality theory and person-perception (Asch, 1946; Chapman & Chapman, 1967, 1969; D'Andrade, 1965; Passini & Norman, 1966; Schneider, 1973) demonstrates that people tend to confuse conceptual or semantic associations with empirical or observational associations and that individuals may be quite insensitive to comparatively strong but non-intuitive empirical correlations. People also may be unaware of the role of situational factors (Ross, 1977) or even of their own self-presentation strategies (Snyder, 1974) in producing apparent traitlike consistency in their behavior.

There are basically two criteria used by personality psychologists to infer traits: cross-situational consistency and construct validity (or the evaluation of alternative explanatory variables). Both criteria involve *probabilistic* assessments of behavior as well as the identification of relevant behavioral parameters. Accordingly, research on subjective probability estimation may yield hypotheses about the nature of self-inference processes. Kahneman and Tversky (1972, 1973; Tversky, 1977; Tversky & Kahneman, 1974) have conducted a number of studies investigating the intuitive strategies that people use to solve probabilistic problems of prediction and explanation. They show that individuals, when confronted with problems of the sort "Did *A* cause event *B?*" or "Was *B* an effect of *A?*" use judgments of similarity between *A* and *B* to estimate the probability of the causal relation. That is, people tend to make predictions by selecting an outcome that represents or incorporates the essential features of the cause or to construct explanations by selecting a cause that represents or incorporates the essential features of the effect. Kahneman and Tversky (1972) term this strategy the *representativeness heuristic*.

Nisbett and Wilson (1977) demonstrated that people can be unaware of the true causes of their own behavior. They raised the possibility that people may use the representativeness heuristic to infer causes for their own behavior. Although they were not concerned with trait inferences per se, it is possible to apply their hypothesis to the problem of how people form beliefs about their own personality traits or characteristics. Trait constructs may be viewed as possible causes of behavior, and behavior may be viewed as possible effects of traits. Thus our prior formulation of self-inferences as answers to questions like "What is the probability that I have the trait x?" can be translated into questions like "What is the probability that my behavior is an effect of the trait x?".

Obviously, people acquire a vocabulary of trait terms as one aspect of general language acquisition. One aspect of mastering the usage of trait terms entails learning how to describe or classify behavior in approximately the same way that other members of the same linguistic culture would describe or classify the behavior. Thus the acquisition of trait concepts includes some process of abstracting and storing in memory the sets of categories of behavioral features that correspond to particular trait terms.

Clearly, behavior varies in the extent to which it resembles or incorporates a set of features that correspond to any discriminative trait construct. We can apply Kahneman and Tversky's (1972, 1973) term *representativeness* to designate this aspect of behavior. Behavior thus may be more or less representative of any given trait construct. We propose that people regard their own behavior as informative about their personality characteristics to the extent that it is representative of personological constructs. To put the hypothesis more formally:

> People will infer that they might have a trait x, when they observe themselves behaving in a way which is representative of or includes the essential features of the trait construct, x.

Two qualifications of this hypothesis must be noted. First, the term *might* is used because we assume that people rarely form an enduring belief about their own traits on the basis of a single observation. The point of the hypothesis is to suggest that people do employ trait categories when encoding observations or remembering instances of their own behavior, to the extent that their behavior is representative of a trait category. It is worth recalling in this context that several studies (Festinger & Carlsmith, 1956; Ross, Amabile, & Steinmetz, 1977; Ross, Lepper, & Hubbard, 1975) have found significant effects on self-description of a single behavioral observation.

Second, we assume that the hypothesis holds only in situations in which an *intuitively plausible* and *intuitively sufficient* situational cause of the behavior is not present and is not salient for the actor. It seems clear that in the presence of a plausible, sufficient, and salient situational cause individuals discount the probability of a personological cause for their own behavior (Lepper, Green, & Nisbett, 1973). Kelley (1971) formalized this proposition about causal reasoning for a single behavioral observations. His discounting principle states that the probability that a particular cause produced an observed effect is lessened when other plausible causes are also present. It is interesting to consider the implications of the discounting principle for self-inference processes. People will regard their behavior as uninformative about their personality characteristics to the extent that it can be attributed to other plausible causes. This strategy could lead to two possible errors. First, from a normative statistical perspective, the presence of more than one possible cause does not affect the probability value for any one cause; it merely means that additional information is required to discriminate the true cause. If people classify their behavior as uninformative about themselves when several possible causes are present, they may exclude such behavioral instances from any retrospective "sampling" of their behavior for self-inference purposes. Such a strategy could exaggerate a retrospective impression of traitlike consistency in one's own behavior. Second, actual dimensions of individual differences elicited in the presence of stimuli that happen to be plausible causes of behavior may remain undetected. For example, Schachter (1959) found that firstborns respond with greater anxiety in fearful situations than those born later. Because the situation offers a plausible and sufficient cause of anxiety, firstborns may not infer that their arousal is informative about their own characteristics.

Our first hypothesis concerned only the origins of an individual's hypothesis that he or she might have a particular trait. The question arises as to how people become confident or certain that they do indeed have a particular trait; that is, how do people decide that they are extraverted, or intelligent, or aggressive, or independent? Presumably some sort of retrieval process occurs in which people scan their behavioral history and make an inference about their personality characteristics. What kinds of evidence do people look for in their own behavioral history? What temporal parameters are involved in this retrieval process? What "sampling" strategies do people use?

From a methodological standpoint, such interior retrieval processes are notoriously difficult to investigate systematicaly, although it should be noted that they are potentially amenable to investigation. No one has yet explored such experimental strategies as creating a miniature "behavioral history" in the lab to enable investigations of how subjects combine or use several behavioral observations for self-inference purposes (as opposed to the single behavioral observation usually manipulated in laboratory studies). In any case, we can only speculate at this point about the nature of this retrieval and inference process. An assumption that provides a fruitful point of departure is that people treat their memories of their own behavior in much the same way they treat available information about another person's behavior, at least with respect to self-inferences about traits. That is to say, the inference criteria used by a person in scanning his or her own behavioral history may be assumed to be the same criteria used by a person in the presence of information about another individual's behavioral history. Essentially, this assumption represents only a logical extension of the framework initially provided by Bem's (1972) self-perception theory. Bem argued that actors treat their own behavior in the same way that observers do when making inferences about their internal states and other characteristics. We are suggesting that, other things being equal, actors treat their memories of their own behavior like observers when making inferences about their own personality characteristics.

Given this assumption, several lines of research on intuitive induction and subjective probability yield hypotheses about the nature of self-inference processes. A number of studies suggest that individuals use positive instances of a class of events to estimate or infer associations between variables, and ignore negative instances (Chapman & Chapman, 1967, 1969; Ross, 1977; Smedslund, 1963; Ward & Jenkins, 1965; Wason & Johnson-Laird, 1972). This bias in attention to positive instances has been demonstrated also in a set of studies by Snyder and Cantor (1979). They asked subjects to use information about a stimulus person to test hypotheses about her personality attributes. They found that subjects consistently evidenced a confirmatory hypothesis-testing strategy; that is, subjects looked for the presence of trait-consistent behavior and ignored other aspects of the information about the stimulus person, including available disconfirmatory instances of behavior. Snyder and Uranowitz (1978) demonstrated a similar effect in a memory study. They presented subjects with a narrative of a woman's life history. The narrative contained details that would be intuitively perceived as predictive of a lesbian sexual orientation as well as details that would be intuitively predictive of a heterosexual orientation. Afterward, subjects were told that the woman was either a lesbian or a heterosexual. One week after reading the narrative, subjects were administered a memory test. It was found that subjects' recall was biased in the direction of the outcome. Subjects ''remembered'' background details that were consistent with the sexual orientation information they had been given. The results of this study indicate that, at least for social inferences; memory for past information about behavior may exhibit similar effects of the confirmatory evidence searches already demonstrated in concurrent use of behavioral information (Snyder & Cantor, 1979). This bias may be characteristic of self-inference processes as well. Markus (1977) found that subjects who think of themselves as independent can cite many more instances of their own independent behavior than subjects who don't. Although she is concerned with already formed beliefs about the self, rather than with the formation of beliefs, her findings at least indicate that memory for behaviors may be organized in terms of its trait characteristics and that positive instances can readily be brought to mind. Also Estes (1976) has demonstrated relatively good prediction of subjects' probability estimates with a model that assumed that frequency information is represented categorically as well as episodically; that is, frequency information may be independently represented in terms of the category of the event as well as in terms of the context in which it occurred. This raises the possibility that behavior may appear to be more traitlike in memory than at the point of its original occurrence—an hypothesis consistent with the results of a study that found that actors described themselves in more traitlike terms when characterizing themselves in the past than in the present (Lenauer, Sameth, & Shaver, 1976).

These several lines of research suggest the hypothesis that, other things being equal, actors make an inference about having a particular trait on the basis of retrieval of representative instances of traitlike behavior and that the frequency of those instances will predict the probability of a self-inference with respect to the trait. We surmise that the relationship between frequency representations and the formation of beliefs about the self is not linear but asymptotic, such that the contribution of each actual instance to the inference process decreases after a certain point at which the belief is formed with some certainty.

In general, then, we are suggesting that actors encode their behavior with trait categories when their behavior is representative of a trait category and that the frequencies of traitlike behavior are represented categorically (or in terms of the relevant trait category) and essentially form the basis for self-inferences with respect to a given trait. For example, suppose an individual is wondering whether or not he or she is an extravert. If he or she can retrieve a number of instances in which he or she behaved like an extravert, we suggest that he or she will infer that he or she is an extravert. That there may have been as many or more times when he or she could have behaved like an extravert but did not may not enter into the inference process.

Although negative instances may not enter into the inference process, contradictory instances may. If representative behavior is encoded with trait categories, then semantically or conceptually associated categories might be activated in the actor's retrieval process. Suppose the actor, when scanning his or her behavioral history for instances of extraverted behavior, suddenly remembers instances of introverted behavior. Instances of introverted behavior may come to mind either because it is a dimension of behavior that shares similar contexts with extraverted behavior (e.g., being shy or being gregarious at a party) or because it is semantically associated as an opposite characteristic. In either case, it seems reasonable to assume that when instances of semantically or psychologically inconsistent traitlike behavior come to mind, actors either qualify their inferences by searching for discriminative characteristics between the behavioral instances (e.g., "I'm gregarious with friends but shy with strangers") or decide they don't have the trait, depending on the relative frequencies of the relevant behavioral instances.

To summarize the argument, we are hypothesizing that individuals regard their own behavior as necessarily informative about themselves to the extent that it is representative of a personological construct and that the simple frequency of occurrences of representative behavior comprises the set of data for personological self-inferences. We are suggesting that actors make personological self-inferences on the basis of some kind of frequency estimation of positive instances of their own traitlike behavior, that actors will not make a given trait inference about themselves when no positive instances have occurred in their own behavioral history, and that actors will qualify their inferences when some number of positive instances of semantically or psychologically inconsistent traitlike behavior has occurred *concurrently* in their own behavioral history.

Undoubtedly, processes of self-inference are more complicated than these hypotheses would imply. Nevertheless, these hypotheses represent an attempt to formulate systematically testable characteristics of self-inference processes. Attribution theorists have shied away from this problem for reasons discussed in the foregoing. But the problem is too important to be neglected. For methodological reasons alone, self-inference processes warrant investigation. Psychologists, especially those involved in personality research, have relied extensively on self-ratings of trait characteristics without considering the nature of the psychological judgments required by the task of self-description. To the extent that subjective criteria for trait ratings depart from scientific criteria, the utility of self-report measures for personality-trait research becomes questionable. In this connection, it should be noted also that the criteria developed by personality psychologists provide a normative model for trait inferences that can be compared to subjective criteria. It is somewhat surprising that the primary criterion used by personality psychologists, namely cross-situational consistency in behavior, fails to appear in the most prevalent model for causal attribution (Kelley, 1967, 1971, 1973). In any case, it would be of value to know whether, to what extent, and in what ways, processes of both social and self-attributions of traits depart from the scientific criteria used by personologists to infer traits. Such a comparison would certainly facilitate the attempt to develop a descriptive theory of trait inference processes.

One interesting difference between the hypotheses presented in the foregoing and available attributional theories is that the former emphasize features or descriptive characteristics of observed behavior itself more than the latter, which tend to emphasize logical characteristics of patterns of behavioral information. This shift in emphasis suggests further hypotheses about two general problems, one being actor–observer differences in attribution, briefly discussed previously, and the other being the role of motives in attributional processes. We would like to discuss briefly the implications of the hypotheses presented here for each problem in turn.

With respect to the first problem, the argument we have presented suggests that whether or not actors and observers agree about the causes of the actor's behavior is at least partially a function of the extent to which the array of information available to actors and observers does not differ with respect to the representativeness of the actor's behavior. When the array is equally representative of a dispositional or trait construct, then both actors and observers should make dispositional attributions. When it is not, then actors' attributions should diverge from observers' attribution.

There are two major ways in which the dispositional representativeness of behavior may be decreased. One is to alter the context of the behavior in such a way that a plausible situational cause is also present.

Research on oversufficient justification (Lepper & Greene, 1978) and insufficient justification (Festinger & Carlsmith, 1956) indicates that the presence of a plausible situational cause for the actor's behavior will dilute its personological information value. Studies that have compared actors' and observers' inferences in the insufficient and oversufficient justification paradigms have found results supporting our hypothesis about the actor–observer effect. For example, Bem's

(1967, 1972) original application of self-perception theory to the cognitive-dissonance paradigm demonstrated that observers' inferences about the actor's attitudes paralleled the actor's inferences. And Ross et al. (1977) found no differences between actors' and observers' inferences about the actor's intelligence in a quiz game in which the situational cause of the actor's performance was implausible for both actors and observers.

The second major way to affect the representativeness of behavior is to alter the set of behavioral features in such a way that they no longer correspond strongly to or share predominantly similar features with a trait or dispositional construct (Nisbett & Zukier, 1979). Interestingly, one of the strongest demonstrations of the actor–observer effect presented in Jones and Nisbett's (1971) article was a study (Jones, Rock, Shaver, Goethals, & Ward, 1968) comparing actor–observer attributions of actors' performance on a pseudo-intelligence test. In that study, feedback was rigged in such a way that high proportions of correct responses clustered at the beginning of the test (descending performance condition) or at the end of the test (ascending performance condition). Jones et al. (1968) found that observers exhibited a primacy effect, attributing high intelligence in the descending condition and low intelligence in the ascending condition. Actors did not make self-inferences about their ability, believing instead that the test became more difficult if they were in the descending condition and less difficult if they were in the ascending condition. From our perspective, the results could be interpreted as a consequence of the fact that the feedback manipulation differentially affected the representativeness of the actor's behavior. Because of the primacy effect, observers, in essence, had a representative and stable set of data for an inference about the actor's intelligence. However, actors had to maintain their attention on feedback throughout the test. As a result, they experienced or observed a variable set of data about their own performance. This interpretation suggests that when performance feedback is consistent for both actors and observers no difference will occur in their ability attributions. Consistent with this prediction, Ross et al. (1975) did not obtain any differences between actors' and observers' dispositional inferences when feedback concerning an actor's ability to discriminate between real and fictitious suicide notes remained consistent throughout the testing phase.

The second problem we would like to discuss briefly is the role of motivation in trait-inference processes. Motivation is often treated as a source of bias in attributional and judgment processes. There are potentially more fruitful approaches to the problem of what role motivational factors play in both self- and social-inference processes, which do not assume that motivational factors literally distort interpretations of actual behavioral observations. For example, Festinger's (1954) theory of social comparison proposes that people are motivated to obtain information about themselves. Festinger hypothesizes several effects of this motive, including a preference for interaction with simialr rather than dissimilar others, which may bias the sample of behavioral observations available to the actor but does not lead to literal distortions of the meaning of the behavioral observations themselves. Similarly, Berglas and Jones (1978) and Lenauer (1979) have conducted several studies demonstrating a "self-handicapping" effect. In the relevant conditions, subjects are led to expect that they will not be able to repeat a highly successful performance on a pseudo-intelligence test. The experimenters find that the subjects manipulate the attributional context for their expected failure in order to minimize its implications for their own intellectual abilities. It is interesting that these subjects are behaving as though "actions speak louder than words;" that is, the subjects are treating the potential information value of their performance as a given and are manipulating the inferential context in order to reduce its implications for the self. These experiments also demonstrate the role of context or situations in self-inference processes. Certain contexts can activate a trait dimension even before an individual observes his or her own behavior in that situation. For example the anticipation of a test can activate the dimension of intelligence. Or the anticipation of going to a party of strangers can activate the dimension of extraversion. Motivational aspects of self-inference may involve avoiding or seeking out situations (to the extent that one has control over accessing situations) according to their implications for self-perception rather than involving literal distortion of the meaning of actual behavior. We may improve our investigations of motivational factors in self-inference processes if we consider what kinds of informational gains an individual may be interested in obtaining. So far the predominant formulation of motivational factors has emphasized emotional gains (e.g., enhanced self-esteem or positive self regard). Informational gains are at least as important as emotional gains. People treat their beliefs about their own abilities and traits as highly relevant for all sorts of major and minor life decisions. It follows that increments in self-knowledge would be perceived as desirable and that individuals may prefer some increments over others, according to their current situation.

To sum up, we have proposed a formulation of self-inference processes that emphasizes the role of representativeness judgments of observed behavior in the formation of actors' summary impressions of their own personality characteristics. This formulation suggests consideration of the role of observable behavioral characteristics in attributional and inferential processes, in addition to the logical characteristics of patterns of behavioral information that have usually been emphasized in attribution theory (Jones & Davis, 1965; Kelley, 1967, 1971, 1973). This formulation can also be investigated in contrast to a normative model for trait inference that has been developed by personality psychologists over the past fifty years and that enables the investigator to assess whether or not actors make optimal usage of available behavioral information and, if not, to determine possible inferential errors. Finally, we have suggested that the investigation of effects of motivational factors be expanded to take into account needs for information about the self in addition to needs for positive feelings about the self.

ACKNOWLEDGMENTS

The authors are grateful to Chris Hepburn, Gary Brill, and Vilma Ortiz for their contributions to various aspects of this argument and to Nancy Cantor for her comments on an earlier draft of this manuscript. Preparation of this manuscript was supported in part by NIH grant BRSG RR07062 to the senior author. Requests for reprints should be sent to Anne Locksley, Department of Psychology, New York University, 6 Washington Place, New York, N.Y., 10003.

REFERENCES

Asch, S. E. Forming impressions of personality. *Journal of Abnormal and Social Psychology*, 1946, *41*, 258–290.

Bem, D. J. An experimental analysis of self-pursuasion. *Journal of Experimental Social Psychology*, 1965, *1*, 199–218.

Bem, D. J. Self-perception: An alternative interpretation of cognitive dissonance phenomena. *Psychological Review*, 1967, *74*, 183–200.

Bem, D. J. Self-perception theory. In L. Berkowitz (Ed.), *Advances in experimental social psychology* (Vol. 6). New York: Academic Press, 1972.

Bem, D. J., & Allen, A. On predicting some of the people some of the time: The search for cross-situational consistencies in behavior. *Psychological Review*, 1974, *81*, 506–520.

Berglas, S., & Jones E. E. Drug choice as a self-handicapping strategy in response to noncontingent success. *Journal of Personality and Social Psychology*, 1978, *36*, 405–417.

Cantor, N., & Mischel, W. Traits as prototypes: Effects on recognition memory. *Journal of Personality and Social Psychology*, 1977, *35*, 38–48.

Chapman, L., & Chapman, J. The genesis of popular but erroneous psychodiagnostic observations. *Journal of Abnormal Psychology*, 1967, *72*, 193–204.

Chapman, L., & Chapman, J. Illusory correlations as an obstacle to the use of valid psychodiagnostic signs. *Journal of Abnormal Psychology*, 1969, *74*, 271–280.

D'Andrade, R. G. Trait psychology and componential analysis. *American Anthropologist*, 1965, *67*, 215–228.

Estes, W. K. The cognitive side of probability learning. *Psychological Review*, 1976, *83*, 37–64.

Festinger, L. A theory of social comparison processes. *Human Relations*, 1954, *7*, 117–140.

Festinger, L., & Carlsmith, J. M. Cognitive consequences of forced compliance. *Journal of Abnormal and Social Psychology*, 1956, *52*, 384–389.

Heider, F. *The Psychology of interpersonal relations*. New York: Wiley, 1958.

Jones, E. E., & Davis, K. E. From acts to dispositions. In L. Berkowitz (Ed.), *Advances in experimental social psychology* (Vol. 2). New York: Academic Press, 1965.

Jones, E. E., Rock, L., Shaver, K. G., Goethals, G. R., & Ward, L. M. Pattern of performance and ability attribution: An unexpected primacy effect. *Journal of Personality and Social Psychology*, 1968, *10*, 317–340.

Jones, E. E., & Nisbett, R. E. The actor and the observer: Divergent perceptions of the causes of behavior. In E. E. Jones, D. E. Kanouse, H. H. Kelley, R. E. Nisbett, S. Valins, & B. Weiner (Eds.), *Attribution: Perceiving the causes of behavior*. Morristown, N.J.: General Learning Press, 1971.

Kahneman, D., & Tversky, A. Subjective probability: A judgment of representatives. *Cognitive Psychology*, 1972, *3*, 430–454.

Kahneman, D., & Tversky, A. On the psychology of prediction. *Psychological Review*, 1973, *80*, 237–251.

Kelley, H. H. Attribution theory in social psychology. In D. Levine (Ed.), *Nebraska Symposium on motivation, 1967.* Lincoln, Neb.: University of Nebraska Press, 1967.

Kelley, H. H. Attribution in social interaction. In E. E. Jones, D. E. Kanouse, H. H. Kelley, R. E. Nisbett, S. Valins, & B. Weiner (Eds.), *Attribution: Perceiving the causes of behavior.* Morristown, N.J.: General Learning Press, 1971.

Kelley, H. H. The processes of causal attribution. *American Psychologist,* 1973, *28,* 107-128.

Lenauer, M. *Uncertainty and the avoidance of diagnostic information about ability as components in the organization of fear of success and fear of failure.* Unpublished doctoral dissertation, Department of Psychology, New York University, September, 1979.

Lenauer, M., Sameth, L., & Shaver, P. Looking back at oneself in time: Another approach to the actor-observer phenomenon. *Perceptual and Motor Skills,* 1976, *43,* 1283-1287.

Lepper, M. R., & Greene, D. (Eds.), *The hidden costs of reward.* Hillsdale, N.J.: Lawrence Erlbaum Associates, 1978.

Lepper, M. R., Greene D., & Nisbett, R. E. Undermining children's intrinsic interest with extrinsic rewards: A test of the "overjustification hypothesis." *Journal of Personality and Social Psychology,* 1973, *28,* 129-137.

Markus, H. Self-schemata and processing information about the self. *Journal of Personality and Social Psychology,* 1977, *35,* 63-78.

McArthur, L. A. The how and what of why: Some determinants and consequences of causal attributions. *Journal of Personality and Social Psychology, 1972, 22,* 171-193.

McGuire, W. J., & Padawer-Singer, A. Trait salience in the spontaneous self-concept. *Journal of Personality and Social Psychology, 1976, 33,* 743-754.

Mischel, W. *Personality and assessment.* New York: Wiley, 1968.

Monson, T. C., & Snyder, M. Actors, observers, and the attribution process: Toward a reconceptualization. *Journal of Experimental Social Psychology,* 1977, *13,* 89-111.

Nisbett, R. E., & Ross, L. Human inference: Strategies and shortcomings. Englewood Cliffs, N.J.: Prentice Hall, 1980.

Nisbett, R. E., & Valins, S. Perceiving the causes of one's own behavior. In E. E. Jones, D. E. Kanouse, H. H. Kelley, R. E. Nisbett, S. Valins, & B. Weiner (Eds.), *Attribution: Perceiving the causes of behavior.* Morristown, N.J.: General Learning Press, 1971.

Nisbett, R. E., & Wilson, T. D. Telling more than we can know: Verbal reports on mental processes. *Psychological Review,* 1977, *85,* 231-259.

Nisbett, R. E., & Zukier, H. *The dilution effect: Producing "regressive" predictions by exposure to nondisgnostic information.* Unpublished manuscript, The University of Michigan, Department of Psychology, 1979.

Passini, F. T., & Norman, W. T. A universal conception of personality structure? *Journal of Personality and Social Psychology,* 1966, *4,* 44-49.

Quine, W. V. O. *Word and object.* Cambridge, Mass.: MIT Press, 1960.

Rogers, T. B., Kuiper, N. A., & Kirker, W. S. Self-reference and the encoding of personal information. *Journal of Personality and Social Psychology,* 1977, *35,* 677-688.

Ross, L., Lepper, M. R., & Hubbard, M. Perseverance in self-perception and social perception: Biased attributional processes in the debriefing paradigm. *Journal of Personality and Social Psychology,* 1975, *32,* 880-892.

Ross, L. The intuitive psychologist and his shortcomings: Distortions in the attribution process. In L. Berkowitz (Ed.), *Advances in experimental social psychology,* (Vol. 10). New York: Academic Press, 1977.

Ross, L., Amabile, T. M., & Steinmetz, J. C. Social roles, social control, and biases in social perception processes. *Journal of Personality and Social Psychology,* 1977, *35,* 485-494.

Ross, M., & Sicoly, F. Egocentric biases in availability and attribution. *Journal of Personality and Social Psychology,* 1979, *37,* 222-336.

Schachter, S. *The psychology of affiliation.* Stanford, Calif.: Stanford University Press, 1959.

Schneider, D. J. Implicit personality theory: A review. *Psychological Bulletin*, 1973, *73*, 294–309.

Smedslund, J. The concept of correlation in adults. *Scandinavian Journal of Psychology*, 1963, *4*, 165–173.

Snyder, M. Self-monitoring of expressive behavior. *Journal of Personality and Social Psychology*, 1974, *30*, 526–537.

Snyder, M., & Cantor, N. Testing hypotheses about other people: The use of historical knowledge. *Journal of Experimental Social Psychology*, 1979, *15*, 330–342.

Snyder, M., & Uranowitz, S. W. Reconstructing the past: Some cognitive consequences of person perception. *Journal of Personality and Social Psychology*, 1978, *36*, 941–950.

Tversky, A. Features of similarity. *Psychological Reveiw*, 1977, *84*, 327–352.

Tversky, A., & Kahneman, D. Judgment under uncertainty: Heuristics and biases. *Science*, 1974, *185*, 1124–1131.

Ward, W. C., & Jenkins, H. M. The display of information and the judgment of contingency. *Canadian Journal of Psychology*, 1965, *19*, 231–241.

Wason, P. C., & Johnson-Laird, P. N. *Psychology of reasoning*. London: Batsford, 1972.

Wilson, G. Introversion/extraversion. In T. Blass (Ed.), *Personality variables in social behavior*. Hillsdale, N.J.: Lawrence Erlbaum Associates, 1977.

V PERSONALITY IN SOCIAL INTERACTION

12 Toward an Interaction-Centered Theory of Personality

Michael Athay
John M. Darley
Princeton University

INTRODUCTION

In the common usage of psychologists, the term *personality* has traditionally been taken to refer, in Murray's words, to a "hypothetical structure of the mind," the function of which involves integrating, organizing, and controlling the multifarious aspects of the individual's thought and behavior. The entity usually is thought of as constituted by "establishments and processes" (Murray's terms) that are highly consistent in their operations and in their observable effects through time and across collections of particular situations. These consistent patterns are thought to indicate the existence of underlying propensities of thought and action known as "dispositions" and generally said (or else covertly thought) to have the status of "bona fide mental structures" with "more than nominal existence" (Allport's language, in reference specifically to personality traits.) Moreover, the dispositional properties of particular interest to personality psychology are those which generalize across different individuals of well-specified broad types as well as across situation-tokens within the lives of individuals. (Allport's "idiographic" traits are the well-known partial exception.)

In the last few years, this long-accepted conception of "personality" has been seriously challenged, by Walter Mischel, Daryl Bem, and psychologists who join them in questioning the very existence—or at least, the evidence purporting to demonstrate the existence—of cross-situational consistencies of a "global" or "traitlike" sort. The vehemence of the controversy between Mischel and his opponents is proof that fundamental matters are involved here. Indeed, the underlying issue is the very existence of the entity most of us have taken to be the reference of the term *personality*. For dispositional properties of the "global" sort, be they the "traits" familiar from decades of research, Freud's instinctual drives, Murray's "need-states," or Eysenck's broad personality types, are *constitutive* of personalities. If it is true, as some of Mischel's (1973) formulations seem to suggest,[1] that behavior is so situation-specific as to rule out large-scale cross-situational consistencies, then there can be no sense in positing the existence of "establishments," "institutions," "processes," or any of the other "bona fide mental structures" theorists have long hypothesized to explain what people do.

Our purpose in the present chapter is to come down squarely on both sides of the controversy. We argue for behavioral invariances that are appropriately conceptualized as "underlying structures and processes" comprising "personality." But we also believe that competent actors normally do behave in highly situation-specific ways, manifesting Mischel's (1973) highly developed "facility" for discriminating fine aspects of their immediate situations and for adjusting both their cognitions and performances to take account of them. The global dimensions we find in personalities therefore turn out to look little like the dispositions postulated by traditional theorists. In substantial part, this is because our personality dispositions are determined by the structure of ordinary social action: In order to act effectively, people must define situations, perceive other persons, plan strategically, construct performance patterns, monitor their own self-presentations and interpret those of others, satisfy role demands and enforce them on others, and so on. In order to do these things, they must generalize and routinize their patterns of action, exhibiting a maximum of regularity in dealing with others. But they also must monitor and evaluate their thinking and behaving to adapt to constant changes in circumstances brought on by variations in partners, contexts, projects, and purposes. The general dispositional properties

---

[1]Consider, for example, his following remarks on cross-situational consistencies within the life of an individual: "Whereas discriminative facility is highly functional . . . diminished sensitivity to changing consequences (i.e., indiscriminate responding) may be a hallmark of an organism coping ineffectively. In fact, indiscriminate responding (i.e., 'consistent' behavior across situations) tends to be displayed more by maladaptive, severely disturbed, or less mature persons than by well-functioning ones [p. 258]." ". . . What a person does tends to be relatively specific to a host of variables, and that behavior is multiply determined by all of them rather than being the product of widely generalized dispositions [p. 256]." Mischel (1973) on dispositions that obtain across persons: "Because the conditions under which stimuli acquire their meaning and power are often both adventitious and unique, and because the dimensions of stimulus and response generalization tend to be idiosyncratic, it may be futile to seek common underlying dimensions of similarity on the basis of which diverse events come to evoke a similar response pattern for all persons [p. 259]."

It is essential to recognize, however, that Mischel also takes care to disavow any attempt to deny that *some* sort of general pattern can be found in the behavior of individuals. His project really is to criticize traditional formulations of these general patterns and to suggest other formulations of a more explicitly cognitive sort. He does not, in other words, deny that there are global dispositions; he wants rather to redo the ones we take as basic to personality, hence the "reconceptualization of personality" reference in his title.

comprising their "personalities" must be flexible enough to accommodate easily and smoothly such variations in local conditions. These properties will *not* be the fixed and strongly suprasituational dimensions of classical personality theory, immune to revision in light of the requirements of ongoing social action.

In support of this account, we contend that both traditional personality theorists and their critics overlook a fundamental fact about the subject of psychological investigations: He or she is first of all an *actor* rather than a thinker or a theorist or a bundle of drives, affects, and needs; his or her action takes place in social contexts involving other actors; and, in large part, this action consists of getting the others to do things which fit in with his or her own projects and goals. If there is any point in psychology's accepting the entity "personality," then the point lies in the utility this notion has for explaining ordinary social interaction. "The theory of personality," in other words, is a subdivision of the study of social action, and its task is to construct a representation of the person as actor. Therefore this representation must be constituted by whatever properties (cognitive, affective, need-related, drive-based, etc.) are required in order to account for the patterned ways in which actors organize their exchanges with each other.

According to this perspective, the issue of whether there exist global dispositional properties of thought and behavior can only be settled by first analyzing the structure of social interaction. It is the failure to do this, we contend, which has led traditional personality theory to focus on traitlike dispositional properties— fixed, highly general patterns of thinking and behaving that are applied in a mechanical fashion to all instances of very broad situation types. Now that this familiar construal of "the dispositions constituting personality" has been effectively questioned by Mischel and others, it is possible to focus reconstructive efforts on the analysis of persons as social actors. Mischel (1973, 1977, 1978) has seen that dispositional properties of an explicitly cognitive sort are major constituents of "personality" and has thereby identified an important link between personality theory and the growing interest in "social cognition," especially of the sort now called *attribution theory.*" But he has yet to show us how "cognitive–social learning-person variables" are accounts of interpersonal action. In the present chapter we attempt to do so.

THE STRATEGIC STRUCTURE OF ORDINARY INTERACTION

Everyday action is ego-centered in the sense that ordinary doings are organized in accordance with personal projects, the fulfillment of which is the actor's overriding concern.[2] These projects can be various; they may involve securing the

---

[2]This does not mean that most people are "egotists" most of the time. An actor's egocentric projects may well involve the regular performance of "selfless" (i.e., "altruistic," in one sense of

provision of certain overt performances from specified others, the receipt of positive affect from them, getting them to confirm and/or affirm a self-concept, obtaining their conformity to wishes regarding their behavior for the pure pleasure of exercising influence, and so on. The projects may be of the "occasional" sort, involving the securing of particular responses in some immediate, short-term situation, or they may be "standing" projects, involving the achievement of a particular public persona or life-style, a set of occupational or status goals, an orderly conception of who and what one is, reformation of the world or some small corner of social life.

This ego-centeredness means that projects of different actors normally will diverge. A high degree of congruence, when it obtains, usually is the result of prolonged interaction in which the parties have reached compromises and working agreements through repeated negotiations, or else it is due to the fact that the interaction is of the brief, highly restricted, and role-bound sort that takes place between clerk and customer, official and client, or passersby on the street. The point is not that actors are egotists. Diverging interests and projects are the results of divergences in perspective, and the latter are bound to obtain between actors of different social positions, who belong to different reference groups (occupational, kinship, friendship) and whose educational and/or cultural backgrounds are different. In complex and highly diversified societies like ours, where roles do not interlock in functional harmony, the inevitable outcome is that interactants' interests and projects "naturally" diverge and conflict. Nuclear families are an obvious illustration. Functional interdependence of roles is relatively high in these specialized groups, but, even so, the different roles of wife–homemaker, husband–provider, and child produce radically divergent projects and interests on the part of their incumbents. To take one currently salient example: Dissatisfactions accumulated in the course of filling their traditional "homemaker" roles have led more and more married women to demand occupational roles as well. Enacting the traditional role has led them to generate projects that are at odds with those of the husband and employer, both of whom, more often than not, see wives as properly finding fulfillment in the unpaid job of ensuring their hus-

---

the term) acts which benefit particular others or even the adoption of an altruistic stance toward the world in general. But, however "prosocial" his or her programs of interaction are, he or she will still put their realization ahead of others' realizations of their own egocentric programs. The terms *altruistic* and *prosocial* behavior can be taken to mean the performance of specific acts which *the performer* believes are beneficial to the other and costly to himself. Such a program of "doing what is in the best interests of the other," whatever said other may think about it, is an egocentric program which may well involve overriding the other's own self-assigned projects and interests. Alternatively, these terms may be taken to refer to a pattern of regularly putting the other's self-assigned interests and projects ahead of one's own. We are denying that people ordinarily are altruistic in this deeper sense. We agree with Kelley and Thibaut (1978, chap. 7) that such prosocial behavior ordinarily is adopted as part of a longer-term program of dealing with specified others (e.g., within a given long-term relationship with some individual recipient[s] of the benefits)—a program which is evaluated as a whole on the basis of its utility in bringing about the fulfillment of egocentric projects.

bands' readiness to perform paid occupational functions (Darley, 1976; Zellman, 1976).

Instrumental Manipulation

Where actors' projects conflict, an element of instrumental manipulation inevitably is a part of ordinary interaction. Differences in aims and in strategies for fulfilling them (also the product of role experiences) mean that each actor, in order to carry out his or her particular programs, usually is in the position of requiring from others the provision of performances, manifesting of attitudes, and so on that they would not otherwise undertake— or just as importantly, could not be *counted* on to undertake at just the needed times and places. In a culture like ours, with its democratic legal and political values, this manipulation necessarily takes the special form of getting the other to see it as in his or her self-interest to do what is wanted. Manipulation of the other consists of persuading him or her to "volunteer" the desired treatment; actors secure voluntary compliance from each other by operating on the other's cognitions of the joint situation in such a fashion as to bring the other to adopt an account of what is going on that dictates to him or her (given his or her own interests and programs) that he or she perform in the desired way.

Given the premise of "naturally" divergent interests and projects, this process must usually involve bringing others to adopt perspectives they would not adopt on their own. In rather a broad sense of the term, the manipulation of ordinary interaction thus amounts to a form of "persuasion." People get what they want from each other by attempting to influence each others' situation definitions, including, most especially, each one's definition of the other's projects and his or her likely strategies for securing them. Each acts in such a way as to convince the other that some particular view or views of what is happening to them are correct ones and that other possible accounts, less useful from the manipulator's strategic point of view, are not. (This is perhaps the most important sense in which "social cognition" is at the very foundation of everyday interaction: Cognitions of the shared social situation are the basic "handles" by which people attempt to manipulate each other into providing strategically useful responses.)

Erving Goffman (1959, 1972), using the rubric *self-presentation*, has studied many of the techniques actors commonly employ to influence each others' situation definitions. His work is useful from our point of view because he makes it very clear that the "persuading" and "convincing" of instrumental interaction usually is not, and never need be, a matter of argument or even of explicit verbal communication. He shows that actors present themselves to each other mainly by way of actions that have multiple imports. Nonverbal acts as well as verbal ones—we might usefully think of both as "utterances"—convey information, in a nonliteral mode, about the utterer and his definition of the interaction situation.

Actions that, on the surface, have narrowly utilitarian motives and consequences are read, in context, as conveying information about their authors and their authors' perspectives. Verbal utterances, the literal construals of which convey information about one topic, also convey, in a nonliteral mode and in light of the context of utterance, quite different information about speaker and situation.[3] Actors standardly use these resources to carry on elaborate dialogues of "symbolic action" without ever bringing up, in so many words, the strategic issues treated—dialogues in the course of which each actor communicates to the other an account of the situation that serves his or her strategic purposes and attempts to convince the other of its essential validity. ("Symbolic action" as a nondiscursive process of persuasion and conviction obviously offers a rich, and to our knowledge largely untouched, field of investigation for "the social psychology of cognition.") And if it is granted that the objectives of self-presentation ordinarily are instrumental in the special sense we have been giving the term (Goffman uses the word "strategic"), then his analyses can be taken as support for our contention that much of what people do most of the time has a broadly instrumental motivation.

Interpersonal manipulation of this voluntaristic "noncoercive" sort depends to a large extent on skillful exploitation of the normative principles of action recognized by interactants. We have argued that smooth, confident, and effective action (as well as cognition) requires that the actor have a high degree of subjective certainty about *what* his or her alters will do *when*.[4] He or she must be able to see alters' performances as regular enough so that he or she can plan his or her own strategies of interaction without fear of having to revise repeatedly and

---

[3]Goffman's introductory chapter (1959) describes the symbolic or expressive character of concrete actions, and Chapters 1 and 6 provide numerous examples. Labov and Fanshel, in *Therapeutic Discourse* (1977) effectively make the point about verbal utterances carrying meanings other than their literal meanings.

[4]Goffman graphically describes the consequences of one or more interactants becoming hesitant and uncertain in their performances. (*Frame Analysis,* 1974, chapter 10.) He points out that ordinary interaction is governed by a specialized set of norms which pertain to what might be called the "formal" features of interpersonal behavior. These norms dictate, for example, that a certain pace or flow of action and response be maintained, that a high degree of smoothness and readiness of response be sustained by all participants, and that all exhibit an appropriate degree of involvement or absorption in the interaction. Breaking them, Goffman contends, has the effect of sounding an alarm signal: It is a social fact about the nature of interaction in our and similar societies that violations of these norms has the public significance of something's being wrong with the interaction. Unless remedial action is taken by one or all parties immediately (i.e., action to reassure that no difficulties are developing), the alarm signals inevitably lead to a focusing of attention on the nature of the interaction itself and hence away from the subject matter of the interaction. This is in itself highly disturbing to both parties, and unless successful remedies are quickly supplied, the interaction is likely to suffer a more serious "frame break," as Goffman calls these disruptions, and dissolve altogether. Notice that the requirement for a high degree of subjective certainty is not the same as requiring that actors expectations about others be *objectively* adequate. Our point here concerns the necessity of the actor's *feeling* that he is in control of his situation.

suddenly. But the most reliable patterns of conduct on the part of another are patterns imposed by normative principles that he recognizes as binding. All competent actors know this in an intuitive way and rely upon it in plotting their everyday doings. As a result, the process of manipulating others (by getting them to see it as in their interests to respond in a specified fashion) standardly takes the form of getting them to see the situation as one in which it is *incumbent* upon them to perform in the desired way. The instrumental objective is to bring the other to adopt a definition of the shared situation that will activate in him or her certain normative principles of action he or she already holds—principles that (in the estimation of the manipulator) will oblige him or her to provide performances the manipulator desires of him or her for strategic reasons. Strategic planning thus consists, in large measure, of forming estimations as to what principles of action alter regards as normatively binding, how he or she would apply them in the given case, and what actions on ego's part would activate particular ones among them.

We have placed special stress on two aspects of instrumental manipulation in ordinary social action—the fundamental role of normative principles of action held by the other and the necessity of appealing to and working within his or her self-assigned interests—in part because we want to counter at the outset a commonplace tendency to construe all interpersonal manipulations on what might be called ''the con man model.'' Goffman (1959, 1974) is to some extent responsible for this tendency, having permitted his evident fascination with the techniques of espionage agents, bunco artists, impersonators, and other experts at delusion to influence overmuch his choice of illustrations of the basically quite mundane practices of ''strategic interaction.'' The error here consists in thinking that ordinary actors, like professional con men, adopt the *project* of deluding others, of deceiving them in such a fashion that they will do something which, if they fully understood the nature of the interchange or relationship, they would not do. From the point of view of ordinary actors, however, efforts at instrumental control over others will count as interaction moves of the sort all competent actors legitimately employ every day. They are not seen as instances of conning or defrauding because they are built into the normative structure of everyday interaction.

Jones' (1975) work on ingratiation illustrates and provides some support for the view of interaction we have been presenting. His concept of ''ingratiation,'' as we interpret it, formulates one familiar and commonplace class of strategies for carrying out instrumental manipulations of others in the way we have described. The attraction-seeking behaviors he describes are directed toward the other's cognitions of the actor's beliefs, skills, competencies, and other attributes relevant to the content of their interaction. The actor uses them to influence the other's definition of that most basic component of the interaction situation—the actor himself or herself—in a way that will dispose him or her to provide a favorable exercise of whatever control he or she can exert over the actor's outcomes in their interchange. It is no accident that, as Jones points out, attraction-seeking techniques are particularly appropriate in relationships of differential power and status.

From our point of view, the significance of the two experiments Jones reports (1975, chapter 5) lies in their clear demonstration that the subjects: (1) recognized characteristics of their situations that were crucial for the effective manipulation of their partner's cognitions of them on dimensions concerning the content of the interaction; and (2) adjusted their performances in the situation to fit these instrumental exigencies. These subjects were clearly aware that powerful partners could be manipulated by operating upon the latter's cognitions of the situation (i.e., of the subjects themselves), and they were prepared to take advantage of whatever opportunities the experimental situations afforded for action that stood a plausible chance of influencing their partners' cognitions in ways that would facilitate their own goals in the interchange. These subjects, in other words, conformed to our instrumental model of social interaction.

Social Exchange

The elements of strategy and manipulation that we have identified in the interaction process comprise one of two sets of features that we believe are fundamental determinants of everyday social interchanges and relationships. The other set involves what sociologists call *social exchange*. It is a commonplace that in the advanced capitalist democracies, with their highly rationalized and highly industrialized economies, economic relations have come to permeate and determine substantially all aspects of social life. In particular, the structure of ordinary social interaction has come to be modeled on practices usually thought to fall within the "economic sphere" narrowly defined. As Marx and the classical political economists long ago pointed out, capitalistic economic relations are founded on the exchange of commodities in a "free market" situation. One fundamental manifestation of this modeling is the social fact that the economic practices and relationships comprising "commodity exchange" serve, for every well-socialized actor, as a kind of paradigm for the organization of interpersonal relations.

Sociologists like Blau (1964) and Homans (1961) have recognized this fact in formulating an account of "social exchange" as the fundamental feature of interaction (Lempert, 1972–1973). The basic point is that actors regard their treatments of each other as so many benefits to be exchanged for benefits provided in return. The patterns of action they provide in response to each other's performances and self-presentations count, in effect, as "commodities"— entities produced specifically to be exchanged for other such items produced by interactants. Moreover, actors seek to exchange treatments on a basis of maximal advantage to them, providing treatments that cost as little as possible to produce (i.e., for which the investment of time, effort, thought, affect, self-esteem, public prestige, etc., is as small as possible) in exchange for treatments that have the greatest possible value to them (i.e., that are maximally facilitative in the realization of egocentric projects). They seek, in other words, to maximize their profits, both in particular exchanges and in the long run. Considerations of the instrumental utility of particular courses of action take the form of calculations of their "exchange value" and come to be of paramount importance in making decisions to provide or withhold treatments desired by others. Processes of negotiation modeled on bargaining in commodity exchanges, likewise become of central importance in interaction. Interchanges routinely have something of the structure of offer and counteroffer, with each party seeking to raise the value of the other's treatment offers while keeping down the value of his or her, own. Contractual relations in the economic sphere, both formal (as codified in the law of contract) and informal, provide paradigms for the exchange agreements reached in the course of such negotiations. Stable interaction requires that interactants feel they can count on each other sufficiently to permit confident planning. Within the exchange structure of ordinary interaction, this condition is fulfilled by informal norms imposing and enforcing a contractual character on actors' understandings with each other. The capacity to make and sustain contractual agreements (although perhaps not an essential property of human nature, as Locke (1973) argued) is acquired in the course of basic socialization into the action patterns of our society and counts as a fundamental mark of social competence.

The "commodities" figuring in these exchange processes will be as various as the projects and competencies of individual actors. The different "psychological commodities" we have mentioned in connection with instrumental manipulations comprise a large subset (symbolic acts of affirmation and confirmation, expressions of affect and interest, helping actions of a "therapeutic" sort, as when people assist each other in reducing tensions, managing depression, etc.). Of course actors often seek from each other specific concrete performances they require as means to the fulfillment of goals—as when supervisors in work relationships require that their subordinates perform specified tasks according to set standards. Virtually any treatment of another person, however diffuse or specific, concrete or abstract, can become a commodity figuring in an exchange relationship. The interactants themselves (operating within boundaries imposed by the normative principles of their larger communities) determine what is to count as an exchangeable commodity in a given interchange or relationship as well as the exchange values that are fairly to be assigned them. Indeed, negotiations in social action often are concerned as much with defining the content of the commodities bargained about as with determining their relative values.

Our contention is that such social exchange processes are universal, or very nearly so, in advanced industrial societies. "Social exchange" does not refer to one of many interesting patterns employed by actors in organizing their relationships; virtually all ordinary interaction, we claim, has an exchange structure.

Jones' (1975) perceptive remarks about the *mutual* dependence of more and less powerful interactants provide one good set of reasons for thinking this is so. (Kelley & Thibaut, 1978, make a similar point in taking *inter*dependence as the norm in social action.) Jones points out that even persons in clear possession of high relative power are dependent on subordinates, as supervisors depend on their underlings to provide task performances living up to the productivity standards of the larger organization they all belong to. And all actors, powerful and weak, depend upon each other for confirmations of their perspectives, affirmations of their performances, and other "psychological commodities." The relatively weak can and do exploit these dependencies for instrumental gain as do their more powerful alters, though of course with less overall success. Social psychologists have long taken an interest in cooperative behavior of all sorts, but usually without recognizing that if actors require each other's assistance in achieving desirable outcomes then each is in a position to exert power over the others. Jones' point (and the unexplicit lesson of the Kelley and Thibaut analysis) is, in effect, that relations of interpersonal power enter into and govern virtually all social interactions. But wherever actors are in a position to exert control over each other's outcomes, then negotiation and exchange is appropriate—and in our society, very likely—as the basis for organizing their relations.

The specific attraction-seeking strategies Jones (1975) describes provide some interesting concrete illustrations of how exchange can work between persons in situations of differential power. "Complimentary other enhancement" and "conformity to the other in opinion, judgment, and behavior" are best regarded as patterns of performance designed to secure from the other some favourable disposition of outcomes he or she controls within an interaction. In Jones' analysis, such "ingratiation" behaviors are, in effect, tactics of self-presentation—acts of selectively communicating information about self, skills, competencies, values and beliefs, projects, dispositions, action strategies, etc., with the specific intention of increasing, in the eyes of the other, the desirability of sustaining an interaction or relationship with the ingratiator. Thus their function is to define the larger exchange situation in a way that will facilitate advantageous bargaining for the actor employing them. In presenting his or her evaluations as "other-enhancing", his or her judgments as "other-conforming" (hence confirming), and so on, he or she seeks to raise their exchange value (and by implication, the exchange value of all the commodities he or she can produce) in the other's eyes—thereby leading the other to offer, in exchange, instrumentally valuable treatments over which he or she has control.

A further and stronger set of considerations supporting our account follows from our earlier remarks concerning the "voluntaristic" nature of the norms governing everyday social action. Within these values, we argued, others can be manipulated *legitimately* only by leading them to see it as in their own egocentric interests to provide the commodities one desires. The most effective way to do this is to offer, in exchange for the desired performances, particular commodities that the other requires in order to fulfill his interests. Where egocentric projects and "voluntaristic" ground rules govern interaction, exchange is the natural way to go about securing what one wants from others, powerful or not. Interaction strategy thus involves operating on the other's perceptions of his or her interests and of the situation in order to lead him or her to see that a particular exchange for performances on his or her part counts as advantageous or as otherwise desirable in "cost–benefit" terms. Those normative principles of action on the other's part that one seeks to activate to one's instrumental advantage are, broadly speaking, principles of exchange.

"Global Dispositions" Implied by the Social Exchange Perspective

Our objective in developing this account of the instrumental nature and commodity-exchangelike structure of social interaction has been twofold: (1) We wanted to provide a basis for establishing the explanatory utility of some sort of "global dispositional concept," thereby rescuing a remnant of psychology's traditional notion of "personality"; and (2) we wanted to establish some broad parameters for use in determining what these dispositions might be, given our position that the concept of "personality," properly construed, is a tool for explaining interpersonal behavior in social contexts.

The framework for this endeavor is the current criticism of the idea of a personality trait as conflicting with a growing body of empirical evidence which suggests that ordinary actors are so responsive to the minute details of particular situations that we cannot generalize reliably their behavior patterns across large classes of particular situations or across large classes of particular persons. In the course of decades of research, the construct "personality disposition" has been burdened by psychologists with more than its share of misleading connotations, with the result that it has become difficult not to think of the term as a synonym for "personality trait." From our point of view, however, this is an extremely unfortunate equation. We take the concept of a "psychological disposition" to be a very general notion referring to virtually any constant or invariant factor which underlies and structures phenomenal variations in behavior. On our account, the question of whether we should expect to find actors exhibiting dispositional properties becomes the question: Do the structural characteristics of social action we have described somehow necessitate that actors sustain such invariances in thought and action? And the question of whether actors exhibit "global" dispositions becomes one of how "general" such invariances must be if actors are to operate this system of interaction effectively: Must they generalize across many, few, or just quite a lot of situations for each actor; must they generalize across many, few, or a middle-sized number of actors?

Our answer to the first question must be affirmative. This is clear once it is recognized that two considerations must come to be of overriding importance to every actor who operates a system of interaction governed by instrumental motivations and organized in terms of exchange: (1) The actor must be able to maintain a sense of *cognitive* mastery over the ongoing interaction situation, a sense that his or her conception of what is happening is essentially sound enough to permit confident attributions of social cognitions to alters and reliable predictions of their behavior. (2) He or she must feel *instrumentally* in command of the situation: He must feel that he can without great stress and in a matter-of-course way, produce the performance routines that his or her situation definitions indicate are instrumentally necessary in order to secure the treatments required to fulfill his or her projects. A feeling of cognitive competence is essential because, in accordance with our earlier formulation, the social cognitions of others are the principal "handles" by which actors manipulate each other. So construed, the process of instrumental manipulation cannot be initiated without a sound sense of how the other views the particular situation at hand. Because manipulation, in addition, depends on selectively activating normative principles of action in the other, it is equally necessary to have a sound sense of the content of these principles, of the conditions of their application (in particular, the treatments one must provide in order to activate them), and of the concrete performances they will lead him or her to in the given circumstances. Over and above these planning skills, the actor must feel that he or she actually can carry out the performance-and-response sequences comprising social exchange. He or she must feel able to manage the elaborate signaling, mostly in the form of symbolic actions, involved in bringing the other to adopt instrumentally useful perspectives; he must feel able to negotiate the terms of his exchanges effectively; and he must feel able to live up to the performance expectations of the other when exchange agreements are reached.

Our point is that a system of interaction of the sort we have been describing demands of actors a very high degree of *calculability*—calculability of oneself and one's capacities and calculability of the beliefs, values, intentions, and capacities of one's interactants. The instrumental orientation of action by itself places a heavy premium on the "manageability" of persons and situations. When we review the formidable list of factors which comprise the actual process of interpersonal manipulation, we can see that maintaining or losing one's sense of mastery over one's immediate social world must be dominant in the planning of every actor.

The required calculability of social life, we contend, is secured by a mechanism which we shall call *routinization*. In the course of acquiring the skills and practices which define a socially competent actor, members of our society develop a strong generalized disposition to make routines of patterns of performance and cognition which they find workable. Given a new situation and new partners, they "assimilate" to familiar situations, attempting to apply cognitive and performance patterns that they have employed satisfactorily in such situations in the past.

Our notion of routinization of thought and action patterns is really just another way of talking about the underlying invariances that comprise the entity *personality*. Our claim is, in effect, that actors seek to establish and sustain invariances in their cognitive and performance patterns in order to sustain the sense of competence and control that can come only from operating familiar procedures. Moreover, competent actors must learn to regularize their patterns of interaction, within particular interaction contexts, as a way of making themselves calculable to their alters. Each must provide the other with sufficient information about self, projects, strategies, and perspectives to permit the other to plan his or her participation in the interaction with confidence; each must present himself or herself to the other as an individual whose dispositional properties the other can handle, both cognitively and instrumentally, without sacrificing his or her sense of competence, his or her sense of being in control of the situation. The only really effective way for an actor to establish himself or herself as such a safe and calculable creature is to establish and sustain behavioral invariances as the interaction develops. If he or she fails to do this or refuses to do so in the service of some ulterior strategy, then the other's attempts at routinizing his or her participation likely will be thwarted, and interaction will tend to break down under the other's growing sense of inability to cope.

Stable interaction thus requires that people take care to live up to the public expectations associated with the social positions they announce themselves as occupying; that they signal with some accuracy the contents of their basic traits and dispositions and then conform pretty closely to these presentations; that they commit themselves to cognitive formulations of the situation and then pretty much stick by them. Actors can and do violate these normative requirements on interaction, but in doing so they declare themselves dangerous characters who can be dealt with only at high risk.

There are, then, sound psychological and "social–functional" reasons for expecting that actors should develop dispositions of cognition and action which generalize reliably across large classes of similar interaction situations. Moreover, these same considerations provide good social–functional reasons for expecting that dispositions will generalize across particular actors, at least within well-specified communities of individuals who interact frequently. Because stable interaction requires that all exhibit a fair degree of regularity with each other, it is natural that communities should train their members to conform to more or less well-specified patterns in those matters which bear most directly on the business of the community. A main purpose of normative principles and associated sanctioning apparatus is to fulfill just this requirement.

The question of how "global" these dispositions must be probably cannot be answered in general. The needs of particular communities will determine the degrees of regularity required of the incumbents of different roles within them and so will determine the scope of the invariances required of members. Moreover, invariances of different degrees of generality will be required for interactions of broadly different types. Many of the interchanges that get us through our everyday affairs are brief, fleeting, highly formalized, and determined almost wholly by norms defining roles that vary little throughout the society as a whole. These routine interchanges between clerk and customer, official and client, passersby on the street, and so on proceed smoothly because all parties exhibit the same invariances or dispositions in carrying them out. Many others of our interchanges, however, are between intimates and close associates and, by their nature, require careful attention to specialized task requirements, highly particular characteristics of the other, and so on. The invariances appropriate to interchanges at this end of the scale usually will have quite a narrow domain of application—within the life of an individual actor as well as across different actors. The degree of generality probably varies according to a typology of interaction types, arranged on a scale with one pole comprising the highly impersonal and routinized interactions of the clerk-and-customer sort, where highly universalized role requirements determine most of what takes place, and the other pole comprising the interactions between intimates, where the purpose and parameters of interaction will be very highly particularized. Most interchanges, as between occupational colleagues, say, will fall somewhere between.[5]

All these considerations strongly support traditional personality-theory postulation of long-term dispositional properties governing thought and behavior. But they also suggest that many of the basic dispositions are to be conceived as specifically cognitive in nature—hence as fundamentally unlike the trait concepts employed by most traditional personality theorists. We shortly draw the distinction still more sharply by arguing that the behavioral patterns comprising our dispositions, unlike the fixed and largely situation-independent traits of traditional theories, are highly adaptable to situational particularities.

By way of preparation for this argument, we want now to point out that Mischel's (1973) thesis that ordinarily competent actors exhibit a highly developed facility for discriminating and responding to specific details of their situations falls neatly out of our analysis of interaction in instrumental and "commodity-exchange" terms. We have said that competent action, within an instrumental orientation, involves attending to particular characteristics of the

---

[5]Critical readers will have noticed by now that these remarks about dispositions and invariances and their role in strategically organized interaction do not very obviously have anything to do with the special entity "personality." The issue here is a difficult one because psychologists by and large have not defined their notion of personality with sufficient precision to permit saying just what dispositional properties of persons fall within its scope and what do not. But we all have the strong intuition that there is something quite special about the entity "personality" and that we ought to be able to distinguish its constituent invariances from, say, the regularities of thought and action that consist in "merely" living up to the norms of one's community. We are sensitive to these matters and we shall attempt to address them explicitly in what follows. Our position, as we have said before, is that whatever special features might attach to personality dispositions will be determined by the role of this concept as a formulation of specialized features of agents of instrumental action.

other's cognitions of the joint situation, his or her projects and competencies, strategies of interaction, normative principles of action, and position of power relative to oneself. Competent actors are therefore always in the position of having to monitor and interpret particular details of the other's self-presentations and of having to adjust these readings to fit pertinent aspects of the external circumstances. (The responses of a job supervisor will have one meaning in the work setting but probably quite another in informal encounters away from the workplace. The social fact of "audience segregation" [Goffman, 1959] means that adjustments in one's interpretations must be made in light of the dominant audience present at any given time.) "Taking the other's perspective" becomes the fundamental step in securing control of an interaction situation, and that means attending and responding to often quite minor variations of point of view among the various interactants one encounters.

The commodity-exchange structure of instrumental action introduces a further set of situational specificities which must be taken into account if the job is to be done effectively. Actors seek from others responses that are maximally useful for the realization of their own egocentric projects, in return for supplying performances that are minimally prejudicial to their interests and cost as little as possible. But the terms of the best trade will depend on "market" factors: Ego must take what the available alters have to offer in the way of facilitative performances and, in order to effect an exchange, he or she must offer performances that those particular alters desire. Negotiation strategies must be adjusted to suit the supply of available commodities, and they must permit the provision of just those commodities for which there is a demand. All such factors will vary considerably with features of the external situation and with different combinations of interactants. Competence in exchange thus demands that behavior and cognition be closely adjusted to the exigencies of the particular case. The role of negotiation in exchange reinforces the point: Given the divergence of actors' egocentric interests and the variability of their skills and strategies in negotiation, competence requires monitoring and responding to the fine details of the other's self-presentations as they change and develop in the course of the interaction.

Mischel's (1973, 1968) criticisms of standard formulations of "global personality dispositions"—especially his (1973) summaries of the lessons of research on "moderator variables," delay of gratification, and "person–situation interactions [pp. 255–257]"—indicate that considerations of the sort we are here advancing are at the bottom of his program of "reconceptualizing personality." He argues that:

> The overall results [of person–situation interaction research] suggest, as Endler and Hunt [1968, p. 20] noted with regard to their own findings for anxiety, that behavior 'is idiosyncratically organized in each individual. . . .' A similar conclusion emerges from Moos's (1968) studies of self-reported reactions by staff and patients to various settings. . . . (p. 255) The concept of "moderator variables" was

introduced to trait theory to refer to the fact that the effects of any particular disposition generally are moderated by such other variables as the subject's age, his sex, his IQ, the experimenter's sex, and the characteristics of the situation (Wallach, 1962). When one examines closely the interactions obtained in research on the effects of dispositions and conditions, the number of moderator variables required to predict behavior and the complexity of their interrelationships (e.g., McGuire, 1968) tend to become most formidable. . . . This seems to be another way of saying in the language of moderator variables and interaction terms that what a person does tends to be relatively specific to a host of variables, and that behavior is multiply determined by all of them rather than being the product of widely generalized dispositions . . . [p. 256].

From our point of view, the really interesting feature of these passages lies in Mischel's use of them to justify his belief that ordinary actors must be seen as standardly exhibiting a highly developed facility for distinguishing and taking account of situation specificities. He argues further that:

the "specificity" so regularly found in studies of noncognitive personality dimensions accurately reflects man's impressive discriminative facility and the inadequacy of the assumption of global dispositions, and not merely the distortions of measurement. . . . The findings remind us that what people do in any situation may be changed dramatically even by relatively trivial alterations in their prior experiences or by slight modifications in the particular features of the immediate situation [pp. 258–259].

Actors exhibit a highly developed "discriminative facility," because the failure to develop such a facility makes it impossible to operate effectively within a social system of interaction structured by instrumental manipulation and commodity exchange. The possession of this facility is a minimal condition of social competence in our sort of society, and all agencies of socialization conspire to generate and sustain a substantial degree of it in every adult actor who obtains full membership. Mischel's (1973) passages on moderator variables and person–situation interactions stress that behavior patterns standardly vary: (1) with idiosyncratic characteristics of individual actors; (2) with individual actors' beliefs about the particular situation confronting them; (3) with particular characteristics of the particular alters he meets in the situation; (4) with aspects of the external setting, such as task demands.

Although Mischel is not exhaustive in his articulation of the relevant types of specificities to which actors are attentive, we think his list is definite enough to suggest that instrumentally relevant factors are of great importance, especially, in categories 3 and 4. Mischel's reference to the role of "individual differences in children's beliefs about their ability to control outcomes in determining goal-directed behaviour [p. 256]" is particularly suggestive of an instrumental orientation as underlying the situation specificity of behavior. His further remark that "the relationships hinge on extremely specific moderating conditions both with regard to the type of behaviour and the type of belief [p. 257]" suggests to us that his young subjects were selecting behavior patterns according to relatively fine-grained matches between aspects of the situation and the competencies they felt themselves to possess.

The Tension Between Routinization and Contextualization

We have been referring to actors' performances as "commodities" in order to stress that performances are produced specifically for purposes of exchange. Actors, we contend, are properly conceived as producers of commodities to barter for the treatments they require of each other to facilitate realization of their various egocentric projects. We stress this formulation because it expresses in a vivid way what we think is the lasting significance of Mischel's critique of personality traits. For to say that interaction consists in the production of commodities is to emphasize that actors *construct* their performances to suit the exigencies of the immediate situation. The weight here is on the active and potentially innovative character of ongoing interaction. Competent actors do not mechanically apply fixed profiles of "what to do when." Instead, the instrumental orientation and exchange structure of ordinary interaction demand a highly developed capacity for discriminating fine aspects of particular situations. Interaction situations vary greatly as the external circumstances and the actor's projects and competencies vary. Therefore, the corollary of this "highly developed discriminative facility" is the capacity to construct cognitive patterns (situation definitions) and patterns of performance—out of familiar elements, to be sure—that have not been employed in just that form or fashion in the past. As we suggested earlier, actors are strongly motivated (by these same factors of instrumental orientation and exchange) to routinize their interpersonal doings in so far as possible. Now we are adding the other side of this point, viz. that it is in the nature of actors and social situations to thwart routinization to a considerable degree.

So much is the lesson of our discussion in the section just concluded—and, we think, the lesson of Mischel's criticisms of trait concepts. It is thus a mark of competent interaction that actors have not only a well-developed discriminative facility but also a highly developed capacity for what Piaget calls "accommodation" of familiar patterns of thought and action to the everchanging particularities of immediate situations. Yet at the same time this notion of the actor as a producer of commodities effectively brings out the other term of the dichotomy we have been developing. Mutual calculability of actors is supremely important, both from the actor's subjective point of view *and* as a functional condition on stable social action, exactly because actors who produce performances in order to make advantageous exchanges must be able to count on their alters to a high degree. This critical need for calculability is satisfied by a socially induced drive to routinize and regularize patterns of cognition and performance. It is satisfied, in other words, by the very opposite of the necessity we have just described for ''contextualizing'' cognition and behavior by actively constructing new patterns to meet whatever particular exigencies are at hand.

This troublesome state of affairs, we argue, does not reflect a contradiction in our theoretical position, but points instead to a tension between conflicting drives to routinize and to contextualize performance and cognition—a tension which is fundamental to interaction exhibiting the social structure we have been describing. The instrumental orientation and commodity exchange structure of ordinary social action demands both that the actor proceed in a routine mechanical fashion to apply thoroughly familiar and unproblematic programs of action and cognition and that he or she constantly reconstruct his or her standardized profiles to meet everchanging circumstances and the strategic requirements they impose. Every situation definition, every plan and performance, is a more or less felicitous compromise between these ultimately quite inconsistent demands. As we have been saying in a number of slightly different ways, the contradiction is built into the system of action itself: Calculability of others and of one's own abilities in the face of given demands is essential to strategic success; yet conflicting projects and interests, and the instrumental orientation of all properly socialized actors, ensures that each will not act exactly in accordance with the other's profile of whatever situations they share.

PERSONALITY DISPOSITIONS AS INTERACTION COMPETENCIES

Our purpose throughout has been to develop an account of social interaction from which we could derive principles indicating how the ''institutions and structures of personality'' must be conceived if they are to play a role in understanding human beings qua social actors. We contend that the permanent tension between drives to routinize and to contextualize patterns of thought and action constitutes one such parameter. Thus the pure situationalist position and the traditional trait theorists are equally wrong: Actors do not, as the latter often imply, organize their cognitions or performances in accordance with fixed profiles, learned in the course of prior socialization and determined independently of the immediate situation. Nor do they create brand-new patterns to fit the unique details of every new situation, as Mischel's (1973) formulations occasionally seem to suggest. The awkward fact is they do both at once, maximizing the fit between the here and now and long-established conceptualizations and performance routines, but at the same time accommodating those preestablished patterns to immediate particularities which lead them to think and act, as often as not, in ways that are genuinely new. This is the basic difficulty confronting any attempt to model the dispositional properties of a person, whatever the further explanatory demands we may care to make on these concepts.

The way out, we propose, is to take as the fundamental characteristics of personalities a specialized type of disposition which we shall call "interaction competencies." By this we mean abilities or capacities to construct innovative patterns of performance by reconstructing familiar practiced paradigms to meet the instrumental demands of constantly varying interaction situations. In Piaget's language, the skill in question involves the ability to organize new situations, often containing elements not before encountered or dealt with in just their given form, by assimilating them to long-established profiles of "what to do and think when." Unlike Piaget, we derive this demand for cognitive assimilation from the social structure of interaction and, in particular, from the premium that structure places on calculability of self and others: It is *only* by assimilating the unfamiliar to what has long been thought and done in a routine way, that actors can achieve the all-important feeling of control over their situations.

In sum: Our contention throughout this chapter has been that "personality" is a useful concept exactly insofar as it helps to explain how and why actors think and interact as they do in social situations. The constituents of "personality", however they are conceived, must therefore explicate some fundamental dimensions of the person as agent of instrumental action.[6] We are now claiming that this requirement has two concrete applications: First, the dispositional properties of persons that we single out by the term *personality disposition* must be so constructed as to square both with the propensity of actors to routinize their cognitions and performances and with their constant need to contextualize these routines. (Personality dispositions must thus be seen as structuring and bounding the actor's efforts at constructing situationally adequate patterns but without closely determining what patterns he or she will employ in the given case.) Second, personality dispositions must be understood as competencies in the active, in situ, construction of patterns of cognition and performance rather than as fixed profiles applied in the mechanical fashion of rule-following behavior.

---

[6]This formulation implies, and we intend it to imply, that the *general* characteristics of the entity "personality," not merely their realization in the form of particular dispositions common in particular communities, are socially determined. We do not, as do most traditional theories of personality, think of 'personality' as a way of talking about asocial, extra-historical human nature. In our view, even the most general laws we can formulate about the constitution and workings of personality ultimately will be a function of social and historical circumstances. The entity is conceived by us entirely as a tool for articulating certain fundamental dimensions of social interaction, and its nature will therefore inevitably vary with the basic structure of interaction in the communities of the actors studied. For psychologists of the more highly developed capitalist democracies, "personality" will refer to fundamental features of persons qua participants in and operators of the social system of instrumental action organized as a process of commodity exchange. The strictures on their theories of personality which follow from this fact may or may not apply to persons living under fundamentally different social arrangements.

We recognize, however, that it is not sufficient to characterize personality dispositions simply as interaction competencies, even if this concept were much clearer than we have been able to make it so far. Psychologists have always, and quite rightly, attached a special status, within the thought and behavior of the individual, to those of his dispositional properties supposed to comprise his "personality." As Allport's and Murray's talk about "institutions" and "structures" of the mind suggest, "personality" is construed by psychologists, as by common sense, to refer mainly to dispositions that somehow constitute the "essence" of the individual—to those properties, in other words, without which he would not be *that* individual, hence to properties that are fundamental in the explanatory sense that we must understand most of his or her behaviors as manifestations or outcomes of them. To capture this notion, it is not enough to look for the invariances that underlie and determine the multiplicity of particular observable behaviors. Personality dispositions are some theoretically special subset of these invariances, postulated because they are most powerful in explaining and predicting what *this* individual will do than are his or her other run-of-the-mill propensities, skills, interests, habits, and so on.[7]

We accept this notion of personality as a set of "core" dispositions marking out the singularity of the individual, and we also accept its usual corollary, viz. the proposition that the core dispositions generalize across classes of individuals. (With the exception of Allport's "idiographic traits" and George Kelly's "personal constructs," personality theories have sought essences of persons that are common to large numbers of them.) There is no genuine inconsistency here with the stress on personality as the core of the individual; the program of personality theory traditionally has been to identify a small set of basic dimensions which generalize across all normal actors and out of which the idiosyncratic makeups of individual actors can be constructed as a set of permutations on the common themes.[8] The job now confronting us, then, is to demonstrate that somewhere in

---

[7]This theoretical tendency is especially evident in personality models like Cattell's, with its use of factor analysis to identify "ergs", "meta-ergs", and other "source traits" (Hall & Lindzey, 1965, pp. 396–399); or Eysenck's, with its emphasis on "trait types" picked out by reference to primary dimensions such as "intraversion," "neuroticism," "psychoticism [pp. 384–389]." But Freud's psychosexual drives and the individual's paradigmatic strategies for satisfying them, fixed in the course of passing through developmental stages, would count as equally clear instances. So would Murray's (1951, p. 168ff) "need-states" and the individual's typical modes and strategies for reducing the "tension" they create or his notion of a "unity thema [p. 189]." Sullivan's "self-system," defined as a set of protection-oriented strategies for exercising supervisory controls over behavior, could also be included along with similar notions common to most of the neo-Freudian ego psychologies.

[8]The resulting program of research has been largely directed toward constructing a typology of people, each type marked by some distinguishing set of core dispositions, with the hope that large numbers of identifiable behavior patterns would correlate each with some one type. By implication, "the uniqueness of the individual" would be understood in terms of permutations on the defining dispositions of one or more types although, in truth, personality theorists have by and large been so

the domain of "interaction competencies" we can locate a set of such basic dimensions in terms of which "particular personalities" can be explicated and the thoughts and actions of their owners understood.

According to the abstract definition we offered in the foregoing, an "interaction competency" is an ability to construct innovative patterns of performance and conceptualization by reconstructing familiar, practiced, and hence thoroughly manageable paradigms to meet the instrumental and exchange demands of constantly varying immediate situations. We propose now that such abilities standardly come in two degrees of generality, best explicated by means of some long overdue concrete examples.

The Ability to Adopt the Perspectives of Other Actors.   Instrumental manipulation in everyday social action proceeds in a very particular way: Actors operate

---

busy generating their types that they have tended to scant the individual—per Allport's lamentations. Empirical work has focused on both the taxonomic project and the correlating project, because the mark of a genuine disposition ultimately just *is* success in correlating with a substantial number of independently measurable behaviors—thereby putatively explaining the behaviors.

We are disinclined to equate explanation with correlation, but our main quarrel with this perspective involves quite another aspect of it. The majority of personality theorists, from Freud to Cattell, assume that the core of dispositions they investigate in a person are fixed in the sense of being relatively impervious to ongoing social experiences. Usually, it is said (following Freud's lead) that a special set of early experiences determines the form of this core for the entire life of the individual. The core dispositions specifically are *not* conceived as fundamentally determined by or as evolving with adult experiences within a system of social interaction. On the contrary, it is thought that adult behavior patterns must be understood as applications and reorientations of character components formed in the early years. The view leaves some room for social influences on personality formation, but it is hard to see how they can include the considerations we have detailed in the course of describing the processes and techniques of instrumental manipulation and commodity exchange. If the concept of personality is to explicate the actor qua agent in this social system of action, then it seems clear that the dispositions comprising it must be susceptible to radical change as the circumstances and demands of the individual's interaction patterns change with age, economic status, and other aspects of social position. Should his social milieu change in sufficiently radical ways, it is entirely possible, in our view, that the individual's personality would undergo a thorough reconstruction.

Traditional personality theories do allow for radical change of personality, it is true, but such changes specifically are not perceived as normal responses to external conditions. Usually deep change is thought to be possible only through therapeutic intervention or else through some cataclysmic impact of the external world (e.g., the death of a loved one, economic or physical disaster, and so on). In our view, a radical change of personality would count rather as a normal response of a competent actor to radically changed needs and demands of interaction. Once the priority of childhood socialization is discounted, there is no theoretical reason why people should not redo their most fundamental cognitive and behavioral dispositions to suit the exigencies of the social environment. The changes usually will not be abrupt, nor will they be planned, nor will the actor necessarily see the discontinuity that would be apparent to an outside observer. The importance of competence in interaction and the drive to routinize ensure that actors will *strive* to maintain continuity and usually will conceive themselves as highly continuous over time. But these facts do not in any way preclude a series of stepwise changes in the course of accommodating established profiles of thought and action to radically changing circumstances, which issue in radically revised personalities.

on each other's cognitions of their shared situations in order to bring the other to a definition of the situation that will activate in him or her normative principles of action issuing in desired performances. Therefore it is obviously of importance to be able to perceive the situation from the point of view of the alter to be manipulated. It is essential for ego to know how alter perceives his or her projects and strategies, the resources and demands of the external situation, and especially the values (to alter) of the interaction commodities it is in ego's power to provide. Yet actors differ enormously in their capacities for picking up the perspectives of others. They differ with respect to the generalized capacity (often called "empathy" by psychologists) for intuiting the perspective of a person not before encountered or not well-known. They also differ with respect to the repertoires of particular perspectives of others that each is competent to interpret readily and accurately. Differences in prior social experience mean exposure to different types of points of view, and actors with divergent backgrounds will differ with respect to the determinate types each is predisposed to recognize and incorporate in his or her strategic calculations. Both levels of perspective-taking ability depend on cognitive skill in detecting and accurately interpreting behavioral cues and verbal communications for information about social position, personal background, and so on. Moreover, actors are faced with applying familiar, long-used perspective types to newly encountered persons and situations. They must therefore be able to accommodate their type concepts to specific details of these situations. At the same time, they must be able to formulate the situations (in line with the routinization requirement we discussed earlier) in such a fashion as to render them assimilable to the familiar types—necessary for preserving the sense of control that goes with assimilation to the routine.

Role-Playing Abilities. In the course of participating in various social groups, actors acquire skills in performing specified social roles—occupational roles, spouse and parent roles, the role of leader or peacemaker or informal advisor in friendship circles, and so on. Individuals can be compared according to the different particular roles each is competent to fulfill, and they can be compared according to how effectively each performs a given role. In addition, actors vary with respect to a more generalized capacity for interpreting and fulfilling role demands. Some are more sensitive than others to the formal and informal demands of new groups whatever they might be and to the probable expectations of familiar groups in new situations; some are more flexible than others in their willingness and in their capacity for interpreting and living up to the criteria of adequate performance that accompany these demands.

These two levels of role-playing ability have been well-researched in areas of social science that seem peripheral to personality theory and therefore have been largely ignored by personality psychologists. For examples, sociologists interested in the mechanisms by which social classes are perpetuated have recognized that institutional contexts available only to upper-class children (the squash courts found only at schools of the St. Grottlesex sort, the "head boy" role in English public schools) provide skills training and role practice which increase the role repertoires of upper class persons in ways wholly unavailable to most of society. Ecological psychologists working within the Barker (1963) tradition have discovered that a similar role repertoire-increasing advantage can occur for other than social class reasons. Barker and Gump (1964) found that an American school in a Midwestern town provided many more "behavior settings" (their term for such roles as "school newspaper editor") than did a comprehensive school in an English community. They also discovered that schools with small enrollments, responding to obvious social pressures, attempted to fill a role set nearly as complete as did larger high schools. Each student of a small high school was more likely to be called on to fill the role requirements of a larger number of behavior settings, gaining performance competencies in wider variety of roles. Some evidence indicates that these competencies developed in school settings are retained later in life (Wicker, 1973). In addition, studies with children generally find a correlation between tests of the ability to take the role of the other and measures of more general social competence, as would be expected from our account. For instance, Rubin (1972) found that early school age children who were better able to take the alter's "point of view into account during communication interaction [were] more popular than their more egocentric age mates [p. 364]." Keller (1976) reports that role-taking ability was a better prediction than IQ of selection for a higher track in a tracked school system.[9]

---

[9]If the conception of personality we are elaborating still does not seem much like "personality" to some readers, it is probably because our account departs in a very fundamental way from the psychodynamic conception that has tended to dominate the field since Freud. According to the psychodynamic perspective, the basic motivators of all thought and behavior are nonrational entities of a highly fixed sort (the product, in Freud's orthodox formulations, largely of constitutional factors)—psychosexual drives, need states conceived as sources of psychic tension, instinctual forces, and fixed affective patterns. Thought and action are conceived as the expression of the actor's attempts to satisfy these irrational and largely implacable demands in a way that will be consistent with limits that his or her social reality places upon acceptable conduct. Conflict is irrevocable, indeed is constitutive of every actor's situation in the world—a claim we wholeheartedly endorse, in this general form. But conflict is conceived in a very narrow way as the confrontation of fixed irrational demands with requirements of social life that are, in their way, equally implacable. The basic dimensions of personality are taken to be the set of such irrational demands, together with characteristic strategies for achieving compromises between the two sets of demands, internal and social. On Freud's original account, even the outlines of the compromise-reaching strategies are predetermined by the psychosexual constitution of human organisms—patterns comprising oral, anal–sadistic, genital, and so on phases of infantile psychosexual development determine in broad outline the actor's programs of drive satisfaction throughout his life. More recent theory has tended to emphasize the role of social learning over constitution; but it has also tended to retain the basic conception of actors as always seeking optimal compromises between the pressing demands of various nonrational needs, drives, fears, anxieties, and other forms of psychic tension, and the limits imposed by communal norms and values. More or less scope is granted to socialization as a determinant of behavior, depending on the theorist considered, but the impact of social processes is nonethe-

Self-Monitoring Abilities.   Snyder (1974) differentiates people in terms of the degree to which they report that they attend to the social context when planning behavior. In doing so he identifies a further case of a competence-centered personality dimension. His high self-monitoring individuals, for example, were quite sensitive to variations in behavioral demands communicated by the groups in which they found themselves (Snyder & Monson, 1975). When the group conveyed that conformity was the most appropriate orientation, the high self-monitors were conforming; when autonomy was appropriate, they were much less conforming. The conformity behavior of non–self-monitors was not significantly affected by variations in group climate.

Our account suggests that several competence-related dispositions are likely to be possessed by the situation-sensitive self-monitor. First, he is likely to hold the essentially correct belief that social contexts frequently alter the desirable tactical means for achieving the same strategic purposes (e.g., autonomy in one setting and conformity in another). In a competent actor, this realization should lead to an orientation toward learning to take the perspective of others, in order that their operational requirements can be determined and taken account of. And it is psychologically likely this orientation would lead to skill in accurately ascertaining these requirements: Because the self-monitor, by our account, is monitoring these situational demands of others in order to achieve his own projects, he will naturally develop skills in carrying out such monitoring.

Snyder (1974) has also shown that high self-monitors are better at the task of simulating the expression of various emotions: When subjects were asked to read a set of lines in a way that conveys anger, happiness, or some other emotion, observers were more accurate in guessing the emotion that the high self-monitor intended to convey. This ability to simulate emotional reactions in a way that others can read is a basic strategic skill. In social exchanges, an essential task is to respond appropriately to the emotional productions of others, answering their sorrow with sympathy, their joy with happiness, and so on. This skill need not be

---

less thought of mainly as affecting the particular form in which the actor goes about reducing his psychic tensions.

The general thrust of these theories, in other words, is to make as much as possible of the actor's thought and behavior strongly independent of ongoing processes of perceiving, inferring, planning, and evaluating and strongly independent of his ongoing experiences of the social system of interaction in which he finds himself operating. Our own conception of personality, as should be obvious by now, reverses these priorities. The point of our construing the basic dimensions of personality as "interaction competencies" is to stress their responsiveness to social experience and, more importantly, their ultimate foundation in the constitution of the actor's community as opposed to the psychological constitution of the organism. We agree with psychodynamics that conflicts between individual and social world are basic determinants of action, but we interpret these conflicts in terms of antagonistic and inconsistent strategic interests on the part of different actors. This permits us to explain the antagonisms as endemic to the system of social action most of us know and study rather than taking them as irrevocable products of biological programming.

cynically construed; the emotions conveyed normally are genuinely felt. It is nonetheless necessary that they be effectively conveyed to the other person, and the high self-monitor is particularly able to do this.

In the same study (Snyder, 1974), marginally significant evidence was found that the high self-monitors were also better decoders of the underlying meanings of other people's attempts to convey emotions. Other research (Snyder, 1979) tends to confirm this. A picture emerges of the high self-monitor as an individual who has grasped the central social fact that achieving one's purposes requires accurate perceptions of the signals sent by others, as well as well-developed signaling capacities of one's own and has therefore developed the skills necessary to do both these tasks.

Here, then, are three sets of basic dimensions of people's behavior which we believe are good candidates for personality dispositions conceived according to our interaction competence notion. The literature of recent experimental social psychology provides a host of further candidates, although in few cases are the investigated variables recognized as determinants and consequents of the social processes of instrumental interaction and commodity exchange. For example: Strongly Machiavellian actors seem to be more skillful than most at mobilizing groups to fulfill their egocentric goals (Christie & Geis, 1970). Sociolinguists studying conversational interaction have found that actors differ in their abilities to channel conversations onto topics of their choice. (This and similar competencies in conversational management may well be an important part of the socially effective actor's skill in group manipulation.) Capacity to delay gratification (Mischel, 1976) clearly counts as a behavioral competence, and it can have an important role to play in instrumental interaction: The actor who can abstain at will is in a position to orient his or her actions toward longer-term projects without deflection in favor of immediate rewards.

As these examples suggest, once one begins to think of persons in terms of competencies in instrumental interaction, many of the specialized topics investigated by social psychologists turn out to be candidates for basic constituents of personality. And much familiar work, in personality psychology and in social psychology generally, turns out to be reinterpretable as analysis of constructs involving the dimension of interpersonal competence. Even more important, the social interactional conception of personality suggests new lines of research and focuses attention on other which have barely begun to attract interest. One very obvious candidate for the role of basic personality dimension would be a generalized skill in conducting interpersonal negotiations within the commodity-exchange format. This competence, like the others we have listed, could be broken down into a number of more specific cognitive and performance abilities. A generalized competence in self-presentation, similarly analyzable into a number of specific constituent skills, is a likely second candidate. Instrumental manipulation of the sort we have described depends on clear and persuasive communication of one's own perspectives and projects, and the treatments one requires of the other in order to realize them. Actors differ enormously in their capacities for this sort of signaling of their concerns, and their success in interpersonal interactions may vary accordingly. A third candidate for a generalized personality competence might involve generalized skills in accommodating one's own egocentric projects to the interests of others. Because actors' interests frequently diverge, the egocentric motivations of others can be made to serve one's own programs and strategies only if one is prepared to reinterpret and reconstruct them. Moreover, one must be able to do so again and again, as one moves among different interaction contexts, without losing a firm sense of one's own projects in the process.

We close with a few brief remarks about the status of this concept, "interaction competency," in a hurried attempt to reassure hardheaded readers that we are talking about a set of constructs which is susceptible to experimental testing—withour denying that the testing will require reorientation of some of the standard paradigms of personality research. First, the theory stresses that personality is essentially constructed for, and therefore revealed in, contexts of interpersonal interaction. It follows that, although assessment devices can be designed which focus on the individual, validation of the assessment requires observing the actions of the assessed individual in a social-interaction situation—or rather, according to the well-known necessity for multiple observation for construct validation, in several social-interaction settings. This is difficult research to do, requiring as it does one or more individuals with whom the assessed individual must come in contact. And because the theory stresses skills at interaction, it is preferable that the other participants be free to engage in genuine interaction, rather than acting as confederates of the experimenter who carry out some preplanned sequence of actions that is not responsive to changes in the assessed actor's performances. Hence this sort of social–action-centered research requires, in addition to the assessed actor, one or more other persons with whom he or she can interact and who can be expected to make their own contributions to the variance of the interactional sequence. The earlier work of Christie and Geis (1970), as well as the more recent work of Snyder, Tanke, and Berscheid (1977), demonstrates that this kind of research is possible and frequently fruitful.

The competency focus of the present theory points toward a class of measurable dependent variables. The outcomes of a social interactional sequence should more closely match the dictates of the instrumental needs of highly competent participants than those of less competent actors. Particular social competencies from our list will have distinctive outcomes, predictable and measurable, within the social interaction sequence. Competence in perceiving the projects of others, for instance, can be experimentally assessed. In general, differences between individuals on the interpersonal competency-based dimensions suggested here can be assessed within research paradigms currently available and in use within cognitive, social, and personality psychology.

REFERENCES

Allport, G. W. *The nature of personality: Selected papers.* Cambridge: Addison Wesley, 1937. (b)

Allport, G. W. *Personality: A psychological interpretation.* New York: Holt, 1937. (a)

Barker, R. *The stream of behavior.* New York: Appleton-Century-Crofts, 1963.

Barker, R., & Gump, P. *Big school, small school: High school size and student behavior.* Stanford: Stanford University Press, 1964.

Bem, D. J. Constructing cross-situational consistencies in behaviour: Some thoughts on Alker's critique of Mischel. *Journal of Personality,* 1972, *40,* 17–26.

Bem, D. J., & Allen, A. On predicting some of the people some of the time: The search for cross-situational consistencies in behaviour. *Psychological Review,* 1974, *81,* 506–520.

Blau, P. M. *Exchange and power in social life.* New York: Wiley, 1964.

Christie, R., & Geis, F. *Studies in Machiavellianism.* New York: Academic Press, 1970.

Darley, S. Big time careers for the little woman: A dual-role dilemma. *Journal of Social Issues,* 1976, 33, 85–88.

Endler, N. S., & Hunt, J. McV. S-R inventories of hostility and comparisons of the proportions of variance from persons, responses, and situations for hostility and anxiousness. *Journal of Personality and Social Psychology,* 1968, *9,* 309–315.

Gibson, E. J. *Principles of perceptual learning and development.* New York: Appleton, Century Crofts, 1969.

Goffman, E. *The presentation of self in everyday life.* New York: Doubleday Anchor Books, 1959.

Goffman, E. *Relations in public.* New York: Harper and Row, 1972.

Goffman, E. *Frame analysis.* New York: Harper and Row, 1974.

Hall, C. S., & Lindzey, G. *Theories of personality* (2nd ed.). New York: Wiley, 1970.

Homans, G. C. *Social behaviour: Its elementary forms.* New York: Harcourt, 1961.

Jones, E. E. *Ingratiation: A social psychological analysis.* New York: Irvington Publishers, 1975.

Keller, M. Development of role-taking ability. Social antecedants and consequences for school success. *Human Development,* 1976, *19,* 120–132.

Kelly, G. A. *A theory of personality: The psychology of personal constructs.* New York: W. W. Norton & Co., 1963.

Kelley, H. H., & Thibaut, J. W. *Interpersonal relations: A theory of interdependence.* New York: Wiley, 1978.

Labov, W. & Fanshel, D. *Therapeutic discourse: Psychotherapy as conversation.* New York: Academic Press, 1977.

Lempert, R. Norm-making in social exchange: A contract law model. *Law and Society Review,* 1972–1973, *7,* 1–32.

Locke, J. The second treatise of civil government. In Cook, T. L. (Ed.), *Two treatises of government.* New York: Hafner Press, 1973.

McGuire, W. J. Personality and susceptability to social influences. In B. F. Borgatta & W. W. Lambert (Eds.), *Handbook of personality theory and research.* Chicago: Rand McNally, 1968.

Mischel, W. *Personality and assessment,* New York: Wiley, 1968.

Mischel, W. Toward a cognitive social learning reconceptualization of personality. *Psychological Review,* 1973, *80,* 252–283.

Mischel, W. *Introduction to personality* (2nd ed.). New York: Holt, 1976.

Mischel, W. On the future of personality measurement. *American Psychologist,* 1977, *32,* 246–254. (a)

Mischel, W. The interaction of person and situation. In D. Magnusson & N. S. Endler (Eds.), *Personality at the crossroads: Current issues in interactional psychology.* Hillsdale, N.J.: Lawrence Erlbaum Associates, 1977. (b)

Mischel, W. *On the interface of cognition and personality: Beyond the person–situation debate.* APA Distinguished Scientist Award address, expanded version in typescript, 1978.

Mischel, W., Zeiss, R., & Zeiss, A. Internal–external control and persistence. *Journal of Personality and Social Psychology,* 1974, *29,* 265–278.

Moos, R. H. Situational analysis of a therapeutic community milieu. *Journal of Abnormal Psychology,* 1968, *73,* 49–61.

Murray, H. A. *Explorations in personality.* New York: Oxford University Press, 1938.

Murray, H. A. Toward a classification of interaction. In T. Parsons & E. A. Shils, *Towards a general theory of action.* Cambridge, Mass.: Harvard University Press, 1951.

Piaget, J. *Biology and knowledge.* Edinburgh: Edinburgh University Press, 1971.

Rubin, K. H. Relationship between egocentric communication and popularity among peers. *Developmental Psychology,* 1972, *7,* 364.

Snyder, M. The self monitoring of expressive behavior. *Journal of Personality and Social Psychology,* 1974, *30,* 526–537.

Snyder, M. Self monitoring processes. In L. Berkowitz, (Ed.), *Advances in Experimental Social Psychology.* (*Vol. 12*) New York: Academic Press, 1979.

Snyder, M., & Manson, T. C., Persons, situations and the control of social behavior. *Journal of Personality and Social Psychology,* 1975, *32,* 637–644.

Snyder, M., Tanke, E., & Berscheid, E. Social perception and interpersonal behavior. On the self-fulfilling nature of social stereotypes. *Journal of Personality and Social Psychology,* 1977, *35,* 656–666.

Wallach, M. A. Commentary: Active-analytical versus passive-global cognitive functioning. In S. Messick & J. Ross (Eds.), *Measurement in personality and cognition.* New York: Wiley, 1962.

Wicker, A. W. Undermanning theory and research: Implications for the study of psychological and behavioral effects of excess populations. *Representative Research in Social Psychology,* 1973, *4:* 185–206.

Zellman, G. The role of structural factors in limiting woman's institutional participation. *Journal of Social Issues,* 1976, *32,* 33–46.

13

On the Influence of Individuals on Situations

Mark Snyder
University of Minnesota

As a personality–social psychologist, I am concerned—almost by definition—with understanding the relationships that exist between individuals and social situations. The social psychologist in me never allows me to forget the extent to which social situations influence the behavior of individuals. In different situations and with different people, I—and many, if not most, other people—may act like very different persons. Cocktail parties bring out the sociable and the gregarious in me; academic symposia bring out the intellectual and the scholarly in me. In fact, demonstrations of the many and varied ways in which people are creatures of their situations are the stock-in-trade of social psychologists. One might go so far as to characterize social psychology as the systematic attempt to verify the proposition that "situations influence individuals."

The personality psychologist in me does not question the proposition that "situations influence individuals." However, it does prompt me to consider the symmetric proposition that "individuals influence situations." After all, individuals typically have considerable freedom to choose to be where, when, and with whom. Accordingly, the situations in which an individual finds himself or herself may be partially of his or her own choosing. Moreover, once in a social situation—whether of the individual's own choosing or not—much of what transpires in that situation is determined by the individual's own actions. Thus, if late on a Friday afternoon, I find myself in a situation that encourages me to behave in serious, reserved, and thoughtful fashion, it may be because I have chosen to attend a research seminar rather than an end-of-the-week cocktail party. Moreover, having entered the research seminar situation, my actions then may influence the nature of the situation that confronts me. To the extent that I behave in appropriately academic fashion, I may help the situation preserve its

309

academic character. However, to the extent that I decide to operate on the situation (if, for example, I convince my colleagues that we really ought to put aside our weighty intellectual concerns and chat instead about movies, sports, and the like), my actions may succeed in transforming that rather formal, serious, and academic situation into one with a somewhat more informal, relaxed, and sociable character.

Of what import might be the processes of choosing and influencing situations? Quite possibly, one's choices of the settings in which to live one's life may reflect features of one's personality: An individual may choose to live his or her life in serious, reserved, and intellectual situations precisely because he or she is a serious, reserved, and thoughtful individual. Moreover, just as one's choices of the settings in which to live one's life may reflect features of one's personality, so too may the influences that one attempts to exert on those settings: An individual may attempt to transform life situations into friendly, relaxed, and sociable situations precisely because he or she is a friendly, relaxed, and sociable individual. From this perspective, individuals are to be understood in terms of the settings in which they live their lives, and the settings in which individuals live their lives are to be understood in terms of the processes by which individuals actively choose and influence their social situations.

This chapter represents one attempt to consider the implications of the processes by which individuals choose and influence situations for conceptualizing and investigating several of the fundamental concerns of the personality–social psychologist: (1) the nature and consequences of an individual's conceptions of self; (2) the nature and consequences of an individual's conceptions of other people; (3) the nature and consequences of characteristic dispositions of the individual; and (4) the nature and consequences of characteristic attitudes and values of the individual. In such considerations, one asks questions of the form: What is the impact of an individual's conceptions of self, conceptions of other people, characteristic dispositions, attitudes, and values on his or her social situations? Or, more generally, what is the impact of the individual on the social world within which he or she lives? The journey from asking these questions to answering these questions begins, of necessity, with the development of appropriate research paradigms for the empirical investigation of the impact of individuals on their social situations.

INVESTIGATING THE IMPACT OF INDIVIDUALS ON THEIR SITUATIONS

Is it possible to structure research paradigms that permit the investigation of how the individual influences situations? To do so would require casting the *individual* in the role of *independent variable* and the *situation* in the role of *dependent variable*. Such a procedural paradigm would, of course, precisely reverse the direction of causal influence typically examined in the traditional empirical investigation familiar to experimentally oriented researchers in personality-social psychology. Characteristically, experimenters manipulate and control characteristics of the situation and observe the impact of these manipulated situational independent variables on dependent variable measures of the behavior of the individual.

The feasibility of performing a paradigmatic reversal and documenting the influence of individuals on their situations may be demonstrated with an example from the domain of person perception, an example concerned with the nature and consequences of an individual's conceptions of other people. A traditional "situation influences individual" experiment might investigate the effects of a target's behavior on a perceiver's impressions of the target. The researcher might find, for example, that if he or she arranges for the target to behave in a friendly and sociable manner, then the perceiver will infer that the target has a friendly and sociable temperament. If so, the researcher would have witnessed an example of the impact of events in the situation (here, the target's behavior) on events in the individual (here, the perceiver's beliefs).

What if the researcher were to attempt to reverse the direction of causal influence? What if he or she were to manipulate and control the beliefs of the perceiver, allow perceiver and target to interact with each other, and observe the impact of the perceiver's beliefs on the actual behavior of the target? He or she might observe that, when perceivers interact with targets whom they believe (erroneously, as a result of the experimental manipulation) to have friendly and sociable natures, those targets actually come to behave in friendly and sociable fashion. If so, the researcher would have witnessed an instance of the impact of events in the individual (here, the perceiver's beliefs) on events in the individual's social situation (here, the target's behavior).

Indeed, it has been possible to investigate experimentally the processes by which an individual's conceptions of other people exert powerful channeling influences on subsequent social interaction between the individual and other people. Actions of the individual based upon preconceived notions about other people can and do cause the behavior of other people to confirm and validate even erroneous and highly stereotyped conceptions of other people. These processes of behavioral confirmation, by which an individual's beliefs about the social world may create their own social reality, have been documented in diverse interpersonal domains (for a review, see Snyder, in press-a).

For example, in one investigation of behavioral confirmation processes in social interaction, Snyder, Tanke and Berscheid (1977) investigated the impact of stereotyped conceptions of physical attractiveness (i.e., "beautiful people are good people") on the unfolding dynamics of social interaction and acquaintance processes. They arranged for pairs of previously unacquainted individuals to interact in an acquaintance situation (a telephone conversation) that had been constructed to allow them to control the information that one member of the dyad (the perceiver) received about the physical attractiveness of the other individual (the target). In anticipation of the forthcoming interaction, perceivers fashioned erroneous images of their specific discussion partners that reflected general stereotypes about physical attractiveness. Perceivers who anticipated physically attractive partners expected to interact with comparatively sociable, poised, humorous, and socially adept individuals. By contrast, perceivers faced with the prospect of getting acquainted with relatively unattractive partners fashioned images of rather unsociable, awkward, serious, and socially inept creatures. Moreover, perceivers had very different patterns or styles of interaction for targets whom they perceived to be physically attractive and those they perceived to be physically unattractive. These differences in self-presentation and interaction style, in turn, elicited and nurtured behaviors in the targets that were consistent with the perceivers' initial stereotypes. Targets who were perceived (unbeknownst to them) to be physically attractive actually came to behave in a friendly, likable, and sociable manner. This behavioral confirmation was discernible even by outside listeners who knew nothing of the actual or the perceived physical attractiveness of the targets.

In this demonstration of behavioral confirmation in social interaction, the perceivers' stereotyped conceptions of other people had initiated a chain of events that had produced actual behavioral confirmation of these conceptions. The initially erroneous impressions of the perceivers had, in a sense, become real. The "beautiful people" had become "good people," not because they necessarily possessed the socially valued dispositions that had been attributed to them but because the actions of the perceivers based upon their stereotyped beliefs had erroneously confirmed and validated these beliefs.

Other important and widespread social stereotypes also can and do channel social interaction so as to create their own social reality within the context of individual relationships. Empirical research has documented the behavioral conformation of stereotypes associated with race (Word, Zanna, & Cooper, 1974) and gender (Skrypnek & Snyder, 1980; Zanna & Pack, 1975). Moreover, the very act of labeling another person may initiate a chain of events that induces that person to behave in accord with that label. Empirical investigations have demonstrated the behavioral confirmation of labeling other people, for example, as hostile or nonhostile (Snyder & Swann, 1978-a) and as intelligent or nonintelligent (Rosenthal & Jacobson, 1968). Even when individuals attempt to use social interaction as opportunities to evaluate and assess the accuracy of beliefs, hypotheses and, theories about other people, their "reality-testing" procedures may channel social interaction in ways that provide behavioral confirmation for the beliefs, hypotheses, and theories under scrutiny (Snyder, in press-b; Snyder & Swann, 1978-b).

The consequences of behavioral confirmation processes in social interaction and interpersonal relationships may be both profound and pervasive. As consequences of behavioral confirmation processes, individuals may construct for themselves social worlds in which the behavior of those with whom they interact reflects, verifies, maintains, and justifies their preexisting conceptions of other people, including many highly stereotyped assumptions about human nature. It is as though, as a consequence of behavioral confirmation processes, individuals construct their social worlds in their own images of the social world. Nevertheless, the reality-constructing consequences of behavioral confirmation processes aside, investigations of behavioral confirmation in social interaction demonstrate the feasibility of empirically and experimentally investigating "individual influences situations" propositions.

UNDERSTANDING INDIVIDUALS IN TERMS OF THEIR SITUATIONS

Of course, in investigations of behavioral confirmation processes in social interaction, it has been possible to manipulate experimentally those aspects of the individual (i.e., their conceptions of other people) of concern to the investigators. Other attributes of the individual (whose impact on social situations the personality–social psychologist might wish to investigate) may not be so readily amenable to experimental manipulation. For example, it is in practice (if not in principle) somewhat more difficult to manipulate and control an individual's conceptions of self, characteristic dispositions, attitudes, and values than it is to manipulate and control his or her conceptions of other people. Nonetheless, one need not be deterred from investigating the impact of individuals on their situations either in the domain of conceptions of self or in the domain of characteristic dispositions. In either case, a consideration of the influence of individuals on their social situations suggests that *it may be possible to characterize individuals in terms of the social world that they construct for themselves to habitate.*

Conceptions of Self

Consider, first, examples drawn from the domain of self-conceptions. It goes almost without saying that some individuals regard themselves as more competitive than other people. What influences might these competitive self-conceptions exert on the social worlds within which these individuals reside? As it happens, individuals with competitive conceptions of self believe that the world is composed homogeneously of competitive individuals; by contrast, those with cooperative conceptions of self construe the world to be composed heterogeneously of both cooperative and competitive people (Kelley & Stahelski, 1970). Furthermore, and perhaps as a consequence of these stereotyped beliefs about other people, individuals with competitive self-conceptions are highly likely to treat all people as if they were competitive individuals and thereby elicit competitive responses from all others with whom they interact, whether these individuals have cooperative or competitive conceptions of themselves (Kelley & Stahelski, 1970). Effectively, those individuals with competitive conceptions of self create for themselves social worlds that not only provide behavioral confirmation for their stereotypic beliefs that all people are competitive, but also justify and maintian their own competitive dispositions. They construct their social worlds in their own self-images. Moreover, these social worlds are ideally suited to expressing or acting out their competitive conceptions of self.

Consider another example drawn from the domain of self-conceptions. Consider the case of those individuals who conceive of themselves as competent, intelligent people. How might such individuals arrange the circumstances of their lives to preserve and sustain these images of self-competence? Jones and Berglas (1978) have proposed that people strive to protect their images of self-competence by actions that make it easier for them to externalize (i.e., explain away) their failures and to internalize (i.e., take credit for) their successes. They have labeled such actions *self-handicapping strategies*. In an empirical demonstration of self-handicapping strategies in action, Berglas and Jones (1978) observed that male college students who have reason to anticipate that they may not perform well on a problem-solving task will choose to take drugs that will interfere with their subsequent problem-solving performance. Should they then perform poorly, they have provided themselves with a readily available explanation for their failure that in no way threatens their images of self-competence. Should they then perform well, they may pride themselves for being sufficiently intelligent and competent to overcome the handicap of the performance-inhibiting drug.

More generally, Jones and Berglas (1978) have proposed that, to the extent that individuals are concerned with maintaining images of self-competence, they will try to choose settings and circumstances for their performances that maximize the implications of success for enhancing their self-competence images at the same time as they minimize the implications of failure for threatening their self-competence images. To the extent that their choices of life settings meet these criteria, they will manage to live their lives in worlds that protect and enhance both their private self-conceptions and their public images of competence.

One can readily imagine similar scenarios in which individuals actively construct social worlds well-suited to the maintenance and expression of other attributes of their self-conceptions. Individuals who regard themselves as liberals (politically and/or socially) may choose to associate whenever possible with other people whom they regard as liberals. They may choose to expose themselves selectively to the messages of liberally oriented newspapers, magazines, books, radio, television, and movies. These individuals may join organizations that are devoted to the advancement of liberal causes. They may pursue careers in occupations that they regard as appropriate for liberals. Such individuals even may choose to live in areas that typically elect liberal representatives to political offices. If so, by choosing to live their lives in ''liberal'' surroundings, individuals who conceive of themselves as liberals would have created for themselves social worlds ideally suited to the maintenance and expression of their liberal conceptions of self. Not incidentally, these individuals would have constructed for themselves social worlds that foster and promote the regular and consistent performances of liberal behaviors in diverse situations—social worlds that would encourage them to display the behavioral features that would appear to the personality psychologist to be representative of a trait or disposition of liberalism. Indeed, the proposition that individuals influence their social situations has considerable implications for conceptualizing and assessing stable traits and enduring dispositions of the individual.

Characteristic Dispositions

Central to the activities of the personality psychologist are the conceptualization and identification of characteristic dispositions of the individual. Consider, for example, the case of sociability. If one assumes that some people are more sociable than others, how is one to identify these differences in sociability? And, having accomplished this identification task, how then is one to conceptualize the origins of these differences in sociability? Perhaps one might identify those behaviors that are manifestations of sociability and tabulate the frequency with which individuals engage in these actions. It might even be acceptable to trust individuals to report accurately the frequency with which they perform sociable actions. One then could identify as sociable individuals those who perform (or who claim to perform) relatively many sociable behaviors. Such an approach is, of course, very similar to traditional assessment strategies in personality psychology, strategies that focus on identifying regularities and consistencies in the *behaviors* that individuals perform.

However, a consideration of the impact of individuals on situations suggests a fundamentally different approach to understanding individuals. This approach focuses, instead, on the processes of *choosing and influencing situations.* Instead of defining sociable individuals as those who perform sociable actions, one would define sociable individuals as those who: (1) when given the choice, choose to enter situations that foster the expression of sociability; and (2) once in a situation, will act in ways that increase the sociability of that situation. Thus, sociable individuals are those who, when given the choice of going to a party or going to the library, will choose to enter the party situation. Similarly, when sociable individuals find themselves with groups of people, these sociable individuals will work actively to mold their situations into ones conducive to the display of sociability.

From this perspective, sociability is defined behaviorally as the processes of choosing whenever possible to enter sociable situations and acting to maximize the sociability of one's situations. In so doing, sociable individuals would be constructing for themselves social worlds most conducive to the expression and manifestation of their sociable dispositions. Not incidentally, as direct consequences of the active and constructive processes of choosing and influencing their social situations in ways that create "sociable" worlds within which to reside, "sociable" individuals would come to display sociable behaviors with high frequency and great regularity across situations and over time. In other words, these individuals would come to display the cross-situational consistency and the temporal stability that traditionally are regarded as the defining features of a "trait" or "disposition" of sociability. However, by understanding sociability in terms of the processes of choosing and influencing social situations, it has been possible to go far beyond the identification of regularities and consistencies in observed behavior to a theoretical understanding of these regularities and consistencies as the consequences of consistencies and regularities in the processes of choosing and influencing situations. This is not to say that the identification of regularities and consistencies in social behavior is not an important or a productive task. Rather, regularities and consistencies in social behavior are not important in and of themselves: They are important because of the processes that generate them. And, from the perspective of one concerned with the impact of individuals on their social situations, regularities and consistencies in social behavior are the product of regularities and consistencies in the social worlds that individuals have constructed for themselves by means of the active processes of choosing and influencing their social situations.

Attitudes, Values, and Preferences

One may adopt a similar approach to understanding and investigating the nature of attitudes, values, and preferences. Consider the case of attitudes toward affirmative action. What does it mean to characterize an individual as one who possesses a "positive attitude" toward affirmative action? What does it mean to say that affirmative action is a prominent feature of that individual's system of "values"? A traditional approach to understanding the nature of attitudes and values might characterize that individual in terms of a set of beliefs (e.g., he or she *believes* that affirmative action procedures increase the representation of minorities in the work force), a set of feelings (e.g., he or she *feels* that it is desirable to recruit minorities actively into the work force), and a set of intentions (e.g., he or she *intends* to take actions that might facilitate the goals of affirmative action). That is, the traditional approach seeks to understand attitudes and values in terms of the specific beliefs, feelings, and intentions that are thought to be associated with global attitudes and general values. Moreover, this traditional approach would lead one to construct measures of attitudes and values that focus on the assessment of beliefs, feelings, and intentions.

By contrast, an approach that seeks to understand individuals in terms of their social worlds would characterize attitudes and values in terms of the processes of choosing and influencing situations. From this perspective, to the extent that an attitude or value is relevant and important to an individual, the consequences of holding that attitude or value will be reflected in that individual's choices of situations and that individual's attempts to influence his or her situations. Thus, when the individual for whom attitudes toward affirmative action are personally important and relevant is given the choice between spending time with a group of people who will be discussing affirmative action and spending time with a group of people who will be discussing baseball teams, that individual will choose to enter the "affirmative action" situation. Moreover, should that same individual find himself or herself thrust into a group that is looking for a topic of discussion, he or she will attempt to steer the topic of the discussion in the direction of affirmative action. As consequences of these activities, that individual would be creating a social world conducive to maintaining and acting upon his or her attitudes and values in the domain of affirmative action.

Even with personal attributes as simple as preferences there may exist considerable benefits of examining the situations within which individuals live their lives. Consider the influence of musical preferences on the situations within which individuals spend their leisure time: Individuals who like rock music go to one type of place to listen to their favorite music; individuals who like disco go to another type of place; individuals who like country music go to yet another type of place; individuals who like classical music go to still another type of place; and so on. Clearly each of these settings both indulges and perpetuates particular tastes in music. In addition, the choice to spend one's leisure time in one setting or another may have consequences far beyond the domain of leisure time activities. One may acquire whole "personalities" as consequences of these choices of settings.

Consider the hypothetical case of two individuals who are identical in all respects save their tastes in music. One individual regularly attends the symphony to satisfy his interests in classical music. The other individual becomes a habitué of discos to indulge his cravings for that type of music. The individual who likes classical music is going to meet, interact with, form relationships with, and be influenced by the type of people to be found in the "symphony situation." The individual who likes disco music is going to meet, interact with, form relationships with, and be influenced by the type of people to be found in the "disco situation." As a consequence of choosing to spend their leisure time in either the "symphony situation" or the "disco situation," these two individuals eventually may live in drastically different social worlds—worlds populated by very different people with very different beliefs, attitudes, and behaviors. As a consequence of their choices of situations, these two formerly similar individuals may develop into very different individuals: One may come to resemble the prototypic disco-person; the other may come to resemble the prototypic symphony-person.

STRATEGIES FOR ASSESSMENT: INDIVIDUALS AND SITUATIONS

For the personality–social psychologist concerned with the assessment and measurement of characteristics of individuals, there are clear and undeniable implications of conceptualizing individuals in terms of their social worlds. Efforts to assess differences between individuals, from this perspective, should be directed at the construction and validation of measures of the situations in which individuals live their lives. Furthermore, if individuals are to be understood in terms of the situations in which they live their lives, then procedures for measuring situations will be necessary tools of the assessor's trade. Consider examples from the domains of self-conceptions, characteristic dispositions, attitudes, and situations.

Conceptions of Self

Consider again the case of individuals who conceive of themselves as liberals. Imagine also a researcher who seeks to develop a measure, say of the paper-and-pencil self-report variety, of self-conceived liberalism. Should that researcher construct a measure of the extent to which individuals who report that they think of themselves as liberals also report that, given the opportunity, they would endorse the "liberal" stand on a variety of personal, social, and political issues? Or should that researcher construct a measure of the extent to which individuals who report that they think of themselves as liberals also report that, given the opportunity, they would choose to live their lives in "liberal" surroundings? Clearly, if one thinks of self-conceptions in terms of their consequences for the surroundings within which individuals live their lives, then one ought to adopt the corresponding strategy of assessing self-conceptions in terms of the surroundings within which individuals live their lives.

Furthermore, if the researcher's ultimate goal in designing a measure of liberal conceptions of self is to identify which of those individuals who conceive of themselves as liberals are the true liberals of this world (i.e., those individuals who faithfully translate their liberal conceptions of self into meaningful liberal actions), then a measure of self-conception that focuses on liberal situations is destined to be more successful than one that focuses on liberal beliefs. After all, individuals who live their lives in liberal surroundings are subject to all of the situational influences that such surroundings can exert to foster and promote the performance of liberal actions.

Characteristic Dispositions

Similarly, from this perspective, one interested in the assessment of characteristic dispositions should direct his or her assessment efforts at constructing and validating measures of the situations in which individuals live their lives. Thus, to return to the example of sociability, should one wish to construct a measure of individual differences in the construct of sociability, that measure should *not* be an assessment of the frequency with which individuals display or claim to display sociable behaviors. Rather, that measure should be an assessment of the extent to which individuals choose to spend time in situations that foster the expression of sociability and an assessment of the extent to which individuals attempt to influence the sociability of the situations that confront them in their lives.

True, an assessment strategy that focuses on the identification of the extent to which individuals live their lives in sociable situations cannot help but identify indirectly the extent to which individuals perform sociable behaviors. Nevertheless, to the extent that the regular display of sociable behaviors is the product of living one's life in sociable situations, any strategy for assessing sociability that is oriented toward life situations cannot help but be a more valid strategy than one that is oriented toward individual behaviors.

Attitudes

The implications of this perspective for measuring attitudes also are clear. Should, for example, one want to identify individuals with positive attitudes toward affirmative action, then one ought to look at the people to be found in situations that promote the maintenance and expression of such attitudes. Not incidentally, such a strategy would succeed in identifying those individuals who are particularly likely to display those behaviors that are manifestations of positive attitudes toward affirmative action. Should one want to develop a paper-and-pencil self-report measure of attitudes toward affirmative action, one might focus one's efforts on soliciting information about situations relevant to affirmative action. One also would present hypothetical choices of situations and hypothetical opportunities to influence situations as other parts of that measure.

Of course, the payoff of any measure of attitudes is its ability to predict behavior. Will a measure of attitudes that elicits statements about real or hypothetical situations be any better a predictor of actual behavior than a measure that elicits statements about beliefs, feelings, and intentions? In the context of the limited ability of self-reports of beliefs, feelings, and intentions to predict actual behavior, the potential certainly is large for alternative approaches to measuring attitudes to outperform traditional approaches.

Assessing Situations

If individuals are to be understood in terms of the situations in which they live their lives, then there exists a crying need to develop techniques for assessing and measuring situations. How, then, are situations to be characterized? One possibility is to characterize situations in terms of the individuals who choose them. Thus, to use the example of sociability one more time, if "sociable" individuals systematically choose to enter "sociable" situations, then perhaps one may characterize a sociable situation as one populated by sociable individuals. In fact, it is not uncommon for individuals to characterize situations in terms of the typical individual to be found in such situations. To use my own favorite example, if I were to tell you that Andy's Bar is the type of place that Archie Bunker and his kind would frequent, you readily would appreciate just what type of place Andy's Bar really is. Indeed, it may be precisely that by identifying the typical individual to be found in a social situation, other individuals read its character and begin to gravitate toward situations that will foster and encourage the expression of their own characteristic dispositions (Alexander & Knight, 1971; Alexander & Lauderdale, 1977; Argyle, 1977; Pervin, 1977; Price & Bouffard, 1974).

If it is the case that individuals choose their situations on the basis of a reading of their character, then it may be possible to construct formal procedures for assessing situations on the basis of the types of persons who would be well-suited to particular situations. The defining characteristic of such an assessment strategy would be the characterization of situations in the same terms that one typically uses to characterize people. The use of the same constructs to characterize situations and people dates back at least as far as Murray's (1938) conception of the "thema." Lewin (1951) too suggested that the same dimensions be used to quantify situations and people. However, only very recently has the notion of a common language for describing situations and people been translated into an empirical strategy. Bem and Funder (1978) have proposed just such an empirical strategy for "assessing the personality of situations."

The approach of Bem and Funder (1978) perhaps is characterized best by their own favorite example of how one might characterize a university to a prospective student. They suggest that one might characterize that university in terms of a set of prototypic individuals: "Students who are hardworking but somewhat shy tend to get good grades but don't have much interaction with the faculty; students who are bright and assertive often get involved in faculty research projects but as a consequence sometimes have little social life and get lower grades than they should; students who . . . [p. 486]." Rather than describing the situation represented by that university in terms of enrollment, size of classes, reputation of faculty, background of the students, and other structural features of the situation, they instead have defined it in terms of sets of *template-behavior* pairs that specify how particular types of individuals will react to that situation. In so doing, they have described a situation in the language that typically is used to characterize people. In their empirical research, they have translated this notion of template-behavior pairs into a procedure for assessing empirically the personality of situations (Bem & Funder, 1978).

STRATEGIES FOR RESEARCH: CHARTING THE STRUCTURE OF SOCIAL WORLDS

Beyond their implications for issues of assessment, considerations of the influence of individuals on social situations have implications for the research strategies of personality–social psychology. To the extent that individuals reside in social worlds that reflect their conceptions of self, their characteristic attitudes and dispositions, and their abilities and competences it may be possible to provide precise specifications about the populations of an individual's social world, the activities, competences, and dispositions of the members of that social world, the nature of the social relationships that exist between the individual and the other members of his or her social world, the settings within which the individual and these other members interact and conduct their social relationships, and so on. With these specifications as guidelines, the personality–social psychologist then may proceed to understand the ways in which the individual influences and is influenced by his or her social world.

How might the personality–social psychologist enact such a strategy for charting the social worlds of individuals? Consider, for example, the case of an investigator concerned with the psychological construct of Machiavellianism (Christie & Geis, 1970). To understand the settings within which individuals high and low in Machiavellianism live their lives, that investigator would begin by identifying: (1) conceptions of the self that differentiate Machiavellian and non-Machiavellian individuals; (2) conceptions of other people that differentiate Machiavellian and non-Machiavellian individuals; (3) characteristic behavioral dispositions and competencies that differentiate Machiavellian and non-Machiavellian individuals. In the case of Machiavellianism, existing research would provide the investigator with knowledge of the conceptions of self, the conceptions of other people, and the behavioral orientations that are characteristic of individuals high and low in Machiavellianism (Christie & Geis, 1970).

The investigator then would attempt to articulate hypotheses about: (1) the characteristics of social worlds that would be well-suited to expressing and maintaining the characteristic orientations of Machiavellian and non-Machiavellian individuals; and (2) the processes by which Machiavellian and non-Machiavellian individuals may create such social worlds for themselves. The investigator then could design appropriate investigations of these hypotheses. The investigator would attempt to determine whether the actual social worlds of Machiavellian and non-Machiavellian individuals reflect the structural organization demanded by his or her hypotheses. When given the opportunity to choose to enter or not to enter social situations, do individuals choose to enter or not to enter the social situations predicted by the investigator's hypotheses about the links between Machiavellianism and processes of choosing situations? Once in a social situation, do individuals operate on that situation in a manner that will transform the situation in ways that are predictable from the investigator's hypotheses about the links between Machiavellianism and the processes of influencing social situations?

As it happens, the research literature is particularly helpful in providing hypotheses about the types of situations in which Machiavellians are to be found, toward which they will gravitate, and into which they may attempt to transform their situations. Specifically, it has been possible to identify some features of situations that are necessary prerequisites for the Machiavellians of this world to translate their Machiavellian beliefs and attitudes into Machiavellian actions. Specifically, Machiavellians are most successfully manipulative in situations that provide face-to-face interaction with their targets, some latitude for improvisation and tailoring their tactics to their targets and goals, and opportunities to use emotional arousal to distract their targets and make them more susceptible to control (Christie & Geis, 1970). The questions then become: Do Machiavellians actually live their lives in situations that possess these features? Do Machiavellians systematically choose to enter situations that possess these features and to shun those situations that do not possess these features? When Machiavellians find themselves confronted by situations that lack these features, do they attempt to transform these situations into ones that possess these features? With empirical answers to these questions, the investigator then could proceed to determine the extent to which individuals live their lives in settings conductive to the expression and maintenance of their characteristic dispositions within the domain of Machiavellianism.

Consider another illustrative example of charting the social worlds within which individuals live: the psychological construct of self-monitoring (Snyder, 1974, 1979). High self-monitoring individuals regard themselves as rather flexible and adaptive creatures who shrewdly and pragmatically tailor their social behavior to fit situational and interpersonal specifications of appropriateness. They tend to define their identities in terms of characteristics of the situations in which they find themselves (Sampson, 1978; Snyder, 1976). It is as if the sense of self for high self-monitoring individuals is a flexible "me for this situation." Moreover, their characteristic behavioral orientation appears to reflect their self-conceptions. They are keenly sensitive and responsive to social and interpersonal cues to situational appropriateness (Snyder & Monson, 1975).

In contrast to their high self-monitoring counterparts, low self-monitoring individuals seem to cherish images of themselves as rather principled and consistent individuals who wish to live their lives according to the maxim "believing means doing." They value congruence between "who they are" and "what they do." Furthermore, they construe their identities in terms of enduring attributes that reside within themselves (Sampson, 1978; Snyder, 1976). For low self-monitoring individuals, the sense of self seems to be an enduring "me for all times." Indeed, low self-monitoring individuals have particularly rich, well-articulated, and readily accessible knowledge of their characteristic selves in a wide variety of trait and behavioral domains (Snyder & Cantor, 1980), and their social behavior typically manifests studious correspondence between private attitudes and public actions (Snyder & Swann, 1976; Snyder & Tanke, 1976).

What, then, are the characteristics of social worlds that would be well-suited to expressing and maintaining the characteristic orientations of high self-monitoring and low self-monitoring individuals? By what processes might high self-monitoring and low self-monitoring individuals create such social worlds for themselves? One might predict that the social worlds of high self-monitoring individuals should be structured in ways that allow them to "be different persons in different situations''—to adopt a wide variety of identities specific to particular social settings and interpersonal relationships; that is, high self-monitoring individuals ought to live in highly partitioned, differentiated, or compartmentalized social worlds, in which they engage in specific activities with specific members of their social worlds. Members of a high self-monitoring individual's social world may have been chosen because they each bring out one of a wide variety of "selves" in high self-monitoring individuals. The social settings of that high self-monitoring individual's social world may be chosen because they have clearly defined characters; that is, because they provide clear specifications of the type of person that one ought to be in those situations. By contrast, one might predict that the social worlds of low self-monitoring individuals should be structured in ways that allow them to "be themselves"—to guarantee a high level of congruence between private self-conceptions and public actions. Members of a low self-monitoring individual's social world may have been chosen because they have personalities and characters similar to or supportive of those of the low self-monitoring individual. The social settings of a low self-monitoring individual's world may be chosen because they call for personalities or characters of the type possessed by that low self-monitoring individual. Indeed, empirical investigations support these characterizations of the social worlds within which high self-monitoring and low self-monitoring individuals live their lives (Snyder & Campbell, in press; Snyder & Gangestad, 1980).

CONCLUSIONS

What is the impact of the individual on the social world within which he or she lives? Questions of this form and answers to such questions constitute the theoretical and empirical core of a personality–social psychology that focuses on the processes by which individuals actively choose and influence the situations and settings within which they live their lives. The underlying theme of this approach to understanding individuals and their social worlds is the proposition that: As consequences of their transactions with the social world, individuals construct for themselves social worlds that are suited to expressing, maintaining, and acting upon their conceptions of self, their conceptions of other people, their characteristic attitudes, and their characteristic dispositions. From this perspective, individuals are to be understood in terms of the social worlds within which they live their lives and, in particular, in terms of the active roles they play in choosing, influencing, and structuring the situations of their lives.

The defining characteristics of this personality–social psychology of the individual and the social world are: (1) its concern with the reciprocal influences and the mutual interplay of individuals and social situations; (2) its definition of "personality" in terms of processes that actually and actively link individuals and their situations; (3) its identification of the antecedents of these processes in individuals' conceptions of self, conceptions of other people, and characteristic attitudes and dispositions; and (4) its identification of the consequences of these processes in the structure of the social world within which individuals reside.

As a general strategy for understanding the relationships that link individuals and their social situations, considerations of the processes of choosing and influencing situations have their intellectual ancestors and their contemporary companions. The classical pragmatic philosophers and self-theorists, most notable Mead (1934), emphasized the active role that individuals play in shaping their social environments and their destinies and regarded individuals as both the causes and the consequences of society. For example, Mead (1934) offered these observations on the interrelationships of the individual and the social world:

> As a man adjusts himself to a certain environment he becomes a different individual; but in becoming a different individual he has affected the community in which he lives. . . . [I]nsofar as he has adjusted himself, the adjustments have changed the type of environment to which he can respond, and the world is accordingly a different world. There is always a mutual relationship of the individual and the community in which the individual lives [p. 215].

Moreover, contemporary statements in the sociology of identity reflect the themes of these classic theories of the construction of the self in and through social interaction. Thus, Goffman (1959), Secord and Backman (1965), Weinstein (1966), and Alexander (Alexander & Knight, 1971; Alexander & Lauderdale, 1977) all have proposed that individuals are sensitive to the identities that they will possess (or at least appear to possess) as a consequence of entering specific social situations or by virtue of acquiring particular social and occupational roles and that situations and roles may be chosen, to some extent, in the service of creating, expressing, maintaining, and bolstering features of identity and self-conception.

Any conceptualization of individuals as active agents who both influence and are influenced by their circumstances owes intellectual debts to Lewin's (1935, 1936, 1951) conceptual propositions about the interplay of persons, environments, and behavior, as well as to Kantor's (1924, 1926) earlier theoretical assertions about the reciprocal influences of persons and their environments and to Murray's (1938, 1951) views on the reciprocity of "needs" (i.e., characteristics of the person) and "press" (characteristics of the environment). Similarly, any attempts to understand individuals in terms of the settings in which they choose to live their lives are reminiscent of Sullivan's interpersonal theory of psychiatry (1953, 1964) that regarded personality as "the relatively enduring pattern of recurrent interpersonal situations which characterize a human life [1953, p. 111]."

The strategy of understanding individuals in terms of the social worlds within which they live reflects the intellectual spirit of the emerging (or reemerging) "interactionist" perspective in personality theory (Buss, 1977; Ekehammar, 1974; Howard, 1979; Magnusson & Endler, 1977). Propositions about the individual as the active creator, as well as reactive creature, of the social world are more than compatible with contemporary assertions by personality theorists about the interaction of persons and situations: "Behavior partly creates the environment, and the environment influences behavior in a reciprocal fashion [Bandura, 1974, p. 866]"; "Situations are as much a function of the person as the person's behavior is a function of the situation [Bowers, 1973, p. 327]"; and "The person continuously influences the 'situations' of his life as well as being affected by them in a mutual, organic two-way interaction [Mischel, 1973, p. 278]; "the understanding of any one person's behavior in an interpersonal situation solely in terms of the stimuli *presented to* him gives only a partial and misleading picture. For to a very large extent, these stimuli are *created by* him" [Wachtel, 1973, p. 330].

This chapter began with the expression of concern about the relative emphasis and attention accorded the two theoretical propositions "situations influence individuals" and "individuals influence situations." In an effort to undo what appeared to be the relative neglect of the proposition "individuals influence situations," the chapter presented an attempt to understand individuals in terms of their impact on the social worlds within which they live. However, in the context of historical and contemporary assertions about the reciprocal influences and the mutual interplay of individuals and situations, this attempt to understand individuals in terms of their social worlds may appear to overemphasize the core proposition "individuals influence situations" to the possible neglect of the symmetric proposition "situations influence individuals." Not so. In fact, an understanding of the proposition that "individuals influence situations" cannot help but add to our understanding of the proposition that "situations influence individuals." For, by choosing and influencing their situations, individuals determine which situations and which settings will have the opportunity to influence their actions. Thus, individuals who choose to live their lives in the intellectual and academic settings provided by university communities will increase the opportunity of intellectual and academic situations to bring out the intellectual and the academic in them. Indeed, it may be precisely because of the influences of situations on behavior that the processes of choosing and influencing situations may constitute the major vehicles for fostering the expression and maintenance of an individual's self-conceptions, social attitudes, preferences, abilities, aptitudes, motives, dispositions, and so on.

Furthermore, the possibility that individuals may knowingly and willingly allow and use situations to influence their own behavior may provide new perspectives on understanding the influence of situations on individuals. Thus, when we witness instances of situations influencing individuals, we ought to ask: "To what extent has the individual chosen to be in that situation?"; "To what extent has that individual chosen to allow that situation to influence his or her behavior?''; ''How might that situation facilitate the expression of characteristics of that individual?''; and so on. Of course, in such circumstances we must distinguish between the known and the unknown, the foreseen and the unforeseen, the anticipated and the unanticipated consequences of an individual's choices of situations. Thus, when a college student chooses to pursue a career as a university professor, he or she may do so in order to live his professional life in settings conducive to acting upon his intellectual aptitudes, interests, and preferences. Yet, that same student may be less aware that his or her intentional choice of vocational setting may have far-reaching consequences for the social world within which he or she will live. After all, as a university professor, he or she will live in a social world populated by rather different people than is the social world of an engineer, an artist, and so on.

Moreover, even when individuals have *not* knowingly and willingly chosen the situations that confront them, we still may benefit from asking a related set of questions: ''What action of the individual may have unknowingly created the situation that confronts him or her?''; ''What characteristics of that individual might have generated those actions that produced his or her current situations?''. Not only may such an approach be beneficial to the researcher who attempts to understand the interaction of individuals and situations, but also such an approach may have considerable utility in therapeutic contexts. Thus, Wachtel (1973) has suggested the possible benefits of educating people about the processes by which their own actions may generate the problematic situations that appear to be the source of their troubles: ''The seductive, hysterical woman who is annoyed at having to face the aggressive, amorous advances of numbers of men has much to learn about the origin of the stimuli she complains she must cope with. So too, does the man who complains about the problems in dealing with his wife's nagging, but fails to understand how this situation, which presents itself to him, derives in turn from his own procrastinating, unresponsible behavior [p. 330].''

In the most general of terms, when considering the relationships between individuals and situations, we must go beyond the asking of questions about the influences of situations on individuals to asking questions about why particular individuals are in specific situations in the first place. Moreover, we must go beyond the asking of questions about the influences of situations to asking questions about what particular individuals have done to mold, shape, and create the very situations that now appear to influence and constrain their behavior. Only then will it be possible to understand the extent to which the situations that seek to influence and that succeed in influencing individuals are reflections of characteristics of the individuals. Only then will the reciprocal influences and mutual interplay of individuals and social situations be truly apparent. Only then will it be possible to construct a genuine personality–social psychology—a true psychology of the individual and the social world.

ACKNOWLEDGMENTS

The development of these ideas and the preparation of this manuscript have been supported by National Science Foundation Grant BNS 77-11346, "From Belief to Reality: Cognitive, Behavioral, and Interpersonal Consequences of Social Perception," to Mark Snyder.

REFERENCES

Alexander, C. N., & Knight, G. W. Situated identities and social psychological experimentation. *Sociometry,* 1971, *34,* 65–82.

Alexander, C. N., Jr., & Lauderdale, P. Situated identities and social influence. *Sociometry,* 1977, *40,* 225–233.

Argyle, M. Predictive and generative rules models of PXS interaction. In D. Magnusson & N. D. Endler (Eds.), *Personality at the crossroads: Current issues in interactional psychology.* Hillsdale, N.J.: Lawrence Erlbaum Associates, 1977.

Bandura, A. Behavior therapy and the models of man. *American Psychologist,* 1974, *29,* 859–869.

Bem, D. J., & Funder, D. C. Predicting more of the people more of the time: Assessing the personality of situations. *Psychological Review,* 1978, *85,* 485–501.

Berglas, S., & Jones, E. E. Drug choice as an externalization strategy in response to noncontingent success. *Journal of Personality and Social Psychology,* 1978, *36,* 405–417.

Bowers, K. S. Situationism in psychology: An analysis and a critique. *Psychological Review,* 1973, *80,* 307–336.

Buss, A. R. The trait-situation controversy and the concept of interaction. *Personality and Social Psychology Bulletin,* 1977, *3,* 196–201.

Christie, R., & Geis, F. L. (Eds.). *Studies in Machiavellianism.* New York: Academic Press, 1970.

Ekehammar, B. Interactionism in personality from a historical perspective. *Psychological Bulletin,* 1974, *81,* 1026–1048.

Goffman, E. *The presentation of self in everyday life.* Garden City, N.Y.: Doubleday-Anchor, 1959.

Howard, J. A. Person–situation interaction models. *Personality and Social Psychology Bulletin,* 1979, *5,* 191–195.

Jones, E. E., & Berglas, S. Control of attributions about the self through self-handicapping strategies: The appeal of alcohol and the role of underachievement. *Personality and Social Psychology Bulletin,* 1978, *4,* 200–206.

Kantor, J. R. *Principles of psychology* (Vol. 1). Bloomington: Principia Press, 1924.

Kantor, J. R. *Principles of psychology* (Vol. 2). Bloomington: Principia Press, 1926.

Kelley, H. H., & Stahelski, A. J. The social interaction basis of cooperators' and competitors' beliefs about others. *Journal of Personality and Social Psychology,* 1970, *16,* 66–91.

Lewin, K. *A dynamic theory of personality.* New York: McGraw-Hill, 1935.

Lewin, K. *Principles of topological psychology.* New York: McGraw-Hill, 1936.

Lewin, K. *Field theory in social science: Selected theoretical papers.* New York: Harper, 1951.

Magnusson, D., & Endler, N. S. (Eds.). *Personality at the crossroads: Current issues in interactional psychology.* Hillsdale, N.J.: Lawrence Erlbaum Associates, 1977.

Mead, G. H. *Mind, self, and society.* Chicago: University of Chicago Press, 1934.

Mischel, W. Toward a cognitive social learning reconceptualization of personality. *Psychological Review,* 1973, *80,* 252–283.

Murray, H. A. *Explorations in personality.* New York: Oxford University Press, 1938.

Murray, H. A. Toward a classification of interaction. In T. Parsons & E. A. Shils (Eds.), *Toward a general theory of action*. Cambridge, Mass.: Harvard University Press, 1951.

Pervin, L. A. The representative design of person–situation research. In D. Magnusson & N. S. Endler (Eds.), *Personality at the crossroads: Current issues in interactional psychology*. Hillsdale, N.J.: Lawrence Erlbaum Associates, 1977.

Price, R. H., & Bouffard, D. L. Behavioral appropriateness and situational constraint as dimensions of social behavior. *Journal of Personality and Social Psychology*, 1974, *30*, 579–586.

Rosenthal, R., & Jacobson, L. *Pygmalion in the classroom*. New York: Holt, Rinehart & Winston, 1968.

Sampson, E. E. Personality and the location of identity. *Journal of Personality*, 1978, *46*, 552–568.

Secord, P. F., & Backman, C. W. An interpersonal approach to personality. In B. Maher (Ed.), *Progress in experimental personality research* (Vol. 2). New York: Academic Press, 1965.

Skrypnek, B. J., & Snyder, M. *On the self-perpetuating nature of stereotypes about women and men*. Unpublished manuscript. University of Minnesota, 1980.

Snyder, M. The self-monitoring of expressive behavior. *Journal of Personality and Social Psychology*, 1974, *30*, 526–537.

Snyder, M. Attribution and behavior: Social perception and social causation. In J. H. Harvey, W. J. Ickes, & R. F. Kidd (Eds.), *New directions in attribution research*. Hillsdale, N.J.: Lawrence Erlbaum Associates, 1976.

Snyder, M. Self-monitoring processes. In L. Berkowitz (Ed.), *Advances in experimental social psychology* (Vol. 12). New York: Academic Press, 1979.

Snyder, M. On the self-perpetuating nature of social stereotypes. In D. L. Hamilton (Ed.), *Cognitive processes in stereotyping and intergroup behavior*. Lawrence Erlbaum Associates, in press. (a)

Snyder, M. Seek, and ye shall find: Testing hypotheses about other people. In E. T. Higgins, C. P. Herman, & M. P. Zanna (Eds.), *Social Cognition: The Ontario Symposium*. Lawrence Erlbaum Associates, in press. (b)

Snyder, M., & Campbell, B. H. Self-monitoring: The self in action. In J. Suls (Ed.), *Social psychological perspectives on the self*. Hillsdale, N.J.: Lawrence Erlbaum Associates, in press.

Snyder, M., & Cantor, N. Thinking about ourselves and others: Self-monitoring and social knowledge. *Journal of Personality and Social Psychology*, 1980, *39*, 222–234.

Snyder, M., & Gangestad, S. *Self-monitoring and the choice to enter situations*. Manuscript in preparation, University of Minnesota, 1980.

Snyder, M., & Monson, T. C. Persons, situations, and the control of social behavior. *Journal of Personality and Social Psychology*, 1975, *32*, 637–644.

Snyder, M., & Swann, W. B., Jr. When actions reflect attitudes: The politics of impression management. *Journal of Personality and Social Psychology*, 1976, *34*, 1034–1042.

Snyder, M., & Swann, W. B., Jr. Behavioral confirmation in social interaction: From social perception to social reality. *Journal of Experimental Social Psychology*, 1978, *14*, 148–162. (a)

Snyder, M., & Swann, W. B., Jr. Hypothesis-testing processes in social interaction. *Journal of Personality and Social Psychology*, 1978, *36*, 1202–1212. (b)

Snyder, M., & Tanke, E. D. Behavior and attitude: Some people are more consistent than others. *Journal of Personality*, 1976, *44*, 510–517.

Snyder, M., Tanke, E. D., & Berscheid, E. Social perception and interpersonal behavior: On the self-fulfilling nature of social stereotypes. *Journal of Personality and Social Psychology*, 1977, *35*, 656–666.

Sullivan, H. S. *The interpersonal theory of psychiatry*. New York: Norton, 1953.

Sullivan, H. S. *The fusion of psychiatry and social science*. New York: Norton, 1964.

Wachtel, P. Psychodynamics, behavior therapy and the implacable experimenter: An inquiry into the consistency of personality. *Journal of Abnormal Psychology*, 1973, *82*, 324–334.

Weinstein, E. A. Toward a theory of interpersonal tactics. In C. W. Backman & P. F. Secord (Eds.), *Problems in social psychology,* New York: McGraw-Hill, 1966.

Word, C. O., Zanna, M. P., & Cooper, J. The nonverbal mediation of self-fulfilling prophecies in interracial interaction. *Journal of Experimental Social Psychology,* 1974, *10,* 109–120.

Zanna, M. P. & Pack, S. J. On the self-fulfilling nature of apparent sex differences in behavior. *Journal of Experimental Social Psychology,* 1975, *11,* 583–591.

VI DISCUSSION

14

General Discussion of Issues: Relationships Between Cognitive Psychology and the Psychology of Personality

Sam Glucksberg
Princeton University

What do cognition and personality have to do with one another? Historically, the study of cognition was a specialty within the field of personality psychology. This is reflected in the composition of study sections within the National Institutes of Health, where experimental psychology and personality/cognition were, and still are, separate. It is also reflected in the people who are most closely identified with the study of cognition up to the 1950s, Gardner Murphy, Sylvan Tomkins, and Herman Witkin, among others.

With the transition from neobehaviorism and verbal learning to information processing and cognitive psychology in the 1960s, modern cognitive psychology developed independently of the personality and social-psychology movement. This volume reflects the completion of a cycle, wherein social psychology and personality again become integrally involved with cognition, but this time drawing from experimental cognitive psychology rather than leading the way.

How has work in personality been informed by cognitive psychology? At the most trivial level, the two fields share a technical vocabulary or jargon. The terms that we use—schema, prototypes, scripts, frames—reflect a second commonality between the two fields, namely, a zeitgeist that not only permits but encourages speculation about mental life and mental processes. Not unrelated to this is the attention, long overdue, that both fields now pay to such important figures as Jean Piaget, for his powerful conceptions of learning and conceptual development, and Frederick Bartlett, for a rich and useful conception of memorial processes.

The chapters in this volume reflect the consensual view that perception, memory, and thinking are active, constructive processes that operate in similar ways across various domains. Perception and categorization of objects involve the same mental activities as do the perception and categorization of persons. Memory for events, memory for persons, and memory for people's actions and characteristics share important structural and processing mechanisms. In short, we have learned—or at least we all seem to agree—that the way we deal with the world of physical objects shares important characteristics with the way we deal with persons and with ourselves. At the level of conceptual knowledge, common mental processes are used irrespective of the specific domains.

Although this agreement is comforting, it is also mildly disturbing. Along with the development of the current zeitgeist has come a shift in the way we interact with one another, and how we do science. First, there is a general trend away from an adversary mode of operation to a consensual and confirmatory mode. Everyone seems to agree, at least in spirit, with everyone else. This may be because, after 100 years of experimental psychology, we have finally found the truth, but I somehow doubt this. It may be partly because, as Walter Mischel put it, our favorite straw men are dead, dying, or retiring, and so there is no longer any need to make a fuss about them. It may also be because we lack good conceptual alternatives at the moment, either in cognitive psychology or in personality.

A related trend is a shift from a research strategy that is aimed at rejecting hypotheses in order to discriminate sharply among theoretical alternatives, to a strategy of finding confirmatory evidence for positions that have a priori or consensual plausibility. This trend is, I think, inevitable when people are just beginning to apply the conceptual tools of cognitive psychology to the domains of personality. The first order of business is to demonstrate the potential utility of the various approaches, and most of the chapters in this volume do just that, arguing that cognitive psychology can provide useful models for the study of personality in at least two specific ways. First, cognitive psychology may be a source of models—both structural and processing—for the psychology of personality. Second, cognitive psychology may be a useful source of experimental paradigms and methods for studying personality and social cognition processes.

The major class of structural models that has been applied to personality and social cognition has come from the literature on abstraction and conceptual categorization. In a sense, we might say that people are like chairs in that the structure of object categories shares important commonalities with the structure of person categories. Natural objects on the one hand—such as furniture, birds, tools, or vehicles—and people, on the other—such as extraverts and introverts—can be classified at various hierarchical levels. In the realm of object categories, the most useful level is usually below a general superordinate like "furniture," and above a specific subordinate like "kitchen table." The middle, or basic level, like "table," is normally the most useful and common level of generality. Category exemplars at this middle level of generality are also the ones that are judged to be prototypical of the category. These two notions, originally developed by Eleanor Rosch (1973) in the context of characterizing natural object categories, have been fruitfully applied to the structure of person categories, notably in this volume by such people as Cantor and Kuiper and Derry. Cantor, for example, argues that our conception of people and personality types is organized very much like our conception of ordinary object categories. Just as a robin may be a prototypical bird, so might a particular sort of reclusive scholar be a prototypical introvert.

In this work, as in Kuiper's and Derry's, the organization and *structure* from one knowledge domain is used as an analogy for another. In similar ways, others have taken not only structures but hypothetical *processes* from the domain of cognitive information processing and applied them to the domain of person perception and social cognition. Examples of this are provided by Cohen (this volume) in the treatment of selective attention in goal-directed information seeking, by Fiske and Kinder (this volume) in their discussion of learning as a function of political involvement, and by Locksley and Lenauer (this volume) in their application of decision-theory constructs to the problem of how people make inferences about the self and about others. In each of these cases, experimental cognitive psychology has provided a language for talking about personality and social cognition, as well as a set of constructs and models.

These constructs, once applied outside their original contexts, no longer depend on those original contexts for their continued worth and utility. For example, once the notion of prototypes is borrowed and applied in a novel context, it can achieve functional autonomy. This autonomy has two aspects. The first concerns the levels of analysis that are appropriate in the respective contexts. Within the original context—in this case the psychology of classification processes—the specific form of a prototype is an important issue. Is it of the sort described by Rosch (1973)? Is it formed via the abstraction of instances as proposed by Posner and his colleagues (Posner & Keele, 1968), or is it more appropriately characterized in terms of specific examplar-based information as suggested by Medin and Schaffer (1978)? These theoretical questions continue to be important and appropriate, but they are not necessarily of central concern within the domain of person perception and categorization. In this latter domain, the more general properties of the construct—including such notions as the probabilistic nature of classification, the distinction between clear, prototypical cases and less clear, poor cases—may be more important. Indeed, one might argue that it is these latter, more general properties of the construct that are the most useful in broader domains of application and that the more specific and detailed issues may be quite irrelevant. I won't push this too far because the fine structure of prototypes may well have implications for how they might be learned, modified, or otherwise manipulated. However, until such implications are clearly worked out, issues about fine structure and detail might safely be ignored. Indeed, the utility of a notion such as prototypes for person classification is, in principle, independent of its ultimate utility in the domain of object classification. If it were suddenly discovered that object categorization involves explicit rule learning and that prototypes have no useful role in models of natural-object classification, would that necessarily imply a parallel shift in our thinking about person categorization? Obviously not . . . the utility of a concept like prototypes should be assessed on its own terms within each of its domains of application.

Michael Posner and I differ somewhat on this issue. I believe that constructs such as selective attention, prototypes, and cognitive reference points etc., attain functional autonomy and independence within each of their domains of application. Posner seems to prefer a closer link between the way selective attention, say, is treated in one domain and the way it is treated in another. We both do agree, however, about a second major class of borrowed items. This is the class of methods and paradigms. As Kihlstrom's (this volume) review clearly demonstrated, experimental methods, paradigms, and inference procedures from experimental cognitive psychology are being widely applied to studies of personality and social cognition.

Two important issues merit consideration. The first concerns the inferential power of selected paradigms and procedures. When an experimental paradigm is borrowed from one domain for use in another, it cannot attain the functional independence that broader theoretical concepts can. The notion of prototypes might prove useless in object classification but remain useful in the domain of person categorization. Not so the logic of, say, the additive factors method (Sternberg, 1969) or the power of reaction-time paradigms to discriminate among alternative processing models. Admittedly, the temptation to apply a method that has been successful in one domain to another domain is very great, particularly when one thinks that important mental processes might be revealed. Techniques and paradigms that purport to discriminate between short- and long-term memory, or between automatic and nonautomatic processing, or between serial and parallel processes, have been useful in specific laboratory contexts. They cannot, however, be routinely and automatically applied to novel task settings where the number and nature of theoretical alternatives are different. Second, their utility within their new domain of application depends critically on their continued utility and validity in their original domains of application. If a reaction-time recognition paradigm proves to be equivocal for distinguishing between theoretical alternatives in the perception laboratory, then it must also be equivocal in other, presumably more complex, contexts. Unlike borrowed structural and processing constructs, borrowed methods and paradigms do rely on their original utilities and contexts. If they prove untrustworthy or useless in their original contexts, then they cannot survive unchanged in their new contexts.

The second important issue is, what do we do if our methods produce data that are incompatible with central, indispensable assumptions? One case in point is the self in the context of information processing. It is entirely possible that the self cannot be distinguished from other constructs by using standard information-processing and memory paradigms. In that event, do we then argue that the self has no unique or important properties? For a personality psychologist, it seems to me that the phenomenal fact of the self is sufficient to differentiate it from other objects of perception and knowledge, and this fact must be dealt with in any adequate theory of personality (see Rogers, this volume). In such cases, prior theoretical commitment must take precedence over the outcomes of particular empirical operations.

This argument might well be applied to one of the central questions of this volume: Is an information-processing approach to the study of personality and social cognition useful? The empirical evidence is equivocal, but the promise, if one is to judge from the volume chapters, is high. The concepts of information-processing cognitive psychology have proved useful and powerful within the traditional domains of human experimental psychology. Used sensitively and imaginatively, many of them might well be useful and powerful in the domains of personality psychology as well. At this early stage of the development of the field of personality and cognition, this is an appropriate theoretical commitment to make.

REFERENCES

Medin, D. L., & Schaffer, M. M. Context theory of classification learning. *Psychological Review*, 1978, *85*, 207–238.

Posner, M. I., & Keele, S. W. On the genesis of abstract ideas. *Journal of Experimental Psychology*, 1968, *77*, 353–363.

Rosch, E. On the internal structure of perceptual and semantic categories. In T. E. Moore (Ed.), *Cognitive development and the acquisition of language*. New York: Academic Press, 1973.

Sternberg, S. The discovery of processing stages: Extensions of Donders' method. *Acta Psychologica*, 1969, *30*, 276–315.

15 Cognition and Personality

Michael I. Posner
University of Oregon

Inasmuch as I have no knowledge of modern work on personality, I wondered why I had been invited to comment on the papers in this volume. However, I am an avid reader of *The New Yorker,* and I saw there a cartoon that pictured two elderly Indians on horses, one saying to the other, "When you get too old to hunt, you teach them how to track the buffalo chips." Perhaps I have been invited to suggest some directions you should take.

I have followed carefully the historical summaries included in a number of the papers. From them I understand that the history of this field goes back as far as 1954. I am not a historian, but I missed any reference to a man I consider the most prominent investigator in the area of personality and cognition. I expected to encounter some citations from Professor Herschel McLandress, consultant for the Noonan Psychiatric Clinic in Boston, whose work goes back to the early 1960s. Most readers, I think, will be familiar with his work from the book put together by Mark Epernay (1963) called *The McLandress Dimension.* If you are not, you will probably want to become acquainted with this very important quantitative approach, and for that reason I quote:

> The dimension along which McLandress has sought to measure human behavior is that of the individual's relation to self. The unit of measurement which he employs, called the McLandress Coefficient, reflects the intensity of the individual's identification with his own personality. No modern scientific tool is ever simple and the McLandress Coefficient—in scientific circles it is referred to as the McL-C (pronounced Mack-el-see)—is a thing of some complexity. But in essence it is the arithmetic mean or average of the intervals of time during which a subject's thoughts remain centered on some substantive phenomenon other than his own personality. By way of illustration, a twenty-minute coefficient—a McL-C of

twenty minutes—means that an individual's thoughts remain diverted from his own personality for periods of average duration of twenty minutes. A sixty-minute McL-C, a fairly large coefficient according to Dr. McLandress' researches, would mean that an individual's thoughts are diverted from himself for intervals averaging one hour [p. 2].

Some prominent people's McL-Cs that you are probably familiar with are: J. Robert Oppenheimer's at 3 hours; Lyndon Johnson's at 2 minutes; and Richard Nixon's at 3 seconds. The work reported under the name Mark Epernay (sometimes attributed to John Kenneth Galbraith) shows that there can be quantitative approaches to cognition and personality.

While I was editing the *Journal of Experimental Psychology* I tried to use the logic of the McLandress Coefficient. Figure 15.1 plots the number of self-citations as a function of the years since the Ph.D. You'll notice it is monotonic, with a peculiar spurt in the 6th and 7th year post-doctoral. (After this work, I was especially grateful to note that there were references to articles besides their own in the presentations by the young investigators whose contributions appear in this volume.)

Cognitive Structures

As I understand it, the central issue of this volume is a reaction to finding that one can't predict cross-situational behavior from a knowledge of personality traits. In some ways this is similar to the findings that drove experimental psychologists inside the mind. We found that simple principles of reflexive and operant behavior did not serve to predict overt behavior very well. It was necessary to look inside the organism for evidence of some sort of invariant reponse to stimuli and, to some extent, cognitive psychologists have been finding invariance. Similarly, many investigators do not want to give up the idea of enduring personality traits. Not finding them predictive of overt behavior across situations seems to have driven many of you inside the mind. We have seen a number of approaches along these lines. Just as cognitive psychology presents the danger of leaving the human subject lost in thought without being able to act, so does the current approach leave unsolved the problem of how action occurs—as Athay and Darley (this volume) and Snyder (this volume) have reminded us. The link between cognition and action is obviously important, both in cognitive psychology and in personality. Nonetheless, I think there are some fruitful reasons to look inside the mind at the types of organization one finds there.

I definitely agree with Glucksberg (this volume) that the treatments presented here on cognitive structure are at a very high level of generality. You write about cognitive structures and use a variety of names but generally are not any more specific than that. Glucksberg hints that perhaps you shouldn't be, and maybe he

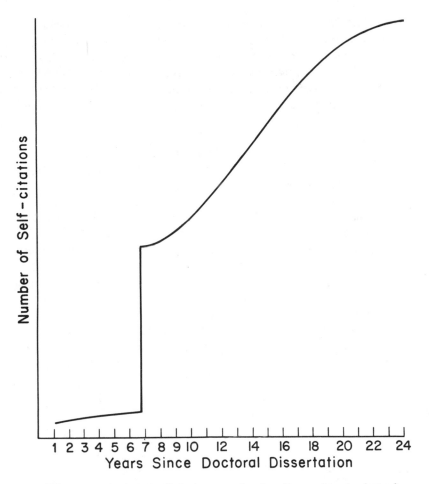

FIG. 15.1.   Number of self-citations as a function of years since the doctoral dissertation (data made up by M. Posner).

is right, but I want to argue that you should be a little more analytic as to the nature of structure as cognitive psychologists have been trying to use it.

Suppose we look at the present volume as it might be viewed in terms of three types of cognitive structures. The most familiar kind of cognitive structure would be a simple list of the chapters. It would not make very much sense to talk about the prototype of this list, nor would it be a very fruitful characterization of a volume to talk about the median contributor in such a list. When material is stored in terms of a list structure, cognitive psychologists have been able to show important consequences. In the social domain, DeSoto (1961) pointed out that there is a tendency when you have things in lists to think that the person who is on the top of one list is on the top of all other lists (the *halo effect*). In the case of this list it could be true. Nonetheless, it is a danger of list-ordering. Many of us go to faculty meetings in which psychologists who *know* that intelligence is multidimensional talk about a job candidate as being the bright candidate, as though intelligence were really unidimensional, with a single list that would serve to rank-order that domain. There are cognitive consequences to even so simple an organization of information as a list.

The editors of this volume did not put this list in anything like a random order; rather, the order of the chapters in the Table of Contents shows that they had a structure in mind. Two other organizational structures also come to mind.

Figure 15.2 illustrates what cognitive psychologists might regard as an alternative structure of the volume viewed in terms of a network or binary tree diagram. A major division of the volume is between those who are looking for some sort of general cognitive principles and those looking at individual differences. It turns out that many contributors have multiple goals, but when you start to organize material this way, you have to choose. Among those working in the area of a general cognitive principle, one major group placed an emphasis upon cognitive structure (for example, prototype [Cantor], perceptual units [Cohen], or stereotype [Borgida, Locksley, & Brekke; Fiske & Kinder]). Another group seems to be telling us about various cognitive processes (for example, activation in memory [Higgins & King] or memory search [Kihlstrom]). Among people working in the area of individual differences, the

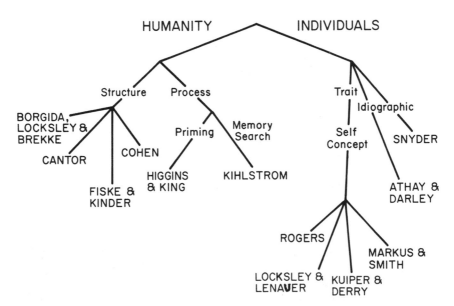

FIG. 15.2. Tree diagram of the volume (constructed from pre-conference abstracts).

trait approach in its traditional form appears to be dead—at least it does not seem to be represented in this volume. Instead, many people deal with the concept of the self (e.g. Kuiper & Derry; Markus & Smith; Rogers). Finally, we have what I call an idiographic approach (Athay & Darley; Snyder), although I don't know if the investigators would see it that way.

A tree diagram is a different organizational structure than a list, and there are certain cognitive consequences in this type of organization. For example, the people in a category look more alike than they should. I doubt that I would confuse them physically, but I might have semantic confusion when I talked about their research. This kind of structure can produce stereotyping because it is economic to assign at one node a property that then is seen as true of all entries at that node, even though not all entries assigned a category have equivalent ideas.

With a different cognitive structure, such as the space illustrated in Figure 15.3, new consequences would arise. This structure has dimensions, one of which is *domain:* individuals versus humanity. I could talk sensibly about a chapter that was the prototype on that dimension. A second dimension, *dynamics,* varies from structure to process. A third dimension, *specificity,* runs from single context to all settings. I don't find this spatial structure a very easy way to remember a volume and will probably revert to the tree. Note that some people who appear close on the tree don't look so close on this space. A special consequence of the spatial representation is that I must assign to every individual a value on all three dimensions. As Allport pointed out many years ago, and Bem and Allen (1974) recently reminded us, that is a difficult problem of nomothetic measurement. If some people are not well characterized on some dimensions, there is a disadvantage of a spatial structure.

There are consequences not only to having made the general choice to go along with cognitive psychologists on structure but as to which cognitive structure one has chosen. Careful choices may help reduce the problem of ambiguity in social-cognitive theory. The word *prototype* used as an average or central tendency might be the key to understanding some particular kinds of cognitive structure, but might not be helpful with others. One place where prototypes might be important is where positive and negative affect is involved. The idea of pooling the positive and negative affect of input information may be a helpful approach to understanding how affect gets tied to cognitive structure (Posner & Snyder, 1975) and why it often tends to dominate other types of information (Zajonc, 1980).

Another point from cognitive psychology that might turn out to be useful when you go a little deeper into the notion of cognitive structure was made in an article by Anderson and Hastie (1974). They tried to examine what seems to me to be one of the most difficult problems in both personality theory and cognition in general: The question of when there is a strain toward *cognitive consistency* between inconsistent beliefs, and when there is *compartmentalization* of these beliefs. Many of us have inconsistent cognitions that don't bother us because

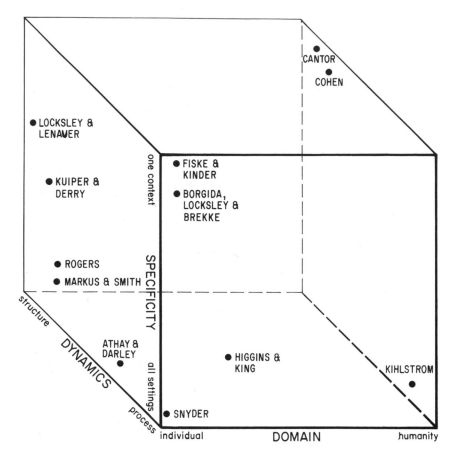

FIG. 15.3.   Spatial model of the volume (constructed from pre-conference abstracts).

they never become related to each other. Anderson and Hastie (1974) explored cases in which structures tie beliefs to the same internal node and might therefore produce a pressure toward consistency and cases in which the beliefs would be built into separate nodes. Their ideas presume the existence of structure and seek to determine the consequences of different cognitive organizations. I think this is the level at which contact between cognition and personality theory can lead to new advances.

Psychological Processes

I would like to turn now from structure to the problem of psychological process. In cognitive theory, the *reason* that structure is thought to be important is that structures guide the direction of psychological processes. The work of Higgins and King (this volume) with priming examines activation patterns that occur automatically. They go to great lengths to try to make sure the subject is not actively dealing with the primed material. The chapter represents one effort to deal objectively with the distinction between conscious and unconscious processes. Although there are some people working in cognitive psychology who would resist this distinction, I think a more typical view would be one that accepted conscious and unconscious processes as part of normal cognition. For example, many investigators studying word recognition in reading divide the process between conscious and unconscious components (Posner, 1978). A vivid illustration of this is in the studies of a type of acquired dyslexia resulting from brain injury in which the patient is unable to read a word correctly, but produces instead semantic associates to it (Marshall & Newcombe, 1973)— for example, *mouse* for *dog*. Although you might think the patient is trying to fool you, the literature has accumulated to reduce that possibility and to indicate that this is a genuine effect of brain injury in which the patient is not able to bring the phonetic representation to consciousness, although he or she is able to report on the activation pattern in semantic memory. Even in normal reading, the distinction between what occurs consciously and what does not has been a powerful one and has helped us in relating normal and brain-damaged functioning (Marcel & Patterson, 1978).

The interesting question for personality theory is not to ask if there is an unconscious but to ask what it does. Most of the people in experimental psychology have been content to show that unconscious processes look up the meaning of words or perform other routine processes involving highly familiar pathways. That is not exactly what Freud had in mind when talking not just about unconscious processing but about *the* unconscious. The techniques may not be available for trying to look at more of the exotic affective aspects of the unconscious processing of information. An understanding of cognitive structure should help us to open these questions to further analysis.

A second kind of process discussed in this volume and about which there is a good deal of interest in cognitive psychology is the effect of arousal on memory (Kihlstrom, this volume). The idea of arousal and its effect on memory has been a difficult area in cognitive psychology. One reason for its difficulty is the need to distinguish between arousal as a background state present at the time information is presented to the organism and arousal that arises as a result of processing that information. Rehearsal is itself a condition that produces arousal, but there is not too much interest in showing that rehearsal affects memory. On the other hand, arousal changes spontaneously with such things as time of day or sleep. It is quite interesting to show that this type of arousal affects memory. The use of concepts of arousal in personality theory will have to build upon careful distinctions between level and source of the arousal if the extant information from cognition is to be useful.

The largest area of process represented in the volume is the idea of comparisons with the self (Kuiper & Derry; Locksley & Lennauer; Markus & Smith;

Rogers). I agree entirely with Glucksberg's point that the self ought not to be dismissed even if one finds that memory for other items can be made as good as the memory for self-reference. Clearly, there must be some mechanisms by which the self-reference effect that Rogers discovered occurs. Maybe it's because the self produces a lot of affect or because it contains much information, and so on. As Rogers uncovers these mechanisms, experimental psychologists can unleash an army of memory drums and find non-self-reference items that use the same processes and thus duplicate Rogers' memory finding. That will not convince me or anyone else that the self is just another concept. The self is surely an important field of study and already, in the hands of Kuiper and Derry (this volume), we have some rather surprising results with respect to automatic self-comparison as part of comparing against other people. It's not so surprising that one doubts it, but it certainly is not obvious that one is going to compare trait adjectives that relate to a well-known "other" by first referring to oneself. I wouldn't give up on that result, even if some avid reaction-time freak instructed subjects first to compare with John F. Kennedy, for example, *before* they made the assignment to the other and then showed that you find the same results for Kennedy as you do for self. That would not be a sufficient result because the interest is in the fact that the reference is "automatic" (i.e., without any deliberate instruction or cognition on the part of the subject). The fact that it could be duplicated by an instructed effort of the subject does not take it away.

In short, there are some very interesting possibilities in the study of personality processes. It's an area in which there is active work in cognition and it will require people to keep up with that work as well as carry on with their own.

Action

What about the problem of action? As a lay person, when I become interested in how people behave and want some of the inspiration that we acquire through studying the lives of others, I don't go to the cognitive or personality literature, but instead to biography. I read about how people with limited capacities and particular mental structures face the situations of life, particularly the dramatic ones that confront public figures. So I am an avid reader of Erikson (1958, 1969) because I am interested in how Luther and Ghandi each faced and brought about changes in their social environments. I like to read psychobiography, but I think it is a very limited approach that you should change.

There are at least two great conceptions of how personality influences cognition. One of them is by Freud, who points to early experience as dominating later life—that is the view that has been captured by Erikson in his psychobiographies. But there is another conception: The view of Karl Marx, in which our unconscious is shaped by the economics of the working environment. I think that modern cognitive psychology suggests that both are likely to be true and that everyday life experiences written into cognitive structure are important for the behavior of individuals as they go through life. I'm looking forward to seeing people like Snyder (this volume) and Athay and Darley (this volume), who are interested in the interaction between cognition and social situations, lead us toward a genuinely cognitive psychobiography. There are already some fairly good examples, although they are not by professional psychologists. For example, there is no more psychologically oriented work on cognitive processes working in interesting situations than the biography of Lyndon Johnson by Doris Kearns (1976). In part, she was motivated by her psychoanalytic background, but she had to face the fact that Lyndon Johnson was probably shaped as much by his experience at Southwest Texas Teacher's College as he was by his early interactions with his mother. Cognitive psychologists like Hunt, Lunneborg, and Lewis (1975) and Lyon (1977) are trying to look at an enduring mental skill that characterizes individuals. With the sophisticated techniques that are emerging from psychological laboratories, we ought to see more of an effort to look at lives in progress. I agree with Snyder (this volume) that if you are good at language you will put yourself in situations where language is important; and if you have enduring skills with respect to spatial ability, you will probably gravitate to situations where such skills are important. The study of interactions between cognitive skills and strategies of individuals seems to open exciting possibilities for personality theory to build upon cognition in a way that does not view the individual only in terms of mental structure but looks at actions as well.

REFERENCES

Anderson, J., & Hastie, R. Individuation and reference in memory: Proper names and definite descriptions. *Cognitive Psychology,* 1974, *6,* 495–514.

Bem, D. J., & Allen, A. Predicting some of the people some of the time: The search for cross-situational consistencies in behavior. *Psychological Review,* 1974, *81,* 506–520.

DeSoto, C. The predilections for single orderings. *Journal of Abnormal and Social Psychology,* 1961, *62,* 16–23.

Epernay, M. *The McLandress dimension.* Boston: Houghton-Mifflin, 1963.

Erikson, E. H. *Young man Luther.* New York: W. W. Norton, 1958.

Erikson, E. H. *Ghandi's truth: On the origins of militant noviolence.* New York: W. W. Norton, 1969.

Hunt, E., Lunneborg, C., & Lewis, J. What does it mean to be high verbal? *Cognitive psychology,* 1975, *7,* 194–227.

Kearns, D. *Lyndon Johnson and the American dream.* New York: Harper & Row, 1976.

Lyon, D. Individual differences in immediate serial recall: A matter of mnemonics? *Cognitive Psychology,* 1977, *9,* 403–411.

Marcel, A. J., & Patterson, K. E. Word recognition and production: Reciprocity in clinical and normal studies. In J. Requin (Ed.), *Attention and performance VII.* Hillsdale, N.J.: Lawrence Erlbaum Associates, 1978.

Marshall, J. C., & Newcombe, F. Patterns of paralexia: A psycholinguistic approach. *Journal of Psycholinguistic Research,* 1973, *2,* 175-198.

Posner, M. I. *Chronometric explorations of mind.* Hillsdale, N.J.: Lawrence Erlbaum Associates, 1978.

Posner, M. I., & Snyder, C. R. R. Attention and cognitive control. In R. Solso (Ed.), *Information processing and cognition: The Loyola symposium.* Hillsdale, N.J.: Lawrence Erlbaum Associates, 1975.

Zajonc, R. Feeling and thinking: Preferences need no inferences. *American Psychologist,* 1980, *3,* 151-175.

Author Index

Subject Index